blue
rider
press

TRUMP

is F*CKING CRAZY

ALSO BY KEITH OLBERMANN

Pitchforks and Torches

Truth and Consequences

The Worst Person in the World

The Big Show

TRUMP

is F*CKING CRAZY

[THIS IS NOT A JOKE]

KEITH OLBERMANN

BLUE RIDER PRESS · NEW YORK

blue
rider
press

An imprint of Penguin Random House LLC
375 Hudson Street
New York, New York 10014

Library of Congress Cataloging-in-Publication Data

Names: Olbermann, Keith, author.
Title: Trump is f*cking crazy : (this is not a joke) / Keith Olbermann.
Other titles: Trump is fucking crazy
Description: New York : Blue Rider Press, an imprint of Penguin Random House, 2017.
Identifiers: LCCN 2017028965 | ISBN 9780525533863 (hardcover) |
ISBN 9780525533887 (epub)
Subjects: LCSH: Trump, Donald, 1946– . | United States—Politics and government—2016– . | Presidents—United States—Election—2016.
Classification: LCC E913 .O43 2017 | DDC 973.933092—dc23
LC record available at https://lccn.loc.gov/2017028965
p.   cm.

Printed in the United States of America
1   3   5   7   9   10   8   6   4   2

Book design by Gretchen Achilles

In memory of Ted and Marie Olbermann,

who would be way *more pissed off than their son is*

Contents

CHAPTER 3 • November 2016, pre–Election Day

PART II

After: THE RESISTANCE

CHAPTER 4 • November 2016, post–Election Day

CHAPTER 11 • June 2017

TRUMP

is F*CKING CRAZY

Introduction

efore my flabby, almost flatulent words about Donald Trump were out of my mouth, I knew Bill Maher was going to beat the crap out of me for saying them.

This was November 6, 2015. To alter a soon-to-be cliché, I had been taking Trump literally but not seriously and figured the Republicans would do what they always did: poll crazy but nominate boring. But now I found myself on Maher's HBO show, hopelessly lost in a Trump story. I had mentioned that I'd first met him in 1984 and had since run into him in the hallways of NBC as well as the lobby of the apartment building that bore his name where I owned a condo. I had observed that—contrary to this hybrid of Huey Long, Mussolini, and Buzz Windrip that seemed to inhabit Trump's body during the campaign—the conversations were low-key, rational, pleasant each time *I* had talked to him. Even accounting for the likelihood that he was sucking up to me because you don't want an unhappy condo owner with a public profile, these conversations were, stunningly, about *me* and not *him*. He had even written me a fan letter at ESPN.

I was confessing to Maher of having been conned.

I could not stop the self-incrimination. Even though I managed to express the point that the two personalities—Benito Trumpolini and Eddie Trump-Haskell—were both incredibly convincing and the longer he used them both, the less it mattered which was the "real" Trump, I knew Bill; after all, we'd originally run into each other in college in 1978—and within seconds we were arguing, with him calling me a "corporate sellout" at a juncture in my life when all the corporations in the history of the world had paid me about $100 in total. Now, thirty-seven years later, Maher was going to call me a lot worse than a corporate sellout.

Only, he didn't.

He completely agreed with me.

He couldn't have agreed more with me and my assessment of Trump's in-person non-Mussolinism had he said, "Golly gumption, Keith, you're right, he was super neato pleasant!"

That was my Trumpian tipping point.

I was born with a pretty solid bullshit detector, honed by twenty years covering sports for a living and nearly twenty more after that covering politics and news and sports, often all at the same time. But Bill's bullshit detector was so much better than mine that it was weaponized—and somehow even *he* had been taken in by Trump. If you see the video of my appearance that night on Bill's show you'll notice a little tic in my left eye as it registers in my head: *Trump was able to fool Maher?*

When I walked off his stage that night, the thoughts came as fast and as loud as any I had ever had. It wasn't implausible that Trump had conned me. But Trump had conned *Maher*? Those aren't two integrated personalities Trump wears interchangeably like different penis-draping ties. These are manifestations of acute mental illness. Trump isn't just a scam artist and he isn't merely a reincarnated P. T. Barnum. This is a psychopath. This is a clear and present danger. *Soylent Green is people. They're after you, they're after all of us, our wives, our children, everyone! They're here already! You maniacs! You blew it up! Damn you! God damn you all to hell! You're gonna need a bigger boat!*

I'll spare you the full details of the process that ten months later led to my election-year commentary series that was supposed to keep the car alarm bleating and help my old nemesis Hillary Clinton seal her victory. Besides me, there was one other guy who was asking the question "Why isn't Olbermann doing commentaries about this?" and he was Geoff Gagnon, the articles editor at *GQ* magazine. At our first meeting about doing a series we called it *The Closer* because we were still beholden to pre-11/8 thinking that all Hillary needed was somebody to close the deal for her.

*

When the perfect Russian storm hit and the nightmare came to life on Election Day, Geoff and I, and *GQ*'s video executive producer, Dorenna Newton, and photographer-editor Peter Calvin and Noel Howard and Luke Leifeste and the rest of the crew talked for literally a couple of minutes about shutting the thing down. And then we all said: To hell with that, so what if this will be used against us in court, after two months of this guy we aren't going to get a trial—and we renamed the series *The Resistance* and persisted.

The commentary scripts were not designed as a narrative of the closing stages of the campaign and the opening months of this Ray Bradbury Funhouse Mirror of a presidency. But when I read them in order, it was shocking to me how they formed themselves into one. It's like digesting a diary rescued from the *Titanic* and actually finding yourself hoping against your better judgment that *this* time the damn boat won't hit the damn iceberg.

I'd love to say I planned it that way, but I didn't. I don't think it's been noted anywhere, but views for each commentary began to rival, then surpass, the high-water-mark ratings of cable news—the total audience for the series eventually exceeded 300 million. I never got a dime out of the videos—I asked *GQ* only for a few charitable contributions in my name and some (much-needed) fashion help. I hoped all along that the project would be put out of business because the grown-ups would ultimately stop this lunatic from being elected, or from being confirmed by the Electoral College, or from being sworn in, or from *not* being removed by the fourth clause of the Twenty-fifth Amendment the *first* time he showed he was crazier than Ted Bundy, Ted Kaczynski, and Ted Cruz put together.

Tragically, there *weren't* any grown-ups, only opportunists who were too busy leveraging Trump's election to their own advantage for political power or ratings or for paying off mortgages. Crazy old John Brown hastened the coming Civil War and said the crimes of this guilty land would never be purged away but with blood. I don't think we're nearly at that point—yet—but I'm just as confident as he was, that the crimes of this self-absorbed land will never be purged away but with everything from Lexuses to the repossession of personal freedoms.

This may seem like an odd point to make here, but bear with me for a moment. By marriage and adoption, I'm Mike Tyson's distant cousin (he was adopted by his first trainer and manager, Cus D'Amato; D'Amato's late niece Gerry was my uncle's wife). Thirty years ago, Trump—who was then involved in the boxing-promotion business because of his casino venues—and the infamous promoter Don King squeezed Cus's protégé trainer Kevin Rooney and other D'Amato disciples out of Tyson's coterie. They also told Mike—forgive me, *cousin Mike*—that he was the champ now and he no longer had to do the things that Cus and Kevin used to insist he do. You know, like taking the cocktail of medications that kept him surprisingly stable and unexpectedly kind and even sweet-hearted but harshed his buzz, or sticking to a diet, or training, or not attacking people, or not giving away $200,000 cars to strangers. King and Trump came into a situation that was seemingly permanently under control, disabled the brakes and busted the headlights and painted over the speed-limit signs, and within a few years, Tyson was in prison, convicted of rape.

The point of this book is to chronicle how Trump managed to get America to choose him to do to our country what Trump helped do to my cousin Mike. These commentaries are *about* what Trump's mixture of illness, hucksterism, amorality, and manipulative cunning has done to the United States, so I won't belabor you with some long meta-analysis right here. But I will say that I suspect you'll reach the same kind of conclusion I did after reading all these scripts at once. Trump's immeasurable ego and his "Wheeee! The Rules Don't Apply to Meeeeee!" attitude (which mirrors the bravado of the opioid abuser—plus whatever else is wrong with him) found a partner in that less than half of the electorate that ultimately doesn't give a shit about anybody they don't know personally (and not a lot of people they *do* know personally, either).

Trump gives them permission to ignore whatever principles they might have. Trump gives them permission to believe that laws and invoices and religions apply only to others. Trump gives even the lower-incomed among them confirmation that they can act with vengeance against the less fortunate because he's going to make his "fans" rich. Trump gives them the right to dispute facts. Trump gives them the right to ignore warnings. Trump gives them the right to hate. Trump gives them the right to stop doing what other people and common sense and common decency tell them to do. Trump gives them the right to say, "We don't have to have any more black people or women running this country." Trump gives them the right to do what he does when he's caught lying, stealing, obstructing, or selling out the country: just make up a cover story, the wilder the better—the rubes will believe it. Trump gives them the right to be stupid and goddamned proud of it.

Just remember as you read, that this can be fixed whenever we will it. We who have seen him for what he is, and fought him and the driving-morally-drunk America still cheering him, are not some fringe group scuttling in the darkness.

We are the majority.

Let's act like it.

PART I

Before:

I'M KEITH OLBERMANN and this is

THE CLOSER

Chapter 1

SEPTEMBER 2016

176 REASONS DONALD TRUMP SHOULDN'T BE PRESIDENT

Post date • TUESDAY, SEPTEMBER 13

In brief, the Trump presidential campaign so far:

The Republican Party has actually nominated for president a man who attacked the Pope.

Who attacked John McCain for being captured by the North Vietnamese.

Who attacked Gold Star parents Khizr and Ghazala Khan and then juxtaposed their names with the phrase "Radical Islamic Terrorism."

Who attacked Hillary Clinton as a "bigot."

Who attacked her as "brainwashed." As "unhinged." As "a monster." As "the devil." As "the most corrupt candidate ever"—showing her face on piles of hundred-dollar bills and the Star of David.

Who attacked her as someone whom "Second Amendment people" should do something about.

As someone whose religion "we don't know anything about"—after *he* had explained he had never asked God for forgiveness.

*

The Republican Party has actually nominated for president a man who attacked President Obama and implied he was a traitor. Who attacked him as having been complicit in the Orlando terrorist attack. Who attacked him for having lower approval ratings than Vladimir Putin, as if Putin's were real. Who attacked Obama as being born in another country.

Who attacked him as the founder of ISIS, then said it was sarcasm, then said it wasn't sarcasm, then attacked him again as the founder of ISIS.

Who attacked Carly Fiorina for her face. Hillary Clinton for her nonpresidential "look."

Heidi Cruz for her appearance. Heidi Cruz for her past *depression*.

Megyn Kelly for having "blood coming out of her wherever."

Mika Brzezinski as "very crazy and dumb," "neurotic," "not very bright," "a mess."

Who attacked the women harassed by Roger Ailes.

Who attacked women who choose abortion—and said they must be "punished."

*

Who attacked a *New York Times* reporter because he had an illness that made his arms look atypical; who attacked Judge Gonzalo Curiel because he was of Mexican descent; who attacked Senator Elizabeth Warren over allegedly lying about her heritage to get into Harvard, when she never *went* to Harvard.

*

The Republican Party has actually nominated for president a man who attacked U.S. troops in Iraq and claimed they stole millions; attacked Ted Cruz's father and claimed he helped to kill President Kennedy; attacked Bill Clinton and claimed he was a rapist.

Who attacked *Mexicans* as rapists, bringing drugs and crime; who attacked African Americans and claimed they were all living in poverty, with no jobs, and schools that were no good; who attacked Harrisburg, Pennsylvania, as a "war zone" and attacked the United States of America, claiming it is in a "death spiral."

*

The Republican Party has actually nominated for president a man who lied about opposing the war in Iraq, when there is a tape of him supporting it. A tape recorded on the first anniversary of 9/11 . . .

Who lied about opposing the war in Iraq during a speech in which he insisted, "I will never lie to you."

Who lied about $6 million in charitable donations to veterans' groups from his telethon; who lied about his charitable donations from *The Apprentice*; from *The Celebrity Apprentice*; from Trump: The Game; to St. Jude cancer center.

Who lied about debating Bernie Sanders for charity.

Who lied about why he wouldn't release his taxes because he was being audited, and proved himself a liar by saying he *would* release his taxes if Secretary Clinton released emails; who lied about how much money his father gave him, or helped him get, coming out of college; who lied about sending his private jet to ferry stranded U.S. servicemen; who lied about talking to the attorney general of Florida about pay for play.

Who lied about his business in Russia; who lied about meeting Putin; who lied about Putin's using the n-word about Barack Obama, when that n-word was actually "nuclear."

Who lied about offering childcare to his employees, when it was childcare for his hotel guests; who lied about a moment of silence for the murderer of five Dallas policemen; who lied about seeing thousands of Muslims in New Jersey celebrating 9/11; who lied about 9/11 hijackers sending their wives and girlfriends home to Saudi Arabia.

Who lied about thousands of Syrian refugee terrorists being secretly admitted to this country; who lied about the Chicago police urging him to cancel a rally; who lied about the Chicago police saying they could solve crime there with "tough tactics"; who lied about how there was no drought in California, how he never said Japan should have nuclear weapons.

How he opposed the ouster of Egyptian president Mubarak.

How the unemployment rate is 42 percent.

*

Who lied about ISIS making millions a week selling Libyan oil; who lied about dozens of secret terrorist cases in this country.

Who lied that a protester who tried to rush onto his stage had "ties to ISIS"; who lied about refugees entering this country carrying cell phones with "ISIS flags on them" and phone plans prepaid by ISIS!

Can you hear me now?

*

The Republican Party has actually nominated for president a man who congratulated himself in two tweets and a press release for predicting terrorist attacks like Orlando, while bodies still lay in the Pulse nightclub . . .

Who congratulated himself after the murder of Dwyane Wade's cousin.

Who congratulated himself on predicting Brexit, even though three weeks earlier he had never heard of Brexit.

Who congratulated himself on Republican Convention TV ratings, even though those for his closing speech were the lowest since 2004.

Who congratulated himself by disseminating a video showing how much of that speech's total running time was taken up by . . . applause.

*

Who congratulated himself on having "the world's best memory," then three weeks later testified in a deposition that he had no memory of saying that.

*

The Republican Party has actually nominated for president a man who has proposed that Russia or China should enact a Watergate-like hacking of Hillary Clinton's emails; who has proposed banning Muslims from entering the country, then said it was only a suggestion, then proposed it again; who has proposed banning members of other religions; who has proposed open racial profiling; who has proposed banning people from "terror nations," saying, "Look it up: they have a list." Who has proposed "ideological certifications" for immigrants; who has proposed worse than waterboarding while praising how Saddam Hussein, Vladimir Putin, Kim Jong-un, and the Chinese government handled protest and terrorism; who has proposed that American citizens be tried by military commissions at Gitmo; who has proposed killing the families of terrorists or suspected terrorists.

A man who has proposed teaching patriotism in schools; proposed that his supporters act as vigilantes on Election Day; proposed making American protection of fellow NATO members COD; proposed purging the government of all Obama appointees.

Proposed avoiding government debt by printing *more* money.

Proposed reducing national debt by paying *less* than we agreed to.

Proposed eliminating all financial regulations by executive order—and then, in the same speech, proposed eliminating . . . all executive orders.

*

A man who has proposed a wall along the Mexican border to keep out undocumented immigrants; and proposed mass deportation of undocumented immigrants.

Proposed a smaller wall and fewer deportations during a taped television interview that played at the same moment he was giving a speech insisting on a *larger* wall and *more* deportations.

A man who has proposed immediately expelling at least two to three million undocumented immigrants, even though this would be like trying to evacuate the city of Chicago in a day; proposed *immediately* expelling any others not convicted but merely *accused* of a crime.

A man who has proposed to enact all this by executive order, bypassing Congress—even though he employed undocumented immigrants in the building of Trump Tower; even though those immigrants say he not only knew *of* them but hired them personally; even though his own modeling agency and television shows enabled and employed undocumented immigrants; even though his own wife may have been an undocumented immigrant; even though his own grandfather was not merely a fraudulent immigrant to this country but also was denied reentry to Germany because he was a draft dodger.

*

The Republican Party has actually nominated for president a man who has claimed he understood the sacrifice of a child in war because he had spent money to hire employees.

Who has claimed he understood prejudice against African Americans because the system is also rigged against *him*; claimed the election will be rigged against him; claimed the opinion polls are rigged against him; then praised one of the exact same polls when it favored him; claimed he would be leading those rigged polls by twenty points but for rigged media; claimed Democrats are voting ten times each; claimed that his crowd in Colorado Springs would've been larger if the fire marshal hadn't been a Democrat; claimed that his speech in

Washington would have drawn more than Martin Luther King's "I Have a Dream" speech, but "they wouldn't let them in."

A man who has claimed he was his own best foreign policy adviser; claimed that Putin will not go into Ukraine, when he already invaded Ukraine in 2014; claimed the United States is paying rent for a military base in Saudi Arabia, when the last one there closed in 2003; claimed that to avoid hacking, the military should stop communicating "on wires" and return to using messengers.

A man who has claimed that any candidate using a teleprompter should be ineligible, then himself began using a teleprompter.

Who claimed that he doesn't use notes for speeches during a speech he gave primarily from notes; claimed he will fix the problems of African Americans, then the next day suggested that an African American athlete protesting police shootings should leave this country.

*

The Republican Party has actually nominated for president a man who was revealed to have asked his foreign policy advisers three times in one hour why this country can't use nuclear weapons if we *have* nuclear weapons—after having asked a television interviewer the same question; who was revealed to have not known what the nuclear triad is.

A man who was revealed to have been the beneficiary of fake internet accounts underwritten by the Kremlin; revealed to have improperly sought campaign contributions from foreign nationals, including officials of foreign governments.

A man who was revealed to have erased all his emails, including those sought in a lawsuit, for five years; revealed to have improperly repurposed hotel mailing lists into campaign fund-raising lists; revealed to have plagiarized twenty pages in his "Trump Institute" handbook; revealed to have employed the purported author of his wife's convention speech, which plagiarized a speech written for Michelle Obama by Hillary Clinton's speechwriter; revealed to have said on his 2008 radio show that Hillary Clinton would "make a good president."

A man who was revealed to have used the pseudonyms "John Barron" and "John Miller" while pretending to be his own press spokesman and boasting of his sexual conquests in the 1980s.

Revealed to have used the pseudonym "John Baron" while his company threatened his undocumented workers; revealed to have telephoned one television network to alert it to something positive being said about him on another television network.

A man revealed to have millions in outstanding loans to the Bank of China; revealed to have tried to make investment deals with Muammar Qaddafi.

Revealed to have once kept a book of Hitler's speeches in a cabinet near his bed.

*

The Republican Party has actually nominated for president a man who has *allied* himself with his campaign adviser and delegate who said Hillary Clinton should be shot by firing squad for treason; who has allied himself with another campaign adviser who wants to *waterboard* Hillary Clinton; who has allied himself with an African American pastor who disseminated an image of Hillary Clinton in blackface; who has allied himself with his own son who follows a series of white supremacist Twitter accounts.

A man who has allied himself with at least seven campaign staffers who have disseminated racist and/or violent messages on social media; who has allied himself with a state campaign chairman who tweeted, "Lynch Loretta Lynch"; who has allied himself with an *Illinois* Trump delegate who is a white supremacist; a *California* Trump delegate who is a white nationalist leader; a former personal butler who wrote on Facebook that President Obama should be "hung for treason."

A man who has allied himself with three different campaign chiefs: the first who manhandled a woman reporter, then lied about it; the second who received $12 million from a pro-Russia political party in Ukraine; the third who has been accused under oath of anti-Semitic comments and domestic violence.

A man who has allied himself with a *foreign policy adviser* accused under oath of anti-Semitic comments; with a New York State co-chair who asked if Khizr Khan supported ISIS and was a member of the Muslim Brotherhood; with an adviser who says a Clinton aide could be a "Saudi spy" or "terrorist agent."

A man who has allied himself with a campaign state chairman accused of drawing a gun on another campaign staffer; with a conspiracy theorist radio host who claims the Newtown school shooting was an inside job; with a political operative so corrupt he was once fired—by Republicans—for falsifying evidence against Hillary Clinton.

＊

The Republican Party has actually nominated for president a man who has offered to pay the legal fees of any supporter who becomes physically violent against a heckler; who encouraged crowd members to harass and threaten reporters, some of whom he has called out by name and who thus needed Secret Service protection.

Who accepted a military medal from an audience member and said, "I always wanted to get the Purple Heart. This was much easier"; who conducted a news conference to introduce his running mate, only to spend the first twenty-five minutes talking only about himself; whose Latino outreach director warned that Mexican immigration would put "taco trucks on every corner"—four months after the nominee commemorated Cinco de Mayo by tweeting a photo of himself eating from a taco bowl.

The Republican Party has actually nominated for president a man who tweeted thanks to singer Billy Joel for dedicating a song to him, never realizing that Joel was, by doing so, mocking him; who gave a trade speech in Monessen, Pennsylvania, standing in front of a wall made of bales of compressed garbage; who gave a television interview while seated in front of a photograph of himself wearing the same suit, shirt, and tie; who appeared, in a joint news conference with the president of Mexico, with two bobby pins visible, holding his hairdo in place.

＊

The Republican Party has actually nominated for president an irresponsible, unrealistic, naive, petulant, childish, vindictive, prejudiced, bigoted, racist, Islamophobic, anti-Semitic, misogynistic, fascistic, authoritarian, insensitive, erratic, disturbed, irrational, inhuman individual named Donald John Trump.

This . . . is madness.

＊

Any questions?

THE RUMORMONGERING ABOUT HILLARY'S HEALTH IS . . . DEPLORABLE

Post date • WEDNESDAY, SEPTEMBER 14

Even in a campaign built out of unintended irony, there has been nothing *more* ironic than questions about Hillary Clinton's pneumonia—and whether she's fit to serve—still coming from the campaign of an opponent who will not denounce or even distance himself from supporters who often shout that she should be killed or hanged or shot for treason.

"We want you dead, but we're concerned that your health disqualifies you from being elected."

Well, there *is* one thing *more* ironic than that:

That Donald Trump's point man on Secretary Clinton's health is Rudy Giuliani.

Rudy! Seriously?

The media "fails to point out several signs of illness by her. All you've got to do is go online and put down 'Hillary Clinton illness.' Take a look at the videos for yourself."

Doctor Rudy Giuliani!

Rudy, do you even *remember* when *you* ran for president yourself, starting in 2006—when you were still considered a short-term survivor of prostate cancer?

Do you remember anybody saying it was disqualifying in any way?

Do you remember anybody saying that the possibility of recurrence, or the chance that you might have cancer anywhere else in your body, might make you unfit to seek the office?

Did any of your opponents have the gall to *attack* you over your own health?

Did any of your opponents do that when you were first diagnosed?

While you were running for the Senate seat from New York? Who were you running against again?

Oh, right! Hillary Clinton!

The New York Times, April 28, 2000: "Mrs. Clinton spoke to the mayor by phone yesterday while campaigning in the Finger Lakes district and wished him, according to her press secretary, Howard Wolfson, a 'speedy recovery.' The mayor, who has been sharply critical of both Mrs. Clinton and the Clinton administration in recent weeks, said, 'Thank you,' according to Mr. Wolfson. The conversation, Mr. Wolfson said, lasted one minute."

What the hell, Rudy?

That doesn't sound like an attack on *you* for not addressing your health sooner or having the media cover it up for you!

What about when you had to drop out because of the cancer?

The New York Times, May 20, 2000: "Mrs. Clinton, who telephoned the mayor shortly after his announcement, said afterward, 'I certainly hope and pray, as I know all New Yorkers do, that he will have a full and speedy recovery.'"

Whaddya mean she didn't say you were hiding something?

Whaddya mean she didn't start chanting, "Lock him up! Lock him up!"?

More from sixteen years ago: "Asked if she would miss the mayor as an opponent, Mrs. Clinton replied, 'Well, I think we should just wish him well as a person.'"

Wait—where's the reference to your marital scandal that was going on at the same time?

You mean she *didn't* accuse you of using your health as an excuse? She *didn't* claim that you were really dropping out because ten days earlier you had announced you wanted a separation from your wife and you left her to conduct a tearful news conference outside the gates of the mayor's mansion?

And Rudy, if *you* have permission to diagnose Secretary Clinton from videos *you saw on the internet*—maybe you got it from Trump's physician, Dr. Vinnie Boombatz—may *I* suggest that having seen you in person several times over the past fifteen years (to say nothing of all those videos), it sure looks to me from my completely and utterly unqualified position as a *not-doctor* that you've been waging a losing battle against ever-increasing symptoms of post-traumatic stress disorder.

Rudy Giuliani!

The only reason he kept the job as chief Clinton health rumormonger was that, while Newt Gingrich was on the air spewing to Sean Hannity about Clinton's coughing fits, Gingrich had . . . a coughing fit.

And Tom Brokaw. Dr. Tom Brokaw! Who in 2008, threatened by the Republicans that their candidate wouldn't show up to the debate he was moderating unless he got me and Chris Matthews thrown off MSNBC coverage of the debates, not only *carried* that barrel of GOP water but then boasted about it in the papers . . . Tom Brokaw saying, an hour after the pneumonia overcame Secretary Clinton inside the 9/11 ceremony:

"Just this morning I had a rather detailed message from a Republican who was inside, and he was raising questions as well, saying, 'I didn't know if this is true, but here are the incidents that we are all watching.' . . . I think that she should go to a hospital, see a neurologist, and get a clean report if it is available to her."

Hey, Tom. I worked with you for nine years. Brought you back from the professional dead to work with us on the cable coverage. *I* think *you* should go to a mirror and see if you have any journalistic credibility left.

It was *pneumonia.*

Bad! Guess! Tom!

*

For crying out loud, Hillary Clinton has been campaigning with pneumonia since at *least* last Friday, and making more sense per minute than Trump has in his entire campaign.

"How's her *health*?"!

She's frickin' Wonder Woman!

THE DEPLORABLES REDEPLOY

Post date • THURSDAY, SEPTEMBER 15

Not to applaud tricks from the poli-sci-fi movie *The Manchurian Candidate* too loudly, but anybody notice that—five days later—we aren't debating *whether or not* Trump supporters are "deplorable"—we're debating how *many* of them are?

And by the way, Hillary Clinton was dead wrong about this.

"*Half*"?

*

The Trump Gang is trying to pull off the neat trick of making "deplorable" into a red badge of courage while *simultaneously* scoring martyr points by insisting it was an inappropriate attack.

It's not going well.

Somebody asks Mike "I, Robot" Pence if he would agree merely that *David Duke* is deplorable, and Pence seems offended by the question and says he's not in the name-calling business, whereupon his buddy Mike Lee, Republican senator from Utah, tells Pence that he at least must call Duke's *racism* deplorable and that the Trump campaign must repudiate the alt-right.

Then campaign manager Kellyanne Conway tries to pivot away to Hillary's health by claiming that Secretary Clinton "lied" about her pneumonia. Unfortunately, when pressed about whether Trump should release his full medical records, *she* seems offended and says that everybody—even Trump—has a "right to privacy"—apparently completely unaware that less than three weeks ago, Trump *offered* to release his full medical records.

And while *that* gaffe is still echoing, the Deplorables again steal the stage. Video spreads of a protester getting grabbed by the neck and punched by a Trump supporter during his speech in Asheville—whereupon they ejected . . . not the choker . . . but the *choked*.

And *then* a sixty-nine-year-old woman, after the same speech, tells a Trump supporter that if Trump gets elected, the guy had better learn Russian, and the first words he *should* learn should be "ha-ha-ha"—so he decks the woman, who is injured when the punch sends her crashing into her portable oxygen tank.

And this kinder, gentler Trump campaign—well, it *is* kinder, gentler: the Trump supporters aren't all wearing the same-colored shirts yet—this comes the same week the hapless campaign manager number three (perhaps out of four), Conway, had convinced her boss to do fewer big events with dangerous crowds, and thus tamp down all the noise about "deplorable."

*

What was that Hillary Clinton said about them again?

"Racist, sexist, homophobic, xenophobic, Islamophobic."

Annnnnnd . . . your point?

*

But forget the *supporters* for a moment . . .

What about the *advocates*?

Racist?

A co-chair of Trump's campaign in New York, Carl Paladino, former Republican nominee for governor, on Twitter: "Lynch Loretta Lynch." It was a typo by a staffer, they explained. Ah, but six years ago he sent out a video of an African tribal dance. The email was titled "Obama Inauguration Rehearsal."

Sexist?

Trump himself talking about Megyn Kelly? Or Mika Brzezinski? Or Heidi Cruz? Or Carly Fiorina?

Homophobic?

Robert Jeffress, the Texas megachurch pastor who led the prayer at a Trump rally in June, a year after he said gay rights "will pave the way for that future world dictator, the Antichrist, to persecute and martyr Christians without any repercussions whatsoever"?

Islamophobic?

The New York co-chair Paladino again, on Khizr Khan: "I mean, if he's a member of the Muslim Brotherhood or supporting the ISIS type of attitude against America, there's no reason for Donald Trump to have to honor this man."

And *xenophobic?*

Ubiquitous campaign spokeswoman Katrina Pierson, four years ago: "Perfect Obama's dad born in Africa, Mitt Romney's dad born in Mexico. Any pure breeds left?"

If you say "pure breeds" and you're not in a Harry Potter film or at a dog show, you have a screw loose.

These are campaign leaders, surrogates, friends of Mr. Trump—if they're not talking to a basket of deplorables, who *are* they talking to?

Why would you have them there? You say stuff like that at work, you get fired. You say it at school, you get suspended.

But happily, Trump is there to say, "No, it's okay to hate. Better than that, you can hate out loud! We'll just call it 'freedom of speech' and 'Make America Great Again'!"

*

Secretary Clinton originally postulated that *half* of Trump supporters were *not* deplorable.

And *that's* where she screwed up.

Because if you support Trump . . .

If you think he should be president *regardless* of how much he and his advocates *hate* . . . and mock . . . and punch old women with portable oxygen canisters . . .

If you're not condemning this madness and repudiating these deplorable people and you are *not* racist, or sexist or homophobic or xenophobic or Islamophobic . . .

If you're supporting him not *for* those things but *in spite* of them . . .

You are even *more* deplorable.

The correct number, Secretary Clinton, is not 50 percent . . .

But a hundred!

KING LEAR

Post date • **TUESDAY, SEPTEMBER 20**

Beware the demagogue who knows everything.

Because nearly every demagogue, ever, has actually known . . . nothing.

Donald Trump is a demagogue.

You tweet him that I just called him this.

Then tweet him again, explaining to him what a demagogue is.

This is a demagogue.

Late last Saturday, a dumpster blew up on Twenty-third Street in New York.

The perfect 2016 campaign analogy, of course.

Also the perfect *opportunity* for Donald J. Trump, Demagogue, to, per the definition, be "a political leader who seeks support by appealing to popular desires and prejudices rather than by using rational argument."

So he got off his plane in Colorado Springs and told the crowd there that "a bomb went off in New York and nobody knows exactly what's going on. But boy, we are living in a time—we better get very tough, folks. We better get very, very tough.... It's a terrible thing that's going on in our world, in our country, and we are going to get tough and smart and vigilant."

Trump said that *before* any official had confirmed it was a bomb.

Before any expert, literally, could *have* any idea what was going on.

He couldn't wait.

He couldn't wait *literally* because he is a compulsive talker, a gossiping child.

He couldn't wait *metaphorically* because he clearly knows that terrorist attacks benefit him. He needs them. Alone in this country, to him they are preferable to—you know—no more terrorism. They fit his product: this vast, free-floating sense of panic and the need for vigilance—or is the right word "vigilantism"?—that he is so successfully selling.

It *had* to be a bomb.

It *had* to be evidence of the vast plot against his voters that—to use his words—only he can fix.

"Nobody knows what's going on," Donald Trump said.

*

True.

Least of all...Donald Trump.

"We're going to have to do something extremely tough," he said Monday morning.

"Like what?" he was asked by the other guy accused by Gretchen Carlson.

"Over there. Like, knock the hell out of them. And we have to get everybody together and we have to lead for a change, because we're not knocking them..."

Trump has no idea what to do except "knock them."

There's no plan, secret or otherwise.

There is nothing he is concealing.

There is no deal for him to make.

Trump! Confused?

Actually, Trump is just Shakespeare's King Lear.

"I will have such revenges on you both
that all the world shall—I will do such things!,—

What they are, yet I know not; but they shall be
The terrors of the earth."

No plan, no clue.
Just a lot of "knocking them."

*

Donald Trump has had no plan against terrorism, ISIS or otherwise, for a long time.

He has been doing his "terrors of the earth" King Lear bit for at least sixteen months, when in reality, to paraphrase Winston Churchill, he wouldn't know the difference between a first lieutenant and a Mark 48 torpedo.

May 27, 2015. To Fox News: "I do know what to do, and I would know how to bring ISIS to the table or, beyond that, defeat ISIS very quickly. And I'm not gonna tell you what it is tonight."

Even the Fox host was appalled: "Why won't you tell? We need all the help we can get!"

"I don't want the enemy to know what I'm doing. Unfortunately, I'll probably have to tell at some point, but there is a method of defeating them quickly and effectively and having total victory."

Hate him or love him, there is a small germ of logic in that.

Or there would have been, had Trump not been lying.

He wasn't keeping the plan from *ISIS*—he was keeping it from Ted Cruz and Marco Rubio.

The next month, to *The Des Moines Register*:

"The problem with politics is if I tell you right now, everyone else is going to say, 'Wow, what a great idea.' You're going to have ten candidates go and use it, and they're going to forget where it came from, which is me. But no, I have an absolute way of defeating ISIS."

Because Trump's plan to defeat ISIS was an "absolute way," but he would keep it a secret for a year and a half, rather than tell America's generals right then, in June 2015.

So instead, we had the June beheading in France, the November Paris attacks at the Bataclan and the stadium and the restaurants, the German attacks, the San Bernardino attack last December . . .

Those all would not have happened if Donald Trump, Super Genius, had said, "This will work, General."

Even if he demanded public credit for it afterwards.

Which he would have gotten.

April 2016. Trump's clownish foreign policy speech:

For Isis: "I have a simple message for them: their days are numbered. I won't tell them where and I won't tell them how . . .

"But they're going to be gone. ISIS will be gone if I'm elected president. And they'll be gone quickly."

So if he'd gone to the generals *then* with his plan, no ISIS.

No attack on the Pulse club in Orlando in June.

No suicide attack at Ansbach, Germany, in July.

No priest killed in Rouen, France.

No ISIS lunatic driving a truck down the boardwalk in Nice during holiday fireworks, killing 86 and injuring 434.

No whatever-this-was in New York and New Jersey last weekend.

All because Donald Trump wanted to keep his foolproof plan a secret, *from* the generals, from the public, *from* the families of those who would yet suffer.

And finally, *this* month, we get an inkling of the plan.

Trump, at Greenville, North Carolina:

"We are going to convene my top generals and give them a simple instruction. They will have thirty days to submit to the Oval Office a plan for soundly and quickly defeating ISIS. We have no choice."

Trump could've also added: ". . . and we have no *plan*."

The secret plan, the foolproof plan, "the absolute way of defeating ISIS," the one he wouldn't tell and thus hundreds of people who could've been saved by it were instead murdered—the one he alone could devise, because, as he said, he knows more about ISIS than the generals . . . The big plan is to tell the generals they have to think up a plan.

*

Trump had no plan. He has no plan. He *will* have no plan.

He is not a leader. He is not tough. He is not concerned about ISIS except as a sales tool to get your vote.

He knows nothing.

He has nothing.

Except a tweet: "Once again someone we were told is ok turns out to be a terrorist who wants to destroy our country & its people- how did he get thru system?"

Well, my understanding is, his grandfather emigrated from Bremen in 1885, and then changed the family name from Drumpf, and the guy you're referring to is that man's grandson.

Donald Trump is our national shame.

ASSASSINATION

Post date • **WEDNESDAY, SEPTEMBER 21**

Donald Trump has *repeated* the worst thing he has done in this campaign— worse than the smearing of African Americans or the self-congratulations over the Orlando nightclub shooting or even the display of madness as he petulantly backed away from the lifeblood of his campaign, birtherism.

Worse than *all that.*

Worse than anything any other candidate for president has done in our history.

And it is the second time he has done it.

And after he did it, he reminded everybody he did it on Twitter.

And because you may have already forgotten it.

Because within twenty-four hours, with the atrocity of his message already in the ears of those to whom it was music, Donald Trump did what he always does. To prevent getting called in by the grown-ups, he changed the subject. He did something else. He shot off his big bazoo about another topic— in this case, about the terrorism here in New York—and suddenly he got us yelling at him, as he always does, over something not . . . quite . . . as bad . . . as what he had said the day before.

Trump, you again dog-whistled for somebody to assassinate your opponent.

You did it in a speech in Miami. Then you went back to a hotel and obsessed over what they were saying about you online like you were a fourteen-year-old, like you do every night and every morning, and there wasn't enough praise for the omniscient, omnipotent Trumpness of your being—so you dog-whistled again, on Twitter.

What kind of sick bastard are you, Trump?

Again, predicating this on another one of your lies—that Hillary Clinton wants to eliminate the Second Amendment . . . I wish! As if somebody could!—you said:

"I think that her bodyguards should drop all weapons. They should disarm. I think they should disarm immediately; what do you think, yes? Take their guns away, she doesn't want guns. *Take them, let's see what happens to her.* Take their guns away, okay? It will be very dangerous."

Trump, what do you think those idiots out *there* think you meant?

It'll be dangerous, Trump, because . . . the Secret Service dropping its weapons will . . . damage the floor?

It'll be dangerous because without guns the Secret Service wouldn't be able to protect crowds from escaped circus animals?

The people who heard you say, "Take their guns away, let's see what happens" will think you meant: "Somebody should shoot her. See what she thinks of gun control *then.*"

And they will think that, Trump, because that's what you meant.

Because that's also what you meant when you said it in North Carolina in August. "If she gets to pick her judges, nothing you can do, folks. Although the Second Amendment people—maybe there is, I don't know."

You meant . . . shoot her.

You meant kill her.

You meant assassinate her.

And even when the former director of the CIA said that anybody else who said what you said would "be in the back of a police wagon now with the Secret Service questioning him," you went back and did it again, two months later.

Trump, you don't know this, because it's not on Twitter at the moment, but the theme of this country's political history is not greatness, nor growth, nor compromise—it is assassination.

President Reagan: shot—survived.

President Ford: shot at twice in seventeen days—not injured.

President Andrew Jackson: shot at, point-blank. Both guns misfired.

President Truman: *saved* from being shot by White House police.

President Nixon: gunman Arthur Bremer removed by Secret Service. So he shot George Wallace instead a month later.

President *Franklin* Roosevelt: shot at, three weeks before his inauguration. Gunman missed, killed the mayor of Chicago.

President *Theodore* Roosevelt: shot while campaigning to regain the White House.

President Taft: gunman apprehended along his parade route.

President Clinton: gunman shot toward the White House twenty-nine times, thinking a man he saw on the lawn was the president.

President Lincoln: shot dead.

President Garfield: shot dead.

President McKinley: shot dead.

President Kennedy: shot dead.

*

Thirteen of our presidents, Trump.

Thirteen of our presidents—30 percent, nearly one in three—shot and killed, or shot and injured, or shot at but escaped harm, or *very nearly* shot at.

And you—three times in two months—*you* dog-whistle to the worst dregs of this gun-crazed, death-wish society—that the "Second Amendment people" should do something, that "guns be taken from her heavily armed Secret Service detail," that we should "see what happens to her."

*

When, eight years ago, Hillary Clinton merely *mentioned* that she hadn't ended her Democratic nomination bid yet, because a previous front-runner like Bobby Kennedy had been assassinated, she was excoriated. She was shunned. *I* shunned her. It remains her low point.

And she apologized within hours. The same day, Trump.

And she never dog-whistled for somebody to shoot her *opponent*, as you did.

And she didn't just change the subject.

She didn't do what you did.

Enraged as you were that you had to admit to your lie about birtherism, *you* went out and brought up assassination the same night.

To wish, to incite, to dog-whistle—to do anything *but* repudiate and fight against—physical violence against a political leader in this country is beyond despicable.

With our history, with our political annals stained with the blood of everybody from Martin Luther King to Ronald Reagan to Harvey Milk!

And I pity you, Trump, that you have so little humanity or decency inside you that you could so cravenly and dismissively say it . . . "Let's see what happens to her."

But *I* know what should happen to *you*, Trump.

That ex–CIA director, General Michael Hayden, was right.

August 9, after you did this. The *first* time.

Because of "the prevalence of political assassination inside of American history and how that is a topic that we don't ever come close to, even when we think we're trying to be lighthearted.

"If someone else had said that outside the hall, he'd be in the back of a police wagon now, with the Secret Service questioning him."

You made a call for violence against the other candidate for president, Trump, less than two months before the election. Repeated it three times, once on social media.

And the Secret Service should take General Hayden's cue.

And you, Trump . . . you should be in the back of a police wagon now, being questioned.

And then, you know what? Let's see what happens.

IS TRUMP LOYAL TO THE UNITED STATES?

Post date • **WEDNESDAY, SEPTEMBER 28**

Is Donald Trump *knowingly* acting as an agent of the Russian government?

Or is he just such a stooge that it only *looks* that way *by accident*?

We are running out of other explanations.

And we need an explanation *now*, about an investment banker named Carter Page.

He didn't come up in the debate—too much time was wasted because of the defective automatic sniffling microphone they gave the Republican nominee.

But Carter Page *should* have come up.

And we need him explained by *you*—Trump.

Because Carter Page is one of *your* guys.

Because U.S. intelligence agents are sifting through reports that Page has met with a top aide to the Russian dictator, Vladimir Putin, *in* Moscow—a man who is Putin's deputy chief for internal policy and whom this country believes is responsible for the information collected by the *Russian* intelligence agencies about... the U.S. presidential vote.

Translation: your guy reportedly met with the *Russian* guy spying on our election. *In Moscow.*

This is a problem, Trump.

This... is *your* problem.

And before you say your people have resolved this...

Because Kellyanne Conway said, "He's not part of our national security or foreign policy briefings that we do now at all, certainly not since I have become campaign manager. If he's doing that, he's certainly not doing it with the permission or knowledge of the campaign, the activities that you described."

Or because another guy said that, relative to the campaign, Carter Page "has no role. We are not aware of any of his activities, past or present."

What your toadies *just* said about Page, Trump...

Is different from what a different toady said about Page last *month*...

When she called him your "informal foreign adviser."

And it's different from what Carter Page now tells an opinion columnist from *The Washington Post*...

That "he is taking a leave of absence from his work with the Trump campaign due to the controversy," and that in his travels to Russia this July, "Page said he made clear that he was acting in his personal capacity and not as a member of the Trump campaign."

So now *all four* of these quotes are different from what you said, Trump, in March.

The Washington Post asked you for the names of your foreign policy team, and the second guy *you* named... was Carter Page.

Who our spies think met with Russian spies about spying on the U.S. election.

Who is on your foreign policy team. Or isn't on your foreign policy team. Or is an informal adviser. Or is acting without the campaign's knowledge but has to take a leave of absence from the foreign policy team he isn't on.

*

We all already know, Trump, about the day you encouraged the Russians—at a live news conference—to hack Hillary Clinton's emails . . .

To, you know, commit a kind of electronic-age, international version of Watergate that would have benefited *you* . . .

And we know how you tried to worm your way out of that by calling it "sarcasm" . . .

And we already know about our government's belief that the Russians *have* already hacked into the Democratic computers—a conclusion you mocked during the debate, suggesting that the real culprit might be a four-hundred-pound guy sitting on a bed.

And we already know about the day you looked like a complete moron when you said that Putin—a *dictator*—was a greater leader than President Obama, because Putin—who is a *dictator*—had higher approval ratings. Because you're too stupid to realize that the "approval ratings" in Russia—for the Russian *dictator*—may not . . . exactly . . . be *legit*.

And we already know about your second campaign manager, this slimy Manafort guy, and the strings that connect him to Putin and a pro-Russian political party in Ukraine.

But we need to know about this Carter Page, and why his name was the second one on your lips when you were asked for your foreign policy advisers.

Because, Trump, you probably won't understand any of this, but Carter Page may have also done something even *worse* than allegedly meeting with the Russian in charge of spying on our presidential elections.

Yahoo News reports that the government is investigating whether your man Carter Page also met with people in the Russian hierarchy to talk about possibly lifting our economic sanctions against the Russians if you become president—talk which might violate federal law.

Carter Page says of all this, "All of these accusations are just complete garbage." Which would be easier to believe, Trump, if your campaign hadn't put out four *separate* statements about who he is and what he's doing for you.

You have to explain this buccaneer *now*, Trump, because if you don't—if you don't explain this continuing embrace of the murderous regime of a malevolent country like Russia—you will face far bigger questions than "Who is Carter Page?"

Those questions are simply these:

Trump!—Do you believe *our* elections are sacrosanct and must not, under any circumstances, be influenced by any other government?

Trump!—Do you already have a deal in place to reward a country that may have already hacked the political party of your opponent in this election?

Trump!—Are you loyal to the concept of *democracy*?

Trump!—Are you loyal . . . to the United States of America?

THE ATLANTIC WALL

Post date • THURSDAY, SEPTEMBER 29

If you watch the speeches, if you read the tweets, if you survived the debate, you probably saw something obvious and disqualifying: like when Sniffy Trump went after Rosie O'Donnell, or said we can't defend Japan, or gave his string of answers in which he did *not* deny his tax returns would show he didn't pay anything, and then he said *that* made him smart, and then said if he *had* paid them, they would have been squandered.

And as the post-debate polls now come out in force, you are probably saying, "What? How? How is the margin not bigger?"

It's because some people saw in that debate, in those speeches, in that hatred and stupidity . . . their ideal president.

Why? How? Huh?

The answer is in something not addressed in that debate Monday: the Trump Wall.

Not *that* wall.

The *other* wall.

There *is* another wall—and it may be the most underreported slice of madness in this ceaseless fifteen months of electoral id.

Public Policy Polling (PPP) is one of the few players in this Kafkaesque farce to have maintained some sense of humor. It will ask whom you're voting for, but also, "What do you have a higher opinion of: Donald Trump or middle seats on airplanes?" Middle seats win, by the way, 45 percent to 42.

And in one poll it asked . . . Question 12.

"Would you support or oppose building a wall along the Atlantic Ocean to keep Muslims from entering the country from the Middle East?"

No, you didn't just hallucinate that.

But . . . *yes*—we should look at that one again.

Question number twelve: "Would you support or oppose building a wall along the Atlantic Ocean to keep Muslims from entering the country from the Middle East?"

As you know—there is only one correct answer to that question and it is: "Are you out of your goddamned mind?"

But "Are you out of your goddamned mind?" was not one of the choices.

Yes, no, or not sure.

And this is how those participants identifying themselves as Trump supporters came out on this vital question of . . . the *other* Trump Wall.

Thirty-one percent said yes, they *were* in favor of an Atlantic Wall to keep out the Muslims . . .

Fifty-two percent said no, they were not . . .

Seventeen percent said "not sure."

A . . . wall.

To keep Muslims from entering the country.

Via . . . the Atlantic.

How are they—how are they—I can barely say it.

How are they supposedly breaching our present Atlantic fortifications? Rowboating in from Syria, are they? Swimming from the ISIS-infested region of Molenbeek, in Brussels, straight to Myrtle Beach, South Carolina?

Even assuming some spark of humanity and intelligence among these 31 percent of Trump supporters . . . getting from the so-called Islamic State to Cuba somehow . . .

And then coming up from Cuba on a 1951 Chevy pickup truck repurposed into an oceangoing vessel?

The more you think about this question—and the nearly one in three Trump supporters who don't know enough about geography or about construction or about how deep the water in the ocean might be or about, you know, *life*—the less LOL-worthy it gets and the more it takes on a shape resembling the entirety of Donald Trump's campaign.

Start with a threat that exists only in theory—since 9/11, no act of terrorism has been conducted in this country by people who were here illegally. Add to that a nonexistent paranoid fever—that terrorists are streaming into this country from every corner. Multiply it all by fear and an unthinking desire for mindless revenge and a demagogue happy to exploit it so he can take over this country, and you get Question 12: Do you support an Atlantic Wall to keep out them Muslims? Yes—*31 percent!*

Let me be clear. Donald Trump has not actually *proposed* building a wall along the Atlantic, which would have to be 2,069 miles long—or ten times that long if you wanted to be really safe and block off all the rivers, lakes, and other bodies of water that *connect* to the Atlantic. *He* has not proposed destroying every beach and every harbor and every marina and every dock and every pier and every bit of shipping and every business and every city dependent on tourism and beachgoers.

He didn't say it. The people who want to vote for him did!

Wall off Miami. All of Florida. Georgia. The Carolinas. Virginia, Maryland, Delaware, New Jersey, New York, Connecticut, Rhode Island, Massachusetts, New Hampshire, and Maine. Two thousand sixty-nine miles.

*

They don't like immigrants, and they don't like anybody who's not white, and they don't like facts, and they don't like things they don't understand, and they don't like Hillary Clinton.

And that's why he's still in the race.

He is *indeed* their ideal president.

What we do about their proud, defiant stupidity—short of finding these 31 percent who want an Atlantic Wall to keep out . . . surfboarding Muslims . . .

in burkinis, and forcing them back to second grade to start all over again— I don't know.

But between now and November 8, do not count them or him out.

Trump and his idiot supporters do not know the meaning of the word "beaten."

Well, actually, they don't know the meaning of a lot of words, and therein lies the problem.

Chapter 2

OCTOBER 2016

TRUMP AND DOGS

Post date • MONDAY, OCTOBER 3

"Until one has loved an animal," wrote the journalist and author Anatole France, "a part of one's soul remains unawakened."

There is no evidence that Donald Trump has ever ... loved an animal.

"If Trump has ever in his life had a pet," wrote Gail Collins of *The New York Times*, "his campaign doesn't know about it. There's some question, in fact, about whether he's ever even had an animal friend."

In fact, none of the books about Trump, including his own, refer to a pet dog.

The coauthor or ghostwriter of *The Art of the Deal*, Tony Schwartz, told me he never heard Trump *reference* a pet, as adult or child.

Google it, fact-check it, do a LexisNexis search on it and you come up blank—save for an apocryphal story about him tweeting asking for prayers for a Labrador named Spinee. There were no tweets, no entreaties, and, for all we can determine, no Spinee.

A man running to lead a nation of 324 million people—and, while we're at it, 78 million dogs and 76 million cats—and there are solid reasons to believe he's never had a dog.

Never. Had. A. Dog.

*

But it's worse than just *that*—isn't it?

July 2015: "I hear that sleepy eyes @chucktodd will be fired like a dog ..."

October 2015: "Wow, great news! I hear [Erick] Erickson of Red State was fired like a dog."

December 2015: "@GlennBeck got fired like a dog . . ."

This January: "Union Leader refuses to comment as to why they were kicked out of the ABC News debate like a dog."

Twelve days later: "@BrentBozell, one of the National Review lightweights, came to my office begging for money like a dog."

Huh?

When was the last time you saw a dog begging for money? In an office?

February: "Wow was Ted Cruz disloyal to his very capable director of communication. He used him as a scape goat - fired like a dog!"

March: Erick Erickson again: "got fired like a dog from RedState . . ."

Eleven days after that: "@DavidGregory got thrown off of TV by NBC, fired like a dog!"

June: "Mitt Romney had his chance to beat a failed president but he choked like a dog."

Huh? What the hell's wrong with this guy?

Fired like a dog?

Have you ever fired a dog?

He's also tweeted that Egyptian president Mubarak was "dropped" like a dog, that Reverend Jeremiah Wright was "dumped" like a dog, that Mark Cuban was "thrown off television" like a dog, that Kristen Stewart cheated on Robert Pattinson "like a dog."

And, worst of all, he said after one of the Republican debates that Senator Marco Rubio had been "sweating like a dog."

Dogs don't sweat.

In theory, they *could* get fired, cheat on someone, beg for money, or get dropped, dumped, kicked out, or thrown off television. But they physically *can't* sweat.

Donald Trump has no understanding of this.

No evidence he's ever *had* a dog.

No evidence that he understands even the kinds of basic facts that people who don't have dogs still know *about* dogs.

What the hell? Is he from Mars?

*

Look, until four years ago last week, I had never had a dog. Allergies as a kid, never at home as an adult, never thought myself mature enough to assume the responsibility.

And then it happened.

And it didn't change me much.

I only got one *more* dog. And got two other dogs for my girlfriend's parents. And started working with a rescue shelter for injured and sick dogs. And started giving out dog books for Christmas. And saw that most of human behavior can be explained by watching dogs. And called all my dog-world friends from before I was blessed and asked, "Why didn't you *tell* me?" And realized that dogs explain enough of the meaning of life that you don't *need* to know any of the *other* possible meanings of life.

No biggie.

I was just born again.

*

And Donald Trump ... no dog.

As Anatole France said, part of his soul, unawakened.

Even so, this was still just philosophy.

And then the Trump campaign put out, and almost as quickly pulled back, a proposal to eliminate what it called the "FDA Food Police."

Citing as one of its supposed government overreaches that the agency "even dictates the nutritional content of dog food."

Well, it *does* dictate the nutritional content of dog food.

It dictates the nutritional content of dog food so the dog food doesn't kill the dogs.

As *The Daily Beast* reported, in the past year, eleven of the twenty-three FDA pet-food recalls were to remove *poisoned* pet food from shelves.

To save dogs' lives.

*

And Donald Trump, who tweets "fired like a dog," "cheated on like a dog," "begged for money like a dog," and all the other put-downs as his go-to insult, as if a dog were somehow a *bad thing* . . .

Donald Trump has given a hint that, if elected, he would protect a businessman's right to poison dogs.

Maybe your dogs.

Maybe mine.

Maybe any of the other 78 million.

Because . . . you know . . . profits.

*

Hey, Don.

Fuck you.

THE ELECTION IS INVIOLABLE, TRUMP

Post date • **TUESDAY, OCTOBER 4**

The first question to Mike Pence in tonight's vice presidential debate should *not* be about Donald Trump's tax avoidance.

It should be: Does Donald Trump believe in democratic elections? In *this* country?

*

It was, perhaps, the first sane moment of his campaign.

It appears it was his last.

Within ninety-six hours he had repudiated that moment. And that repudiation was the most craven and cowardly act not just of this election, not just of this campaign, but by any presidential candidate since the Civil War.

And it was lost in the shuffle.

Something un-American, something unbelievable, something unconscionable—and it barely registered . . .

Buried amid the emotional debris of an unstable megalomaniac raining down upon the nation: the "genius" who claimed that poor people weren't paying enough taxes when he might have paid none for eighteen years; a debate over nonexistent sex tapes; controversy over who will tweet at three a.m. invocations of marital infidelity, cheating at charity, cheating at illegal trade with foreign nations...

Lost in the avalanche of stupidity and self-obsession and hypocrisy from this idiot Trump...

Missed—in large part—because there are a dozen things a day, any one of which should disqualify him from *residency*, let alone presidency.

And yet—he said it, as glibly as if he were unhappy about a zoning board decision.

"One of you will not win this election," debate moderator Lester Holt had said. "Are you willing to accept the outcome as the will of the voters?"

And Trump could not simply answer it. He first had to wade through the involuntary egotism and spasmodic salesmanship with which he thinks he cloaks the most insecure man of our times from public view. But finally he said it. "If she wins, I will absolutely support her."

The first thing he has yet said that indicated that for a moment, just for a moment, he could put America ahead of his own ego, his own naked lust for power and control. Control not just of a company or a television show, where what *he* says is the rule, but of a *nation* in what *he* says is the law.

And it *was* just for a moment.

For then the impact of his failures at the debate hit him, and the pattern of whatever is wrong with him stopped waning and started waxing, and Trump... took it back.

Late last Friday, Trump told *The New York Times* that he was rethinking his statement. Rethinking whether or not to recognize the outcome of the presidential election next month. "We're going to have to see. We're going to see what happens. We're going to have to see."

No presidential candidate, no political party, no leading government figure, no member of the military, no prominent commentator nor leader of any kind is *permitted* to raise such doubt. The sanctity of the election is the bedrock of this country—not the Constitution, not the Bill of Rights, not the military, not the Founding Fathers.

There is only one permissible response to a question about the outcome of the election: acceptance. Merely to hesitate, in the most trying of circumstances, in the midst of legal actions by both sides, in the immediate aftermath of as close a vote as could be imagined, is to change one's reputation forever—as it did that of Al Gore. To hesitate and be judged in the legal right *still* eternally alters a man's place in history—as it did that of George W. Bush.

Richard Nixon, who craved the presidency more—and more ominously—than any other man who attained it ... even *he* did not move to formally contest the razor-thin margin of 1960, and he certainly did not imply that he would not—nor others *should not*—recognize it.

Samuel J. Tilden, denied the presidency in 1877 in a fateful bargain between the Democrats and Republicans that sanctified Jim Crow for eighty years, still walked away. Even with the sitting president quietly strengthening the military presence in Washington over rumors of armed revolt no matter *who* won—even as members *of* the U.S. military supposedly offered Tilden support to overturn the election by force—*he* obeyed.

Abraham Lincoln, when he thought, as late as September 1, 1864, that he would lose reelection to General George McClellan and the Democrats, was ready to leave office—in the middle of the Civil War.

And Nixon and Gore and Hubert Humphrey in 1968 and Charles Evans Hughes in 1916 and Andrew Jackson in 1824 and all the other losers in all the other impossibly tight elections in our history not only never raised a serious doubt about the legitimacy of their own defeat *after* it happened—even when, as in Tilden's case, the flaming torch of Civil War had been one side's recourse just four elections previously—but none of them ever would have *dreamed*, in a dozen lifetimes, to threaten not to recognize it *before* it happened.

Trump: You are a child throwing matches at a gasoline can.

You are pulling on the loose thread that every winner, every loser, every saint, every devil, and everyone else who has ever sought the presidency has known better than to touch.

You are denying *the* fundament of democracy; betraying the history of your party, your people, your nation.

Trump: You are fomenting revolution.

There is no margin for error here.

Because, no, Trump, we are *not* "going to have to see."

What *we* are going to do, we *Americans*—after this remark, I don't *know* what *you* are—what *we* are going to do is honor the fifty-seven elections that have gone before. Even if they're hacked by the Russians, whom you like far too much to make thinking men and women do anything but cringe. And if we don't like the outcome, we will act to remedy it, within the Constitution. Opposition, protest, impeachment, even formal contestation—all of it legal, ethical, often necessary to the life of the nation.

But nobody, Trump, who believes in democracy—Republican or Democrat, conservative or liberal—first says he will "absolutely support" the free elections that have kept *us* free for 240 years and then, within the week, because he doesn't like the polls, because he doesn't like the commentators, because he doesn't get his way, suddenly switches to "We're going to have to see."

Trump, you are—by yourself and as a representative of a brutal minority in this country—a threat to the very democracy that permits a savage like you to rise this far and get so close to the life-and-death power of the presidency. In the kind of nightmare country you invoke just by using the very phrase "We're going to have to see," your presidential aspirations would have ended long ago, and not by legal means.

But this is America, and this is democracy, and even when nearly two and a half centuries' worth of process and law and good fortune comes to a sudden end and the system spits up someone wholly unqualified for office, nowhere is it written that the rest of us can simply say "we're going to have to see" if we will support the outcome of this election, even if it led to the cataclysmic nightmare of *your* administration, Trump.

We would stay and fight you.

Through the law.

Through the Constitution.

Through the Constitution, and *for* those things, the Founding Fathers risked their lives, their fortunes, their sacred honor; for those things, every soldier who ever wore this nation's colors fought; for those things, every patriot willingly offered up all they knew and loved.

And the *first* of those things, Trump, is the sanctity of the election.

If you cannot now hold to a pledge to honor and accept its outcome for more than ninety-six hours, you are not a president, you are not a man of freedom, you are not an American. Get out—out of this race—now, before you damage this democracy still further. Get out—out of this country—now, before the cowards and fascists and bigots who have rallied around you for a year begin to believe that their subversion of democracy will be permitted here.

You'd fit in perfectly in the new government of the Philippines.

You like *Russia*? I'm sure they can find people for you to dictate to and oppress *there*.

Get out, Trump.

For once in your life, recognize that something is not *about* you.

Nor is it about your opponent, nor the Democrats, nor the Republicans.

It is about the essence of the United States of America.

And you do *not* have the option of saying, "We're going to have to see."

*

Two hundred forty years of patriots' blood and respect for law will *not* be sacrificed at the gold-plated altar of your sick and demented—and treasonous—ego.

DONALD TRUMP'S TOP FIFTY EXCUSES

Post date • **WEDNESDAY, OCTOBER 5**

We have excuses from Donald Trump about apparently not paying taxes—"That makes me smart" and the amazing "I know our complex tax laws better than anyone who has ever run for president and am the only one who can fix them."

Nevertheless.

We begin day five of our wait for Donald Trump to come up with an excuse for why he accused a woman who is *not* in a sex tape of *being* in a sex tape . . .

When he himself *was* in a sex tape . . .

Please note how remarkable it is that Trump has *not* blamed his agent, or a celebrity look-alike service, or claimed he didn't know *Playboy* even *made* sex tapes, or simply insisted that the Second Amendment protects his right to bear arms and legs and the rest.

Because Trump . . . has an excuse . . . for everything.

*

The top fifty of them?

I mean . . . *recently*?

His excuse for not releasing his taxes? "I'm being audited, so I can't."

But he will "when *she* releases her 33,000 emails."

But "I don't think anybody cares."

But "there's nothing to learn from them."

Plus, his tax rate is "none of your business."

*

His excuse for his bad poll numbers? The "Google search engine was suppressing the bad news about Hillary Clinton."

Without the "disgusting and corrupt media," he'd be leading by 20 percent.

And he's *not* losing: "I certainly don't think it is appropriate to start changing all of a sudden when you have been winning."

*

Trump's excuses about Russia:

Hacking into Democratic National Committee computers? "It could be Russia, but it could also be China. It could also be lots of other people. It also could be someone sitting on their bed that weighs four hundred pounds, okay?"

Shooting down Malaysian Airlines flight MH-17: "They say it wasn't them."

Going on a Larry King TV show carried by Russian-owned television and saying Vladimir Putin was a great leader: he thought it was for a Larry King *podcast*.

*

His excuses for supporting the invasion of Iraq in September 2002:

A 2004 interview proves he *didn't*.

He told Sean Hannity he *didn't*.

When Howard Stern asked him, he said, "I don't know," even though the tape shows he actually said, "Yeah, I guess so."

"By the time the war started, I was against it.

"And shortly thereafter, I was *really* against it."

Regardless, when he said it, he "was not a politician."

*

His excuse for his performance in the first debate:

"They also gave me a defective mic," but he wasn't sniffing, because also, "the mic was very bad, but maybe it was good enough to hear breathing."

His excuse for not attacking the Clintons' marriage: "I really eased up because I didn't want to hurt anyone's feelings." Then he attacked anyway. Then he questioned whether Hillary had been loyal to Bill.

Also: Moderator Lester Holt? "Lester is a Democrat. It's a phony system. They are all Democrats."

No, he's a registered Republican, and "he did a great job."

No, he deserved a "C, C minus," but "I'm not complaining."

No, Lester Holt rigged it. "What a rigged deal. I tell you, we're in such a rigged system."

Trump's excuse if he loses the election: "I'm afraid the election is going to be rigged."

Before then? "The polls are rigged."

His opponent cleared by investigators? It's a "rigged system."

But "it's not just the political system that's rigged. It's the *whole economy*."

*

But not everything is *rigged*.

Trump's excuse when he asked Russia to hack Clinton's email? "Of course I'm being sarcastic."

Trump's excuse when he called President Obama the founder of ISIS? Quote: "THEY DON'T GET SARCASM?"

*

Small crowd size in Colorado Springs? The fire marshal was a Democrat.

Small crowd size in Washington? Six hundred thousand would've been there, but "they wouldn't let them in."

*

How his wife, Melania, got into the country despite apparent immigration ir-regularities? She'll hold a news conference.

Why Melania hasn't held a news conference? They released a letter from her lawyer.

*

His excuse for claiming that global warming was a hoax perpetrated by the Chinese? "I did not say it."

He tweeted it.

His excuse? "I often joke that this is done for the benefit of China. Obvi-ously, I joke.... But this is done for the benefit of China."

Trump's excuse for his connection to alt-right white supremacists? The term "was just made up" by Hillary Clinton.

The excuse for violence at his rallies? It adds "excitement."

His excuse for not disavowing white supremacist David Duke during a TV interview? "A very bad earpiece."

His excuse for proposing a Muslim ban: "It was just a suggestion."

His excuse for saying he could shoot people on Fifth Avenue in New York City and not lose any support: "Obviously it was a joke."

His excuse for calling Ted Cruz a pussy: "We were all just having fun."

His excuse for disparaging *Heidi* Cruz's appearance: "*I* didn't start it."

His GOP debate excuse for disparaging remarks toward women: "Often-times, it's fun; it's kidding; we have a good time."

His excuse for commenting that if Ivanka weren't his daughter, he might be *dating* her: "Cute. It was cute."

His excuse for abusive remarks about former Miss Universe Alicia Ma-chado: "She had gained a massive amount of weight."

His excuse for disparaging Machado after she endorsed Hillary Clinton: "Check out sex tape."

His excuse for the three-to-five-a.m. overnight tweetstorm that included the *phrase* "check out sex tape": "At least you know I will be there, awake, to answer the call."

*

And lastly, his excuse for making all of his harsh remarks:

"I do regret it, particularly where it may have caused personal pain."

That was August 19.

Before the Washington Hotel Birther News Conference; before he talked about disarming Hillary Clinton's Secret Service detail; before he physically mocked Hillary Clinton's pneumonia collapse; before the "Raise your hand if you're not a Christian conservative" thing; before he said he might not recognize the outcome of the election; before he slammed the entire African American community, Mika Brzezinski, Maureen Dowd, ex–CIA director Robert Gates, Colin Kaepernick, Obama's poll numbers compared with Putin's, Alicia Machado, the Federal Reserve System, Jeff Zucker, Elizabeth Warren . . . and Rosie O'Donnell. *Again.*

"BECAUSE YOU'D BE IN JAIL"

Post date • MONDAY, OCTOBER 10

On the thirtieth of September 2007, the Russian chess master Garry Kasparov declared that he would run against Vladimir Putin's handpicked successor in the presidential election in Russia.

His platform was simple: he led a coalition of anti-Putin groups called "Other Russia," and they vowed to establish a "democratic and just" government.

Less than two months later, Garry Kasparov, Russian presidential *candidate,* was arrested at a Moscow rally by police loyal to . . . Vladimir Putin . . . Russian *president.*

Last night, on the ninth of October 2016, in the United States of America, on live national television, Donald Trump, *American presidential candidate,* stared at his opponent and said:

"If I win, I am going to instruct my attorney general to get a special prosecutor to look into your situation . . . We're going to get a special prosecutor and we're going to look into it, because you know what? People have been, their lives have been destroyed for doing one-fifth of what you've done."

Secretary Clinton replied, "It's just awfully good that someone with the temperament of Donald Trump is not in charge of the law in this country."

Trump then erased any doubt about what he meant—or who he is—or what he has *planned.*

He shot back.

"Because you'd be in jail."

*

Make no mistake what you heard between the sniffs and the snorts and the mindless wandering around the stage.

Make no mistake what you heard amid the swirling, strutting egotism and the cacophony of insults.

Make no mistake what you heard—and put aside for now even the lie about opposing Iraq and the mindless, heartless claim that Captain Humayun Khan would still be alive if *Trump* had been president. . . . Put aside even the disavowal of his own running mate's position on Syria, and the bobbing and weaving about the "grab them by the pussy" tape.

You heard a would-be president of the United States, the twenty-eighth different nominee in the long history of his party for the most important job on earth, who heretofore has left this ominous, dire, dictatorial threat to the bleating of his ravenous rally crowds—*you heard* Donald Trump threaten to not merely *defeat* his opponent but to then put her in prison.

"Instruct my attorney general . . ."

"Special prosecutor."

"Because you'd be in jail."

Afterwards, last night, his surrogates tried to palm it off as a joke. Except Trump actually said it twice. Later, Trump said to her, "You'd be *put* in jail."

That was no joke.

Make no mistake . . . what you heard.

*

There are no other conclusions here, Trump, are there?

It is not the *presidency* you are running for. Not, at least, the presidency as we have known it since 1789.

Not, at least, as we have known it as a *free* country.

The kind of presidency *you* want to have, Trump, already exists.

It is called a Putin-style dictatorship.

And the kind of America *you* want to lead, Trump, is *not* the America we live in now.

This other America already exists. It is called Russia.

＊

Trump: men and women you often invoke, but none of whom you have understood for a moment, have died for this country in order to prevent . . . *you.*

They have died—and others have lived and sacrificed in other ways—to prevent exactly the kind of one-man rule in which a president, or a candidate for president, can threaten to imprison his opponent.

All the patriots of our hallowed history have given and lost and self-abnegated so that *you* could not *say that* . . . last night.

And . . . they have also given all of themselves so that *Hillary Clinton* could not look at *you* last night and say, "You admitted to sexual assault on that tape. If I'm elected, I will appoint a special prosecutor to investigate you"—so that she could not look at *you*, Trump, and say, "You just admitted to writing off $916 million in losses to avoid taxes. If I'm elected, I will appoint a special prosecutor to investigate you."

But *she* didn't *say* either of those things.

Because she believes in our democracy.

And our democracy rests on the same razor's edge that has permitted a bully and a lunatic like you to get this close to having the power to destroy it.

Because it is very simple, Trump.

When you personally promised to put Hillary Clinton in jail last night—when you made her "imprisonment" part of your *campaign*, in your own words—you killed a part of our democracy.

When you threaten to jail *one* of your political opponents, you have threatened to jail *all* of your political opponents. It is, by itself, the outskirts of a Russian pseudo-democracy in which the act of opposition to the ruler becomes a crime or, worse yet, becomes a reason to fabricate evidence of an extant crime against the opponent.

It is dictatorship.

And the power you seek might still carry the *title* "president," but with the threat of the legal power of the United States of America being brought down on your opponents, you might as well be *Chancellor* Trump . . . or *Chairman* Trump . . . or *Protector* Trump . . . or *Generalissimo* Trump . . . or *Führer* Trump.

*

"Because . . . you'd be . . . in jail."

*

Because, Trump, if you are elected, *we* would *all* be in jail.

Your threat last night, to merge political opposition with legal prosecution, has no place in a free country.

And *you*, Trump . . . have no place in *this* free country.

TRUMP'S THIRTY CRAZIEST DEBATE EVENTS

Post date • TUESDAY, OCTOBER 11

We have sunk to this.

We can now rank the thirty craziest things done by one presidential candidate.

Just in the debates.

Just in *two* of the debates.

We have the thirty craziest things by Donald Trump even leaving out the apology for the "grab them by the pussy" tape. The apology in which the first half of the first sentence was "I've never said I'm a perfect person," which was a lie, because he once tweeted, "I consider myself too perfect and have no faults."

The apology in which the *second* half of the first sentence was "nor pretended to be someone that I'm not," when he used to pretend to be his own press spokesman, named John Barron and John Miller, and didn't even change his voice when he pretended to be someone he was *not*!

We're *leaving those out*—and many, many more.

Number 30, from Sunday night: "ICE just endorsed me." First, it sounded like "ISIS just endorsed me." Second, ICE is a branch of the government involved in immigration; it can't endorse anybody. He meant either the union representing employees *of* ICE, or *Vanilla* Ice.

Number 29, in the first debate, he brought up Rosie O'Donnell and added, "I said very tough things to her, and I think everybody would agree that she deserves it and nobody feels sorry for her."

What are you, nine?

Number 28, in the first debate, he claimed the DNC hackers, believed by our government to be Russian, "could be someone sitting on their bed that weighs four hundred pounds, okay?"

Number 27, Sunday night, same topic, he said, "Maybe there *is* no hacking."

Number 26, also debate 2, without apologizing for crapping all over the parents of Captain Humayun Khan, insisted that if he had been president then, their son "would be alive today, because unlike her, who voted for the war without knowing what she was doing, I would not have had our people in Iraq."

Number 25, first debate, he denied that there's a 2002 tape of him supporting the invasion of Iraq. "Wrong." Then Hillary Clinton said, "That is absolutely proved over and over again." He replied, "Wrong. Wrong."

Number 24, second debate, she said his claim that he hadn't said *what is on the tape* had been debunked. His reply? "That's not been debunked," "That has not been debunked," and "Has not been debunked."

Number 23, first debate, he offered proof he was against Iraq by saying that people should call Sean Hannity, because he told *him*! He mentioned Hannity by name *seven* times in a presidential debate—a debate that he was trying to *win*!

Number 22, Sunday night, about terrorism: "You know, there's always a reason for everything."

Well . . . you've got me there.

Number 21, first debate. Denied he had ever said global warming was a Chinese hoax. "I did not. I did not. I do not say that."

No—he only *tweeted* it.

Number 20, debate 2: "She *also* sent a tweet out at three o'clock in the morning, but I won't even mention that."

You just mentioned it!

Number 19, first debate, explaining the time he settled government prosecution for racial discrimination in renting apartments: "There was no admission of guilt."

Number 18, first debate. Clinton noted that he rooted for the 2008 housing collapse. "That's called business, by the way," he replied.

Number 17, first debate. Admitting that he paid low or no taxes: "That makes me smart."

Number 16, first debate. Then he said that if he *had* paid more tax, "It would be squandered, too."

Number 15, first debate, she mentioned his father got him $14 million. He called it a "small loan."

Number 14, Sunday. Complained to the moderator: "I'd like to know, Anderson, why aren't you bringing up the emails?" . . . When they had just finished a question *about the emails*!

Number 13, also debate 2: Claimed truthfulness was "the big difference between Abraham Lincoln and you. That's a big, big difference. We're talking about *some* difference."

Number 12, Sunday. Again lied about the 2008 Clinton campaign starting birtherism . . .

Number 11, first debate. Asked what he had to say to people of color about his birtherism, replied: "I say nothing. I say nothing."

Number 10, Sunday, asked by a Muslim American for help with rising Islamophobia, he told her to inform on her fellow Muslims and then lied: "In San Bernardino, many people saw the bombs all over the apartment . . ."

Number 9, first debate. Insisted he could not release his tax returns, then immediately said he *would* release them "when she releases her 33,000 emails that have been deleted."

Number 8, Sunday. Asking why, in the Senate, Clinton hadn't repealed "carried interest" and getting the answer that there was a *Republican president* at the time, he seemed not to know what that meant. "If you were an effective senator, you could have done it. If you were an effective senator, you could have done it. But you were not an effective senator."

Number 7, first debate: Claimed he had a better temperament than Clinton, while clearly showing he had no idea what the word "temperament" *means.* "I think my strongest asset, maybe by far, is my temperament. I have a winning temperament. I know how to win."

And then, Number 6, Sunday, twice threatened Clinton with a special prosecutor, saying, "You'd be put in jail" and "You'd be in jail."

Number 5, Sunday, asked why he had tweeted, about Alicia Machado, "Check out sex tape," he said, "No, there wasn't 'check out a sex tape'"—when he tweeted, "Check out sex tape"!

Number 4, Sunday, asked about the "grab them by the pussy" tape, said it was "locker room talk." Five times. "Locker room talk." Because *all* locker rooms feature two men wearing microphones in a bus while they know they are being videotaped.

Number 3, Sunday. Pivoted from the tape—which by itself cost him the support of at least thirty-three elected Republicans—by saying, "Certainly I'm not proud of it. But this is locker room talk. You know, when we have a world where you have ISIS chopping off heads . . ."

He segued from "grab them by the pussy" to "chop off their heads!"

Number 2, Sunday, said *sniff. Sniff, sniff, sniff!* After doing it throughout the first debate, he sniffed at least eighty *sniff* times in *sniff* the second *sniff* debate *sniff* alone!

He was so loud he was just this side of Darth Vader!

Eighty times!

In just over ninety minutes!

That's once every sixty-eight seconds!

What's with the goddamned sniffing?

Buy a handkerchief!

See your doctor, Dr. Vinnie Boombatz!

*

And the Number 1 craziest thing yet by Trump in the debates . . . how could he have *not* known this? How could somebody have not *seen* this? How could somebody have not *stopped* this?

In a debate, the whole point of which was to change the narrative from the "grab them by the pussy" tape, do you know what they call the shirt that his wife Melania *wore* to the debate?

It's a *pussy-bow* shirt!

That's what it's called by the designer, Gucci!

A *pussy-bow silk crepe de chine shirt*!

Pussy bow!

The woman wore a *pussy bow* to the event at which her husband was trying to get people to stop thinking about "pussy"!

And if all of this bullshit is not bad enough...

Worst of all... *worst of all*... this sniffling, sniveling, pacing, threatening, preening, bullying, nitwitted would-be dictator... made it necessary for me... to find out what a pussy-bow silk crepe de chine shirt is!

CAMPS, WITH CONCENTRATION

Post date • WEDNESDAY, OCTOBER 12

They were once not just the centerpiece of the Trump campaign; they were the first evils out of its Pandora's box.

The wall along the Mexican border...

And the deportation of around eleven million undocumented Americans.

The starting line of this whole wretched, hateful, bigoted nightmare. What empowered the alt-right and inflamed xenophobia and imperiled something fundamental to this nation since slavery ended: the idea that if you were born here, you were an American.

The *wall* comes up now and again. But... what was the other thing?

Oh, yeah.... mass deportation.

How exactly would that work?

How exactly would you take eleven million people and make them, you know, *leave*?

Especially if—and I'm going way out on a limb here—they, you know, didn't *wanna leave*?

Eleven million people.

Eleven million people is... the population of the entire state of Ohio.

Three and a half percent of the population of... all of us.

Even now, a year and three months into this triumph of delusion and ego, over reality and stuff like math and science, there is no policy or guidance about this to be gleaned from the Trump website or the campaign . . . other than his surrogate Chris Christie's declaration that about two million people would be targeted for *immediate* deportation, and Trump's claims that he would deport any undocumented American *accused* of a crime—not convicted, just accused—and the original plan to "triple the number of immigrations and customs enforcement agents," with Trump's insistence that he would "do it humanely."

A generous estimate is that there are a hundred thousand agents now.

So we triple that, to three hundred thousand.

Three hundred thousand to humanely round up eleven million undocumented Americans.

That's thirty-seven undocumented Americans per agent. *If* you triple the number of agents.

If somehow the whole process—from finding these people to apprehending them to giving them whatever is left of due process to maybe an appeal to transportation to expulsion—takes *only* six months per undocumented American, Trump's Deportation Force could humanely get the job done . . . in only nineteen years.

Presuming, that is, all of the undocumented Americans cooperate. And all of their friends cooperate. And relatives cooperate. And employers cooperate. And ordinary Americans—who think it's the work of the devil to round up and expel people who risked their lives to *get* here and are willing to *live* their lives in the shadows to *stay* here—presuming *they* also cooperate when the trucks come for their friends and neighbors.

And it would still take one agent about nineteen years to get "his" thirty-seven undocumented Americans out of America.

Now if, say, each case required the work of *three* members of that 300,000-person Trump Deportation Force, the project wouldn't be completed until about the year 2072. And that still assumes that those who are forced out do not come back in.

Now, no matter what numbers and dates are actually realistic (there is another scenario in which Trump's ethnic cleansing—I'm sorry! I meant to say "humane deportation"—could be concluded by 2027), there is still one giant problem looming in the background.

These eleven million people are not simply going to line up on a given day and march out of the country.

You are going to have to *take* these people and remove them from society. Go to their homes and—for want of a better word—*capture* them. Capture as many people as now live in the state of Ohio—and take them somewhere else... until the process of expulsion from the country is complete.

Is Donald Trump thinking of humanely keeping them in... his hotels?

No.

There would have to be humane deportation centers of some kind.

These would in fact be camps of some kind, and the living arrangements would necessarily be cramped, crowded, congested, confined—oh, what *is* the word I'm looking for?

Concentrated!

That's it!

The camps would be concentrated.

Where people would be humanely held in, you know, concentrated places.

Where the deportee-residents were in a—humane—state of being concentrated.

Where these humane camps had the quality of concentration.

Camps. With concentration.

And unless you want these *camps, with concentration* to just hemorrhage money, there are going to have to be a *lot* of *camps, with concentration* all around the country, to make transportation easier.

Places to round up and humanely keep the 400,000 undocumented immigrants from Dallas alone. Or the 400,000 more from Houston. Or the 500,000 more from New York City—more New Yorkers than live on Staten Island.

You know, in *camps, with concentration.*

Some of them big enough to fit all the residents of Atlanta in them. Or Kansas City. Or Cleveland. Or New Orleans.

Now, you might not need to house all *eleven* million, because some of the people would kill themselves rather than go back, or would resist the roundup and would *be* killed—humanely, I'm sure.

Still, you'd better make the *camps, with concentration* just a little better, because, well, sorry, it'd be necessary—to make the process go more smoothly and more humanely—to make it illegal to, you know, *help* or *hide* anybody accused of being an undocumented American. Maybe Trump would make it illegal to *not* turn in . . . any undocumented Americans, and anybody guilty of one of these crimes would go into the camps, too.

You know, the *camps, with concentration.*

But don't worry. Trump intends to do it "humanely."

These would be *humane* camps. With concentration.

And what could possibly go wrong . . . in them?

It'll be *done* humanely!

MELTDOWN

Post date　•　THURSDAY, OCTOBER 13

At the start, I'd just like to reiterate Donald Trump's laudable interruption of his now four-day-long temper-filibuster to offer his now famous public service announcement at Panama City, Florida, about the importance of voting: "So go and register, make sure you get out and vote November 28."

In fact, I'll go further. If you're voting on November 28, I say: vote for Donald Trump.

What the hell is wrong with *this guy*?

November 28 is Cyber Monday, the online Christmas-shopping apex. November 28!

*

Quick! A diversion!

Maybe Trump could attack a prominent Republican—like Mike Pence!

Maybe Trump could say Bill Clinton had an affair with Nancy O'Dell!

Maybe Trump could claim that he is appalled by that tape on which Hillary Clinton is heard using coarse sexual language about women in a conversation with Billy Bush.

Because that's about all we are missing from the Trump meltdown that began early Monday afternoon.

There have been Trump tweetstorms before, and Trump rages before, and even Trump attacks on other Republicans before, but this one has taken on a kind of "Mr. Smith's Evil Twin Goes to Washington" quality.

It has gone deeper and deeper into a kind of campaign psychosis, and yet it is being treated as if it were some kind of campaign *strategy* . . .

"Donald Trump's New Attack Strategy: Curb Clinton Vote," wrote *The Wall Street Journal* late Tuesday.

Trump "plans to renew the nationalist themes that built his base and amplify his no-holds-barred attacks against Hillary Clinton to try to depress Democratic voter turnout, his advisers said."

So it's full-on, no-holds-barred, absolute war against Hillary Clinton. Throw anything at her, use any means, by hook or by crook, just keep pounding away that she's the worst person in history, and all efforts must begin with the understanding that she is the source of every evil in the world, and not only is nothing and no one more deadly than her, but that nothing and no one *could* be, ever, under any circumstances.

"Disloyal R's are far more difficult than Crooked Hillary. They come at you from all sides. They don't know how to win—I will teach them!"

So how does *that* work?

If you read that and you're a—you know—Trump voter, you think: "Trump says Hillary's bad but Paul Ryan is worse."

But if you read that and you're a—you know—Hillary voter, you think: "Trump says Hillary's bad but Paul Ryan is worse."

Only *one* kind of voter could read that and *not* think, "Trump says Hillary's bad but Paul Ryan is worse"—that would be the voters who actually *are* Donald Trump.

Quick! A diversion!

"The very foul mouthed Sen. John McCain begged for my support during his primary (I gave, he won), then dropped me over locker room remarks!"

Once again—locker room remarks, because *everybody* talks that way in their locker room, and *everybody's* locker room is a bus on a Hollywood film lot in which all the men are wearing microphones and know they are being videotaped for a television show.

So *that* didn't work against McCain.

Quick! A diversion!

He torched McCain again, then said, "I wouldn't want to be in a foxhole with a lot of these people, that I can tell you."

That deft bit of strategy reminded anybody still listening that there was no way he ever would have *been* in a foxhole with John McCain, because while McCain was a pilot who was tortured inside a North Vietnamese POW camp, at exactly the same time, Trump was getting draft deferments for a hangnail or whatever it was.

Quick! A diversion!

That crazy wandering stuff during the debate? Tuesday night, "she came into my territory ... I never walked near her. She stands right in front of me."

Yesterday, NBC reported that, as all this is happening, two big-money Trump donors—responsible for tens of thousands of dollars—have asked for their contributions back. And the bundler who gathered about a million says he's done raising money for Trump.

Quick! A diversion!

So back to the greatest hits, and late Tuesday he stands up in front of a rally and blows that dog whistle. Again.

"Hillary Clinton wants to really dismantle our Second Amendment, so maybe she should start with her security people not carrying weapons."

Mr. Trump.

I don't know if you've noticed, but I don't like you. I think you're the most dangerous political figure in our country's history—although on *sunny* days, I begin to think you're only the most dangerous political figure since the 1864 Democratic presidential nominee who ran on a platform of giving up on the Civil War and repudiating the Emancipation Proclamation.

So, politically, I don't care if you melt in the hot sun.

But personally, all human life matters to me. So let me say this, just on a basic "ask not for whom the bell tolls" level:

Get some help.

See a doctor, do some meditation, take a brief leave of absence, read a book on ten quick steps to a healthier mind ... *Do* something.

This is not innovative brilliance. This is not campaigning. This is not self-advocacy. And there is no brand-new political strategy by which one wins ... by getting fewer votes.

Get. Some. Help.

I will even, on the premise of "It tolls for theeeee," offer you a little cover. When you said:

"Make sure you get out and vote November 28"?

You were . . . referring to the campaigns for mayor, city alderman, township supervisor, and township assessor of Bloomington, Illinois—because November 28 is the deadline there for filing petitions to run for those offices.

That's what you meant.

It tolls for theeeee . . .

FROM RUSSIA WITH LOVE

Post date • THURSDAY, OCTOBER 13

Donald Trump is—at best—being played by the Russians like the proverbial two-dollar banjo.

Donald Trump is—at worst—the spokesmodel of the Russians in this country, fronting for their dictator, Vladimir Putin.

There is now hard evidence of this. Not just Trump's advocacy of Putin's dubious poll approval numbers, nor his admiration for his leadership style, nor his excuses for the opponents and reporters jailed or hurt or worse on his watch.

There is now hard evidence of this, and it does not even require invoking the name of the shadowy investor Carter Page, nor the Russian bureaucrat believed to be in charge of his government's efforts to intervene in our presidential election.

This is much simpler, and much stupider, and it reinforces my oldest theory—that democracy survives not as much because of the efforts and sacrifice of the noble to preserve it as it does because of the sloppiness and imbecility of those who seek to destroy it.

On October 21, 2015, *Newsweek* printed a story called "Benghazi Biopsy," by a very good reporter named Kurt Eichenwald.

Benghazi—the lone obsession fully shared by the Republicans and the right wing and the alt-right and Donald Trump.

Eichenwald wrote:

"One important point has been universally acknowledged by the nine previous reports about Benghazi: The attack was almost certainly preventable. Clinton was in charge of the State Department, and it failed to protect U.S. personnel at an American consulate in Libya. If the GOP wants to raise that as a talking point against her, it is legitimate."

On Monday of this week, the tenth, Sputnik, an online news and radio service created by Russia's government-controlled news agency, posted what it called "a major revelation" from the emails stolen by WikiLeaks from the hacked account of Clinton campaign chairman John Podesta.

Sputnik claimed that in one Podesta email, Sidney Blumenthal—the other *shared obsession* of the whole spectrum of right-wingers—had secretly written that Benghazi was preventable.

Sputnik claimed that Sidney Blumenthal had written *this*:

One important point that has been universally acknowledged by nine previous reports about Benghazi: The attack was almost certainly preventable...

Clinton was in charge of the State Department, and it failed to protect U.S. personnel at an American consulate in Libya. If the GOP wants to raise that as a talking point against her, it is legitimate.

It's exactly what Kurt Eichenwald wrote in *Newsweek* a year ago ... minus one instance of the article "the."

Otherwise, it's word for word. What Kurt Eichenwald wrote, WikiLeaks stole out of John Podesta's emails and published as something Sidney Blumenthal said.

Well, *that's* a helluva coincidence.

Of course, it *isn't* a coincidence.

A Blumenthal email included those words because Blumenthal was *emailing* Eichenwald's story.

He didn't say them, he didn't write them, yet they go from Podesta's hacked email account to a Russian propaganda site and are then presented to the world as a blockbuster confession by Sidney Blumenthal.

A fake blockbuster designed to alter the outcome of our presidential election, brought to you by WikiLeaks and the propaganda arm of the Russian government.

But it gets worse, and it gets scarier.

And here is where Donald Trump is either knowingly serving as an agent for the Russians, spreading disinformation . . .

Or he's just a moron reading stuff he doesn't understand that somebody found on the internet.

Trump, addressing a crowd at Wilkes-Barre, Pennsylvania, hours after the Sputnik forgery went online, on Monday of this week:

> So Blumenthal writes a quote—this just came out a little while ago, I have to tell you this. "One important point has been universally acknowledged by the nine previous reports about Benghazi."
>
> This is Sidney Blumenthal, the only one she was talking to. She wasn't talking to Ambassador Stevens, even the six hundred calls, probably desperation.
>
> "The attack was almost certainly preventable." Benghazi.
>
> "Clinton was in charge of the State Department, and it failed to protect the United States personnel at an American consulate in Libya." He meant Benghazi.
>
> "If the GOP wants to raise that as a talking point against her, it is legitimate."
>
> In other words, he's now admitting that they could have done something about Benghazi. This just came out a little while ago.

Trump was reading the paragraph from the Kurt Eichenwald article in *Newsweek*, falsely and obviously turned by the Russians into a fake Sidney Blumenthal quote, and shoved under this idiot Trump's nose.

He read it aloud.

And the crowd started chanting, "Lock her up."

Donald Trump—speeches written by the Russian government.

But why should you think that, and not that it could be a coincidence or just the typical sloppy thinking of a slob like Trump?

Because of a very strange man named Roger Stone. He is a longtime Trump confidant and had been a formal adviser to his campaign.

Stone tweets on Sunday, October 2: "Wednesday @HillaryClinton is done. #Wikileaks."

The next day?

"I have total confidence that @wikileaks and my hero Julian Assange will educate the American people soon #LockHerUp."

But neither of those is a smoking gun.

In fact, Assange canceled a much-touted news conference for Wednesday. Besides which, it's not as though Stone actually specifically referenced John Podesta or anything.

Oh, right. He did.

On August 21, Stone had tweeted:

"Trust me, it will soon the [*sic*] Podesta's time in the barrel."

Eichenwald writes it, WikiLeaks hacks Podesta's email, Stone threatens Podesta, Stone promises Clinton is done thanks to WikiLeaks, WikiLeaks produces an email, Eichenwald's article is misidentified as something Sidney Blumenthal said, and Trump reads it to the red-meat crowd hours later—like a good puppet.

And it sure looks like Stone knew it was going to happen.

Six weeks ago.

Only he was too stupid to keep his mouth shut, and the Russians were too stupid to realize that the guy who really wrote the quote would recognize his own words when he read them.

And on top of everything else, Trump then complained because it *wasn't* the October surprise he'd been promised.

Wednesday, 9:46 a.m.: "Very little pick-up by the dishonest media of incredible information provided by WikiLeaks. So dishonest! Rigged system!"

True—only the system in question is Vladimir Putin's.

*

Democracy survives not as much because of the efforts and sacrifice of the noble to preserve it as it does because of the sloppiness and imbecility of those who seek to destroy it.

Kindly *pray* that this continues to be true.

TO TRUMP'S SUPPORTERS: YOU KNOW THIS MAN

Post date • MONDAY, OCTOBER 17

Three weeks from today, we will stage the most important presidential election since the Civil War.

Three weeks *until* that election and one candidate has spent the past forty-eight hours insisting there is already voter fraud happening at polling places that don't exist yet.

Three weeks *until* that election, which that candidate says is rigged—unless he wins—because of voter fraud, which has happened thirty-one times out of the past *one billion* votes cast in this country.

Three weeks *until* that election and the leaders of one party are still chained, of their own volition, to the captain of the *Titanic*.

Three weeks *until* that election and their candidate has proved himself, more and more, hour by hour, day by day, to be manifestly unstable, sexually criminal, deranged, bigoted, and despotic.

Yet—to paraphrase Winston Churchill—these so-called leaders have been given the choice between shame and loss of office. They have chosen shame. They will *get* loss of office . . . later.

But it is not to them I want to speak at this three-week mark before the election. It is to those who *will* vote for *Trump*.

More important, it is to those who *may* vote for *Trump*.

To those who, bluntly, can still hear me.

If you're thinking of voting for Donald Trump, I'm sorry this country and your life in it are not what you thought they would be, nor what you thought was promised to you.

I'm sorry that you think you have been denied something by Americans who don't look like you or pray like you. I would remind you that when your grandfather or great-grandfather or whoever came here—and whenever they came here—*they* were blamed, identically, because they were Catholic or Italian or Irish or just foreign.

I don't doubt you have grievances, or that our system of government has been so overcome by the *political industry* that you see no chance that you will get what you really want. I have felt that way, too, nearly every day of my adult life.

But I'm not here to agree or disagree with your grievances. I'm here to urge you to recognize that what you see as your solution will, in fact, end with your slavery.

Because . . . you know this man.

You have *always* known this man.

Voting for Donald Trump is like not getting the car you want, so you instead take the car you have—and you drive it into a wall. While you are in it. While your family is in it. While your *country* is in it.

This election is not a question of policy or political correctness or rebellion against the machine. This is sanity versus insanity, and freedom versus a police state.

This man is crazy.

He is violent against women, he has been violent since he was a child, he hates and disparages people based on how they look or where their parents are from. And anyone and anything who goes against him is not treated the way *you* would treat them, or it. He does not move on. He does not work harder. He does not find another way. He says it's fixed, it's a plot, it's a lie, it's the fault of Mexicans, it means war.

He has uncontrollable anger.

And *you* want to give him nuclear weapons?

*

You *know* this man.

You have *always* known this man.

He is the lying used car salesman across town. He is the contractor who puts a hole in your wall and then vanishes. He is the fast-talking huckster on the late-night television commercial. He is the husband or the wife or the girlfriend or the boyfriend who promised you forever and ran off with your heart and your money—and your life.

You may not like Hillary Clinton or her policies or anything about her, but if she's elected, you will have four years to find a presidential candidate of your own whose true goal is *not* to rob you blind, and four years from now you will still have a presidential *election* and a vote—and a country.

Trump will give nothing to you but shame and regret and shackles. He will take, and he will keep, whatever he can get his hands on. It is the story of his life—he boasts about it. He says that giving employees a paycheck is the equivalent of your neighbors sacrificing their son in war. You really think he will give *you* anything? You really think he will give you a better job? More money?

From women to business, he is "grab first and ask questions later," and you *know that.*

And in the rubble—the rubble of *your* life in a political-science-fiction nightmare version of a fascist America made real—this will be on *your* conscience. It will be your fault, not his.

He is merely the con man who is fattening you up for the kill.

He comes onstage to the Rolling Stones song "You Can't Always Get What You Want."

He is telling you in advance.

How much more warning does he have to give you?

*

You *know* this man.

You have *always* known this man.

*

There has been a lot of time wasted on trying to understand the nature of the *strategy* Donald Trump has used since his profile as a serial sexual criminal began to emerge two Fridays ago.

Well, there *is* no strategy.

This is the point. This is not strategy—this is *him.*

He has been acting in this campaign—especially in the past two weeks—as if he has already been elected, already is president, and the rest of us are just annoying him by asking him about these harrowing tapes and accusations. He behaves as if we are being rude to him by not simply agreeing with him and praising his countless amazing skills and wonderful accomplishments and vast piles of money—as if on your deathbed or after it, the question you will ask, or that you will *be* asked, is "How much money did you make?"

Donald Trump is defending himself by claiming that his victims were too unattractive to attack—not as some kind of political strategy; not as some kind of clever answer. He is doing this because *that is who he is*, and *that is what he expects to be able to do as president.*

The presidency would be the same as his current life—seventy years of hedonism and selfishness and abuse—except backed up by the power of the presidency and the military. He has been the dictator in *his* life—and now he intends to become the dictator in *your* life.

*

You *know* this man.

You have *always* known this man.

You have seen him, and you have seen him recently.

He is Bill Cosby. He is O. J. Simpson. He is Bernie Madoff.

In nearly every individual thing Trump says to you, he is lying, distorting, rationalizing, contorting, blaming, and self-martyring. But in one sense, he is the most truthful candidate we have ever had. The awful, dishonest, egomaniacal, dangerous, hateful candidate he shows the world—that is *really him.*

He is not putting on an act. He is not hiding anything more than details. He is—every day—showing you his soul. The monster you see is the monster you will get—only this monster will now have the power to issue executive orders and pull that funny guy José you know, who works at the restaurant or on that farm, out of his house and throw him into a detention camp, and if you protest, he'll have the power to throw *you* in the detention camp alongside José.

Elect him and you will spend the rest of your life trying to undo your vote. You already know that this man promised to honor the outcome of this election if he loses—and then said he was backing out of that promise. You have already heard him spend hours explaining that if he loses, it will *not* be because he and you have been rejected—it will be because he and you have been defrauded.

What makes you think he believes in the things about this country that you *love*? That you have believed in and depended on and taken for granted since you were a kid? What makes you think he would not say, in his inaugural address, "The people have spoken—so there is no need for any more elections"?

Why on earth would you think that—having gotten you to give him your vote, your money, and your freedom—he would ever again bother to ask you what *you* want? Why would he listen to you? Why would he do anything for you? Who would *make* him?

If you want to vote for him because nobody pushes him around—what are you going to do when he does something you don't like? What makes you think that if you dare to raise a complaint, he would not treat *you* as he has treated those who during the campaign have opposed him or criticized him or merely pointed out what he has *said*?

You cheer now when the reporters at his rallies are booed and threatened; you high-five when somebody sucker-punches a protester. How do you think *President* Trump will treat *you* if you feel like he's broken his promise to you? How do you think *President* Trump will treat you if you do not jump when he says jump? How do you think *President* Trump will treat you if you do not applaud when he says applaud?

He has already shown you how.

*

You *know* this man.

You have *always* known this man.

You *know* that this is the kind of man whom oppressed people around the world have spent their lives trying to escape from, and have *lost* their lives staging revolutions against. Elect him and you are signing the death warrant to your own freedoms.

*

But even if you think he's going to lose but you must vote for him anyway—in protest—you still will have opened Pandora's box. Because this *might* be the most skilled and dangerous con man ever to rise up to try to cheat us out of the democracy you and I cherish.

But he might *not* be. The next one may be far worse, and far more skilled. And whichever is the case, he *certainly* will not be the *last* of the con men.

And when the first one finally soft-sells enough of your friends to gain that sacred office of the presidency, *you*—as much as I—will be at his mercy. If Trump merely "does well" while losing this election, it will be open season for demagogues and fascists and white supremacists to try to take over this country. *Your* country.

You have already seen it diagrammed for you. Donald Trump has shown his math. He has gotten this far—gotten to within three weeks of the presidency—based on summoning hate and fear and directing it toward a given group—Mexicans, Muslims, Jews, liberals, reporters. It doesn't matter *which* group, and nothing guarantees that the next time, it won't be *your* group.

*

You *know* this man.

You have *always* known this man.

*

And among all the things you know *about* this man—out of all that has gone on since Trump started it in June of last year—one statement he made should jump out and grab you by the throat. And it should ask you, very softly but very firmly: Why would you ever, ever consider turning over this country to this man? Why would you ever, ever consider encouraging his type just by giving him your vote?

When the woman on the plane thirty-five years ago, Jessica Leeds, accused him of groping her, he tried to defend himself not by getting a believable witness, not by proving he wasn't on the flight, not by the way *you* would defend yourself against such a charge if it were not true and your whole life were at risk because somebody had slandered you.

No.

Trump said you should know he didn't do it because "Believe me, she would not be my first choice, that I can tell you."

*

"She would not be my first choice."

So ask yourself one question before you vote for this man.

Who *would* be his first choice?

Your daughter?

GIVE US YOUR ANSWER!

Post date • THURSDAY, OCTOBER 20

The debates are over.

That is to say, Donald Trump's debates against *Hillary Clinton* are over.

But Donald Trump's debates against *America* and democracy . . . may only be beginning.

*

Last night he made a statement—in front of tens of millions of Americans— that should, by itself, end not just his candidacy for, but his eligibility to *be*, president.

Throughout the media last night and this morning, it was treated as something new and shocking. It is neither. It is just that this time, it was not hidden by the breathing barrage of stupidity and arrogance and delusion this man is.

In short . . . Trump did not get away with it *this* time.

Moderator: "Your running mate, Governor Pence, pledged on Sunday that he and you—his words—'will absolutely accept the result of this election.' Today your daughter Ivanka said the same thing. I want to ask you here on the stage tonight: Do you make the same commitment that you will absolutely accept the result of this election?"

Trump: "I will look at it at the time. I'm not looking at anything now. I'll look at it at the time."

*

At that exact moment, he lost the election.

If Trump still had a chance, it vanished, right then.

And then, if he had a chance to perhaps regain some dignity, to not pull down his supporters and his party with him, he blew that as well.

Moderator: "There is a tradition in this country—in fact, one of the prides of this country—is the peaceful transition of power, and that no matter how hard-fought a campaign is, that at the end of the campaign, that the loser concedes to the winner—not saying that you're necessarily going to be the loser or the winner, but that the loser concedes to the winner and that the country comes together, in part for the good of the country. Are you saying you're not prepared now to commit to that principle?"

Trump: "What I'm saying is that I will tell you at the time. I'll keep you in suspense. Okay?"

*

Burn in hell.

Some days ago in this space, I quoted Donald Trump's whiny interview with *The New York Times* on September 30. Having had it drawn out of him only with rhetorical pliers, in the *first* debate, that he *would* support Hillary Clinton if she were elected, he reneged on that promise twenty days ago, saying, "We're going to have to see. We're going to see what happens. We're going to have to see."

It was, as I observed then, the first time in American history—through dozens of venomous, painful campaigns and a series of impossibly close elections—the first and only time the candidate of a major party had violated the fundamental precept of our democracy.

It shakes every one of our freedoms.

It mocks every dead soldier.

It spits at every sacrifice made under our flag.

It has no comparison—not to Al Gore. Not to Samuel Tilden. Not to Andrew Jackson.

It foments revolution.

It was and is the moral equivalent of treason.

*

And this time it slipped past no one. Not the moderator. Not Fox News.

No one.

It was not a flash of anger from a man who gets angry once an hour.

It was not another slab of red meat thrown to his crazed supporters.

It was not another outrageous statement to throw up against the wall in this cheap reality-game-show version of a presidential campaign.

He meant it.

He *means* it.

He meant it on September 30 to *The New York Times,* and he meant it last night when Chris Wallace asked him about it, and he meant it last night when Chris Wallace gave him a chance to back away from it.

Donald Trump is not invested in democracy.

Donald Trump is not invested in the Constitution.

Donald Trump is not invested in America.

Donald Trump is not invested in preventing people from being killed on the streets after an election as if this were a third-world police state.

"I will look at it at the time. I'm not looking at anything now. I'll look at it at the time . . . What I'm saying is that I will tell you at the time. I'll keep you in suspense. Okay?"

Burn.

In.

Hell.

*

Last night, this moved beyond Trump and his ego and his mental illness and his inability to understand that the other people in this country, the other people on this planet, are not just props in some sort of television series starring Donald Trump.

This is now about the Republican Party, and *its* responsibility to the democracy . . . and *its* responsibility to the Constitution . . . and *its* responsibility to America.

Reince Priebus, Mitch McConnell, Paul Ryan, John Cornyn, John Thune, Kevin McCarthy, Marco Rubio, Jeb Bush, George W. Bush, George H. W. Bush—this man will not promise he will honor the sanctity, the inviolability, of our election—*your* election—*your* candidate—*your* party.

Right now, this moment, uncorrected by you, this man is advocating violent or passive resistance to a presidential election, and if you do not act against him, you will be blamed for him, and you will fall *with him*.

This is bigger than who is the next president, or who is the next RNC chair, or who is the next Speaker of the House. This is our democracy imperiled from within, by a man you have permitted to speak for *you* and for millions of loyal Americans who suddenly realize that the nominee of *their* party is willing to subvert the election and to subvert democracy itself.

Compel him to withdraw.

Now.

Litigate against him.

Find enough doctors and have him declared psychiatrically incompetent.

At minimum, cut off his funding, and denounce him in the strongest possible terms.

Because this nightmare, this fascist, this *Trump*—is now *your* responsibility.

And after what he said on September 30, and after what he said last night, and after what he *repeated* last night, it is no longer *enough* for him to simply *lose* this election.

He must now . . . *not* be given the opportunity to "keep us in suspense."

He must now . . . *not* be given the option to "look at it at the time."

The defense and viability and future of this democracy now depends on this man being removed—by any legal means—from being able to further act *against* this democracy.

Whether the Republican ticket or the Democratic ticket gets the most votes on Election Night and in the Electoral College is, in this context, *incidental.*

The issue *now* is a man who has, on three occasions, assailed the most precious component of our 240 years of freedom—and, by so doing, encouraged others to also subvert and ignore it—and whether you, the Republican Party, will permit him—in the next nineteen days—to do it a fourth time, or a fifth, or a hundredth, or a thousandth time.

Will you?

Or—will you act on behalf of the United States of America?

Give us your answer!

IMAGINE

Post date • SUNDAY, OCTOBER 23

Imagine if we were not two weeks and one day away from a presidential election, but rather two weeks and one day away from a threatened invasion by a foreign cult figure of some kind.

Imagine if that foreign invader intended to take over control of our government, and had already declared that when he did, he intended to remove eleven million people who lived here and put them first in camps and then presumably in other countries.

Imagine if that foreign invader had already declared that he would, upon taking control, put up a *wall* along one of our national borders.

Imagine if that foreign invader had already declared that he intended to institute a religious test for anybody entering into our country, and intended to bar any members of a certain religion from coming here, and said that others coming here would have to be granted "ideological certifications."

Imagine if that foreign invader had already declared that he would have his troops kill the families of terrorism suspects, and would institute racial profiling to *find* terrorism suspects, and would institute national stop-and-frisk racial profiling to find *criminal* suspects.

Imagine if that foreign invader had already made dog-whistle threats about "international bankers" against members of the Jewish faith in this country, and if that foreign invader had once kept, in a cabinet near his bed, a book of the speeches of Adolf Hitler.

Imagine if that foreign invader had repeatedly praised the leadership of such dictatorships as Russia and North Korea, then went on national television here, in front of tens of millions of Americans, and explained that the dictator of Syria was "much tougher and smarter" than American leaders.

Imagine if that foreign invader were connected personally and by members of his gang, past and present, *to* the Russian dictator, and imagine that he then said that, even before he solidified his control over our country, he might personally meet *with* the Russian dictator.

Imagine if that foreign invader had asked, publicly, on live television, why the country he intended to take over *had* nuclear weapons if it did not intend to *use* those nuclear weapons.

Imagine if that foreign invader had declared that all of our treaties—economic and military—would be abrogated or canceled or subject to renegotiation, and that our primary military treaty—NATO—would apply only to countries that paid us protection money.

Imagine if that foreign invader had declared our elections rigged, our debates crooked, and the leaders of both of our main parties dishonest, and three times had refused to say that the loser of the most important of these elections was obligated to honor the outcome.

Imagine if that foreign invader had implied that groups of Americans should try to intimidate other groups of Americans from voting, and that those Americans with guns should act in some manner *against* leaders of whom they did not approve.

Imagine if that foreign invader had spent four years constantly insisting that our foremost elected leader was ineligible for the office and was actually the cofounder of the most heinous terrorist group in the world.

Imagine if that foreign invader had already promised to—when he took over—put at least one of our leading political figures *in prison*.

Imagine if that foreign invader had declared that our freedom of the press should no longer be protected, that "freedom of the press" does not include printing things *he* believes are not true, that he would make it easier to sue the media, that readers should cancel subscriptions to the newspapers that criticize him, and that even *entertainment* programs that displeased him should be "retired."

Imagine if that foreign invader had questioned why a suspect in a minor terror attack should be granted access to a lawyer. Or access to a doctor. Or access to food.

Imagine if that foreign invader had already declared that our country was rife with lawlessness and race riots—especially where the members of minority groups live—and that he was going to fix that by whatever means were necessary.

Imagine if that foreign invader had declared that some of our inner cities were more dangerous than Afghanistan, and that "drugs are a very, very big factor" in protests in those areas.

Imagine if that foreign invader had declared that America was a "third-world country" in a "death spiral."

And imagine if that foreign invader had surveyed all of the problems—real and imagined—of the country he intended to take over two weeks from tomorrow and declared, "I alone can fix it," and then said he "will protect you," because he is "the only one who can."

Imagine if all *that* was what we faced two weeks from tomorrow.

It truly *isn't* hard to do.

Because that *is* . . . exactly what we *do* face . . . two weeks from tomorrow.

TO JOHNSON AND STEIN SUPPORTERS

Post date • TUESDAY, OCTOBER 25

The polls have been all over the map, and the numbers in *specific* polls have also been all over the map, but it is safe to say that as of this week as many as 8 percent of Americans say they plan to vote for Gary Johnson or Jill Stein for president.

If you're one of them—especially if you're a millennial—give an old liberal five minutes to try to explain to you why you should not.

I am not going to try to sell you on Hillary Clinton. I am not going to invoke Ralph Nader. I am not going to wax nostalgic about my nearly voting third party in 1980. I am not going to linger on how *I* want three or four major parties.

What I *am* going to tell you is that all of these points—valid, invalid, or somewhere in between—*cannot* be the priority this election. Not my priority, and not yours—especially not when *your* vote may decide whether it's Clinton or Trump who becomes president.

This is really simple.

If you vote for Gary Johnson or Jill Stein, you need to assume that it will be the last presidential vote you ever cast.

I am not being symbolic, and I am not being hyperbolic.

I am pointing out simple realities.

In every swing state, a vote for Johnson or Stein is one fewer for Hillary Clinton, and her victory over Donald Trump—as big a victory as possible, by as large and indisputable a margin as possible—is vital to your safety; is necessary for assuring that the country . . . still *exists* four years from now; essential to make sure *your right to vote* still exists *one* year from now.

The difference between Clinton and Trump is that stark.

Whatever is wrong with Donald Trump emotionally or psychiatrically, the healthiest diagnosis would probably be: extreme anger management problems. He's asked why this country doesn't *use* its nuclear weapons. He has repeatedly talked about putting his election opponent *in prison*.

He gave a speech at Gettysburg last Saturday—at Gettysburg! Abraham Lincoln!—where he said what his first hundred days as president would be like, and it was all about who would be going to jail, and who he was going to sue, and which news organizations he was going to shut down.

Three times, he refused to promise that he will accept the election outcome if he loses. The one truly, timelessly, eternally noble part of this very flawed democracy of ours—the peaceful transition of power—and he is deliberately leaving doubt about it and encouraging his supporters to believe the election is—or may be—rigged, and even dog-whistling about how they should go to the polling places in inner cities on Election Day and act as a kind of vigilante group against minority voters there.

The man is a bigot. He has shown no commitment to free elections in this country; he is a bully with severe anger management problems, combined with a desire to have and use nuclear weapons—and he's running not for president but for dictator.

Hillary Clinton? Strengths, weaknesses, potentially our first woman president, all of it—and all of it nearly secondary to the fact that she's sane and she believes in our form of democracy.

It's that simple.

You vote for Stein or Johnson and it's one vote fewer for Clinton—but it's also one vote fewer that Trump has to match. Because of how this election will play out in the swing states, your vote for Stein or Johnson *might as well be* a vote for Trump—it will have the same effect.

*

I read not long ago two pieces at *Vox* by a pair of twenty-one-year-old voters—one for Johnson, one for Stein.

One part of each piece—twin mirror images of dissent—jumped out at me.

This is from the Stein voter, Shawn Schossow, a student at Simpson College, in Iowa:

His vote, he writes, "is a deliberate stand against the two-party system."

And this is from the Johnson voter, Stephanie Page, who's at Ohio State.

"I understand that Johnson has little to no chance of becoming president, but I need to use my voice to tell our government that we need to change the way things are done."

"We need to change the way things are done."

No argument here.

My generation failed at it.

You are getting your chance.

"A deliberate stand against the two-party system."

Amen.

And in any other election—Bush-Gore or Obama-McCain, or if this one had been Bush-Clinton—I'd say: Enjoy.

But there is an assumption in both of these statements: We need to change the way things are done—a deliberate stand against the two-party system.

Why do you assume that if you get rid of the two-party system, the only option then is . . . a *three*-party system? Or four? Or five?

What if it's *one*?

What if you get your wish: change the way things are done—no more *two*-party system.

And you instead get . . . a *one*-party system?

What if you vote Johnson or Stein—and Trump gets elected?

What about this Trump guy suggests that he *cares* about what happens after he is elected? Why are you so sure that even *this* democracy can withstand a crazy man with the authoritarian style of a 1930s dictator and a campaign undertone of putting his opponent in prison?

What makes you think he is *not* going to put his opponent in prison? Or put his other opponents in prison? Or the media? Or Muslims? Or the LGBTQ community? Or you?

"People tell me to compromise and vote for the lesser of two evils," the Stein voter, Mr. Schossow, also wrote, "but I cannot compromise when it comes to my beliefs, especially when they involve human rights and systemic oppression."

The point this year is *not* "Are *you* compromising your beliefs?"

The point this year is that you could wind up electing a president . . . who will compromise your beliefs *for* you—and who will make your complaints now about human rights, or oppression, or the two-party system, look to you in retrospect like a quick dance in the spring rain.

You want to change our system?

Please do.

My generation failed.

If *you* fail on November 8 and Trump gets elected, nobody's going to pull you or me out of it.

Change all this—at the *midterms*. Do it in the state legislature. Do it in 2020.

The guy who *wants* to change all this right now—and whom you may help to become president—has no interest in human rights, especially not yours.

You want *more*?

He wants *less*—although I'm sure "systemic oppression" sounds pretty good to him.

If you want to *vote* for Trump, I can't stop you; nobody can.

Just remember, though. If you are voting for Jill Stein or Gary Johnson . . . you are *also* voting for Donald Trump.

TO HILLARY CLINTON VOTERS

Post date • WEDNESDAY, OCTOBER 26

There was some confusion as to exactly what that *was*, bobbing above the Trump crowd at Virginia Beach, Virginia.

Even those who recognized its physical components were more than surprised about what they were actually seeing.

Finally, even those who had covered this sixteen-month kaleidoscopic mix of those Americans who have only vague and loose bonds to reality, and others who dwell in a fantasy world made up of equal parts video game and television horror series—those who had been benumbed by the public emergence of the dregs of our society—even *they* were appalled when they figured out what it was *supposed* to be.

From the Twitter account of Emily Stephenson of Reuters.

From the Twitter account of Jenna Johnson of *The Washington Post*.

From the Twitter account of Ellie Hall of BuzzFeed.

A Hillary Clinton mask, stuck on the end of—what close examination proves to have been—an adjustable cane.

In short: Clinton's head on a metaphorical pike.

As if she had been beheaded.

As if this were the French Revolution and she was the governor of the Bastille prison.

As if—as Ms. Stephenson pointed out—we were living in *Game of Thrones.*

*

This is mentioned by way of reminding you, if you are a Hillary Clinton supporter, or if you don't want to see Donald Trump become president, or *both* . . .

Take nothing for granted in these next thirteen days.

Take no poll at face value.

Take no comfort in trajectories.

Take no break because Clinton has done *this* well or Trump has done *that* disastrously.

Assume . . . the worst.

Assume . . . that the ABC tracking poll giving her a dozen-point lead is the outlier, and the *L.A. Times* tracking poll showing them tied is the baseline.

Assume . . . that whatever you think is a safe margin to save this country from democracy-suicide in two weeks, it is actually too low, too close, too dangerous.

*

Hillary Clinton's head—on a pike.

*

And, in fact, not for the first time.

From the Twitter feed of Emily Schultz on August 31.

It's in the foreground.

The stick just isn't very long.

This was a rush job.

The guy in Virginia Beach? He took his time.

Whoever he is, he planned it out, got his materials, assembled it slowly.

He is the symbol of the Donald Trump gang of bullies.

He is the symbol of what will be *recorded* as a political campaign, but which, for an alarming number of its participants, long ago ceased to be anything but an enabled venue for violent fantasies and hatred based on—well, based on the need *to* hate.

It *seems* specific to Hillary Clinton, but if it had been Bernie Sanders, there would've been another motif—and we know what it would have been. If it had been Michelle Obama, there would've been another motif—and we know what *that* would have been. If it had been Joe Biden, there would've been another motif—and we can't even *guess* what it would have been, because it doesn't matter. It is the *fantasy of normalized violence* that *is* the motif—and that keeps the Trump crowd together.

He stands there blaming Hillary Clinton and the Muslim faith because ISIS has beheaded victims . . .

His supporters show up carrying images depicting Hillary Clinton, beheaded.

*

I don't know what to do about them if he loses.

I suspect most of them will scurry back under the floorboards and other places where bullies hide when their protection disappears and their cowardice is exposed.

But I *do* know that the greater the margin, the more states, the more votes . . . the greater will be the chance that some few of them will get the message that this unthinking orgy of fantasy violence is not acceptable in real life, and that the man who has said it has been sent to crushing, humiliating, historic defeat.

*

So if you want to stop Trump and you feel relieved by recent news, sleep *better*, but do not sleep longer.

If you have viewed the outcome of the election—correctly, I think—as life or death for the Republic . . . you must *now* view the *margin* of the election as life or death for the Republic.

Vote; get others to vote; vote in groups; look up and carry with you the various voter intimidation hotline numbers; be ready to photograph anybody who tries to impede you when you *go* to vote.

And one more thing. Remember Donald Trump's ceaseless, tireless, classless repetition of the claim that the election is "rigged"—but remember it in the context of what one of this year's great patriots, his *Art of the Deal* ghostwriter, Tony Schwartz, observed about Trump and projection.

Remember that Schwartz tweeted that "most negative things he says about others are actually describing him."

Since Trump has endlessly bleated this charge that Hillary Clinton and others are trying to "rig" the election—since his interests and those of the Russian hackers and WikiLeaks are running on parallel tracks, if not the same one—go into the last stretch assuming that Trump's charge of rigging is actually an *admission* of an attempt to rig the election *for* him, not *against* him.

Does this make you uncomfortable?

Good.

Trump imperils our democracy and is now the proverbial wounded wild animal in the corner. From him—incapable of conceiving of himself as mistaken or rejected or failing—anything, in these last thirteen days, is possible.

And if that still is not motivation enough to fight this with every fiber of your being until the last vote is counted . . .

Just remember where this piece began.

On a *pike*.

TO WOMEN VOTING FOR TRUMP

Post date • WEDNESDAY, OCTOBER 26

Depending on the poll, Hillary Clinton is leading Donald Trump among women by either 55 to 35, or 53 to 41.

The startling part is that Trump has any number larger than *zero*.

If you are a woman planning to vote for him, this question: How much *worse* does his record *about* women need to be?

Doesn't it bother you that Donald Trump claimed again this week that all the women who have come forward with sexual allegations against him are doing it for the money, yet *none* of them are suing him—while he says he will sue them *all*?

Doesn't it bother you that he keeps insisting that, as he phrased it in the last debate, "nobody has more respect for women than I do"? Yet when a pornographic actress claimed he grabbed her, Trump said: "Oh, I'm sure she has never been grabbed before."

There he goes . . . respecting women again.

Doesn't that *bother* you?

Even if he *didn't* do anything, and she and the others are all lying—doesn't *that* bother you?

*

Doesn't it bother you that when a woman employee he body-shamed in public came out for Hillary Clinton, he accused *her* of *also* being a pornographic actress, calling her "disgusting (check out sex tape and past) Alicia M"?

Doesn't it bother you that *before* Alicia Machado, and before all those women—long before that Billy Bush tape—back in March, his campaign manager shoved a woman reporter to the floor and *Trump* said she had made the story up . . . and he hinted at *prosecution*?

"Victory press conference was over. Why is she allowed to grab me and shout questions? Can I press charges?"

Doesn't it bother you that he wanted to fire women who worked for him at his golf club in Rancho Palos Verdes, California, for not being "pretty enough"?

Doesn't it bother you that days after Anna Nicole Smith dropped dead, he went on national radio and said: "She had the best hair, but she had the best face and the best body. . . . Now, when she opened her mouth, it was different. Let's face it."

Doesn't it bother you that when one of his advocates gets into an on-air argument with a woman newscaster, his spokesman . . . accuses her of attacking Trump and makes the thinly veiled threat "Watch what happens to her after this election is over"?

Doesn't it bother you that he dismissed one woman seeking to become the first-ever presidential nominee of his party by saying, "Can you imagine that, the face of our next president"?

Doesn't it bother you that after he attacked a Gold Star father—who lost his son as he fought for this nation in Iraq—*for* criticizing him, he then attacked a Gold Star mother . . . for *not* criticizing him?

None of this bothers you?

When he claimed that American troops stole cash while serving in Iraq?

When he said that John McCain wasn't a war hero because he got cap-tured?

When he said he had never asked God for forgiveness?

If none of this bothers you—none of it—none of it makes you think twice about voting for this crude, abusive, sexist, disrespectful, nonreligious man . . . than I have just one more question.

Does the idea of a man like this as president appeal to you because it some-how makes a similar misogynist in your own life seem more okay? I mean, if there's a President Jackass, does that make the *Mr.* Jackass *you* know some-how *acceptable*?

And he *is* a jackass to women.

If you didn't know that, or you won't admit it, consider one last thing. The magazine *Mother Jones* has just found this on the archives of a blog Trump wrote for his infamous Trump University.

This entry is dated January 6, 2009, and it's about the actress Kelly Pres-ton. It's pretty pathetic on its face, but after you read it, I'll tell you why I think that this—by itself—makes Trump ineligible to be taken seriously by any woman, let alone voted for by one.

I have always respected people who were loyal and faithful—which brings to mind Kelly Preston. A long time ago, before I was married, I met Kelly Preston at a club and worked like hell to try and pick her up. She was beautiful, personable, and definitely had allure. At the time I had no idea she was married to John Travolta.

In any event, my track record on this subject has always been out-standing, but Kelly wouldn't give me the time of day. She was very nice, very elegant, but I didn't have a chance with her, and that was that.

When I later found out she was married to John, I liked and re-spected her even more. Some people have values that matter to them, and she is one of them. Her loyalty was unwavering and I have always remembered that about her.

Being true to someone is very close to being true to yourself. That's a valuable attribute in today's world.

Why on earth was he blogging about the time, years before, when he struck out with Kelly Preston? What does the arrogance of the phrase "My track record on this subject has always been outstanding" have to do with *her*?

This was a blog post . . . about Kelly Preston's . . . son dying.

Jett Travolta. Sixteen. A seizure, while on a family vacation.

This self-absorbed boasting about his brilliance at picking up women . . . is his idea of a *condolence note* for the devastating death of a sixteen-year-old boy . . . a subject he finally gets around to in the last of the twelve sentences he wrote:

"I'm sure she was a wonderful mother to Jett and my thoughts are with her and her family after their terrible loss."

No, they weren't!

His thoughts were about . . . himself.

His thoughts are *always* about . . . himself.

*

If you can still vote for a man like this, explain your reasons to your maker, not to me.

TRUMP PRAISES ANOTHER DICTATOR

Post date • THURSDAY, OCTOBER 27

So, Donald Trump, you have now sided with *another* dictator, *against* the United States.

And people probably didn't hear about it because (1) for sixteen months you have generated a dozen stories a day that would've caused any other candidate to withdraw and flee to the Caymans, and (2) you have almost run out of new dictators to praise.

I'm going to let the reader here try to guess who the new addition is.

We know it can't be Kim Jong-un . . .

You already praised him last January . . .

"If you look at North Korea, this guy—I mean, he's like a maniac, okay? And you gotta give him credit. How many young guys—he was like twenty-six or twenty-five when his father died—take over these tough generals? You know, it's pretty amazing when you think about it. How does he do that? . . .

"He goes in, he takes over, and he's the boss. It's incredible. He wiped out the uncle, he wiped out this one, that one—I mean, this guy doesn't play games . . ."

"Incredible" . . . "amazing" . . . "you gotta give him credit."

Sure, you do, Trump—if you are more interested in a despot killing people the way Stalin used to kill people than you are interested in *us* and how we deal with a psychopath who rules his country on the premise that he will eventually stage nuclear war against this country.

So it's not Kim Jong-un.

*

So—Putin?

Can't be Putin, can it, Trump?

Three weeks ago, Homeland Security and the director of national intelligence said both agencies are "confident that the Russian Government directed the recent compromises of e-mails from US persons and institutions, including from US political organizations."

In simpler language, Trump: the Russians hacked us. Just like you invited them to, at your last news conference.

And the intelligence community told you that—presumably in much more detail.

And then Hillary Clinton brings it up in the last debate, and you say . . .

"She has no idea whether it's Russia or China or anybody else. Our country has no idea."

She explains it, and you interrupt her to say, "I doubt it."

So you've said Putin and Russia are probably right—and *our* intelligence agencies are probably wrong.

How many times is that, that you've defended Putin and Russia, Trump? I've lost count!

And how many times have you *praised* Putin? Over Obama? Over Clinton? Just this week, you did it again . . .

You told Reuters you had questions about "how she is going to go back and negotiate with this man who she has made to be so evil."

"*Made* to be so evil?"

He *is* evil, you disloyal bastard!

*

So the new strongman whose side you took isn't Russian.

Chinese, maybe?

No. You already praised them—twenty-six years ago!

In *Playboy*!

"When the students poured into Tiananmen Square, the Chinese government almost blew it. Then they were vicious, they were horrible, but they put it down with strength. That shows you the power of strength."

If you are an actual American, Trump, after you call the Chinese at Tiananmen Square "vicious" and "horrible"—there is no "but."

There is *just* vicious and horrible, Trump.

*

So is it Saddam Hussein?

No, you already praised him, too.

July: "You know what he did well? He killed terrorists. He did that so good. They didn't read them the rights. They didn't talk. They were a terrorist? It was over."

Once again, Trump, your stupidity about foreign dictators—dead or alive—is rivaled only by your naiveté. If, somehow, the only people Saddam Hussein killed *were* terrorists, then what you said might make sense.

But he killed at least 200,000 of his own citizens. I'm guessing the children he killed probably weren't terrorists, Trump.

*

So your new candidate for BFF isn't Iraqi . . .

But we have actually finally gotten warm.

Rodrigo Duterte, the lunatic elected in the Philippines on a mandate of shooting first and asking questions later about possible drug dealers, drug *addicts*—basically anybody he thinks should die now, without a trial. Or often without an arrest.

Approximately two thousand dead in his first hundred days in office.

Oh, and in August, Trump, this buffoon said to Secretary of State Kerry that ... "your ambassador is a gay son of a bitch."

A month later, he said of President Obama, "Son of a whore, I will curse you."

So now, in an interview with Reuters, who did you blame for this murderer Duterte insulting our leaders and damaging his country's relationship with us?

Him?

Of course not! He's showing power, right?

Only you, Trump, could blame this on Obama, because you think our president "wants to focus on his golf game" rather than engage with these tyrants, so it's Obama's fault that Duterte showed—again quoting you—"a lack of respect for our country."

"Our ... country," Trump?

I hear that and I think—which country do you *view* as *your* country?

For all the flag hugging, figurative and literal, when it's North Korea versus the United States, you side with North Korea.

When it's Russia versus the United States, you side with Russia.

When it's China versus the United States, you side with China.

When it's Iraq versus the United States, you side with Iraq.

And now, when it's the Philippines versus the United States, you side with the Philippines!

Trump, I've asked *this* before and I have to ask it again:

Are you loyal to the United States of America?

WORSE THAN WATERGATE

Post date • MONDAY, OCTOBER 31

Donald Trump is—for once—correct.

It *is* worse than Watergate.

And, as *in* Watergate, the director of the FBI must resign.

First—he must retract his statement, *then* resign.

*

There are only two alternatives:

Either James B. Comey knowingly tried to tamper with a presidential election, eleven days out, on a hint of a possibility of a rumor of an inference of a chance of Clinton emails that reportedly aren't *from* Clinton and aren't *to* Clinton, which his bureau hadn't bothered to tell him about, nor gotten a warrant for, until last night . . .

Or James B. Comey had no idea that his statement would impact a presidential election in such a way that there would not be a chance to disprove the negative he threw against the wall, like the shit—by all accounts—that it is.

In the former case, Comey—once that rarest of individuals, the nonpartisan legal hero from the Bush administration—is a criminal who has desperately and personally and at the last minute tried to deliver this country and its 240 years of democracy into the hands of a self-obsessed, compulsively lying fascist with no respect nor interest in anyone or anything besides himself and no understanding of the real world and the billions he could kill in a fit of pique over something somebody said about him on TV.

In the latter case, Comey is merely criminally *stupid*—a man who did not foresee that his actions were the equivalent of crying "Fire!" in a theater, without saying *which* theater he means and with no evidence that there is any fire *anywhere*.

Regardless of which—stupidity or criminality—his viability as the head of the FBI ended the moment he sent his note last Friday to, among others, the chairman of the United States House Committee on Oversight and Government Reform.

Who should *also* resign—today.

Because this is far worse than just an FBI director swinging the mighty weight of his bureau against *one* presidential candidate while refusing to confirm that it is even investigating the *other* presidential candidate and his staff and former staff for their manifestly obvious ties to Russian propaganda and disinformation.

Far worse.

The actions of the chairman of the United States House Committee on Oversight and Government Reform—before and after FBI director Comey's letter—imply either *collusion* . . . or guesswork on the chairman's part that rises to the level of extrasensory perception.

Because on Friday, on Saturday, yesterday, and even this morning, the timeline of how that chairman, Representative Chaffetz of Utah—former wrinkle-cream spokesman—came to know about the investigation has been almost utterly ignored . . . and it is, at best, disturbing.

On the night of Friday, October 7, hours after the release of the *Access Hollywood* tape of Donald Trump boasting about his preferred *methods* for sexual assault, Chaffetz spoke of his fifteen-year-old daughter:

"Do you think I can look her in the eye and tell her that I endorsed Donald Trump for president when he acts like this, and his apology? That was no apology, that was an apology for getting caught. . . . So I'm not going to put my good name and reputation and my family behind Donald Trump for president when he acts like this. I just can't do it."

*

The morality of Chairman Chaffetz lasted exactly nineteen days.

At 9:05 p.m. Eastern Daylight Time last Wednesday, October 26, Mr. Chaffetz—out of nowhere—suddenly tweeted:

"I will not defend or endorse @realDonaldTrump, but I am voting for him. HRC is that bad. HRC is bad for the USA."

So much for Mr. Chaffetz's fifteen-year-old daughter.

Sometime around noon last Friday, Mr. Chaffetz received his communication from FBI Director Comey about a hint of a possibility of a rumor of an inference of a chance of Clinton emails that aren't *from* Clinton and aren't *to* Clinton, which his bureau hadn't bothered to tell him about, nor gotten a warrant for, until last night.

Immediately after receiving Comey's ode to vagueness, Mr. Chaffetz put two essential, critical, devastating words in Mr. Comey's mouth.

At 12:57 p.m. Eastern Daylight Time last Friday, October 28—thirty-nine hours and fifty-two minutes after he repudiated his own moral stance and declared his support for Trump—Chaffetz tweeted:

"FBI Dir just informed me, 'The FBI has learned of the existence of emails that appear to be pertinent to the investigation.' Case reopened."

*

That, of course, is *not* what Comey said.

Mr. Comey did not *say* he had reopened the case.

Of all the pernicious, anti-FBI, anti-American, anti-democracy things James B. Comey did last Friday (and before), saying he had "reopened the case" . . . was not one of them.

Jason Chaffetz said that.

And that made it easy for people to *think* Comey had legally reopened the case.

And then *Donald Trump* said that—and lied!

And then television—with the exception of my former colleague the noble Pete Williams of NBC—said that, and broadcast a lie!

And then newspapers, with almost no exceptions from left or right, said that—and printed a lie!

And by the time they started backtracking, the toothpaste was out of the tube.

Except this was probably *imaginary* toothpaste. If we take Director Comey at his word, he had no idea. He still doesn't. His agents reportedly knew of the emails at the beginning of October, yet he didn't get a warrant until last night! He may not have the slightest idea before the election, and he has nothing with which to undo his malfeasance, or misfeasance, or betrayal of the democratic process.

*

But ignore not Chaffetz.

Why, after nearly three weeks of righteous indignation at Trump's barbarism toward women—indeed, toward *people*—why, late Wednesday night, did he suddenly pivot back to supporting him?

Why did he reverse, thirty-six hours before Comey's historically slovenly, craven note that left Pandora's box unjustly unlocked so that a sniveling little coward like Chaffetz could peek inside, then deliberately exaggerate what he saw, and then fuel Donald Trump's latest delusional rage?

Most assuredly, Jason Chaffetz is a prophet worthy of his religion's Joseph

Smith. *Or* he is the recipient of an accident of timing so unlikely as to be almost biblical.

Or . . . he knew or suspected that Comey's note was coming.

How ever would he have found out about *that*?

FBI agents who reportedly knew.

An FBI director who was reportedly suddenly terrified of leaks.

And if Chaffetz knew that Comey's note was coming, then he and Comey or other sources in the FBI have colluded to try to manipulate the election, in which case Mr. Chaffetz and Mr. Comey may need the best criminal defense attorneys money may procure.

And if Chaffetz knew that Comey's note was coming—did he tell Trump?

And who can clear this up a week and a day before the most important election since the Civil War?

Oh, and that fifteen-year-old daughter Mr. Chaffetz isn't so worried about anymore? She has far more to worry *about* than listening to the psychopath Trump boast about grabbing pussies.

Because she may soon be looking for a paternity test to prove that Jason Chaffetz is *not* her father—because he and James Comey may have been the linchpins in a plot to turn over the country—by treachery—*to* Donald Trump.

And it is a plot that is indeed—as Trump *boasted*—worse than Watergate.

Chapter 3

NOVEMBER, PRE-ELECTION DAY 2016

THE TRUMPCHURIAN CANDIDATE

Post date • TUESDAY, NOVEMBER 1

- "I think"—says the *loyal* senator in the 1962 film *The Manchurian Candidate* about his paranoia-mongering colleague—"if John Iselin were a paid Soviet agent, he could not do more to harm this country than he's doing now."
- "Putin," says Donald Trump in his speech at Grand Rapids, Michigan, yesterday about his opponent Hillary Clinton, "who she likes to say bad things about—you wonder why the world hates us."
- "A former senior intelligence officer for a Western country," writes David Corn in *Mother Jones* this morning, has "provided the [FBI] with memos, based on his recent interactions with sources, contending the Russian government has for years tried to co-opt and assist Trump . . ."
- "If," said Donald Trump about Russia during the third debate, "we got along well, that would be good . . ."
- "The FBI," reports NBC News, "has been conducting a preliminary inquiry into Donald Trump's former campaign manager Paul Manafort's foreign business connections."
- "Wouldn't it be nice," Trump said in a speech at Virginia Beach nearly two months ago, "if we got along with Russia?"

- "A Group of Computer Scientists," reads a headline at Slate.com, "Believes a Trump [Computer] Server Was Communicating with a Russian Bank."
- "At least," Trump said last December when asked about Putin allegedly killing opponents and journalists, "he's a leader, unlike what we have in this country.... I think *our* country does plenty of killing also."
- "The speech is short," says the wife of the Senator Iselin character in *The Manchurian Candidate*. "But it's the most rousing speech I've ever read. It's been worked on, here and in Russia, on and off, for over eight years ... rallying a nation of television viewers to hysteria, to sweep us up into the White House with powers that will make martial law seem like anarchy."

*

Yes, I have employed the theatrical sleight of hand of conflating two movie quotes with four actual Trump quotes and three separate actual Trump/Russia-scandal quotes being reported today.

I have done this because one of the fascinating, terrifying joys of that political-science-fiction classic *The Manchurian Candidate* is that once you buy into the premise that the Russians would go to any lengths to influence who becomes president of the United States, the rest of the plot quickly lines up behind a kind of inevitable logic.

And once you buy into the premise that not the fictional film version of the *Soviets* of 1962 but the *real-life* version of the post-Soviet *Russians* of 2016 would go to any lengths to influence who becomes president of the United States, the kaleidoscopic chaos of Donald Trump's fever dream of a campaign *also* quickly lines up behind a kind of inevitable logic.

So think of the inevitable logic of the plot points in the screenplay of what we might title *The Trumpchurian Candidate* ...

Two weeks ago, Trump, who has continually—again and again, even *during* the debates—defended the Russians against charges that they have hacked American political-related computer systems, elevated his bizarre loyalty to Putin to a new level by disputing the classified briefings he's gotten in which our spies drew him the proverbial map.

Trump continues to say he would restructure the greatest wedge against Russia—NATO—and lend American help to NATO countries menaced by, say, Russia, only if they *paid up.*

During the September presidential *forum,* Trump said Putin was a greater leader than Barack Obama and, with no apparent irony, or awareness that Putin is a dictator, cited Putin's approval ratings of 82 percent.

The same month, the second man Trump named as a foreign policy adviser, Carter Page, was investigated by our intelligence agencies for allegedly meeting *in Moscow* with the Russian who supposedly supervises their attempts to mess up our election.

After years of boasting, "I do have a relationship with him"—Trump is recorded on video saying that—he switched in September to a full denial that he even *knows* Putin.

And Trump has defended Putin's anger at the use of the phrase "American exceptionalism," and Trump has refused to say anything when his own running mate, Mike Pence, called Putin "small and bullying," and Trump denied that the Russians had anything to do with Malaysian Airlines Flight 370, and Trump has insisted that Putin will never go into Ukraine, even though he *went* into Ukraine in 2014!

Anybody seeing the plot lines of our movie *The Trumpchurian Candidate* taking shape yet?

*

There is one other writer's trick to which I must now confess:

I omitted from my collection of quotations anything from *The New York Times'* reporting this morning that the FBI looked but found nothing necessarily nefarious about that reported direct line between a computer server in Trump Tower and the Russian company Alfa-Bank.

Nor, the *Times* says, has the FBI found anything that ties Trump or anybody near him to the conclusion of American intelligence agencies that the Bureau now seems to be finally, grudgingly agreeing with: that the Russians *are* trying to disrupt the presidential election.

But I would point out that the *Times* report also confirms that "the FBI's inquiries into Russia's possible role continue." And the *Times* also quotes an op-ed in its own pages from this past August in which former CIA acting director Michael Morell said simply, "In the intelligence business, we would say that Mr. Putin had recruited Mr. Trump as an unwitting agent of the Russian Federation."

In sum, there is only one flaw that would result from altering that line from *The Manchurian Candidate* to insert into our script for *The Trumpchurian Candidate*, so that it would read, "I think if Donald Trump were a paid Russian agent, he could not do more to harm this country than he's doing now."

That flaw is . . . Trump may not be a *paid* Russian agent. . . . He may be stupid enough, or disloyal enough, or anti-democracy enough . . . or just *evil enough* . . . to be doing it for free.

DESCENDING FROM THE CLOUDS

Post date • **WEDNESDAY, NOVEMBER 2**

As a student of history—and as an individual of largely German heritage—I have wondered since my teens what it would have been like—what it *must* have been like for distant relatives I will never know—to have been a German and watch what seemed like a strange but evidently unimportant political movement rise up from the fringes of my society and from the unsound mind and evil soul of one individual.

What would it be like to watch a man, laughed at more than feared, spew bizarre but hardly earth-shattering invective, year after year, in the shadowy corners? And then to see him—in real time and in my native language—double down on his rhetoric and hate and convoluted revenge fantasies, and then triple down on them, and quadruple, and quintuple.

What would it be like to watch in amazement, from your home, from the only society you and your family had ever known, to see the country you thought you knew react not with trebled laughter and quadrupled outrage—but with growing acceptance and enthusiasm?

What would it be like to see and hear, in your own language and time, the *hate* in which the man trafficked and the power he sought to usurp become part of your daily life?

What would it be like to hear a demagogue, a monster in the making, campaigning for office and promising to disband opposition parties and jail the opposing candidate?

What would it be like to hear those who follow him see their most secret, violent fantasies come to life, burnished with the authenticity and authority of a man who had moved the bar between right and wrong toward himself, who could, with a few words, *validate* their desires to hate and exclude and kill?

What would it be like to see it unfold, in preliminary elections and in increasingly fevered rallies, as millions handed over their votes, never dreaming that they would be repaid only with fear and privation and death, and the destruction of their country?

What would it be like to watch as the sober agencies of government gradually became corrupted, first to influence the outcomes of elections, then to separate a minority from the day-to-day life of my country, then to remove them to camps and uncertain fates there?

What would it be like to watch as the police became first militarized and then politically aggressive and partisan—as they literally adopted the logos and the clothing of the rising mob?

What would it be like to watch the figure at the center of this ever-darkening storm begin to promise accords—on my behalf, on my country's behalf—with dictators around the world?

What would it be like—and when would it have hit home—that what I was watching was no longer politics, nor the governance of a country, but the normalization of repression and horror?

All this I have wondered.

What would it be like to see my country devolve and deteriorate from democracy to mindless, soulless cult worship?

Thanks to Donald Trump, I am getting the chance to find out.

*

Last Saturday: A rally-goer in Phoenix spits at the media pen and starts shouting, "Jew S.A.! Jew S.A.!" and is captured on video as he does so.

Day before yesterday: He self-identifies as George Lindell, of Phoenix, and he claims it was not an anti-Semitic chant, but empathy for a group of Hispanics at the Trump rally who pronounce "USA" that way.

Because that's what you *do* at Trump rallies: empathize with Hispanics.

Lindell does not explain why his empathy was followed by telling reporters and photographers that they were "going down" and adding, "The Jews run the country anyway."

*

In Cleveland on October 22, a man shouts *"Lügenpresse"* at reporters. It's an alt-right term that was used to describe anything Western in the East Germany of the 1960s; it even dates back to the propaganda of the Kaiser in the First World War. But it gained an added meaning—"liar press," or "lying Jewish press," or just "lying Jews"—in the Germany of the *1930s*.

*

Last Sunday: Another man at another Trump rally yells at the press pit, "Put the camera on us, faggot! Put the camera on us, queer!"

He self-identifies as Matt Fox, of Palm Springs, and he explains that he's proud to have said it, and besides, "Queer isn't a bad word. Queer means happy."

*

Yesterday: A member of Trump's Agricultural Advisory Committee tweets a poll result that reads, "TRUMP 44 Cunt 43."

*

Last Sunday: As that rally begins in Las Vegas, an opening speaker named Wayne Root almost sounds like he's fantasizing about the death of Hillary Clinton and then says, "We're putting the D.C. elite on notice. We're coming to tear it down. We're coming to rip it up. We're coming to kick your ass. And we're coming to put you in prison."

*

Since a year ago June, and in the campaign that has followed, Trump crisscrossed the country in an airplane, descending from the clouds into the arms of growing numbers of fanatics, at ever larger rallies. He gave them a positive message, promising something for everyone, then ascended back into the clouds.

A week ago tonight, he descended at Kinston, North Carolina, his plane taxiing toward the crowd of fanatics. A huge spotlight was directed on the door, right next to the giant letters spelling TRUMP, and he walked down the airplane stairs and began to speak.

Soon, an older man in a dress shirt and jacket and sunglasses moved slowly toward the stage and got to within twenty feet of Trump. He waved a piece of paper in the air and shouted, "Donald, Donald..."

Trump spotted him and pointed him out to security, and as the man was removed, Trump said, "We have a protester. By the way, were you paid one thousand five hundred dollars to be a thug?... You can get him out. Get him out... Out!" Trump went on to riff about what a disgrace it is, and how tough *his* people are.

The man turns out to be an ex-Marine. And he's sixty-three years old. And he's named C. J. Cary. And he's... a Trump voter. And he's corresponded with Trump since 1992. And he's had thirty-six different Trump signs in his North Carolina yard, and they keep getting vandalized. And he keeps getting new ones.

And the piece of paper in this ex-Marine's hand was a note urging Trump to not lose the election by continuing to be impolite and unwelcoming . . . to minorities.

But to Trump, he wasn't one of *his* people.

As Mr. Cary approached, Trump did not see the veteran, nor a pen pal, nor a man with thirty-six Trump yard signs, nor a supporter. All *Trump* saw was that Mr. Cary... is African American

So Trump called him a *thug*.

*

Called him a thug, the same way George Lindell called the reporters Jews from Jew S.A....

The same way Matt Fox called them faggots and queers...

The same way the Trump mob in Cleveland called them *"Lügenpresse."*

The same way Wayne Root called *all* of Trump's opponents "D.C. elite" to be "put in prison."

*

What would it be like to see my country devolve and deteriorate from democracy to mindless, soulless cult worship?

Thanks to Donald Trump, I am getting the chance to find out.

I close with a paragraph from a website called HistoryPlace.com. I've played a little trick here. I've already quoted this paragraph, a minute ago.

I have changed just two words in it, both of them proper nouns.

"In the campaign that followed, [he] criss-crossed [the country] in an airplane, descending from the clouds into the arms of growing numbers of fanatics, at ever larger rallies. He gave them a positive message, promising something for everyone, then ascended back into the clouds."

HistoryPlace.com then adds that the candidate who descended from the clouds in his own airplane made his fanatics more and more ludicrous promises.

Such as: "In the Third Reich every German girl will find a husband!"

TRUMP TV—YOU THINK IT'S FOR WHEN HE LOSES?

Post date • THURSDAY, NOVEMBER 3

It is not breaking news.

He will do it again today, at least once.

Donald Trump will attack the media.

Did it in Miami yesterday. Said, "Another important issue for Americans is integrity in journalism. These people are among the most dishonest people I've met, spoken to, done business with. These are the most dishonest people."

The crowd booed lustily.

"There has never been anywhere near the media dishonesty like we've seen in this election. Don't worry, they won't spin the cameras and show the kinds of massive crowds. They won't do that."

He says this every single day.

Yesterday he singled out, for the third time, one reporter—my ex-girlfriend, incidentally, Katy Tur of NBC, still a dear friend. She was harassed by the simpering bullies who populate Trump crowds, but she's fine, because unlike them, or Trump, she's neither a coward nor a fascist.

Still, abusing the media, inciting physical harm against them—that always whips up the crowd.

But it's also . . . a preview.

His son-in-law, Jared Kushner, was reported this week to be using personnel recruiters to try to staff up . . . "Trump TV."

Which starts the obvious cognitive dissonance echoing again.

Trump TV means his family expects him to lose.

Right? Already in the proverbial "soft launch" on Facebook, it's a cynical exploitation of the past sixteen months of relentless self-promotion and reality show plot lines and network enablers and the accumulation of a database of at least twelve million email addresses.

But it is *based* on that one premise: *President* Trump would have no time for his own political television apparatus, right?

What would a president of the United States *need* his own television network *for?*

What would a president of the United States, elected purely as a cult figure and facing enormous opposition from the moment of his inauguration, *do* with his own television network?

What would a president of the United States with no apparent commitment *to* nor understanding *of* democracy, with only a stated insistence that "I alone can fix it," *put on* his own television network?

*

Trump TV isn't designed as a fallback in case he *loses*!

Trump TV is designed as a ready-made propaganda outlet in case he *wins*.

Trump TV isn't a consolation prize—it's a means of consolidating power once he's in the White House. It may not even *remain* "Trump TV." It may morph into something like "*Official State* TV."

What more could he ask for—indeed, what would he *need* more—than a media outlet that *always* agrees with his decisions and whims, and insults and then demonizes and then organizes action against those who criticize him, and ultimately can be amped up to outshout the *unofficial* American broadcasters—the disloyal ones like CBS and NBC and ABC and CNN and Fox News and every nascent operation from *The Closer* to Breitbart TV—if they won't toe the line.

Hell, why bother "outshouting" them for very long?

Trump has already threatened all media, all those protected by libel laws, all free speech. He has threatened CNN and *The New York Times* by name. Nine days ago, his henchman Dan Scavino threatened Megyn Kelly. "Watch," he tweeted, "what happens to her after this election is over."

Why would you assume that Trump would bother sticking to the laws when he believes—as no president in our history has ever believed—that he can just nullify them with executive orders? Why not cut to the chase and just announce that you can't broadcast news without a license from the government, and we will let you know when your license application has been reviewed?

In the age of satellites and internet, it's doubtful that Trump TV—as *State TV*—could totally drown out outside voices. Even when the Nazis took over all of German radio in 1933, and then in 1939 made it a criminal offense to listen to foreign stations, words of dissent made it through.

But not from within the country.

And ask the Chinese or the North Koreans how unfettered the internet is. They are told, and eventually most of them come to actually believe, that in blocking them from seeing half or more of all websites, their governments aren't denying them truth, but *protecting* them from external brainwashing.

Happily, that could *never* happen here!

Not with Trump having demonized the current American media during virtually *every* one of his speeches, like yesterday, to the point that, on the thirteenth of last month in Cincinnati, the entire traveling press corps had to be escorted to safety by police dressed in riot gear.

Happily, that could never *happen* here!

Not with Trump having advocated for restrictions on the internet to keep terrorists from communicating. Or from brainwashing American minds. And then *he* decides who's a terrorist.

Happily, that could never happen *here!*

Not with Trump's toady Newt Gingrich having gone on record as long ago as 2008, saying that part of the internet needed to be turned off and the First Amendment should be reconsidered.

No, no, no, Trump TV is his *backup* plan—just to cash in on his indisputable popularity with the average American.

The average American!

Who believes what Trump tells him, that the "rigged media" is conspiring against him—and against Trump. Who shouts *"Lügenpresse"* and yells homophobic and racist slurs at the reporters and who does so with impunity!

Who *wants* to hear that Trump is right and Trump is good and Trump is winning and Trump has gotten them all better jobs and Trump has made America great again and Trump has gotten rid of those filthy immigrants and Trump is happy to raise the chocolate ration to twenty grams a week and Trump has killed the terrorists and Trump alone fixed it and Trump recognizes which group is the next threat and Trump is acting to protect you from it and Trump has good news about the fighting and Trump is right: we have *always* been at war with East Asia.

But no—Trump TV is just his backup plan if he loses.

Besides, even if he is elected, and even if he wanted to do this, he couldn't, you know, establish his own Trump TV network and shut down all other media in this country?

Who would stop him?

GODDAMNED FASCIST MORONS

Post date • FRIDAY, NOVEMBER 4

This is Friday, November 4, four days until the 2016 presidential election between Secretary Clinton, representing the Democrats, and Donald Trump, representing the Russians.

*

As we sit here waiting for *today's* newest story about the FBI improperly, immorally, and illegally trying to interfere with next Tuesday's elections, this question:

When should we reclassify the form of the government of the United States from "democracy" to "fascism"?

I mean, do we wait until the prospective inauguration next January of a president who doesn't seem interested in the Constitution . . .

Or—if the FBI is already trying to help one party seize control of the government, technically, is that good enough to just cut to the chase and say we are already living in a goddamned fascist state?

Should we just admit that next Tuesday isn't an election to try to *prevent* fascism and a dictatorship here, but one to try to get a woman elected who will fight back against the national detectives who have already decided that freedom is secondary to what *they* want and who *they* like?

The latest FBI nightmare broke last night—although a newer one might have broken since this commentary was posted. Reuters reported that the Bureau is so out of control that its hapless director, James Comey, shouted "Fire!" in a crowded theater a week ago today for fear that if he didn't, somebody else in his clown college would, by means of a leak.

The news service also reported:

"Two law enforcement sources familiar with the FBI's New York Field Office, which initially discovered the emails, said a faction of investigators based in the office is known to be hostile to Hillary Clinton."

To me, this constitutes grounds to—you know—close the FBI's New York Field Office, fire everybody in it, and bring in some placeholder agents to investigate actual—you know—*crimes*, while a special prosecutor investigates how many of the fired New York Field Office employees have violated the Hatch Act by acting politically during an election season.

And I mean if they're acting politically for Trump *or* for Clinton. The moment a nationwide policing operation is corrupted by politics—right, left, or middle—it's goddamned fascism.

But of course, all the other nightmares from the FBI suggest that they are *not* acting "left" or "middle." Even earlier yesterday, the estimable Wayne Barrett of *The Daily Beast* underscored a timeline that nearly all of the rest of us missed.

As Barrett noted, last Wednesday, goddamned Rudy Giuliani—who has, face it, gone crazy—told Fox News that his boy Trump had "a surprise or two that you're going to hear about in the next few days. I mean, I'm talking about some pretty big surprises. We've got a couple of things up our sleeve that should turn this thing around."

Two days later—Comey's statement.

Coincidence—no doubt.

*

Reporter Barrett also noted that Giuliani and his friend, former New York FBI chief James Kallstrom, had both boasted of being in contact with active FBI agents *about* Secretary Clinton. Active agents are not supposed to be talking to a man employed as a surrogate by a political campaign. Active agents are not supposed to be talking to *anybody* outside the agency about a presidential candidate. Active agents are certainly not supposed to be talking to a man like Kallstrom, who runs a charity that took $100,000 from Trump's hissy-fit charity telethon during the Iowa Republican primary. It's against the goddamned law!

Although why would they worry about the law? They're goddamned FBI agents, and they think they should run this country without annoying interference from you or me or the goddamned *laws*.

Some of them also appear to be idiots.

Tuesday, *The New York Times* revealed that in August, the Bureau had descended to the stage of—to borrow Generalissimo Trump's phrase—"All I know is what's on the internet."

The FBI's poking around the Clinton Foundation, which found nothing, "was based mostly on information that had surfaced in news stories and the book 'Clinton Cash,' according to several law enforcement officials briefed on the case."

Clinton Cash?!

Clinton Cash the book—written by Peter Schweizer, the editor of the right-wing nut-job goddamned fascist website Breitbart?

Or *Clinton Cash* the movie—produced by Stephen Bannon, then *chairman* of the right-wing nut-job goddamned fascist website Breitbart before he took a cut in prestige to run Trump's goddamned campaign?

Basing an investigation on *Clinton Cash*?!

Because there weren't any comic books available on the subject?

This is not just fascism—this is *idiot* fascism.

And it's the one shining hope on the ever-darkening horizon.

Yes, Trump admires dictators and was saddened that arrested terror suspects get food or medical care, and he calls protests by abused minority groups "race riots," and he wants to automatically deport any undocumented American merely *accused* of a crime, and he wants national stop-and-frisk and racial profiling and a religious test for people entering the country, and he wants to curb the First Amendment.

But he's also . . . *stupid*!

Stupid enough to still say in Jacksonville yesterday, "I'm also honored to have the greatest temperament that anybody has"—as if he won an *award* for it, or there were a worldwide ranking of all seven billion people. Well, hell, maybe one of those voices in Trump's head actually told him he *had* received an award, and all we should be hoping for is that one of the *other* voices in Trump's head will tell him he has no effing clue what the word "temperament" means.

And while I won't walk back an inch my contention that the best historical match to the campaign that this Macy's Thanksgiving Day Parade balloon in a suit is running is the one Adolf Hitler ran in 1932 and 1933, I'll also continue to insist that Trump is still far dumber than he looks—and he looks radiantly dumb.

It was neither irony nor subtle strategy that made Trump send his spectacularly dense wife onto the campaign trail yesterday, where she vowed that as First Lady she would advocate against the parts of social media that are "too mean and too tough" and filled with insults based on "looks and intelligence," and 318 million Americans simultaneously wondered if this woman had ever met her own husband and whether she was capable of understanding that if abusing people's looks and intelligence on Twitter were a crime, he would be serving the first of 147 consecutive life sentences!

So, yes! We already live in a goddamned fascist state, with the FBI trying to choose the next president, and the would-be First Lady coming out and advocating some kind of First Amendment–altering monitoring of social media. And that should make you . . . *angry!*

To paraphrase one of the great speeches of film, all I know is that first you've got to get mad! You've gotta say, "I'm an American citizen, goddammit! My democracy has value!"

But when you get mad this weekend, get mad with gusto and vigor and confidence instead of depression or anxiety or panic!

These people—Trump, Giuliani, Bannon, Comey, the FBI, that Madame Tussauds version of a would-be First Lady—these people *are* fascists . . . *fearful* fascists.

But they are also *morons.*

And we can *beat* morons!

We can beat morons with the weapons still left to us—the ballot . . .

The ballot *and* your efforts to convince just one other person you know to vote in defense of their birthright and in defense of democracy, and against . . . *morons!*

Against *goddamned fascist morons!*

ANOTHER FUCKING TRUMP LIE

Post date • MONDAY, NOVEMBER 7

It was in *The New York Times* yesterday.

It was about Stephen Miller, senior Trump policy adviser, and Corey Lewandowski, fired Trump campaign manager, meeting with Trump campaign chairman Stephen Bannon.

It was Friday, October 28, Manchester, New Hampshire. And they had just read the letter from FBI Director Comey—the letter that was an attempt to throw the election to Trump, *not* the letter yesterday that was an attempt to save Comey's ass and the asses of the fascists who have caused the FBI's New York office to "go rogue."

Adviser Miller and fired campaign manager Lewandowski and this baboon Bannon were trying to figure out what Trump should say in a speech just minutes away—when it happened.

As the *Times* wrote it:

"As the aides agonized over which words to feed into the teleprompter, they [became] so engrossed that a hot light set up next to the machine caused Mr. Bannon's Kühl hiking pants to begin smoldering.

"'I think my pant leg is on fire,' he said after noticing the acrid smell."

The chairman of this Friday the 13th Movie Marathon of a presidential campaign—and his pants are . . . literally . . . on fire.

Trump, when the go-to metaphor about lying . . . the go-to metaphor about *political* lying . . . suddenly happens, *for reals* . . . to your campaign chairman . . . in something just this side of spontaneous combustion . . .

Trump, when your campaign chairman's clothing *becomes* "liar, liar, pants on fire"—imagery, analysis, probity have all lost their ability to correctly qualify or even quantify your campaign's dishonesty. You have defied description. You have eluded art. You have beggared the imagination.

Trump: You, your campaign, and everything around you are, simply, a lie.

Another lie.

Another fucking Trump lie.

The first Comey letter?

The worst attempt to throw the election by a government agency since a morals charge against an LBJ aide in October 1964 was leaked . . . by—golly— the FBI!

And your exploitations of it—exploitations now rendered pathetic and transparent by Comey's desperate second letter yesterday? Clinton's going to be indicted. Clinton's going to jail. Clinton would be impeached.

Each one of those . . . a lie.

Another lie.

Another fucking Trump lie!

*

And that was hardly the worst of the lies just this weekend!

On Friday, at a North Carolina Clinton rally, a protester interrupted President Obama. The crowd booed the older man, but the president told them—*his own side*—to "sit down and be quiet for a second." He then told them to respect their elders and respect the man's rights and the uniform he wore, which suggested he was a veteran.

That night in Pennsylvania, you, Trump, claimed that Obama "spent so much time screaming at a protester, and frankly it was a disgrace."

A lie.

Another lie.

Another fucking Trump lie!

*

The *next* night in Nevada, you, Trump, upped the ante.

Now you said the president had yelled at *multiple* protesters:

"Wherever I go, I see him screaming at people that are protesters . . ."

And now, during the same speech, in Nevada, a guy unveils a Clinton poster and you say, "Oh, we have one of those guys from the Hillary Clinton campaign. How much are you being paid? Fifteen hundred dollars? All right, take him out."

Your crowd promptly . . . takes him out.

He is jumped, punched; he says he was grabbed by . . . the groin.

And then, Trump, somebody says, "Gun!"

A lie.

Another lie.

Another fucking Trump lie!

There was no gun, just a guy with a sign getting beaten up by *your* crowd. Secret Service rushes you off the stage—fine, good, bless them, glad we haven't yet descended to violence against candidates.

But *while* you are lying, Trump, about how *Obama* handled a protester, *you* incited your own crowd to *beat up* a protester.

And the special projects director of a group called Citizens for Trump promptly tweets, "Hillary ran away from rain today. Trump is back on stage minutes after an assassination attempt."

A lie!

Another lie!

Another fucking Trump lie!

And *that* lie was promptly retweeted by your son Idiot Junior and your social media director, Dan Scavino.

Your people turned a guy with a *sign* into an assassination attempt.

And then at your next speech, Saturday night in Denver, the priest introducing you says you just survived attempted murder.

A lie!

Another lie!

Another fucking Trump lie!—from a priest!

The next morning, confronted on CNN with this succession of lies, your campaign manager, Kellyanne Conway, refuses to back away from the lie that this was an assassination attempt instead of what it really was—a piece of cardboard—but she does complain about a list of CNN stories she doesn't like—and offers to *trade*.

"You guys retract that, and I will give a call to Dan Scavino about the retweet."

Not "Thank goodness there was no assassination attempt." Just . . . a lie.

Another lie.

Another fucking Trump lie!

*

This weekend, Trump, was an unintentional and almost complete preview of what a Trump presidency would be like. You and your little fascist friends, like Rudy Giuliani, manipulating the levers of government to try to win elections. Presenting a universe designed to replace truth with imaginary menaces and phony assassination attempts and political prosecutions and the demonizing of criticism and the insane defiance of reality.

Lies instead of truth.

Lies instead of reality.

Lies instead of life.

*

And yet, with all of these lies, the *biggest* lie of the weekend, Trump, nearly flew under everybody's radar.

It's impossible to say for sure just how far you'd go to punish undocumented Americans. You've already insisted that millions will be deported. There are laws on the books right now about what happens to immigrants—even those who have become naturalized citizens—if they have lied in any way to gain citizenship. But the government rarely pursues these liars, unless they are involved in war crimes or terrorism.

But you, Trump, you want to expand prosecution of those who have worked here illegally.

Like, perhaps, the twenty-six-year-old woman who was revealed by the Associated Press on Friday night to have been here in 1996 on a visitor's visa and yet worked here illegally, getting paid for ten modeling assignments that were not permitted by her visa.

Having violated immigration rules, Trump, she later became a citizen. If she tried this on the first day after you took over the government, you would presumably prosecute her and revoke her citizenship.

You may know her story.

She is your wife.

And *her* story . . . is a lie.

Another lie.

Another fucking Trump lie!

NATIONAL SUICIDE

Post date • TUESDAY, NOVEMBER 8

This is Tuesday, November 8 . . .

The day of the 2016 presidential election between Secretary Clinton, representing the Democrats, and Donald Trump, representing . . . national suicide.

*

The calendar says 2016, but for all intents and purposes, this might as well be November 8, *1864*, because not since that day, exactly 152 years ago, have we Americans voted on whether or not . . . to put ourselves out of existence.

For all the existential national crises of the intervening century and a half since Abraham Lincoln was reelected—none of those moments when the United States of America could have perished, included . . . national suicide.

That's how deadly serious today is.

Go forward with Hillary Clinton, who at the worst will be a good president hamstrung by an obstructionist Congress and by the same kind of clutched-pearls, nonsensical investigations that hindered but never came close to defeating her husband . . .

Or put the full power of the government into the hands of an overwrought child, an amateur who believes he is God's gift to mankind and always had too much money to be impacted by his own failures, a sadistic bully with a cult but not a clue, who indeed can be baited by a tweet, who spent much of the last three days of his campaign complaining that Beyoncé and Jay Z had appeared at a Clinton rally—and onto whom 40 percent or more of this country has projected its personal grievances and prejudices and fears, and many of whom support because of blinding and ill-timed party loyalty.

Stock markets will crash, the world balance of power will be ruined before the inauguration, Russia's influence will immediately double, the Constitution's guarantees will become coin flips, and the lifeblood of this country since before its founding—immigration—will be spilled, metaphorically or otherwise, on the streets.

All because of the ego of one American and the incapability of tens of millions of other Americans to understand that all that they like and love about our country can vanish nearly overnight—that a vote to burn it all down does not just mean the *purge* they want, of minorities and immigrants and the media and anybody else they want to blame—that it also means that *their* America burns; that *their* homes burn; that *their* possessions burn; that the futures of *their* children burn.

That's how deadly serious today is.

*

Most Americans who know our history think of the *1860* presidential election as the last one that chose life or death for the country. The famous Senator Stephen A. Douglas, Tennessee senator John Bell, Vice President John C. Breckenridge—who was pro-slavery—against an obscure ex-congressman from Illinois named Abraham Lincoln.

Lincoln.

To whom, at Raleigh, North Carolina, yesterday, Donald Trump compared himself, boasting he got more Republican primary votes than Lincoln. Even though the population in 1860 was a tenth of what it is today. Even though there *were* no Republican primaries in 1860. "I got more than Honest

Abe." Tens of millions of people will actually vote for this diseased narcissist today.

The 1860 vote *was* crucial, but civil war was likely despite the outcome. It-was the *1864* election, four years later, that was life-or-death. As late as August of that year, some Republicans were talking about holding a second convention, withdrawing their renomination of Lincoln, and finding somebody else.

They, and the leadership—and Lincoln himself—were convinced that as things stood, Lincoln would *not* be reelected, and would lose to the Democratic candidate, George McClellan. McClellan was the general who had nearly *lost* the Civil War to the South, had been twice replaced, and was now running on a Democratic platform of immediately ending the war, negotiating a settlement of any kind with the South, and repudiating the Emancipation Proclamation, which had freed three million Americans *from* slavery barely eighteen months before.

And it was believed—nationwide—that Lincoln was going to lose to him. In a landslide.

Then, on September 2, 1864, the Union Army, led by General William Tecumseh Sherman, took Atlanta—at which point, from the North to the South, the outcome of the Civil War became a foregone conclusion.

The political fortunes of Lincoln and McClellan changed violently. One hundred fifty-two years ago today, Abraham Lincoln was reelected by 212 Electoral College votes, to McClellan's 21 votes. The tragic war was seen through to its conclusion, slavery was *not* restored, the United States of America was *not* split in two, the nation did *not* commit suicide.

And yet, in the popular vote, nearly all of it from only the northern states, *45 percent* of our ancestors . . . still voted *against* Lincoln. Voted *against* finishing the war they were winning. Voted *against* freeing the slaves. Voted *for* national suicide.

Forty-five percent.

That's how deadly serious today is.

*

There have been other moments when democracy could have died. The Revolution itself. The British burning of Washington in 1814. The Civil War, obviously, especially at Gettysburg, where Lincoln became immortal; where

Trump threatened to file vengeance lawsuits. The Great Depression and the prospect of a full-on Communist revolution, or a full-on right-wing military coup. Both world wars. The Cuban Missile Crisis. Watergate. September 11 and the proposal by one elected official that in the aftermath of terror, the end of his term should be delayed by three months. (That elected official was, of course, the mayor of New York City, Rudy Giuliani.)

The democracy—the country—are more fragile, and have faced more perils, than most of us ever choose to admit. But nearly always, these perils have been external and have unified us, and have not been the result of a kind of cancer not merely growing from within the country, but fed and fueled and nurtured and exploited by a psychopathic liar who has *gamed* democracy and is still, this very day, positioned to *destroy* democracy by means of the very freedoms it provides—freedoms that he would happily, and immediately, extinguish.

That's how deadly serious today is.

*

Each life-or-death moment in our 240 years as the closest thing to true freedom in the history of this planet has been met with courage and wisdom and unity, and especially sacrifice the likes of which few of us personally know, or can truly imagine.

And in none of them—not the British invasion, not the Civil War, not the Depression, not World War I, not World War II, not the Cuban Missile Crisis, not Watergate, not 9/11—were we afforded such an easy means of escape, such a simple method of protection, as rests in every man and every woman in every voting booth in every community in this country today.

We do not have to go to war.

We do not have to force a president from office.

We do not have to forestall a revolution.

We do not have to keep nuclear missiles from flying.

We do not have to recover from terrorism.

The Trump Crisis of 2016—national suicide—the death of the United States of America—can be prevented . . .

By voting.

That's how deadly serious today is.

THE TERRORISTS HAVE WON

Post date • WEDNESDAY, NOVEMBER 9

I'd like to begin by congratulating the FBI on its successful coup against the electoral process of the United States of America. You've been working on one of these for a while, boys, and I know everybody at the Bureau's just delighted that the "F" can now also stand for "Fascist."

Also let us acknowledge something a little larger and a little less removed from treasonous malfeasance:

The terrorists have won.

This, after all, was their goal, fifteen long, sad years ago.

To strip from the world's foremost power its traditions of relative and growing tolerance. To hamstring the international influence of a country that rarely stuck to the double white line of the moral road but came closer than any other. To take our energies from trying—more or less—to help the world move forward, and instead to make us direct those energies inward, at one another, within our own borders.

To divide us so, to complete the rupture of our settled, bizarre culture that for so long had been based on the inner monologue of "I really can't stand those people in the other party, or the other state, or of the other color, but my strongest emotion is going to remain annoyance rather than hate, because we are all Americans and we are all in this together."

Today—officially—*that's* gone.

Obviously, the perpetrators of 9/11 had other designs that have yet to come to pass—the destabilization of all the secular states of the Middle East, the rising up of a caliphate, etc.—but for the moment, that's not important to our discussions here.

Because the premise of the 2001 terrorism *here* was to take those divisions that were already then apparent in American society and multiply them by *fear*—fear of more attacks, of sedition, of disloyalty, of weakness, of difference, of immigrants, of minorities, of the loss of the playing field that was still tilted toward white people but was leveling just a little more every year.

It took a long time.

A long time for hatred and fear to find some figure here who would pander to it. Someone whose ego and lust for power would be the perfect vessel to exploit our collective post-traumatic stress disorder. Someone who would say anything, do anything, have an answer for everything even if the answer was made up out of whole cloth and on the spot.

The goals of those who attacked us in 2001 finally found an outlet. And last night, Americans—certainly half of them with no more sense of the permanence or importance of their decision than they brought to their votes for *American Idol*—opened the door and put the spokesman for hate and fear and bluster and, most of all, incompetence . . . in charge of the nation.

Collectively we have slit our own throats. We ordered, mixed, drank, and paid the bill for our own poison.

There is an irony that might be noticed in our upcoming months and years of free fall—namely, that the *first* victims of this act of mass madness will be many of those who pushed hardest for it and put the most faith in it. The economic impacts will be felt long before the inauguration in January—hell, long before Thanksgiving—and the Rust Belt states that turned against democracy and diversity yesterday will doubtless be the first to be consumed by job loss and financial panic and privation.

Cold comfort, indeed.

So what is next?

If you look for transformation within the new elected leader, fat chance. Nothing has changed him in seventy years, and if there is anything to *guarantee* that he will not temper his Hitlerian personality, that he will *not* be restrained by any remaining adults among Republican leadership in the House or the Senate, that he will *not* reach out to those who did not vote for him—if *anything* could actually *increase* his obstinacy and refusal to share or delegate—it would be this extraordinary, unprecedented development in American history.

Right now he thinks he is Superman.

*

But of course, he is not. The economy will be a complete shambles by the time the oath is administered, and there will be no fix available from making great deals, corner-cutting, or bellowing, "I'm not paying for sloppy work."

He, of course, will insist that everything is great and that his mere presence will assure we have made America great, and anybody who thinks otherwise is disloyal or an ISIS sympathizer or somebody he's going to sue.

As the standard of living plummets, he will try a diversion—the wall or the deportations—but boy, those things take time, so he'll probably do what they *all* do when there is no fix to the vital day-to-day issues: a war, or some bizarre gambit in the Middle East that will in fact restore ISIS and destabilize the world just a little bit more every week.

It will be bad. It will be very bad. Americans, and others, will die.

But, necessarily, there will be blowback.

There always is.

Blowback against the good—as this election just showed.

But also blowback against the *bad*. And at some juncture, soon, there will be a Resistance. Those of us who warned against and pleaded against and fought against this madness will find avenues for dissent that will have enough support to at least impede the monster. Put any title you like in front of his name and this is still an *aggressively* self-destructive man, and it will be the goal of the Resistance to help him in that task.

At some *other* juncture, soon or late, probably even before the midterms of 2018, a tipping point will be reached. Whether it's war or the economy or some wild card we can't see yet that is bouncing around in that great stash of funhouse mirrors in his head—it will be the *Republican* governors and the *Republican* senators and the *Republican* congressmen who *will* see the crowds of *Republican* voters demanding action against the irresponsible and delusional president, and an impeachment will begin—of what is nominally a Republican president, *by* a Republican Congress.

None of that is guaranteed, but it should be noted that Richard Nixon was not forced from office until his Republican colleagues acted in concert with Democrats to remove him. Moreover, the political history of this country for the past fifty years has been a series of wild pendulum swings—from the Civil Rights Acts to Richard Nixon in three years, from Bill Clinton to George W. Bush in three seconds . . . from Barack Obama to *this* creature in less than three months.

And if this creature is still in charge of this government and has not yet fled the country, then there *are* those midterms in 2018 and the attempt to begin a Restoration. Unless he acts in the interim against free elections, and I would never assume that in a nightmare like this, the Freddy Krueger in chief suddenly starts obeying the laws.

In any event, I leave you with two quotes. It's H. L. Mencken from 1926, and the long form actually is: "No one in this world, so far as I know . . . has ever lost money by underestimating the intelligence of the great masses of the plain people."

The other, of course, is: "You can fool all the people some of the time, and some of the people all the time, but you cannot fool all the people all the time." This is attributed to Abraham Lincoln, and it pretty much sums up that phase of the American experiment that the electorate ended last night. Because there's no real evidence that Lincoln ever *said* that.

In short, you *can* fool all the people just long enough to become the first anti-democracy president of the United States.

That's . . .

Oh, wait—one more thing. Conceit, probably. Whistling past graveyards, perhaps. A little Churchill, adjusted to the occasion.

Even though large tracts of America and many old and famous states have fallen or may fall into the grip of Trump and all the odious apparatus of Trump rule, we shall not flag or fail.

We shall go on to the end. We shall fight in state legislatures, we shall fight in the stores and the banks, we shall fight with growing confidence and growing strength in the air, we shall defend our America, whatever the cost may be.

We shall fight online, we shall fight in the press and on the television, we shall fight on the street corners of public opinion. We shall never surrender.

PART II

After:

I'M KEITH OLBERMANN and this is

THE RESISTANCE

Donald J. Trump ✔
@realDonaldTrump

 ✿ Following

I am working hard, even on Thanksgiving, trying to get Carrier A.C. Company to stay in the U.S. (Indiana). MAKING PROGRESS - Will know soon!

RETWEETS	LIKES
3,828	14,292

10:11 AM - 24 Nov 2016

↩   ⇄ 3.8K   ♥ 14K   •••

Chapter 4

NOVEMBER, POST–ELECTION DAY
2016

POST-ELECTION, *THE CLOSER* BECOMES *THE RESISTANCE*

Post date • **WEDNESDAY, NOVEMBER 16**

What do we do now?

This evil is unfolding, like it or not.

It can unfold, and you can lie there.

Or it can unfold, and you can resist.

There *are* practical means, things you can *do*.

I intend to offer some in each volume of this new series.

And we start—with something you can accomplish by *not* doing.

*

It is a week.

We were asked to give him a chance.

This is how he has wasted that chance.

Thirty-three hours after Hillary Clinton's concession:

"Just had a very open and successful presidential election. Now professional protesters, incited by the media, are protesting. Very unfair!"

The morning he was to announce his first staff appointments:

"Wow, the @nytimes is losing thousands of subscribers because of their very poor and highly inaccurate coverage of the 'Trump phenomena.'"

"The @nytimes sent a letter to their subscribers apologizing for their BAD coverage of me. I wonder if it will change—doubt it?"

"The @nytimes states today that DJT believes 'more countries should acquire nuclear weapons.' How dishonest are they. I never said this!"

Sixty-eight days until his inauguration.

Still bitching about his paranoid fantasies about the media.

Still lying about what he said during the campaign.

Still referring to himself in the third person.

Still obsessing over one newspaper as if he were fifteen and it had refused to go with him . . . to the junior prom.

*

Give him . . . a chance?

What? In the hope that he will someday grow up enough to be able to see over the top of the Oval Office desk?

We do not have time for the White House edition of *Celebrity Apprentice* starring President-elect Pussygrabber!

*

Give him a *chance*?

Because we're all supposed to pretend that *this* is a normal man and *that* was a normal election?

Because we're all supposed to forget that the Russians interfered with the election, and the involvement of the FBI—at minimum—affected the outcome?

Because we're all going to follow *The Washington Post* and call them "populists" instead of "white supremacists," even though Trump's new chief strategist . . . ran a white supremacist website?

*

Give him a *chance*?

All we are saying is: Give fascism a chance!

Who knows? It *might* not be as bad as we think!

It might *not* be a bottomless pit!

*

This is not my president, and judging by the margin by which Hillary Clinton won the popular vote—at this rate it'll be larger than Kennedy over Nixon in 1960—this is not *America's* president, either.

And so, we will *resist*.

Each statement of substance or policy or intent *will* be met . . . with one of resistance.

Each action and event staged by this man who lost the popular vote . . . *will* be met . . . with protest *by* that resistance.

Each politician whom he fooled with the charm from one of his other personalities—from the Vichy Republicans already lining up to lick his boots to the Democrats like this fathead Joe Manchin—will be *rejected* by that resistance.

*

Since no Democratic or liberal politician has yet stepped forward out of the morass of Politics Inc. to take on the responsibility of the resistance, I— with complete awareness of the presumptuousness and arrogance of this statement—volunteer myself, and will gladly turn over all these burdens to any more legitimate and informed lawmaker or political or cultural leader who has the guts to *take* these burdens.

I do not want violence, and I am not proposing the overthrow of the government by any means other than legal and political. I think protests should be limited to Washington, Trump Tower, and Trump hotels. I have no pie-in-the-sky plan to have the Electoral College alter the outcome. I will even acquiesce to a President Pence—just get . . . this . . . man . . . out . . . of . . . here.

And I will repeat what I said last week: this Trump is a profoundly and proactively self-destructive individual. It is now our sacred duty to help him *finish* his self-destruction.

Whether it is going to be *him* destroyed at his own hands or *democracy* destroyed at his hands . . . it is going to be him.

And the first step is to complete the delegitimizing of his presidency and his election.

Delegitimizing that he *himself* began.

Who said the opinion polling was rigged?

Who said the election *itself* was rigged?

Who refused to say whether he would honor the outcome *of* that election?

Why, the president-elect did!

And he *is* the president-elect! We are supposed to give him a chance! We are supposed to believe him!

*

Fine.

I'll give him a chance. I'll believe what he said. I'll take his word for it: the polling was rigged, the election was rigged, and he is not bound to honor the outcome of the vote.

Oh—and I'll also take his word for it about the Electoral College.

Not his backfilling, cover-your-ass tweet from yesterday about its genius (nor its companion boast—proving that he will never get over being a president who lost the popular vote—that if there were no Electoral College, he would've simply won bigger).

No—his tweets from the night of November 6, 2012, when Big Brother Trump thought Barack Obama would win the *Electoral College* vote and lose the popular.

"He lost the popular vote by a lot and won the election. We should have a revolution in this country!"

"The phoney electoral college made a laughing stock out of our nation. The loser one [*sic*]!"

"We can't let this happen. We should march on Washington and stop this travesty. Our nation is totally divided!"

"Lets fight like hell and stop this great and disgusting injustice! The world is laughing at us."

"More votes equals a loss . . . revolution!"

"The election is a total sham and a travesty. We are not a democracy!"

"Our country is now in serious and unprecedented trouble . . . like never before."

Those tweets the president-elect deleted, that night.

But one other one is still alive, on his account:

"The electoral college is a disaster for a democracy."

"A disaster for a democracy..."

"Lets fight like hell and stop this great and disgusting injustice..."

"More votes equals a loss... revolution..."

So saith the Almighty Trump.

Whatever you wish, sir.

You asked for it.

PRETEND

Post date • WEDNESDAY, NOVEMBER 16

When I was a kid, my dad used to tell me of a dream he had, again and again, starting in the late fifties. He was at his draftsman's desk, looking out his office window in Union Square, in New York, watching a perfect spring day trotting toward sunset, hearing the sounds of life and humanity through the open window and perceiving with his artist's eyes the balance of the contrasting colors in the vivid sky and the city more vivid still, and then noticing—out at the horizon, over the water... the mushroom cloud.

It was a nightmare, but one rooted horrifically in a reality of nuclear annihilation that got just a little bit worse every day, and which, as he noted, you then had to *pretend* wasn't reality and you had to *pretend* wasn't getting worse every day and you had to *pretend* wasn't abnormal and you had to *pretend* wasn't inhuman, and you had to *pretend* it wasn't unacceptable—until you ended the day exhausted by the sheer amount of your life you spent *pretending* that it was just fine.

Better to find ways—small ones, symbolic ones; if possible, *financial* ones—to fight back. You're spending just as much energy.

I was too young to share his nightmare.

And he is gone too many years to share mine.

But wise words stand the test of time. And his words were wise.

*

At the pussygrabber in chief's victory party, a woman named Omarosa Manigault, who was briefly on television, said of people who didn't vote for him:

"I would never judge anybody for exercising their right to and the freedom to choose who they want. But let me just tell you, Mr. Trump has a long memory and we're keeping a list."

We have to *pretend* that isn't abnormal.

Then the chief of the campaign is named the chief strategist in the White House, and he has a track record a mile long of antipathy to women and black people, and all of a sudden you realize Ms. Manigault, who is both, is *herself pretending* . . . that *he* isn't abnormal and *she* isn't a target.

And then we get half a dozen different answers about whether or not the victor in the presidential election is going to shatter all precedent by fulfilling his campaign boast and becoming personally involved in the prosecution of the loser—and all of a sudden the media is *pretending* that this isn't abnormal.

And on Sunday, the president-elect—who lost the popular vote—finally speaks about the Clintons and says, "I don't want to hurt them, I don't want to hurt them. They're, they're good people"—as if the decision whether or not to prosecute somebody in this country is based on how the president personally feels about them.

And now we all have to *pretend* that *this* isn't abnormal.

Then the outgoing minority leader of the Senate, Harry Reid, actually doesn't *pretend*, and says the election "has emboldened the forces of hate and bigotry in America" and is being celebrated by white nationalists, Putin, and ISIS, "while innocent, law-abiding Americans are wracked with fear."

To which the campaign manager Kellyanne Conway replies:

"He should be very careful about characterizing somebody in a *legal sense.* He thinks he's just being some kind of political pundit there, but I would say be very careful about the way you characterize it."

And then Ms. Conway *pretends* she wasn't referring to a lawsuit, even though she used the phrase "legal sense." Which I guess, necessarily, means she was referring not to a lawsuit but to a prosecution, and once again we must *pretend* this isn't abnormal—and the CNN headline actually reads, "Conway, Reid Trade Barbs over Trump," as if criticism and threats against the First Amendment are equivalent—and the *pretending* escalates.

And it is reported that the transition team allegedly asked the White House how the children of this man could receive top-secret security clearance. The children who are supposed to be running the anything-but-blind business trust that we have to *pretend is* a blind trust … a trust for the man who we have to *pretend* did *not* spend the campaign accusing his opponent of mishandling classified information.

And then the radio conspiracy peddler Alex Jones announces that Trump has phoned to thank him and to promise to be on his show soon, and we have to *pretend* Alex Jones hasn't claimed that the massacre at Sandy Hook was staged, and we have to *pretend* that he isn't crazy, and we have to *pretend* that it's not abnormal for a man elected president of the United States to even acknowledge that an Alex Jones exists, let alone to feed his machine of madness and brutality.

And then the cabinet names start falling and we have to *pretend* Giuliani isn't an international political whore who has taken money from repressive elements everywhere from Qatar to El Salvador, and who's now consulting for Uber.

*

But of course—they all have to *pretend* as well. *Pretend* that there *aren't* still avenues open to us for economic blowback.

Giuliani? Uber? Stop using Uber.

Alex Jones? That creature is on a hundred radio stations. Google them. Call them. Identify their advertisers. Boycott them.

The ludicrous media equivalencies and the euphemisms that normalize hate and enable *pretending*? Don't tweet. Don't call the writer. Don't call the editor. Call the president of news, or his boss at his corporation. I promise you, they *always* overreact.

Trump's hidden tax returns and the first *for*-profit presidency? How many Trump businesses can you avoid? How many firms that applauded his election, like New Balance, can you bankrupt?

Just this week, the owners and residents of three New York apartment buildings got the name of the place changed. They are now 140 Riverside Boulevard, 160 Riverside Boulevard, and 180 Riverside Boulevard.

They *were* … Trump *Place*.

These are the kinds of protests against *pretending* that we can make—and the kind that will hit the ego-elect hardest.

That—and forever referring to the fact that he lost the popular vote.

*

And then we gear up for the biggest fight against *pretending*—of our lives.

That man elected by a minority of voters says he will immediately incarcerate or deport two to three million undocumented Americans, which is roughly the same number of people who live in Houston, Texas—which is roughly the same number of people who are *already* in all of the federal prisons and all the state prisons and all the county jails and all the city jails and all the ICE detention facilities and all the Navy brigs and all the Army stockades and all the military disciplinary barracks—all of them *combined*—which leaves no inference possible except that he somehow means to take two to three million people off the streets and keep them somewhere until they can be jailed or deported, and that we again have to *pretend* that this "somewhere"—for a population roughly the same size as all the prisoners in all the jails in this country right now—we have to *pretend* that this will not involve concentration camps.

*

But don't worry.

He's unifying the nation.

Kellyanne Conway said so.

Go back to pretending.

This *isn't* getting worse every day.

This *isn't* abnormal.

This *isn't* inhuman.

This *isn't* unacceptable.

ALIEN AND SEDITION

Post date • TUESDAY, NOVEMBER 22

Somewhere, Benjamin Franklin Bache and Matthew Lyon are saying, "I told you so."

These men went to jail, in this country, under our Constitution, for . . . criticism.

Bache was in new media.

Lyon was a congressman—from the party that wasn't in power.

They were guilty of criticizing . . . the president, and other media that *defended* the president.

And Mr. Bache and Congressman Lyon would remind us that we have *previously* completely and nearly fatally screwed up how to handle resistance.

And they would remind us that the right *to* resist has been destroyed—and the country nearly destroyed with it—by better men than Donald John Trump.

The man behind the imprisonment of Bache and Lyon and twenty or so other publishers and one ordinary citizen who made a joke in public . . . the man Bache and Lyon opposed . . . was President . . . John Adams.

That John Adams.

Founding Father John Adams.

Even a man with the vision of Adams could not see that demonizing dissent and criminalizing resistance could, by themselves, end democracy. The stains upon the Adams legacy were called the Alien and Sedition Acts.

And they threatened jail for anyone daring to "write, print, utter or publish . . . any false, scandalous and malicious writing" against the government.

And fifty-nine days before his inauguration, Trump and his mob are already clearly laying the groundwork for *new* criminalization of your right to publicly criticize that which will begin—on day one—as the worst presidential administration in our history.

Much has been made of the distraction Trump provided by tweeting petulantly about how the cast of *Hamilton* addressed the vice president–elect when he attended their performance last Friday.

The criticism of the coverage paid is valid.

The antimissile crews call it "chaff"—spraying strips of metal in the air to screw up radar.

We spent a day talking about Moron Trump's moronic tweets instead of his confession-in-everything-but-name to fraud accusations in the Trump University lawsuit.

We spent another day talking about *Hamilton* and Pence instead of his totally mixing the presidency with his business.

We spent another day talking about disrespect and respect instead of the anti-Semites, racists, and fascists Trump is appointing to his White House—the Bannons and Giulianis and Sessionses and their ilk, who are so scummy it led the great John Cleese to conclude that it looks as if Trump "is assembling the crew for a pirate ship."

A distraction?

Yes.

But that *doesn't* mean his seeming disbelief at the evidence that he is hated is not real.

Bluntly: if he or Pence cannot handle booing, they should get new jobs in a new country, because whether they hear it or not, they will be booed every day for the rest of their lives.

And, more important, that *also* doesn't mean he isn't intending to create a twenty-first-century version of the Alien and Sedition Acts of John Adams.

A president elected by a *minority* of the voters has again made threats against those who criticize him or his administration-to-be . . . has again made threats against the First Amendment.

Taken out of the context of the antidemocratic anti-criticism snowball already beginning its descent, the takeaways from his tweets—"This should not happen!" and "Apologize!"—would seem merely like more petulance from the man-baby-elect, and the complaint about lack of respect, merely more amazing self-unawareness from President Pussygrabber.

But those tweets did not come in a vacuum.

Before the election, Trump threatened to loosen up libel laws, singled out reporters by name to encourage abuse from the crowds at his rallies, and promised to sue *The New York Times*, while an adviser criticized a television host and tweeted, "Watch what happens to her after this election is over."

Within days of its *being* over, a performer on one of his television shows said of those who hadn't voted for him, "Mr. Trump has a long memory and we're keeping a list." Responding to criticism from Senate Minority Leader Reid, Trump's campaign manager, Kellyanne Conway, said he "should be very careful about characterizing somebody in a legal sense."

In a legal sense.

Nine days after the election, a federal judge in San Antonio, swearing in hundreds of new American citizens, told them that Donald Trump "will be your president, and if you do not like that, you need to go to another country."

He then also lashed out against pro athletes who have not stood for the national anthem, then claimed his remarks were "not political."

If you would like to resist by trying to get the judge ousted, his name is John Primomo, and he can be removed by the U.S. district court.

Or perhaps at least they can send him the copy of the Constitution he appears to lack.

*

But of course, *professional* demonizing of dissent requires blaming the victim. Campaign manager Conway said that dissent, anger, resistance—*your* resistance—is the fault of . . . the media.

"Most of the media did the world a disservice by not preparing them for the possibility of Donald Trump winning the presidency. It simply was not part of the conversation."

So—*fascism* isn't the problem.

American media's reluctance to soften up the public to *accept* fascism is the problem!

Which brings us back to the Alien and Sedition Acts and a state senator in Washington named Doug Ericksen, a loud Trump sycophant—another one of the Banana Republicans whom our friends publisher Benjamin Franklin Bache and Congressman Matthew Lyon would recognize immediately.

"I respect the right to protest, but when it endangers people's lives and property, it goes too far. Fear, intimidation, and vandalism are not a legitimate form of political expression. Those who employ it must be called to account."

Senator Ericksen says he will propose a bill next year that would criminalize protesting—creating a new Class C felony, punishable by fines of up to $10,000 and/or imprisonment of up to five years—crimes to be called . . . "economic terrorism."

"We are not just going after the people who commit these acts of terrorism," he continues—still digging—"we are going after the people who fund them. Wealthy donors should not feel safe in disrupting middle-class jobs."

The "wealthy donors" to whom Senator Ericksen refers would also be liable for any economic loss caused *by* the peaceful assemblies supposedly protected by the First Amendment—or, as Ericksen wants to call those assemblies, "economic terrorism."

*

So. Trump's Twitter tantrum about how Pence was treated at a play about a vice president so incapable of handling criticism that he *shot* the former secretary of the treasury may have been a diversion and may have seemed trivial compared with the other nightmares with which we wake each morning.

But do not mistake them. They are preface to new Alien and Sedition Acts—legal or merely cultural—to new demonizing of dissent, to, *at best*, chilling measures against your right... to resist.

And how do you resist laws designed to *criminalize* resistance?

Happily, there is a method tried and true, and you should prepare for it. It worked in South Africa for Gandhi in 1908, when they tried to create an Indian registry; worked for Gandhi again decades later in India; worked for the civil rights leaders here in the 1960s.

If the laws come to pass, do not seek to evade them; seek to *break* them—have them broken so often, by so many people, that the jails cannot hold all of us, and the infrastructure collapses, with the government begging for our help. Moreover, if resistance is denied us, the act of being arrested *for* resistance *becomes* resistance.

Because we are not going back to the time of the Alien and Sedition Acts. Matthew Lyon and Benjamin Franklin Bache—and, yes, he was Benjamin Franklin's favorite grandson—are alive in our history. Even Adams and those who supported them had an excuse—the country was barely twenty years old.

Trump and his mob have no excuse, no moral ground, no precedent, no right, and no chance of success.

Come after our resistance, Trump—legally or culturally or both—and America will kick your ass.

TWENTY-FIVE, SECTION 4

And what, this worst Thanksgiving week since 2001, do we have to give thanks *for*?

One thing.

The Twenty-fifth Amendment, section 4.

History pays little attention to this, but the first time an American president died in office—William Henry Harrison, just thirty-one days after his inauguration in 1841—nobody was sure what was supposed to happen next.

Incredibly, the Constitution was not specific. Did the vice president become *acting* president? Did his title *remain* vice president, but with executive powers?

The vice president, John Tyler, decided, on his own, to have a judge administer the presidential oath, and he spent the rest of his time in the White House refusing to answer to anything except *"President* Tyler."

But even as six more presidents died in office, the process was still unofficial. Worse yet, twice in the twentieth century, presidents became incapacitated while in office. Not only did Woodrow Wilson suffer a stroke *sixteen months* before the end of his term, but, as we are only now learning, the stroke affected his ability to fully understand that . . . he had *had* a stroke.

President Wilson fought or fired anybody who suggested he should give up the presidency, permanently or temporarily.

Besides which—there were no constitutional *means* for Wilson to give up the presidency temporarily, and the Constitution *still* had no official succession process, not for a resignation and certainly not for a *forced* removal because the president could no longer discharge the powers and duties of his office.

And then, on September 24, 1955, while playing golf, President Dwight Eisenhower had a heart attack. The stock market panicked, lost $14 billion in one day. Eisenhower was hospitalized for seven weeks. And still there was no provision for the vice president—Richard Nixon—to even briefly assume executive powers.

Finally, the assassination of President Kennedy, in 1963, brought the matter to a head. Not only did the succession need to be spelled out in a consti-tutional amendment, but so did temporary transfer of power, and a new idea—that if the vice presidency became vacant, the president should be able to nominate a *new* vice president.

And it also became clear that death or resignation or impeachment could undo an election. If, say, Eisenhower—a Republican—had died or resigned, and Nixon—a Republican—had succeeded him, and then died or resigned or been impeached and removed, the constitutional succession meant the Speaker of the House would then become president.

The Speaker of the House for the last six years of Eisenhower's term was Sam Rayburn—a Democrat. Control of the presidency would have changed parties without an election.

So. In 1965, the Twenty-fifth Amendment to the Constitution was pro-posed, and two years later it was enacted. Section 1 spelled out the succession to the vacant presidency. Section 2 allowed the president to nominate a new vice president—which would promptly happen twice in the next seven years. Section 3 permitted the president to temporarily transfer power to the vice president—which promptly happened for seven hours and fifty-four minutes after Ronald Reagan was shot.

And then . . . there is section 4.

Written nearly fifty-two years ago, with Woodrow Wilson in mind, and yet it might as well have been named for Donald Trump.

Probably easier if I just read this verbatim:

Section 4. Whenever the Vice President and a majority of either the principal officers of the executive departments or of such other body as Congress may by law provide, transmit to the President pro tempore of the Senate and the Speaker of the House of Representatives their writ-ten declaration that the President is unable to discharge the powers and duties of his office, the Vice President shall immediately assume the powers and duties of the office as Acting President.

There's more—but I hope you didn't miss the key point here.
No hearings.

No doctors.

No conferences.

No impeachments.

The vice president and merely *most* of the cabinet write to Speaker Paul Ryan and Senate President Pro Tempore Orrin Hatch, and they say the president is unable to do the job . . . *annnnd* the vice president becomes acting president.

No hearings, no doctors, no conferences, no impeachments.

Just "Bye, Felicia."

Of course, the suddenly suspended president *can* try to regain power.

To resume:

Thereafter, when the President transmits to the President pro tempore of the Senate and the Speaker of the House of Representatives his written declaration that no inability exists, he shall resume the powers and duties of his office . . .

Round one: They say he's unfit.

Round two: He says he's fine—he resumes office.

Not so fast.

There is a round *three*.

He shall resume the powers and duties of his office *unless* the Vice President and a majority of either the principal officers of the executive department or of such other body as Congress may by law provide, transmit within four days to the President pro tempore of the Senate and the Speaker of the House of Representatives their written declaration that the President is unable to discharge the powers and duties of his office.

Yes. Invest in popcorn futures.

If the vice president and his crew *still* say the president is unfit—the president *is not* restored to power.

But wait—there's more. There's a round *four*.

Thereupon Congress shall decide the issue, assembling within forty-eight hours for that purpose if not in session. If the Congress, within twenty-one days after receipt of the latter written declaration, or, if Congress is not in session, within twenty-one days after Congress is required to assemble, determines by two-thirds vote of both Houses that the President is unable to discharge the powers and duties of his office, the Vice President shall continue to discharge the same as Acting President; otherwise, the President shall resume the powers and duties of his office.

Instant impeachment.

Four days for the vice president and the cabinet to state again that the president is "unable to discharge the powers and duties," triggering a vote by the House and the Senate within about three weeks. And a two-thirds vote results in the president remaining in office with the title but without the power.

So it's a crazy-man clause, right?

In the case of Trump, it presumes he behaves as president as he is behaving as president-elect.

Which is a good presumption, because *as* president-elect, he's behaving as he did as a candidate.

For example: twenty-four of his first thirty-eight tweets after the election consisted of the following:

Six complaints about *The New York Times*, four about the cast of *Hamilton* (one deleted), one complaint about *Saturday Night Live*, one complaint about how unfair protesters are, one complaint about a news story, three boasts about who called to congratulate him, two claims he could've won by a larger margin, two lies about keeping a Ford plant from moving to Mexico that was *never* moving to Mexico, two rationalizations about the $25 million he had to pay to avoid a trial for fraud, and two promos for a TV appearance (one deleted).

For my money—he's nuts.

Couldn't pass a sanity test.

Open book.

But of course . . . section 4 of the Twenty-fifth Amendment doesn't say "nuts" or "impaired" or "erratic" or "unbalanced" or "unhealthy" or "bipolar" or "narcissistic" or "sociopathic" or "psychopathic."

It only says that when "the President is unable to discharge the powers and duties of his office, the Vice President shall immediately assume the powers and duties of the office as Acting President."

Ohhhhhh!

Kind of vague, huh?

If he was fine physically, even passable psychologically, the vice president could still clothesline Trump because he was—just to pick a few inappropriate behaviors at random—oh, bringing his daughter to meetings with the prime minister of Japan, or interrupting state business to meet with his Indian partners about "Trump Tower Mumbai," or pocketing profits by gently suggesting to foreign diplomats that the president would really like it if they all stayed at his hotel in Washington, or opening up eight new businesses in Saudi Arabia, or, when the president of Argentina calls to congratulate him on winning the election, asking the guy to clear up some stuck building permits for him in Buenos Aires.

Section 4 of the Twenty-fifth Amendment to our Constitution provides to Vice President–elect Pence and Trump's cabinet the means—if they have the ethics, the patriotism, and the stones to use it—to remove him from office basically as soon as the inauguration is over.

But of course, not only does section 4 not say anything about doctors or health or psychosis—it *also* doesn't say anything about . . . corruption or ethics or disinterest.

It doesn't say anything *at all* about *why* the president might be "unable to discharge the powers and duties of his office"—it just talks about letters and declarations and twenty days and a two-thirds vote!

A Republican vice president and a Republican cabinet and a Republican Speaker of the House and a Republican president pro tempore of the Senate and a Republican House majority and a Republican Senate majority can just *do it*!

Because—they don't trust him.

Because—they don't like him.

Because—it's Thursday!

But, even if you loathe or fear Trump, you must look at this and say, "This can't happen in a democracy! The people voted for him! You can't just *unpresident him!*"

The hell you can't.

How did Margaret Thatcher wind up becoming the *ex*–prime minister of the United Kingdom?

Lost the election?

No!

Decided to retire?

No!

Forced out by the votes of just 356 members of the House of Commons! From her own party. And she got the majority of those votes!

Three of Britain's past five prime ministers *became* prime minister without first being elected!

Winston Churchill became their wartime prime minister in 1940—didn't win an election for the job until 1951!

So don't tell me this isn't democratic!

Not only is there the English example, but, among other things—*this is in our Constitution*!

And on February 23 of next year, it will celebrate its fiftieth anniversary of *being* in our Constitution!

Here's hoping we have a big birthday party that day.

And I have just the right *theme* for it!

And you know who bursts out of the Twenty-fifth Amendment birthday *cake*?

That's right! Acting President Mike Pence!

MADNESS

Post date • MONDAY, NOVEMBER 28

More than thirty-six hours after Donald Trump revealed the full extent of his disconnect from reality—the jaw-dropping, terrifying moment in which the president-elect of the United States of America publicly stated that he still believes the election was rigged against him . . . even though he won it—and we still await the first serious, sober discussion in our nation's media about the exact dimensions of, and the exact *nature* of, Mr. Trump's desperate psychological impairment.

This has long since transcended politics.

This has long since transcended diversions from his corruption, or the FBI, or foreign interference.

This is not left versus right, nor liberal versus conservative, nor alt versus inclusive, nor any of the excuses newspapers and television made Sunday and Monday in hopes of preserving the political-media complex.

This is not funny, and this is not ego, and this is not "He speaks his mind."

This . . . is an existential threat to the United States of America:

The president-elect, Donald Trump, is manifestly, profoundly, and dangerously psychologically imbalanced.

The sooner we acknowledge this, the greater chance we have of averting a disaster that could threaten the safety of every American—indeed, of everybody on this planet.

The sooner those *around him* acknowledge this, the greater chance *they* have of not being remembered by history—if there *is* a history to remember them—as enablers to a cataclysm in which the most powerful military arsenal in the history of the world was placed under the control of a man with no control over himself and his hair-trigger, childish, petulant, peevish, vengeful, hateful, poisonous temper.

The sooner *those who plan to be in his government* acknowledge this, the greater chance they have of summoning the support from all political quarters before it is too late to do anything constitutional about it. A Mike Pence presidential administration is far from the list of my one hundred preferred options, but right now I cling to it as the only realistic prospect of saving ourselves from an insane commander in chief.

A *sane* man does not, on a Wednesday, promulgate a video in which he claims it is his "prayer" that "we begin to heal our divisions and move forward as one country" and then, on a Saturday, insult the losing party as "badly defeated and demoralized."

A *sane* man does not acknowledge the end of a "long and bruising political campaign," and that "emotions are raw and tensions just don't heal overnight," and then three days later brand a fully legal recount—the right to which he reserved for himself not a month earlier—as a "scam," and then a day after *that* insist that there was "serious voter fraud" in three states that "the media" isn't reporting.

A *sane* man does not invoke Lincoln and "a great national campaign to rebuild our country" at one hour and then, seventy-two hours later, insist, "I won the popular vote if you deduct the millions of people who voted illegally."

These are not words of sanity!

These are the rages and the boasts and the madness that we have seen throughout history. Saddam Hussein. Mussolini. Fidel Castro. Mao Zedong. Stalin. Pol Pot. Bin Laden. Hitler.

If there are still doubts about what we face and how our hands are tied just a little more tightly every day—if there needs to be debate about *how* sick this man is, whether this is treatable neurosis or an illness brought on by a physical calamity or injury, or full-on malignant narcissism or paranoia or psycho- or sociopathy—so be it.

We *may* still have time for a national dialogue about exactly *what* is wrong with him.

But in pronouncing, after arguably the greatest upset in American electoral history, that he would have won by more because the vote he won was *still* rigged against him, Donald John Trump has made it inarguably certain that there is something *desperately* wrong with him and he is not psychologically fit to assume the presidency on January 20.

A REPLY TO TRUMP'S VIDEO

Post date • TUESDAY, NOVEMBER 29

It is more than a week now, and yet there is no reply.

Donald John Trump, the first-ever president-elect to begin to try to monetize the presidency and privatize the government and to fill his cabinet with the crew of a pirate ship . . .

Donald John Trump, the first-ever president-elect to insist that an election he *won* was still rigged against him . . .

Donald John Trump, the first-ever president-elect who is a classless guy's idea of real classy . . .

Of course he delivers his first address to the nation . . . in a YouTube video. And worse yet, there is . . . no reply.

As I said two weeks ago, I don't *want* to be at the forefront of the resistance, but the rest of America's commentators and almost all of its politicians are holding back—presumably owing to *Oh, let's give him a chance, another chance, his five thousandth chance,* combined with their deep-seated fears of unemployment and unpaid mortgages.

So somebody has to do this.

And I'll do it line by line.

The official resistance response to President-elect Pussygrabber's Pettysburg Address. On YouTube.

"We are very blessed to call this nation our home. And that is what America is: it is our home. It's where we raise our families, care for our loved ones, look out for our neighbors, and live out our dreams."

I'm sorry—look out for our neighbors?

Our *Mexican* neighbors? The ones you said are "bringing drugs, they're bringing crime, they're rapists"?

Our *African American* neighbors? The ones you said are "living in poverty, your schools are no good, you have no jobs"?

And *America*, where you say we "live out your dreams"? America, which you said last August 27 is in a death spiral?

That America?

"It is my prayer that on this Thanksgiving, we begin to heal our divisions and move forward as one country, strengthened by a shared purpose and very, very common resolve."

Divisions?

You were endorsed by the KKK, your election was celebrated at a neo-Nazi convention with shouts of "Hail Trump" and threats against the *"Lügenpresse,"* and you insisted for week after week after week that the election was rigged and that you were under no obligation to honor the outcome of the vote.

Divisions?

Three days after you recorded that, you were calling the Democrats—whose candidate got more votes than you did—"badly defeated and demoralized" . . .

But—go on, explain to me how we will begin to heal our *divisions.*

Which you personally caused.

"In declaring this national holiday, President Lincoln called upon Americans to speak with 'one voice and one heart.' That's just what we have to do."

Lincoln. Whose words at Gettysburg still inspire the nation 153 years after he spoke them. Gettysburg, where *you* spoke on October 22 and promised that you would sue all the women who had accused you of sexual assault.

Lincoln. Who led this country not *into* civil war, but *out* of one. Civil war started by the political ancestors of the white supremacists who helped to get you elected—by the political ancestors of your campaign chief, now chief White House strategist, who has a history of denigrating women, blacks, and Jews.

"One voice and one heart."

Let me know, Mr. Trump, when you *obtain* a heart.

"We have just finished a long and bruising political campaign. Emotions are raw and tensions just don't heal overnight."

That just fell out of the sky, did it?

After all, it wasn't *you* who said your opponent and the incumbent president were the cofounders of ISIS.

It wasn't *you* who accused the president of complicity in the Orlando terrorist attack.

It wasn't *you* who accused the father of one of your Republican rivals of involvement in the assassination of President John F. Kennedy.

It wasn't *you* who asked a foreign power to hack the email accounts and computers of U.S. citizens.

It wasn't *you* who threatened to imprison your opponent after the election and then, last Sunday, saw your last campaign manager claim that you weren't prosecuting her because of your "graciousness."

Oh, that's right, it *was* you.

You cheated, bullied, lied, attacked, savaged, undercut, and threatened—every week, every day, every hour, for seventeen self-obsessed months—and now you tell us, your victims, that *we* must heal.

"It doesn't go quickly, unfortunately, but we have before us the chance now to make history together, to bring real change to Washington, real safety to our cities, and real prosperity to our communities, including our inner cities. So important to me, and so important to our country."

Nice pointless ad lib just there.

Having exaggerated, exacerbated, and in many cases cut from whole cloth these almost imaginary defects of safety and prosperity, you now call upon those of us who did not swallow your time-share pitchman's snake oil of hate to solve these problems—to which you will obviously give attention only in between efforts to personally profit by exploiting the government of the United States of America.

"But to succeed, we must enlist the effort of our entire nation."

The *entire* nation?

Including the majority of this nation, who voted for somebody besides you?

Including the plurality of this nation, who voted for Hillary Clinton and *not* for you?

All of us, including those of us you have derided in victory as "badly defeated"?

You get nothing from us.

You made this bed, and then you lit it on fire.

Best of luck.

"This historic political campaign is now over. Now begins a great national campaign to rebuild our country and to restore the full promise of America for all of our people."

You mean people like Betsy DeVos, the nominee for secretary of education who doesn't believe in public schools and tried to avoid paying taxes for her local school district?

Or people like Jeff Sessions, the nominee for attorney general, who prosecuted African Americans for voting, and opposed not just *illegal* immigration but *legal* immigration, and is a climate change denier?

Or people like Michael Flynn, the nominee for national security adviser, who claimed that Islam is not a religion, and who tweeted links to a conspiracy nut's claim that Hillary Clinton was involved in "sex crimes with children," and who insanely claimed in speeches as recently as three months ago that legislators in Florida and Texas were trying to impose Sharia law in those states?

The full promise is to be restored *to them*, and to hell with the rest of us.

"I am asking you to join me in this effort. It is time to restore the bonds of trust between citizens."

Trump—you, personally, have damaged and frayed "the bonds of trust between citizens," possibly beyond repair. You have exploited that damage and exploited the weaker-minded of our citizenry.

You have questioned the rights of those here to become citizens, and those guaranteed by the Fourteenth Amendment to *be* citizens, of retaining the citizenship that is legally theirs.

You have been proved again and again a liar, a thief, a scrounger, a corrupt businessman, and a dishonest tradesman.

Where there are bonds of trust, there is no Donald Trump.

"Because when America is unified, there is nothing beyond our reach, and I mean absolutely nothing."

And here, finally, we agree.

We will now see how—when America is unified by your already transparently corrupt and self-aggrandizing subsuming of the presidency as just another division of the Trump Corporation—we will now see how nothing is beyond our reach, and we shall first reach *for* your removal from the White House at the earliest possible moment.

"Let us give thanks for all that we have, and let us boldly face the exciting new frontiers that lie ahead. Thank you, God bless you, and God bless America."

That last little divine touch would be less laughable if there were evidence that you had ever shown a true belief in a God, or even in an understanding of what God, or a God, or just a nameless unifying presence in the universe is perceived to be by most of the fools who voted for you.

At the 2015 Family Leadership Summit in Ames, Iowa, you were asked if you—like everybody from the faithful to the agnostic—had ever asked for God's forgiveness.

"I am not sure I have," you said. "I just go on and try to do a better job from there. I don't think so. I think if I do something wrong, I think, I just try and make it right. I don't bring God into that picture. I don't."

Trump, either stick to that—stop adding insult to larceny by suddenly bringing empty invocations of the creator into the picture . . .

Or get serious about it.

Because, based on the actions of the first three weeks of your transition, it will not be long before the only place to which you might turn for assistance or acceptance—would be to an Almighty.

Because right now the only *honest* end to an address to this nation is "God help us, and God help America."

Chapter 5

DECEMBER 2016

WE HAVE ELECTED AN IDIOT

Post date • MONDAY, DECEMBER 5

We have elected an idiot.

*

For all the insanity, and the stunning self-absorption, and the bullying, and the delusional view of America that would embarrass a high school dropout watching cartoons while strung out on meth . . .

The much more existential threat from the Swiss cheese personality of Donald John Trump roared to the forefront over the weekend, and that existential threat is simply *this*:

In the complex international relations that—like it or not—keep the world from blowing itself up every afternoon, Trump has just proved he has no *earthly* clue what the fuck he is doing.

Just since last Friday, Trump:

Has given aid and comfort to our Russian enemies who are aiming for nothing short of world dominance—with the help of their jackass Trump.

Has undermined this nation's status as the only enforcer on the side of human rights.

Has screwed up—whether inadvertently or, as reported Sunday night, deliberately—nearly four decades of diplomacy balanced on a razor's edge between China and Taiwan.

And just as the China and Taiwan diplomacy began to stabilize—he screwed it up *again.*

On *Twitter.*

Good work, moron.

*

You don't have to live next door to the United Nations to understand why talking to the president of Taiwan, and making it public, and referring to "the close economic, political, and security ties between Taiwan and the United States," just increased the chances that Trump will get some of us—including his supporters—killed.

Since 1979, we have played a silly little childish game with mainland China. If we don't make a big deal about the island of Taiwan, if we don't call it a nation, if we recognize that, psychologically, Taiwan is to the Chinese what Communist Cuba has been to us since 1959, if *our diplomats and presidents and dipshits-elect like Donald Trump* don't rub China's nose in it, the Chinese won't wipe the more-or-less democracy of Taiwan off the friggin' map.

It's that simple. The one billion, four hundred million mainland Chinese Communists will *not* turn the twenty-three and a half million Chinese in Taiwan into a parking lot—all we have to do . . . is *not* do exactly what Donald Nitwit Trump *did* by saying what he did to the Taiwanese president last Friday.

But of course, he did it, because he thinks he knows better than everybody else about the world when he doesn't know *shit.*

And anyway, what's the fate of twenty-three and a half million Chinese in Taiwan compared with what *really* matters?

"The President of Taiwan CALLED ME today to wish me congratulations on winning the Presidency. Thank you!"

"Interesting how the U.S. sells Taiwan billions of dollars of military equipment but I should not accept a congratulatory call."

Because clearly the point of an incoming presidential administration is to see how many leaders around the world *call in to tell him how terrific he is*!

We now see, six weeks out from the inauguration, the outlines of the Trump Doctrine: Congratulate Trump!

*

Sunday, a crowded elevator's worth of Trumpets leaked a story to *The Washington Post* that this was all *planned*—a more "robust" defense of Taiwan—which is, of course, even dumber, especially if the idiot-elect has to publicly disguise his "planned robustness" as naiveté. Because of course he then gets mad when people call him naive, and thus doubles down on the whole thing Sunday night on Twitter.

*

So now, not only are the Chinese pissed off, not only is their help in whatever looms next for us in North Korea in jeopardy, and not only is an actual slow growth in the reliability of the relationship between our two countries at risk—but who *benefits* from uncertainty between the United States and China? We don't win from it. The Chinese don't win from it. In whose interest is the new confusion? The new setback? The new asshattery from Trump?

Russia.

Always Russia.

Russia. And by the way—guess what flooded out of a WikiLeaks dump Saturday that you probably didn't hear about? Ninety gigabytes and 2,420 documents of intelligence related to... Germany. And its chancellor, Angela Merkel. Ahead of *its* upcoming elections.

Germany—which, since Trump's election by a minority of our voters, has already taken our place as the leading democracy in the world and the only Western power able or willing to stand up against the passive-aggressive world war that Russia has been waging for several years—now with the aid and comfort of President-elect Donald Bumbling Amateur Putin Puppet Trump.

*

And yes, I said Trump's election has *already* resulted in Germany taking our place as the leading democracy—the leading enforcer on the side of human rights—in the world.

And if these fiascos with China and Taiwan and WikiLeaks and Germany are not evidence enough, there was a third Trump diplomatic disaster that might actually eclipse the other two.

Philippines president Rodrigo Duterte—the street thug who has had thousands of his citizens murdered by police and vigilantes without trial, and in many cases without even arrest, on the pretext of an anti-drug campaign—Duterte says *he*, too, got on the phone with Trump on Friday and that Trump endorsed the barbarism Duterte has unleashed.

"I could sense a good rapport, an animated President-elect Trump. And he was wishing me success in my campaign against the drug problem," Duterte said. "He understood the way we are handling it . . ."

We are many things in this country, but we have never and must never stoop to murder, disguised as law and order, by a dictator who has compared his own actions to those of Adolf Hitler.

Worst yet, Duterte said this buffoon Trump has invited him to visit New York and Washington, and bluntly, Rodrigo Duterte should not be admitted to this country even in a casket . . . But don't tell Trump that—he knows everything.

*

If this is how this dense, pea-brained little man is going to run things, if this is how far *in over* his own fat, orange head he is going to *be* internationally, if this is how he is going to strut as president—a triple-chinned bull in a nuclear china shop—he cannot be allowed to *become* president.

Because after January 20, if he decides to spend a week prioritizing receiving congratulations for his inauguration and tweeting out his petulance about Chinese taxes—if he can't manage to keep his fucking ego out of these opaque but essential balancing acts, the ones that stitch together the world as it *is*—he could get us all killed before his next appointment with whoever colors his hair.

WE HAVE ELECTED A SHITTY BUSINESSMAN

Post date • TUESDAY, DECEMBER 6

We have elected a shitty businessman.

Amid everything else, from the psychosis to the orange bull in the nuclear china shop, we have elected a guy who doesn't know the first thing about the American economy.

"Any business that leaves our country for another country, fires its employees, builds a new factory or plant in the other country, and then thinks it will sell its product back into the U.S. without retribution or consequence, is WRONG!

"There will be a tax on our soon to be strong border of 35% for these companies wanting to sell their product, cars, A.C. units etc., back across the border."

First of all, that's exactly what he *didn't* do with the Carrier Corporation in Indiana—the thing he is *still* boasting about as if, instead of a tax break for some rich guys, what he had *really* done was give everybody eternal life.

Carrier got $7 million in taxpayer money from the state of Indiana to *not* move eight hundred jobs to Mexico.

And it's *still* moving *one thousand* jobs to Mexico!

And it's *not* facing a 35 percent tax for selling its Mexican-made products in the United States.

Donald Trump. Shitty. Businessman.

*

But of course, it's far *worse* than that.

Consider for a moment what would happen if he really were able to unilaterally and immediately impose this tax.

Don't think about the thousands of jobs at the hundreds of Carrier-style companies around the country.

Think about the jobs as yet uncreated.

Trump—Shitty Businessman—is telling companies, domestic or international, that if they open new plants in the United States, or hire more Americans in their operations *already* in the United States—there is no going back.

Those jobs better be forever.

If another company in Carrier's position—let's call them *Shmarrier*—hires one new employee in this country, then something happens to the economy—of the country, or just *of* Shmarrier—and they have to fire the guy and move his job to . . . Canada, suddenly, according to the Trump Shitty Businessman Plan, there could be a 35 percent tax on Shmarrier products sold in this country.

Explain to me the motive for Shmarrier—or anybody else—ever to expand their U.S. business again!

Explain to me the motive for Shmarrier—or anybody else—ever to hire another American *worker* again!

Add to that—this idiot Trump states, as if there were no laws, as if there was no Congress, as if there were no courts, that "there *will* be a tax," as though he could just make them up as and when he wants them.

What kind of business wants to invest in a country where the economy is predicated not on regulations or just patterns, but on the whim . . . of one Shitty Businessman?

And as if to underscore this, the *vice* president–elect—the one whose home state just bribed Carrier with $7 million of our taxpayer money so Trump can boast about what a *soooooper* genius he is—went even further.

When it comes to punishing companies that move jobs out of this country, Mike Pence says, "The president-elect will make those decisions on a day-by-day basis."

Again—it ain't his call.

There's no reason for *Trump* to know this. He's just a Shitty Businessman.

But Pence has supposedly been governor of a state for nearly four years. A state with laws and a legislature and courts.

And *he* has just told all those businesses that are considering hiring Americans: *Great*, but don't try to fire them, because if he's in a bad mood, Generalissimo Shitty Businessman will slap you with a 35 percent tax because a guy who got over two million fewer votes than the other candidate is convinced he's Moses coming down the mountain with the goddamned Commandments in his hands.

President-elect Shitty Businessman has just thrown the brakes on a huge part of the American economy.

And what's worse, he may have also thrown the economy into *reverse*.

There was a second part of that tweetstorm.

"These companies are able to move between all 50 states, with no tax or tariff being charged."

This is an even dumber deal.

Not only do our imaginary executives at Shmarrier have no motive to *add* jobs in this country, but now, with the economy stalled by the 35 percent revenge tax from Donald J. Trump, Shitty Businessman, they can say to the governments of whatever states their plants are in, "If you don't give us *more* tax breaks or build us *new* facilities—we're moving to Wyoming."

First you cut the legs off the economy by punishing any company that expands its workforce on the logical premise that, yes, in bad times it can *downsize* its workforce.

Then, with jobs scarce, you give all employers everywhere an official sanction to pit one state against another—hell, pit one *county* against another—as if this was a nation of sports teams looking for a new taxpayer-funded stadium.

The states and communities willing to bribe companies the most, and with lower standards of living so employees have to get paid the least, will be able to take this country's economy to the fucking cleaners because ... we ... have ... just ... elected ... a ... shitty businessman!

BATMAN VILLAINS

Post date • WEDNESDAY, DECEMBER 7

The incoming cabinet and White House staff of the idiot-elect is so collectively and individually nefarious, so reeking of financial corruption and moral decay, that it beggars political comparison.

Teapot Dome, the Bush-Cheney-Halliburton Redistribution of Wealth, and the financial scandals of the presidency of Ulysses S. Grant are insufficient.

We literally have to compare this—to again use John Cleese's line—this crew of a governmental pirate ship to *Batman* villains. All *Batman* villains. *All* of them in one movie, like the Adam West movie with the Joker, the Penguin, the Riddler, Catwoman, and the other denizens of what the filmmakers dubbed "United Underworld."

Let's meet them.

And let's dub them *Citizens United* Underworld.

Starting *in* the cabinet—and this first one may be the least offensive.

The nominee for secretary of defense, James Mattis. Who noted that it's fun to shoot *some* people. And who, per federal law, is not eligible to *become* secretary of defense until May 22, 2020, because a secretary of defense must be retired seven years from active military service. Trump's going to get them to *waive* that.

Waive *this*: Mattis is on the board of General Dynamics. Which makes tanks and submarines and other stuff the Pentagon buys.

And he may be the best of them.

Betsy DeVos, secretary of education nominee. Big advocate of spending public money on religious schools and fifteen years ago told a conference of Christians that doing so was an opportunity to "advance God's kingdom."

Secretary of education. Under a president-elect who said we should be teaching patriotism in schools.

The would-be secretary of health and human services: congressman and orthopedic surgeon Tom Price. He is a member of the Association of American Physicians and Surgeons, which opposes vaccination programs in schools, suggested a link between abortion and breast cancer, and once posted an article on its website that postulated that presidential candidate Barack Obama was so popular because in his speeches he was using a hidden form of hypnosis.

A secretary of health and human services who is a member of an organization full of anti-vaxxers, and who believes in Hypnotoad.

The attorney general you know.

Jeff Sessions, the senator representing the Keebler Elf Magic Tree. Prosecuted black voters in Alabama for voting. Allegedly called the ACLU and the NAACP "un-American." Admitted during testimony to the Senate that he believed the NAACP and another group "may have taken positions that I consider to be averse to the security interests of the United States."

The other group was . . . the National Council of Churches.

Transportation secretary nominee Elaine Chao. From the Bush administration, where she was labor secretary and where she drastically cut the roster of mine safety inspectors, and the number of mine inspections, just before eighteen miners and three rescue workers were killed at Sago, West Virginia, and Crandall Canyon, Utah.

Plus she's married to Senator Mitch McConnell, which suggests she has no judgment whatsoever.

Wilbur Ross, Commerce.

The supposed wizard of the distressed assets business.

Except that his funds tanked after he bet on dry bulk shipping . . . and Greek banks.

Greek banks.

Even *I* know not to invest in Greek banks.

Trump's man for Treasury: Steve Mnuchin.

Seven years ago, he and his cronies bought a failed mortgage company, IndyMac. They foreclosed on as many as 36,000 homeowners, including one woman—aged ninety—after a payment error.

She owed twenty-seven cents.

So Mnuchin's company threw her out.

Over twenty-seven cents.

*

Here are a few *Batman* villains mentioned, but not yet named, for other cabinet posts.

At the Department of Agriculture: Sid Miller.

Called Hillary Clinton the c-word.

Also has a Facebook page filled with fake news, including details of the secret Houston jihadist training camp that doesn't exist.

Possible secretary of the interior: former Arizona governor Jan Brewer, who once insisted the desert covering her state's border with Mexico was full of severed heads.

Rumored at Veterans Affairs: Scott Brown. Former Massachusetts senator. Former nude model.

Prospective head of the Office of Management and Budget: Gary Cohn. President of Goldman Sachs.

Goldman Sachs: the company Trump alleged Hillary Clinton was in the pocket of.

Goldman Sachs: which Trump supporters chanted at Ted Cruz.

Goldman Sachs: which reports that current Republican tax plans will increase the debt to $1 trillion by 2020, but that *Trump's* tax plan will increase it to one . . . *and a half* trillion.

At Homeland Security: Milwaukee County Sheriff David Clarke, who has had four deaths in his jail since April and, when a county supervisor criticized him over that, called for the county supervisor to be prosecuted.

Clarke also insisted that the presidential election was rigged, and thus "it is pitchfork-and-torches time in America!"

After Trump *won* the election that Clarke insisted was rigged, Clarke didn't understand why anybody was protesting: "These temper tantrums from these radical anarchists must be quelled," he said. "There is no legitimate reason to protest the will of the people."

Yeah—in a sanity test, I'm not betting on him to *pass*.

Then there's ex–campaign manager Kellyanne Conway, who could wind up somewhere.

She got into a shouting match last week with *Clinton* campaign people. When their manager accused Conway of providing "a platform for white supremacists," Conway feigned shock, said, "Hashtag he's your president," and later whined that she took the comment personally.

She should. If you abetted Trump, you're either a white supremacist or somebody who doesn't *mind* white supremacists, Kellyanne Conway. Which is *worse*.

Named to non-cabinet positions:

Senior counselor and chief strategist: Stephen Bannon.

From Breitbart, a website that makes shit up.

Last week, as the idiot-elect walked near and then amid a group of photographers and reporters, Bannon asked a press aide, "Who are all these photographers and why are they here?"

There came the answer, "This is the press pool."

Chief. Of. Strategery . . . you say?

Deputy national security adviser: K. T. McFarland, who six years ago called a secrets leaker a "terrorist."

That was Julian Assange.

That was *before* Julian Assange started working to get Trump elected.

McFarland's website, Twitter account, and Facebook page were all scrubbed off the internet this week.

*

One overview: This tweet from somebody named Bruce Mehlman, mocking the Bernie Sanders tweet about the Trump administration "of, by, and for the millionaires and billionaires."

"Interesting to see Democrats' selective populism . . ." he writes. "Rich Obama nominees get confirmed, rich Trump nominees get attacked."

The net worth of the nine Obama people there?

A combined $497,600,000. Which is a lot less.

A *lot* less—the combined worth of the nine rich Obama appointees is one-fifth of what Wilbur Ross is worth alone. One-tenth of what Betsy DeVos is worth *alone*.

*

Oh, and one guy I left out.

Former lieutenant general, now national security adviser, Michael Flynn, who thinks CNN and MSNBC are state-run television.

Who has taken payments from the Russians.

And who was, of course, one of those jackasses who spread the false internet story that Hillary Clinton was involved in some kind of child sex ring centered in a Washington restaurant.

A restaurant into which walked—last Sunday—a man carrying an assault rifle, who said he was there to "self-investigate" the story.

"National Security Adviser Michael Flynn."

He could've gotten innocent Americans killed...with his computer; Trump wants him to tell him when to start *blowing things up*.

General Flynn has no business in any government, except perhaps that of North Korea.

But therein lies the problem with *Batman* villains. They're so over-the-top, you think they can't be real. And then along comes Donald Trump.

And for the record, Trump is *not* the Puzzler from *Batman*. That was actor Maurice Evans.

Any similarity is purely coincidental.

RUSSIA

Post date • MONDAY, DECEMBER 12

We are at war with Russia.

Or, perhaps more correctly, we have lost a war with Russia, without a battle.

We are no longer a sovereign nation.

We are no longer a democracy.

We are no longer a free people.

We are the victims of a bloodless coup—*so far* a bloodless coup—engineered by Russia with, at best, the traitorous indifference of the Republican Party and Donald John Trump, a man who, to borrow a phrase from another December long ago, will live in infamy.

In five weeks' time—unless desperate measures are taken—we will hand over the government to a man who lost the popular vote by more than John F. Kennedy and George W. Bush won it by, a man whom the Russians wanted to run our country for them, a man whom the Russians *got* to run our country for them, a man for whom the Russians interfered with our elections—which is an act of war.

And in this country?

We have conceded defeat.

Some experts—John Kasich's strategist, John Weaver, for one—have compared this to Pearl Harbor. Even the hard-right ex-congressman Joe Walsh says, "Republican silence will be tantamount to treason." Some others, too, have proved courageous.

Trump, self-destructive to the last, issued a childish statement mocking the CIA but, as Tim Dickinson of *Rolling Stone* noted, not denying *anything*.

But the vast majority of Republicans have said nothing. And the vast majority of Democrats have said nothing. And the vast majority of the media has said nothing. The president has said nothing *close* . . . to enough.

The CIA and the FBI and Homeland Security—the institutions whose interest in freedom we on the left most frequently distrust—*they* have said something. They said it first to congressional and Senate Republicans and Democrats in September—dire warnings, warnings that Mitch McConnell and other Republicans *buried*—warnings that the Russians, using computer hacking and perhaps other means, were not merely trying to *discredit* the election but to achieve the specific outcome of electing their man Trump.

And finally, at the very last hour, some of those who did the briefings and some of those who received them leaked the details. To *The New York Times*, *The Washington Post*, CBS News, Reuters—in a torrent of anguished honesty.

They said something.

They said something as the president-not-elect began to veer toward appointing as secretary of state—as our diplomatic face to the world—the CEO of Exxon, who three years ago received the Order of Friendship from . . .Vladimir Putin.

They said something as the members of the Electoral College prepared to gather next Monday to finalize this coup, some unaware that half of the states they represent permit them by law to vote for someone other than the candidate to whom they are pledged, and that only thirty-eight of them need to do so to prevent the coup.

They said something as one especially chilling detail in one of the reports sailed by: that "the Russians hacked the Republican National Committee's computer systems in addition to their attacks on Democratic organizations, but did not release whatever information they gleaned from the Republican networks."

It is a short leap from that conclusion—and it is anything *but* a conspiracy theory—to wondering whether the Russians hacked the RNC and have kept what they found, to make sure Trump and the Republicans . . . obeyed.

*

The president of the United States, who at this rate will be the *last* freely elected president of the United States, made, in his measured way, a gesture last Friday that perhaps opened the door for these horrifying revelations of a coup by an outside power, nearly complete. He asked for a full report.

But we do not have time for a full report.

Barack Obama has twice stood in front of America, in front of the world, in front of history, and said, "I do solemnly swear that I will faithfully execute the Office of President of the United States, and will to the best of my ability, preserve, protect and defend the Constitution of the United States."

Today is the time for him to do so!

He must immediately declassify and release all relevant materials held by the FBI, the CIA, the DHS, and the other intelligence and security services, and in the White House, and anywhere else.

And the attorney general must immediately appoint a special prosecutor to investigate what Donald Trump knew and when he knew it, and what, if any, collusive links exist now or existed earlier between the Russian Federation and the Republican National Committee. If Trump does grab power, he can try to dismiss this special prosecutor, but he will at least have to get the courts to sanction it.

*

There are no arguments of security or face-saving or intelligence secrecy or national interest that carry any weight now. How much worse can it get if America is told the unvarnished, unprocessed, unredacted truth about this coup? We are already on the precipice of losing the freedom and independence of this nation!

The attorney general must tell us, so that we may defend ourselves.

He must tell the electors of the Electoral College so that, microscopic as the chance may be, they can still prevent this cataclysm.

There is no time for a full report or a measured analysis or recommendations to prevent interference in our future elections, because permitting Donald Trump to assume the office of president reduces the chance that we will *have* future elections.

The nation and all of our freedoms hang by a thread, and the military apparatus of this country is about to be handed over to scum who are beholden to scum—Russian scum.

As things are today, January 20 will not be an inauguration, but the end of the United States as an independent country. It will not be a peaceful change of power; it will be a usurpation, and the usurper has no validity, no credibility, and no authority under the Constitution.

This is a reality that will become the *only* reality until this country rids itself of Donald John Trump. He is not a president; he is a puppet put in power by Vladimir Putin.

And those who ignore these elemental, existential facts—Democrats or Republicans—are traitors to this country and will immediately—and forever after—be held accountable.

"I'M, LIKE, A SMART PERSON"

Post date • TUESDAY, DECEMBER 13

He has been put into the White House by the evil of another nation, and yet all our politicians will do is promise reports and committees whose words will be too measured and too late . . .

And now he will not listen to the daily intelligence briefings.

"I'm, like, a smart person," he said Sunday—factually correct, incidentally. Perhaps *like* a smart person, but not *actually* a smart person.

"I'm, like, a smart person. I don't have to be told the same thing and the same words every single day for the next eight years."

He will not *attend* the daily intelligence briefings.

"If something should change from this point, immediately call me. I'm available on one minute's notice."

But he would not necessarily *believe* the daily intelligence briefings anyway.

After the wave of reports about the intelligence agencies confirming Russia's intervention in our election:

"These are the same people that said Saddam Hussein had weapons of mass destruction."

No, actually, the intelligence agencies kept insisting that there were no such weapons, and they kept having their reports thrown back in their face by the administration of a president who was, like, a smart person and knew better.

"The election ended a long time ago in one of the biggest Electoral College victories in history."

The Electoral College vote hasn't happened yet.

If no pledged elector changes his vote, his margin will be the thirteenth *smallest* in history.

But he knows better.

He always knows better.

A CIA conclusion that the Russians interfered with our sovereignty, our freedoms, our elections, to put him in office?

"I think it's ridiculous. I think it's just another excuse. I don't believe it."

Who was the last president who would not listen to the daily intelligence briefings?

How many Americans were *killed* because George W. Bush did not listen to the President's Daily Brief from the intelligence community?

Three thousand on 9/11 and seven thousand more U.S. military in Iraq and Afghanistan.

Because what do you need intelligence for if you're...like...a smart person?

*

And still, it is worse.

Because from all that we have covered in this space for three months—the day in October when Trump slipped up and repeated the same mistaken attribution of a quote that a Russian propaganda site had made; the day his confidant praised WikiLeaks and intimated something bad was going to happen to John Podesta just before Podesta's emails were hacked and released *by* WikiLeaks; all the evidence of Russia's personal manipulation of Trump through his cronies, like Paul Manafort and Carter Page and Roger Stone, and now through Vladimir Putin's pals like would-be Secretary of State Rex Tillerson and the putrid Congressman Dana Rohrbacher...

Because all of that—and more—suggests that Donald Trump isn't just a stupid man's idea of what, like, a smart man would be; he is a man whose assumption that *he* has the inside information, and everybody else is just guessing, appears to be based on knowledge provided to him...by Russia.

The CIA said the Russians hacked Americans.

You don't know that, he says. *Could be a fat guy.*

The CIA *now* says the Russians hacked to get him elected.

I don't believe that, and so what? I won in a landslide.

What happens when the CIA *next* says the Russians are absorbing Ukraine?

What happens when the CIA *then* says Putin is so strong he's planning to take back Alaska?

What happens when the CIA *then* says there's an imminent terrorist attack, and it tracks back to Putin?

What happens when the CIA *finally* says Putin has lost his mind and he's launching missiles?

You don't know that, Trump says. *I don't believe it.*

*

The people should know the truth...

They should know that we have sustained a defeat, without a war...

The consequences of which will travel far with us along our road.

They should know that we have passed an awful milestone in our history, when the whole equilibrium of representative government has been deranged, and that the terrible words have, for the time being, been pronounced against our democracy:

"Thou art weighed in the balance and found wanting."

And do not suppose that this is the end.

This is only the beginning of the reckoning.

This is only the first sip, the first foretaste of a bitter cup that will be proffered to us, year by year, unless, by a supreme recovery of moral health and martial vigor, we arise again and take our stand for freedom...

*

Winston Churchill said that, more or less, in the British House of Commons, October 5, 1938, days after Prime Minister Neville Chamberlain, at Munich, gave Czechoslovakia to Hitler in exchange for... a piece of paper.

Chamberlain and much of the world thus thought he had guaranteed that there would be no Second World War—just as supporters of Trump think they have guaranteed some kind of new freedom and more money for themselves.

Churchill, and only a few others, knew that, in fact, Chamberlain had guaranteed there *would* be a Second World War—just as those of us who recognize Trump for what he is know that the voters have guaranteed *themselves* slavery, defeat, economic disaster, and the need to—sooner or later—save this nation and restore freedom by extricating ourselves from a Trump regime by whatever process provides itself.

*

Churchill was *most* prescient when he noted that Munich was only the beginning, just as we must recognize that the administering of the oath of office to Trump—an event to be resisted by any legal means—is only the first and smallest of a series of apocalypses.

Because, just as in Churchill's time, we have a Hitler.

No. It's not Trump. Not yet—certainly not in this context, anyway.

The part of Hitler in our sad reenactment of the months before the Second World War . . . is played by Vladimir Putin.

Trump?

In this remake . . . he is Neville Chamberlain.

He knows better.

He can see the strength in the foreign leader.

He knows how to make a deal.

He can handle him.

He can negotiate with him.

He can hand him our lives, our fortunes, and our sacred honor.

He has already helped hand Putin our sacred right to vote.

He will happily hand Putin a cleared path to the world domination he seeks for Russia.

He will—just so long as Putin tells him he's making a great deal and he's, like . . . a smart person—he will hand Putin . . . this country.

"Treason doth never prosper: what's the reason?" wrote the British courtier and author John Harington four hundred years ago.

"Why, if it prosper, none dare call it treason."

It's treason.

THE ELECTORAL COLLEGE
AND THE COMPROMISE OF 2016

Post date • WEDNESDAY, DECEMBER 14

"The most deadly adversaries of republican government might naturally have been expected to make their approaches from more than one quarter—but chiefly from the desire in *foreign powers* to gain an improper ascendant in our councils.

"How could they better gratify this, than by raising *a creature of their own* to the chief magistracy of the Union?"

*

Not my words.

They are those of . . . Alexander Hamilton.

Writing in the newspaper *The New-York Packet and the American Advertiser* in its issue of Friday, March 14, 1788. *The Federalist Papers.* No. 68. The one explaining how the president of the United States would be elected.

Alexander Hamilton, 83,549 days ago, predicting the Russian attempt to decide our 2016 election for us and install their own stooge, Donald Trump, to the chief magistracy of the Union. "How could they better gratify this, than by raising *a creature of their own* . . ."

A creature of their own . . . indeed.

As if Hamilton was peering through time and seeing Trump's preening face and evil soul. A creature of their own.

In *The Federalist* No. 68, Hamilton was explaining how in the new Constitution, the much-debated concept of the Electoral College would preclude another country from putting its man in the presidency, how it would make bribing the electors nearly impossible, how it would also serve as protection against scoundrels and traitors.

"Talents for low intrigue, and the little arts of popularity, may alone suffice to elevate a man to the first honors in a single State; but it will require other talents, and a different kind of merit, to establish him in the esteem and confidence of the whole Union, or of so considerable a portion of it as would be necessary to make him a successful candidate for the distinguished office of President of the United States."

"Talents for low intrigue."

"The little arts of popularity."

Alexander Hamilton saw everything phony about Donald Trump—except his hair.

*

Hamilton, of course, describes a different Electoral College from that which meets next Monday.

The one Hamilton wrote about in 1788 existed *before* there was any popular voting.

There were no political parties, no pledged delegates, no rubber stamp.

It's a different Electoral College from the one that is our last defense against the end of America—different except in spirit.

For if the Electoral College is not still what Hamilton described, it is still what Hamilton *intended*.

It is there to weed out the unqualified, the unprincipled, the merely famous— and especially to weed out a creature "of foreign powers." Or, in Donald Trump's case, all of the above.

But still, a rubber stamp. A quaint vestige of the fact that you have to win *states*, not just *votes*, to become president.

Oh?

If it is a rubber stamp—why does it *convene*?

If the Electoral College is merely a formality in which the electors vote as the vote totals in their states tell them to—why are the electors *there*? Certainly, the certified results from each state are sufficient to declare, "Trump 306, Clinton 232."

If the Electoral College is merely a vestige of state demographics in which the electors vote as the vote totals in their states tell them to—why is it legal in literally half the states, twenty-five, for the members to vote for . . . whoever they want?

The answer would seem obvious, albeit hard to believe.

Never in our history have any of our leaders *changed* the Electoral College. We have changed the Constitution to permit women to vote and slavery to be ended, and for alcohol to be banned, and then we changed it back so alcohol would be *un*banned. We have changed the Constitution to include something the Founding Fathers quickly discovered they had left out: the entire Bill of Rights.

But never in our history have we changed the fact of the vote *by* the Electoral College.

Thus, there is only one conclusion.

It is there because the Founding Fathers . . . were right.

Someday—we would need it.

Someday, perhaps centuries later, we would need to follow Alexander

Hamilton's version of IN CASE OF EMERGENCY BREAK GLASS. Someday, perhaps centuries later, "talents for low intrigue" and "the little arts of popularity" would combine with "the desire in *foreign powers*" to elect their own president, and only the quaint, irrelevant rubber stamp of the Electoral College—the appendix of the body politic—would stand between us and Armageddon.

Turned out "someday" was December 19, 2016.

*

It is correct that thirty-eight Trump electors voting instead for Hillary Clinton would make *her* president.

It is also correct that it is likelier that the Electoral College will be hit by an asteroid during its convention next Monday than that thirty-eight Republican electors will vote instead for a Democrat.

The country has long since become the land of "me first," and to find thirty-eight political men and women of true, self-sacrificing patriotism and conscience would at least quadruple the number of them I could name right now.

The Russians could have literally, instead of merely *remotely*, swung the election for Trump—they could be standing in Cossack uniforms along Pennsylvania Avenue—and Republican politicians would still think, "But what's in it for me?" before they switched from Trump to Clinton.

*

But there is another way.

There are compromises.

This nation exists—probably to die on January 20, when a foreign-backed usurper seizes power, but for now, this nation exists—because of the second civil war we *didn't* have, the one that threatened to explode in the winter of 1876–77 over the disputed election between Rutherford B. Hayes and Samuel Tilden.

The election was to be decided by Florida. The state sent two entirely separate delegations to the Electoral College: one Republican, one Democratic. And the lame duck president increased the presence of troops in Washington because it was assumed that whoever lost was going to start shooting.

But he didn't.

We compromised.

It was an awful compromise, the impact of which was still felt ninety years later. The Republicans got the White House; the Democrats got the end of Reconstruction in the South and tacit permission to disenfranchise blacks, and there descended upon us ninety years and more of segregation and Jim Crow.

Yet the threat of civil war vanished and has stayed vanished. Until now, at least.

*

Compromise.

A resident scholar from the Cato Institute named Michael F. Cannon wrote in *The Washington Post* on the fifth of this month suggesting that, instead of holding out hope of thirty-eight Trump electors miraculously risking their status in their party for the sake of democracy, the hero this time should be . . . Hillary Clinton.

Her electors—not Trump's—should vote differently.

She should instruct those pledged to *her* . . . to vote instead for a moderate Republican, while patriots in that party find thirty-eight—or more—Trump supporters to switch to that same moderate Republican.

Cannon suggested Mitt Romney. One could make a list—a small list: Romney and John McCain and Evan McMullin, and, for that matter, if he were a little healthier, President George H. W. Bush.

Romney, McCain, McMullin, whoever—presumably with a moderate Democrat as vice president.

Would it be right?

Would it be fair?

Before you answer, answer this:

Would it be a victory over the Russians, who committed an act of war against us by interfering with our elections? Would it be defense against Trump and this Banana Republican government of his, which will turn the rest of the world over to Vladimir Putin and end our democracy?

And before you answer *that*, answer this:

You can't have Clinton . . .

Alexander Hamilton is dead . . .

The alternative is an unelected dictator . . .

Would you, right now, trade Donald Trump for a President Mitt Romney—
or a President John McCain—or a President Evan McMullin?

Me?

In a heartbeat.

And I'd drop to my knees in thanks for . . . the Electoral College.

THE PRESIDENT-ELECT AND TREASON

Post date • MONDAY, DECEMBER 19

Our long national nightmare . . . is starting.

With the Electoral College failing to do its duty as conceived under the
Constitution, Russia's whore is *now* president-elect.

No longer is Donald Trump merely certifiable; now he is *certified*.

So this changes everything.

No.

It changes . . . nothing.

He is *still* president by a minority vote.

He is still wholly unfit for the job—*the* man you would expect to find if you
were searching for the person who could most quickly and efficiently destroy a
democracy and maybe a planet.

He is still a moving, breathing conflict of interest who will likely be guilty
of impeachable high crimes and misdemeanors within hours, if not minutes, of
his own inauguration . . .

He is still a textbook case of corrupt self-dealing come to life . . .

He is still the leader of the most remarkable group of public "serve-yourself
servants" ever assembled.

And, most important: Trump is still—at best—an unwitting pawn of, personal local representative of, and employment recruiter for Russian dictator
Vladimir Putin.

"If you want to shut this down, and you actually love the country enough to
have this peaceful transition in our great democracy between the Obama administration and the Trump administration, there are a couple people in

pretty prominent positions—one's named Obama, one's named Hillary Clinton, since his people are trying to fight over her election still—they could shut this down."

Kellyanne Conway, equating bending to Russian interference with patriotism.

Kellyanne Conway, Trump's campaign manager when he repeatedly refused to confirm that *he* would "shut this down" and participate in a "peaceful transition" if he lost.

Kellyanne Conway, who might as well be a Russian citizen.

"I don't think anyone should complain that the truth did come out. And let's stipulate that Russia *did* cyberhacking. Again, all countries are doing it. We don't like it, we can never condone it . . ."

Republican congressman Chris Collins of New York State, condoning Russia's cyberhacking while saying, "We can never condone it."

"Whether they're Russian hackers or any other hackers, the only information that we were getting from hackers was accurate information, was truthful. And that's not gonna turn the tide. If the American people have been given more truthful information, that's terrific."

Republican congressman Dana Rohrabacher of California, saying the results of a Russia attack on the sanctity of our free elections was "terrific."

"I guess Putin is going to have to do it. RT 'State Dept Won't Release Clinton Fdn Emails for 27 Months.'"

Monica Crowley, whom Trump wants in the communications office of the National Security Council.

No, *our*—not *Russia's*—National Security Council.

And of course, "If Russia, or some other entity, was hacking, why did the White House wait so long to act? Why did they only complain after Hillary lost?"

Trump, on the fifteenth, implying that he'd never heard *anything* about Russia *hacking* and then, less than twenty-one hours later, completely contradicting himself:

"Are we talking about the same cyberattack where it was revealed that head of the DNC illegally gave Hillary the questions to the debate?"

And now Trump and his gang—caviar virtually leaking out of their pockets—are untouchable.

No longer are there evident legal means to prevent his inauguration, other than indictment and arrest for some kind of crime where bail isn't granted.

Hmmm.

For what kind of crime do they not grant *bail?*

"A specter of *treason* hovers over Donald Trump," Ambassador John Shattuck wrote in *The Boston Globe,* in a piece not posted until late last Friday afternoon. "He has brought it on himself by dismissing a bipartisan call for an investigation of Russia's hacking of the Democratic National Committee as a 'ridiculous' political attack on the legitimacy of his election as president."

John Shattuck was this country's ambassador to the Czech Republic from 1998 through 2000, and before that he was our assistant secretary of state for democracy, human rights, and labor.

"Seventeen US national intelligence agencies have unanimously concluded that Russia engaged in cyberwarfare against the US presidential campaign. The lead agency, the CIA, has reached the further conclusion that Russia's hacking was intended to influence the election in favor of Trump."

Ambassador Shattuck graduated from Yale, got first-class honors in international law at Cambridge, graduated from Yale Law, lectured at Harvard Law.

"Why does Trump publicly reject these intelligence agency conclusions and the bipartisan proposal for a congressional investigation? As president-elect, he should have a strong interest in presenting a united front against Russia's interference with the electoral process at the core of American democracy."

The ambassador outlines four answers to his own question: that Trump was trying to "shore up" his political standing before the Electoral College voted; that he was looking for leverage to use against the intelligence agencies once in office; that he was testing his ability to convince the public that he—and not the professionals—knows the truth about national security threats; and/or that he is engaged in a cover-up of prior knowledge—his or his campaign's—of the Russian cyberattack.

"In each case the president-elect is inviting an interpretation that his behavior is treasonous. The federal crime of treason is committed by a person 'owing allegiance to the United States who . . . adheres to their enemies, giving them aid or comfort,' and misprision of treason is committed by a person 'having knowledge of the commission of any treason [who] conceals and does not disclose' the crime."

And now we are brought back to—and must update—John Harington's sixteenth-century couplet:

"Treason doth never prosper: what's the reason?

"Why, if it prosper, none dare *call it* treason."

Except perhaps Ambassador Shattuck.

"By denigrating or seeking to prevent an investigation of the Russian cyberattack Trump is giving aid or comfort to an enemy of the United States, a crime that is enhanced if the fourth explanation applies—that he is in fact seeking to cover up his staff's or his own involvement in or prior knowledge of the attack."

One other note about the ambassador. He is not a desk jockey. He went to Bosnia in 1995 and personally gathered evidence of the genocide there, and he helped the United Nations establish international criminal tribunals for Rwanda and the former Yugoslavia.

We may shortly need international criminal tribunals for *this* country.

"In light of these circumstances, Trump should seek to clear the air by endorsing the proposed investigation of the Russian hacking scandal. For him to continue to deny Russia's cyberattack and resist the investigation invites a specter of treason to hover over the president-elect."

Trump—president-elect or not; presidented or un-presidented, if you will—and still, in the assessment of Ambassador Shattuck, inching closer and closer to the textbook legal definition . . . of traitor.

SOCIAL SECURITY

Post date • **WEDNESDAY, DECEMBER 21**

We all know why *Donald Trump* is doing this.

He has an ego that would make Napoleon blanch and a power lust that would make Stalin back off.

His pimp, Vladimir Putin, has something on him.

He's crazy.

He sees stuff.

Or—best-case scenario—he just exploits. Everyone and everything.

He's the parent to whom the kid shouts out in the middle of the night, crying, "There are monsters under my bed," and he says, "You are correct, there *are* monsters, and only I can save you from them, but first turn over your allowance. And sign this nondisclosure agreement, and don't ever think or say or tell anybody that, in fact, *I* am the monster."

Trump, by now—we *get.*

But why are the *Banana Republicans* who—as recently as two months ago—showed brief, ever-fading signs of standing up to Trump . . . why are *they* doing this?

Why are they becoming the Vichy government who sold out France during the Nazi occupation? Why are they lining up to become Quislings, collaborating with the Germans and helping kill their fellow Norwegians? Why are they applauding a Russian attack on America?

Well, clearly they were standing up to Trump only because they were afraid—afraid he would lose.

Once they won, they saw power, and, as Eric Blair wrote, "we are interested solely in power, pure power . . . No one ever seizes power with the intention of relinquishing it. Power is not a means; it is an end. . . . The object of power is power."

Mr. Blair published, of course, under the name George Orwell.

Still, it's not just about *abstract* power for the Banana Republicans, for the mercenary monsters like Paul Ryan. There is a specific reason they are backing Trump—for *now. Until* he shows signs of losing again, at which point they will kill him and eat him.

For Republicans who think they are using Trump . . . Trump is perpetual chaff.

I've mentioned *chaff* before.

It's metal debris used by bombers and missile crews and pilots to confuse radar. And Trump spews it, every day, every hour, every minute, and as hard as we try, you and I can't avoid *all* of it.

And so, while he's enraging people by appointing a secretary of labor who hates labor, and a secretary of housing who hates housing, and a secretary of energy who once campaigned for president on a promise to dismantle the Department of Energy.

While he's doing all these other Eric Blairish things . . . and while we're raging about ambassadorships reportedly being offered as quid pro quos to get bigger acts at the inaugural, or how the self-dealer-elect is going to stay on as an executive producer of one of the worst shows ever on television, and while we pull out our hair because the self-dealer-elect's last campaign manager, who I'm beginning to think may be a witch, says he'll do that in his spare time . . .

While all that *chaff* is flying, the Banana Republicans are going on a stealth offensive. They have to reveal themselves sooner or later, if only to signal to the corporations who own them that, yes, the fix *is* in, and ownership *will* be getting what they prostituted the government for.

For Paul Ryan, "sooner or later" turned out to be sooner.

Two Thursdays ago, a man named Stephen C. Goss wrote a letter to a man named Sam Johnson, and in so doing, he let the cat out of the Banana Republicans' bag.

Mr. Goss is the chief actuary of Social Security—the man who has to assess the impact of the economy and legislation, and basically everything, on the future not only *of* Social Security but of those who receive it.

And the man he wrote to, Mr. Johnson, is the Republican congressman from the Third District of Texas, who is chairman of the Ways and Means Committee's Subcommittee on Social Security. And on the eighth of this month, Mr. Johnson introduced bill H.R. 6489, "The Social Security Reform Act of 2016."

Mr. Goss's letter is sixteen pages long, plus thirteen more pages of tables and graphs and the kind of calculations that nearly caused me to flunk out of Senior Math in high school, and, but for the generosity of my teacher, Gerry Murphy, I'd be in my forty-second-consecutive year trying to graduate *from* high school.

But it's Mr. Johnson's bill that matters.

It explains why the Republicans are abetting the idiot-elect.

Mr. Goss's letter explains how deeply Johnson and Paul Ryan and all the other corporate whores intend to plunge the knife into the back of Social Security and especially those hardworking fools of Middle America who actually believed the net impact of a Donald Trump presidency would be more money for them and not, you know, poverty in their old age.

The gist is—they're screwed.

Social Security—not just Medicaid and Medicare, on which it's always open season in Republican-land—*Social Security* would be gutted.

Not only no *more* money going *into* Social Security—but actually *less* money going in.

And massive cuts to money going *out* in Social Security checks.

Some cuts starting as soon as December 2018.

Cuts for people *now* getting Social Security.

Cuts for people *yet* to get Social Security. Cuts to the Social Security Trust Fund, designed to meet shortfalls when the baby boomers start to get Social Security.

Hell, money taken *from* the Social Security Trust Fund, cuts made beyond what could ever be necessary to avoid shortfalls, in order to . . . *reduce income taxes for rich people.*

If you're making around $50,000, your Social Security check would be cut between 11 percent and 35 percent. Almost everybody would see their check drop by at least 10 percent.

This bill—or some lesser new version of it that the Banana Republicans would introduce next year, in which, instead of being stabbed to death, you'd just die more slowly by bleeding to death—that's why Paul Ryan and the Republicans are supporting Trump.

Ordinary Americans, particularly those Trump voters who will have taken this Social Security–cut knife and managed to stab *themselves* in the back with it, will be watching whatever Trump is doing at the moment—at some point, his version of Daffy Duck drinking a gallon of gasoline, a bottle of nitroglycerin, a pile of gunpowder, and a glass of uranium 238 and then lighting a match—while in the background, the Republican House and the Republican Senate, now full subsidiaries of the corporations who were able to buy this country after the *Citizens United* decision, will destroy Social Security so the rich can get even richer by stealing a billion dollars, one dollar at a time. And our part-time president will take a quick look away from his Twitter feed to sign where they tell him.

*

Close your eyes for a second.

Imagine you're on a ship that has just sunk, quickly. You have popped up to the surface next to a large, empty lifeboat, stocked with provisions, two oars, and room for several dozen people.

What you do next defines—to me—mankind.

There are generally two responses. In the first, you get in the lifeboat, assess exactly how many other people can safely fit in and how long you all can last, and you begin to pull in other survivors still in the water, trying to bring in women and children and injured, but also people to help you *help* them and row the boat.

In the second response, you get in the lifeboat, assess exactly how long *you* could last if you ate all the food by yourself, and then you pick up one of the oars and start swinging it at the other survivors still in the water, killing them if possible, to make sure *you* are the only one in the boat.

The first response makes you a liberal, also known as a human being.

The second response makes you a conservative.

Open your eyes now.

*

Surprisingly, as seen in the Banana Republicans' Social Security play ... it now turns out ... there's a third response.

In this one, you actually help a couple of other survivors into the lifeboat. And then, as they're leaning over the side trying to help pull up others, you kill them with the oar, and then you steal their wallets off their dead bodies so you can make a profit off them.

That third response?

That makes you Donald Trump.

Chapter 6

JANUARY 2017

WHAT DID TRUMP KNOW AND WHEN DID HE STOP KNOWING IT?

Post date • WEDNESDAY, JANUARY 4

He said, "You'll find out on Tuesday or Wednesday."

He said he knows a lot about hacking.

He said he knows about the hacking of the Democratic National Committee and other computer systems, "things that other people don't know."

"What do you know," he was asked, Saturday night, "that other people don't know?"

"You'll find out," he said confidently, "on Tuesday or Wednesday."

But Tuesday night he tweeted that the intelligence briefing on Russian hacking—he put insult quotes around "intelligence" and "Russian hacking"— had been delayed until Friday, positing "perhaps more time needed to build a case. Very strange!"

Later Tuesday night, CNN reported that there had been *no* hacking review scheduled for Trump by the CIA director nor the director of national intelligence.

NBC reported that there *was* one . . . but it had *always* been scheduled for Friday.

Independent journalist Marc Ambinder reported that there was a scheduled briefing that was delayed from last week by the family emergency of one of the intelligence officials, that the White House would get it Wednesday, congressional leaders Thursday, and Trump Friday—and it was identical to what he *would* have heard last week.

Trump has said nothing except to again attack other Americans and to again pretend he knows everything, and Wednesday morning to—incredibly—again take sides with Julian Assange, who is an enemy to this country and an enemy to democracy everywhere and at best a de facto Russian agent.

"Julian Assange said 'a 14 year old could have hacked Podesta'—why was DNC so careless? Also said Russians did not give him the info!"

And quoting Fox News: "Julian Assange on U.S. media coverage: 'It's very dishonest.' #Hannity More dishonest than anyone knows."

The dishonesty here is all Trump's—with the criminal Assange and the cretin Hannity as fellow travelers.

*

We—the American people, the victims of Trump's disloyalty and his deranged attempt to position himself as the only person who knows the truth—have found out nothing in the four days since Trump began to play his ridiculous, dangerous, un-American game.

We still have no idea what those things are that he supposedly knows, that other people don't, nor who told them to him.

And we are waiting.

*

This was not just his usual boast, not just his usual dismissal of this country's intelligence services, not just his usual lie about the intelligence community and the Iraq weapons of mass destruction—which was not failed intelligence, but rather intelligence manipulated and altered and falsified and turned on its head by the Bush administration.

This was a man, not three weeks before taking power, insisting that this country should *not* investigate what the Russian dictator did to our election, a man demanding that the rest of us, from John McCain to me, need to "get on with our lives," a man suggesting—again (he also said it in July)—that the best response to hacking that might have altered the course of history was to stop using *computers* and go back to using *messengers*.

This is a man, on the eve of ultimate power in our country, still insisting that Russia is right and America is wrong, and that he knows "a lot about hacking" and he knows "things that other people don't know" and "you'll find out on Tuesday or Wednesday."

Trump's silence through Tuesday and then Wednesday and now—based on his tweet—presumably through Friday leaves him very few ways out of his ludicrous boasting...

Unless by Friday *you* have forgotten this.

His incoming press secretary—Sean Spicer—already so far in over his head that he needs a scuba suit—flailed around the other day trying to walk back Trump's boast and suggest that the tinpot-tyrant-elect was really talking about *conclusions* he had *reached* from classified briefings. This excuse *might* have worked if Trump had not spent so much time explaining that he doesn't attend, need, nor worry about classified briefings.

"You'll find out on Tuesday or Wednesday."

Well, we haven't.

※

Of course, even if we *had* found out, even if we yet *do* find out, Trump will still have painted himself into an impossible corner—just a different corner.

About the hacking: "I know things that other people don't know."

Who told you, Trump?

If it's from American intelligence briefers—you said you didn't believe them.

If it's from American intelligence briefers—why are you revealing, or merely referencing, secret classified information weeks before you are legally permitted to do so?

If it's *not* from American intelligence briefers—who was it?

Was it Vladimir Putin?

Did *he* tell you that Russia didn't hack the DNC and try to swing the election so it would have *you* in office?

How long did Putin know?

How long has it been since he told you?

Did he tell you this *before* the election?

Why have you not told America?

Why did you not tell America even last Saturday night? Or Tuesday, instead of another tweet worthy of a snot-nosed teenage boy?

Did Putin *tell* you not to tell *us*?

Why did you agree to conspire with Putin to conceal this evidence, even if it's only been since last Saturday?

Did you inform American intelligence of what Putin told you?

If so, how quickly?

*

What if the things you know that other people don't, Trump, were *not* told to you by American intelligence *or* by Putin?

Who... then?

How do *they* know?

Who told *them*?

Why have you not told America what *they* knew?

*

Is your hacking source General Michael Flynn?

Who reads and believes and disseminates conspiracy theories—bluntly, *insane* conspiracy theories—about pedophilia and Sharia law and Democrats ritually drinking body fluids?

Is your hacking source Julian Assange, who is a thief and an anti-American operative, and has long since lost any credibility among conservatives or liberals?

Is your hacking source Alex Jones, the radio nut? Who believes Sandy Hook never happened? And the dead bodies were child actors?

Is your hacking source the *National Enquirer*? Which you quoted when it claimed that Ted Cruz's father was involved in the Kennedy assassination?

Is your hacking source the individual you have repeatedly cited as a computer expert? Your ten-year-old son?

*

Or—your hacking source, and the things you know that other people don't know, and the part about Tuesday or Wednesday, and the part of a delayed briefing that was reportedly never scheduled—did you just make them up because you thought we were all too stupid to expect you to deliver?

*

In the summer, Trump insisted the election was rigged.

In the autumn, the intelligence community revealed conclusions that maybe he was right.

In the winter, Trump insists we must not have hearings to see whether the Russians subverted our freedoms by remote control.

In a tux on New Year's Eve, Trump insists about the hacking that "I know things that other people don't know" and "You'll find out on Tuesday or Wednesday."

In a peevish tweet on Tuesday night, he describes a briefing that may or may not have ever been scheduled being delayed—when it may very well have been delayed by *him*—and throws up another accusatory smoke screen by writing, "Perhaps more time needed to build a case. Very strange!"

So now we need to have not just hearings about the hacking. We need hearings about what Trump meant last Saturday night, what he knew, why he promised to reveal it, and why he is concealing it now.

In short, to revise a great question from history: What did Donald Trump know—and when did he stop knowing it?

MESSAGE TO A TRUMP SUPPORTER

Post date • THURSDAY, JANUARY 5

So you support Donald Trump.

I'm not going to yell.

I'm not going to say you're wrong.

I'm not going to talk about his policies.

I'm not going to talk about his promises.

*

I'm not going to talk about whether he's going to cut your taxes or raise them.

I'm not going to talk about whether he's going to make America great again or crash it and burn it.

*

And unlike what you probably think, I'm not trying to get the election overturned.

I'm not trying to get Hillary Clinton into the White House.

I'm not claiming the Republican Party won't be there for at least the next four years.

*

No. This is about ... him.

And you.

And the respect for you I start with, because you're following this.

You are thoughtful enough to have gotten this far ...

So let's go in on the assumption that you're smarter than I am ...

In which case you already know what my point is.

*

I don't know who the political figure would be if our places were reversed.

I guess the time I got the closest to the position you're in was with John Edwards, who had a problem, and I didn't see it, and while he wasn't my first choice, I would've supported him for president.

He had what I thought was a great, humane set of policies, and a wife who was so smart and had been through so much in life that she probably should have been the candidate instead of him. And then it turned out John Edwards was a con man who not only had fooled me—he had fooled her, too.

If Edwards wasn't *my* version of this, it would have to be Anthony Weiner. I used to have him on my show a lot. He gave straightforward, damn-the-torpedoes kinds of answers you *never* get from politicians; he disliked the same Republicans I disliked, and he hated the same Democrats I hated.

And even after he crashed and burned the first time, and then tried to run for mayor of New York, I thought, Well, he *has* to have gotten his problem fixed, and he might be a really good mayor, and then it happened again. In fact, it had barely stopped.

And the next time I saw him, a year ago, I literally was afraid to shake his hand, in case (a) somebody took a picture of it or (b) whatever he had, it was catching.

*

So I haven't been where you are right now—but . . . close.

And you are in a terrible position.

A man whose opinions you agree with has been elected president and is about to be sworn in.

And yet—I'm pretty sure you *know* the problem.

You're smart, and generally speaking, the only person who can fool you *is* you.

You're smart enough to recognize something I saw when I first met this man, thirty-three years ago.

And that is *this*: there's something really, really wrong with him.

*

Who does this on Christmas Eve?

His tweet was a plug for a documentary.

A documentary about him.

Not even a new one.

A repeat!

Who *does* this on Christmas Eve?

His Christmas greeting on Twitter was just a photo of himself.

Not the family.

Not the wife.

Not even the vice president.

Not Santa.

Not Jesus.

Just him.

Who *does* this?

Two days later—meaning sixty days after the election—the election is still all he's tweeting about.

"President Obama campaigned hard (and personally) in the very important swing states and lost."

What kind of man does this?

You win, you act like you've won before; you don't waste your energy on the guy who's gone in a month anyway.

Maybe, maybe, if you're a good guy, you're gracious in victory, you're a good winner—at least during the holidays.

"Happy New Year to all, including to my many enemies and those who have fought me and lost so badly they just don't know what to do. Love!"

Would *you* . . . write that?

Would you write that—when you got votes from fewer people than the other candidate?

Would you call everybody else . . . your enemy?

*

Okay. Maybe just because when I interviewed him when I was twenty-five and he owned a football team and I came away muttering to my producer, "What's wrong with *that* guy?"—maybe I'm wrong. Maybe there's nothing really dangerous about a man who has to tell you how much he won by. Again and again. And again. When he actually didn't win by very much.

Maybe that doesn't matter.

Maybe from where you sit, it's *only* about "Make America Great Again" and "America First" and always defending this country because we are right and we need to be loyal to our great nation.

"Vladimir Putin said today about Hillary and Dems: 'In my opinion, it is humiliating. One must be able to lose with dignity.' So true!"

"Great move on delay (by V. Putin)—I always knew he was very smart!"

Who defends a Russian dictator, ahead of an American president, or an American politician, or half of the people *in* America?

I mean, when he was president, as much as I hated George W. Bush, I never took Vladimir Putin's side against him!

Would *you* do that?

*

Maybe you would. I said I wouldn't yell, and I'm not going to. To my mind, it is possible for you to agree with Donald Trump and still be a good person. I just disagree with you. I don't think you're my enemy.

But let me run one last pair of tweets past you and ask you if you think they were written by a normal guy.

"Various media outlets and pundits say that I thought I was going to lose the election. Wrong, it all came together in the last week and . . . I thought and felt I would win big, easily over the fabled 270 (306). When they cancelled fireworks, they knew, and so did I."

So those tweets are from last Monday.

That means it was only three weeks since he got up at one of those victory tour stops—this was in West Allis, Wisconsin, on December 13—and he said . . . he thought he was going to lose the election . . . and he thought so on the *night of* the election.

"I went to see my wife. I say, 'Baby, I tell you what. We're not going to win tonight.' The polls are coming out—I always used to believe in those things. I don't believe them anymore. I said if we're going to lose I don't want a big ballroom."

There aren't a lot of choices here, are there?

He either lied—in the tweets, or at the tour stop in Wisconsin, or to his wife that night—or he forgot that he said it, or . . .

There's *something wrong with him.*

*

To pretend that there *isn't* . . . you have to pretend really hard.

I know you can't say it, I know you don't want to believe it, and I know you won't believe this, either, but I wish it weren't true . . .

But we've elected a man . . . who is not all there.

And that cannot end happily.

His illness—it's an *illness*—is putting you at risk. And your family. And your kids. And my family. And everybody we know, the ones we like—and the ones we don't.

Don't say anything, don't do anything—I don't even want you to admit anything to anybody except yourself.

But you *know* that someday, probably soon, something bad will happen, and whatever he does will make it worse, and it'll all be clear that he's not healthy enough to be president, and they'll have to remove him.

And, by the way, it'll be the Republicans who will have to remove him—either the vice president and the Speaker of the House using the Twenty-fifth Amendment, or the Republican congressmen and the Republican senators impeaching him.

Because this isn't about what he believes in.

This is about the fact that he's . . . not . . . well.

So all I'm asking—all that this has been about—is for you to just think about it, for when the time comes. Because when the Republicans really need to remove him as president, they'll need to do it in a hurry, and as a Republican or a conservative or a Democrat or as an American, or whichever way you describe yourself, it'll be a lot easier—and a lot safer for all of us—if you've prepared yourself, and you help them remove him.

Because he's not well.

HE CANNOT LEAVE IT ALONE

Post date • TUESDAY, JANUARY 10

Any essential distinction between Donald Trump being merely an idiot marionette belonging to Vladimir Putin and Donald Trump being an active Russian agent has been fully erased in the course of just over a week.

And it has been erased by . . . Donald Trump.

*

When the damning stain of illegitimacy grows on this presidency, week by week—hour by hour—when every moment of the political discourse of this nation becomes consumed by a debate over not *whether* he has been placed in office by the efforts of a foreign power, but over how *much* of that subversion he knew in advance—he will have no one to blame but himself.

Because he cannot . . . leave it . . . alone.

Because every move Donald Trump has made *this year* has been politically tone-deaf. He could not make it look more like he is covering up something— something horrifying—if he hung a sign around his neck reading COVER-UP. He *reeks* of cover-up.

And in his neurosis, unsatisfied with having fooled some of the people some of the time, he has not merely ignored the option a *real* president would take—invite a full investigation—he has also waited weeks before trying the option a *skilled traitor* would take: to shut up and change the subject to, say, Meryl Streep.

And still, like a desperate child, he has to keep bringing the subject up, keep shouting those key words that he should never speak again—*Russia, hacking, Assange, Putin*—until he can presumably convince himself that he has convinced everyone *everywhere* that none of it is true, and until he can convince himself that everyone now agrees with him about how strong and powerful he is—and how he has now . . . *won*.

*

It is madness. And it will destroy him.

December 29: "I think we ought to get on with our lives. I think that computers have complicated lives very greatly. The whole age of the computer has made it where nobody knows exactly what's going on."

But saying that "nobody knows exactly what's going on" means . . . even *he* doesn't know exactly what's going on.

And he can't let anybody believe *that*:

December 31: "I know a lot about hacking, and hacking is a very hard thing to prove, so it could be somebody else. And I also know things that other people don't know, and so, they cannot be sure of this situation."

Pool reporter: "What do you know that other people don't know?"

Trump: "You'll find out on Tuesday or Wednesday."

All we found out Tuesday was . . . his willingness to publicly advertise his own paranoia.

Tuesday, January 3, 8:14 p.m.: "The 'Intelligence' briefing on so-called 'Russian hacking' was delayed until Friday, perhaps more time needed to build a case. Very strange!"

The delay was for a family emergency.

The delay was of an intelligence briefing, the likes of which he has reportedly been *skipping* for two months.

Wednesday, January 4, 7:22 a.m.: "Julian Assange said 'a 14 year old could have hacked Podesta'—why was DNC so careless? Also said Russians did not give him the info!"

Trump has here cited—and given credibility to—Assange of WikiLeaks, about whose activities Trump said in December 2010, "I think it's disgraceful, I think there should be like death penalty or something."

Wednesday, January 4, 8:27 a.m.: "Somebody hacked the DNC but why did they not have 'hacking defense' like the RNC has and why have they not responded to the terrible things they did and said (like giving the questions to the debate to H). A total double standard! Media, as usual, gave them a pass."

Trump has now justified international espionage against Americans, provided they are guilty of something—or provided he merely *thinks* they are guilty of something—especially if the espionage involves Julian Assange.

Thursday, January 5, 8:25 a.m.: "The dishonest media likes saying that I am in Agreement with Julian Assange—wrong. I simply state what he states, it is for the people to make up their own minds as to the truth. The media lies to make it look like I am against 'Intelligence' when in fact I am a big fan!"

He cannot . . . leave it . . . alone!

He *must* not only erase what he himself has just done . . . He must also find a new scapegoat.

Thursday, January 5, 7:24 p.m.: "How did NBC get 'an exclusive look into the top secret report he (Obama) was presented?' Who gave them this report and why? Politics!"

He asks about NBC, but does so in his standard way of scapegoating the media: politically, scornfully—not seriously, not officially, not ominously.

The next morning . . . somebody else does all that *for* him.

The tweet from WikiLeaks: "The Obama admin/CIA is illegally funneling TOP SECRET//COMINT information to NBC for political reasons before PEOTUS even gets to read it."

That tweet was from 5:48 a.m. on January 6.

The next tweet is from *11:51* a.m. on January 6:

Trump: "I am asking the chairs of the House and Senate committees to investigate top secret intelligence shared with NBC prior to me seeing it."

He is now desperate enough to try change the subject from his connection to WikiLeaks that he doesn't even seem to realize he has just . . . connected himself to WikiLeaks!

Perhaps somebody pointed *that* out to him, because next, by phone to *The New York Times*:

"China, relatively recently, hacked 20 million government names. How come nobody even talks about that? This is a political witch hunt."

Then comes the briefing on the hacking: a briefing he had avoided, on hacking he had dismissed, from an intelligence community he had undermined.

And after it, a very, very *cleverly* phrased written statement: "I had a constructive meeting and conversation with the leaders of the Intelligence Community this afternoon. I have tremendous respect for the work and service done by the men and women of this community to our great nation.

"While Russia, China, other countries, outside groups and people are consistently trying to break through the cyber infrastructure of our governmental institutions, businesses and organizations including the Democrat National Committee, there was absolutely no effect on the outcome of the election including the fact that there was no tampering whatsoever with voting machines . . ."

Do you see what he did there? Merely through juxtaposition?

The first paragraph describes a meeting with the intelligence community and its work . . .

The second paragraph describes the conclusion that cyberattacks had no effect on the outcome of the election.

Composed *that* way, it *seems* as if the *intelligence community* had concluded the hacking had no effect.

But the conclusion . . . is *Trump's*.

The intelligence community's report doesn't merely offer a different conclusion—it makes Trump's written statement even more deceptive and malicious.

"We did not make an assessment of the impact that Russian activities had on the outcome of the 2016 election. The US Intelligence Community is charged with monitoring and assessing the intentions, capabilities, and actions of foreign actors; it does not analyze US political processes or US public opinion."

When that *real* version of what the report *did not* conclude was officially released, Trump looked like a liar.

So, that night, back to blaming the victim.

Friday, January 6, 10:53 p.m.: "Gross negligence by the Democratic National Committee allowed hacking to take place. The Republican National Committee had strong defense!"

But the intelligence briefing actually concluded the Republicans were *also* hacked by Russia. Russia just didn't *distribute* its RNC data.

So: change the story again.

Saturday, January 7, 6:56 a.m.: "Intelligence stated very strongly there was absolutely no evidence that hacking affected the election results. Voting machines not touched!"

He has just erased the subtle deception and misdirection in his *Friday* statement—and replaced it with a flat-out, transparent, childish *lie*.

He. Cannot. Leave. It. Alone.

Saturday, January 7, 7:03 a.m.: "Only reason the hacking of the poorly defended DNC is discussed is that the loss by the Dems was so big that they are totally embarrassed!"

And here Trump's story spirals out of anything resembling his own control.

It has gone from Russian espionage to him invoking the hacking of voting machines to him disparaging half the country thirteen days before his inauguration . . . to:

Saturday, January 7, 10:02 a.m.: "Having a good relationship with Russia is a good thing, not a bad thing. Only 'stupid' people, or fools, would think that it is bad! We have enough problems around the world without yet another one. When I am President, Russia will respect us far more than they do now and both countries will, perhaps, work together to solve some of the many great and pressing problems and issues of the WORLD!"

In three hours and twenty-eight minutes, Trump has gone from espionage to hacking voting machines to calling tens of millions of Americans "fools" and "stupid" to a promise of cooperation with Russia that reads as if it were written in response to instructions from a blackmailer saying, "You better fix this, Trump. You better make us look good, Trump."

*

And so the desperation escalates, still further.

Sunday, January 8, 1:56 p.m.: "Before I, or anyone, saw the classified and/or highly confidential hacking intelligence report, it was leaked out to @NBC News. So serious!"

The hacking *itself*? We ought to move on with our lives. It's only being discussed because he beat the Democrats.

The possible leak *about* the hacking? "So serious."

And then Meryl Streep changes the topic for him on Sunday night at the Golden Globes—and the last of his campaign managers *changes it right back*, because . . . he . . . cannot . . . leave it . . . alone.

"The fact is," Conway said Monday, dismissing the need for a Russian hack investigation and suggesting that Trump may roll back both President Obama's punishments *of* them *and* U.S. sanctions against Russia, "the Democrats became super-duper interested in this entire issue after the election did not go the way they, quote, wanted and the way they expected."

Trump . . . himself, or his mouthpieces . . . cannot . . . leave it . . . alone.

Neither can he alter his personal connection to WikiLeaks.

Again, the Saturday morning tweet: "Intelligence stated very strongly there was absolutely no evidence that hacking affected the election results . . ."

But even without the Russian element—the hacking . . . *is* WikiLeaks.

And as a review of his speeches by ThinkProgress.org showed, in the last thirty days of the campaign, Trump invoked WikiLeaks at least once . . . every day . . . for a total of at least . . . *164 times in one month*.

October 10, 2016, Wilkes-Barre, Pennsylvania: "WikiLeaks, I love WikiLeaks. And I said, 'Write a couple of them down.' Let's see. During a speech, crooked Hillary Clinton . . . Oh, she's crooked, folks. She's crooked as a three-dollar bill. Okay, here's one. Just came out . . ."

Trump is interrupted by a chant of "Lock her up" . . .

"'Lock her up' is right," he says.

He brought up WikiLeaks in a debate.

He claimed that the WikiLeaks product meant Hillary Clinton shouldn't be "allowed" to run for president.

He complained—in speeches and on Twitter, and it still sits there on his feed—that there wasn't *enough* coverage *of* WikiLeaks.

October 12, 9:46 a.m.: "Very little pick-up by the dishonest media of incredible information provided by WikiLeaks. So dishonest! Rigged system!"

But now Trump says . . . the hacking that produced WikiLeaks . . . had no effect on the election.

And of course, there's no way an American leader could ever compromise himself and suddenly be at Russia's beck and call.

September 6, *2013*, 9:02 a.m.:

"I wonder how much our 'leaders' have promised, or given, Russia in order for them to behave and not make the U.S. look even worse?"

How do we resist this monster?

Just keep quoting him.

Just keep mentioning it.

Just keep remembering: he cannot . . . leave it . . . alone.

WikiLeaks *is* the hacking.

The hacking . . . *is* Russia . . .

And Trump . . . is . . . WikiLeaks.

GUNS AND TRUMP

Post date • THURSDAY, JANUARY 12

In the wake of last Friday's terrorist attack, by another American against Americans at an American airport. At least five dead. At least six wounded. Guns. Gun terrorism.

And a reminder of all the things getting worse in this country that Trump will not even think of, let alone act against, in defense of the American people.

His question would not be: How on earth have we let our country deteriorate to the point that the last three high-profile mass public shootings in this country—San Bernardino, the Orlando nightclub, the Fort Lauderdale airport—

have been accomplished with legal weapons, with legal transportation of those weapons, with *impunity*?

His question would not be: How do we have a system by which anybody—international terrorist or nondenominational psychotic—who wants to kill a lot of people at an airport can have the airline essentially deliver the guns and the ammunition *to* them as if they were ordering a pizza?

His first question would be—*in office*, his first question *will* be—Is it Muslims?

His second question would be—*in office*, his second question *will* be—How can he exploit it to increase his power?

His last question would be—*in office*, his last question *will* be—How can we make sure this latest nightmare doesn't infringe upon the holy Second Amendment?

*

The Constitution, with *all* the amendments, is a patriotic 7,676 words long. 76-76. Two of its clauses mention an exact value in cash and merchandise. And the word "money" appears six times in the Constitution. And "coin" five times. There are ten references to taxes. Eight times you read "duty" or "duties." The word "debt" appears seven times. Four uses of the word "compensation." Two "imports." Two "exports."

And the rest of it, with the non-ownership parts stripped away—the *rest* of the United States Constitution and its amendments reads: *Profit, paid, Treasury, Emoluments, Revenue, Imposts, Excises, Imposts, Excises, credit, Commerce, Bankruptcies, Securities, Exclusive Right, purchased, Capitation, Commerce, Revenue, Treasury, Appropriations, Receipts, Expenditures, Profit, Emolument, Credit, gold, silver.*

Tender, Payment, Imposts, Imposts, Treasury, Profit, Emolument, Bribery, Lands, Grants, Forfeiture, fines, equity, payment, pensions, bounties, pay, obligation, obligations, incomes, manufacture, sale, pay, value, owner, Property, property . . . Private property.

*

Our Constitution . . . is a property document.

Our Constitution is about ownership. Those references just to dollars, money, coin, taxes, duties, debt, compensation, and other ownership? One hundred three of them, all told. In the Constitution, the words "vote," "votes," and "voting" appear only ... thirty-seven times. The words "right" and "rights" ... fifteen times.

Money and ownership: 103 times.

Our Constitution is, first and foremost, a property contract. What the *government* can own and must own and pay for; what the *people* can own and must own and pay for.

*

It is noble, and most of it has held up flawlessly since 1787, and in some places it is sublime. But it does *not* read like the Declaration of Independence. Its closest relative is the contract you sign when you buy a car.

So isn't it funny that in the Second Amendment, the second of all of them ever passed, the one about guns, it doesn't say anything ... about *owning* guns?

Dollars, money, coin, taxes, duties, debt, compensation, import, export, pay, value, owner, Property, property, Private property. A Constitution with as much fine print as a mortgage—a Constitution that mentions ten dollars, and twenty dollars—and yet there isn't *one* of those ownership or property or value *words* in the part about guns.

"A well regulated Militia, being necessary to the security of a free State, the right of the people to keep and bear Arms, shall not be infringed."

Which one of those words means "own"?

None of them.

Which words in the part stating that the Second Amendment is about the well-regulated militia in a free state—are unclear?

None of them.

The Second Amendment is there to keep *state militias* legal.

It does this by keeping legal the rights of private citizens to bear arms. For use in a militia. The Second Amendment guarantees the right to your state National Guard. Doesn't say a thing about prohibiting gun control.

The Second Amendment *is* gun control. It may say you can *bear* one. It may even say you can *keep* one, *in* your own home—if you're using it as part of a well-regulated militia. But it does not say you can *own* one, and if you don't *own* that gun you're keeping and bearing, necessarily somebody *else* does own it, and that somebody has got to be the government, and therefore the Constitution *starts* with the idea that the government controls the guns. All the guns.

And, by the way, the "arms" in the Second Amendment? Those are muskets. Not repeating rifles. Not machine guns. Not automatic killing devices. Saying that the Founding Fathers wanted to protect your right to own an assault rifle is as stupid as saying that they wanted to protect your right to own nuclear weapons.

And we have a history of government gun control that stretches back to the nineteenth century, back to when the musket began the process of evolving into an Uzi. The so-called Gunfight at the O.K. Corral, in Tombstone, Arizona, on October 26, 1881—the epitome of the Wild West—was about . . . gun control. To prevent gun terrorism, it was illegal to *carry a gun* in Tombstone. And the Clantons and the McLaurys were ignoring gun control, and the town marshals, the Earp brothers, were enforcing it.

*

But of course, what does that *matter*?

A man elected president dog-whistled throughout his campaign to the "Second Amendment people." He claims to carry a gun at all times. He is fighting to keep a private bodyguard instead of relying on the Secret Service.

His son, as reported last weekend in *The Washington Post,* is advocating for legislation to end the nine-month waiting period . . . for silencers on guns and rifles.

Oh, and the Second Amendment? This is settled law. The Supreme Court ruled in the *Heller* case, in 2008, that it doesn't matter if the words used are "keep and bear Arms" rather than "keep and *own* Arms" or "*own* and bear Arms."

Supreme Court!

"The Supreme Court is not the Supreme Being . . . While some cowardly politicians will wave the white flag and surrender to the false god of judicial supremacy, I refuse to light a match to our Constitution. We must resist and reject judicial tyranny, not retreat."

Former Arkansas governor and frequent presidential aspirant Mike Huckabee wrote that.

"We've had too many examples in recent years of courts and judges legislating. They're not interpreting what the law *says* and whether someone has violated it or not. In too many instances, they have been actually legislating by legal decree what they think the law should be, and that I don't go for."

Speaking? The fortieth president of the United States, Ronald Reagan. They said it. I didn't.

*

Oh, and one more quote about the Supreme Court and the Second Amendment, this one from *Parade* magazine in January 1990:

"The Gun Lobby's interpretation of the Second Amendment is one of the greatest pieces of fraud, I repeat the word fraud, on the American People by special interest groups that I have ever seen in my lifetime. The real purpose of the Second Amendment was to ensure that state armies—the militia—would be maintained for the defense of the state. The very language of the Second Amendment refutes any argument that it was intended to guarantee every citizen an unfettered right to any kind of weapon he or she desires."

The writer added, "The Second Amendment doesn't guarantee the right to have firearms at all."

Who wrote *that*?

Warren Burger, chief justice of the United States from 1969 until 1986. Appointed by Richard Nixon. Believed that homosexual behavior could be prohibited by law. Thought that sending a man to prison for life for writing a bad hundred-dollar check was just fine. Believed in a strict constructionist reading of the Constitution.

"The Second Amendment doesn't guarantee the right to have firearms at all," he said.

*

The excuses are: hunting, protection against governmental tyranny, and the rights of responsible gun owners.

Bluntly, if you need thirteen guns, or an automatic weapon of some kind, to kill any animal smaller than a kraken, you're no good at hunting. Take up another pastime.

And about protection against governmental tyranny. Ask the interned Japanese Americans of World War II how well that worked.

And "responsible gun owners." I'm sorry for them. But at this point, too many gun terrorists have committed too many gun massacres in this country. And these figures do not include the nearly 10 percent of all the presidents in our history who have been assassinated with guns, or the fifth who was wounded, or the sixth who was wounded while running for reelection, or seven others who survived significant assassination attempts—by guns. That's thirteen out of forty-four presidents. Nearly a third of them.

The BBC noted that on Christmas Day of 2015, we had twenty-seven non-suicide gun deaths in this country. For the entire *year* of 2015, England had . . . *twenty-four.*

"Responsible gun ownership?" *That* ship sailed long ago.

*

And Trump will, actively or passively, call it back to port.

To paraphrase Professor Laurens P. Hickok, of Western Reserve College, speaking of slavery a century and a half ago: The question now before the American citizens is no longer, alone, "Can the schools and public places be made free of the risk of gun massacres?" but "Are we free, or are we slaves under gun mob law?"

Mob law—in which the man seizing the power of the government dog-whistles to that mob, "Remember to bring your guns."

Or have the airline ship them for you.

ANSWER THE QUESTION, TRUMP

Post date • TUESDAY, JANUARY 17

"Thank you, Mr. President-elect. Can you stand here today, once and for all, and say that no one connected to you or your campaign had any contact with Russia leading up to or during the presidential campaign?"

The essential question.

The world-turning question.

The impeachment question.

And then the reporter . . . kept talking. "And if you do indeed believe that

Russia was behind the hacking, what is your message to Vladimir Putin right now?"

And the ball game was over.

Trump got to filibuster for 323 words about how Russia would respect America when he's "leading" and Hillary's reset button and the legal folder props and more of the poisoned word salad constantly being spun, tableside, in that addled mind of his.

And he never answered the question.

And his first news conference in six months . . . ended.

*

If the answer is yes, even in the slightest degree, his presidency is over before it has begun, although it will linger indefinitely as the Republicans continue to put power ahead of country or democracy or even independence as a nation.

And since Trump chose *not* to say whether anyone connected to him or his campaign had—as implied in the independent dossier—any contact with Russia leading up to or during the presidential campaign . . . we will have to answer it for him, by circumstantial evidence.

Michael Flynn, Trump's incoming national security adviser, former director of the Defense Intelligence Agency. Fired in 2014. Within months he was being paid to appear on a Kremlin-sponsored television network, and the next year he was paid to appear at the network's gala in Moscow and to sit next to . . . Vladimir Putin.

The New York Times reports that Flynn spoke to Russia's ambassador to this country this past December 28, the day before this country's sanctions against Russia for its hacking of the Democratic National Committee.

The Washington Post says Flynn and the ambassador spoke "several times" on the *twenty-ninth*.

The international news agency Reuters says they spoke *five* times.

There is a law in this country against individuals—even individuals who are soon to be part of a government—contradicting U.S. government foreign policy or dealing directly with enemy nations, and all we know about these calls is the Trump Gang's claim that Flynn was setting up another phone call for Trump with Vladimir Putin, and unfortunately the Trump Gang has been handing out lies in carload lots.

In December, three veteran intelligence professionals resigned from the Cambridge Intelligence Seminar, at Cambridge University in England, amid "concerns" that the seminar was funded, through intermediaries, by the Kremlin. One of its past speakers was ... Michael Flynn.

Also that month, Bloomberg News reported that Flynn had partnered with a technology company, one of whose chiefs was "once convicted of trying to sell stolen biotech material to the Russian KGB espionage agency."

And the head of Austria's far-right "Freedom Party"—founded in the 1950s by former Nazis—signed what he has described as a "cooperation agreement" ... with Vladimir Putin's political party. The Austrian said that a few weeks earlier he had met with Michael Flynn in New York.

*

And then there's Flynn's boss.

Separating the United States and Germany has been an avowed policy— perhaps the *foremost* foreign policy—of Russia since 1945.

In a joint interview with *The Times* of London and the German newspaper *Bild* over the weekend, Trump called NATO obsolete and said that German chancellor Angela Merkel had made a catastrophic mistake by letting in "illegals," and he threatened Germany with huge tariffs.

Meanwhile, a variety of sources report that the *Israelis* might not share intelligence with the Trump administration, after American intelligence said, in essence: Don't give them anything you don't want to see end up in the hands of Iran, via the Kremlin.

After the revelation of the Trump dossier last week, BuzzFeed News quoted two Israeli intelligence *officers* saying that their nation and at least one European country are separately investigating Trump's ties to—or compromised vulnerability to—Russia.

But—wait—you're not sure about BuzzFeed's reporting now, right?

Because they published the full Trump dossier, mistakes and false leads included, last week?

A question: If that dossier had been about Bill Clinton—lurid details and all—and Donald Trump had a copy of it, and Trump had read it aloud at his campaign rallies—who would have complained about all the networks *televising* those rallies live?

What news organizations refused to publish or broadcast Trump's wildest accusations, or the material he read from WikiLeaks? Who *waited* until it could prove they were all true?

Correct—none.

In our new world in which reporters seek facts and let the *truth* fall where it may, BuzzFeed was entirely right to publish the dossier.

*

Besides which, the key to the dossier is not the perversions and the pee jokes.

It's the money.

To quote the impeccable BBC reporter Paul Wood:

"Last April, the CIA director was shown intelligence that worried him. It was—allegedly—a tape recording of a conversation about money from the Kremlin going into the US presidential campaign."

This eventually led the Department of Justice to get a warrant from the FISA Court, last October.

"They wanted permission to intercept the electronic records from two Russian banks. . . .

"Ultimately, the investigation is looking for transfers of money from Russia to the United States, each one, if proved, a felony offence.

"A lawyer—outside the Department of Justice but familiar with the case— told me that three of Mr Trump's associates were the subject of the inquiry. 'But it's clear this is about Trump,' he said."

And Trump still defends Russia, or lumps it in with China, or just ignores the question.

*

There is a hawkish, Blue Dog Democrat, seven-term former California congresswoman, and ex–undersecretary of state named Ellen Tauscher. Seven years ago, she negotiated the New Strategic Arms Reduction Treaty with the Russians. On January 7, she summed this up on Twitter: "PEOTUS is either traitorously ignoring Russia hacks and provocations or simply naive and weak Com.-in Chief to be."

So, Mr. Trump, let us ask you once again.

Can you stand here today, once and for all, and say that no one connected to you or your campaign had any contact with Russia leading up to or during the presidential campaign?

And if you again choose not to answer . . .

Perhaps you should begin to formulate your answer . . . for the impeachment trial. Or the one for espionage.

PACKING THE COURT OF PUBLIC OPINION

Post date • WEDNESDAY, JANUARY 18

Trump's Banana Republicans have proposed that White House press briefings be moved out of the presidential mansion and held "next door" at the Old Executive Office Building, and why should you care for one damned minute?

Reince Priebus says it's a great thing, because the result would be "about quadrupling the amount of reporters that can cover the White House," and certainly that sounds like a wonderful intensification of the bright, shining light of a democratic free press on the operation of the commander in chief and his staff.

The more the better, right?

Just the way it works in Russia.

A giant crowd of reporters, screaming for the leader's attention, making *signs* indicating what organization they belong to, and even signs and props indicating what questions they intend to ask . . .

Some of them showing exactly the kind of objectivity and respectful skepticism a free press is supposed to bring to the coverage of government at its highest levels, and, yes, she's a self-described journalist *at* a Putin news conference holding a picture of Putin ripping off his shirt to indicate that he's actually Superman.

Just a few steps removed from the contestants trying to get emcee Monty Hall's attention during a taping of the old game show *Let's Make a Deal*.

Though I would never want to insult anybody in a comparison among Vladimir Putin, Donald Trump, and Monty Hall.

I have *respect* for Monty Hall.

*

Look, I don't know the last time anything at a White House news conference, or anything done by a White House *correspondent*, actually contributed anything measurable to the coverage of a president—not since Sam Donaldson used to make news by bellowing questions at Ronald Reagan and Reagan would condemn himself by refusing to answer.

I also think that if traditional journalism contributes in any way to the prevention of dictatorship here, it will be by grunt work: fact-checking the White House news conferences and revealing legislation and departmental orders and checking legalities and confronting an administration's lies with facts. The next Woodward and Bernstein will get there not at the news conferences but through their skill at filing Freedom of Information Act requests.

But the idea of "quadrupling the amount of reporters that can cover the White House" is a Trojan horse with a lot of Trojans in it.

First, there is the Putin-like spectacle. The bigger the room, the more room for staffers and hangers-on and, for want of a better term, Trump plants.

Trump gave this stunt away at last week's news conference. He packed the place with people applauding for him, and they have as much right to be at a presidential news conference as would people *booing* him, and that amount of people is: none.

Quadruple the number of so-called reporters at the news conferences and you have suddenly created another stop on the Trump perpetual campaign rally tour.

Quadruple the number of so-called reporters at the news conferences and you suddenly make it easier to ignore the reporters with actual questions—as opposed to the ones carrying signs showing Trump wearing a Superman shirt.

Quadruple the number of so-called reporters at the news conferences and you suddenly change from difficult to impossible any coordinated action to prevent Trump repeating the stunt he used in New York last week: singling out and attacking one reporter the way the bully picks one kid out of the crowd to beat up while the others say, "Thank goodness it wasn't me," and continue to participate in the farce.

The press corps should've walked out, then and there—but all that would've happened then would have been more questions from Trump staffers.

Quadruple the number of so-called reporters at the news conferences and you lose any sense of who is asking the questions and what their motivations are. You may abhor Fox News as Fox News viewers abhor me, but you don't have any doubts as to why we are asking *what* we are asking.

And you don't have any doubts about whether or not... we have been planted there.

*

It is, in retrospect, so absurd as to be almost unbelievable, and almost forgotten.

His name was Jeff Gannon—or so he said—and he represented something called Talon News, and on February 28, 2003, the Bush White House press office began issuing him day passes to its news conferences.

But then, on January 26, 2005, President Bush held his *own* news conference, and there was Gannon of Talon News, asking him about Senate Democratic leaders: "How are you going to work with people who seem to have divorced themselves from reality?"

Within two weeks the whole stunt had collapsed.

"Jeff Gannon" was actually James Guckert, and the closest thing he'd come to journalism before he began asking friendly questions at the White House was having his naked pictures appear on a series of gay escort websites.

Gannon shuttered his website. The White House never gave him another press credential. His "Talon News" organization tracked back to the owner of the website GOPUSA, and then the Talon site was shuttered. It was also later revealed, but never explained, how Gannon/Guckert had learned of an internal government memo about the outing of CIA operative Valerie Plame.

Just as this was playing out, federal records were revealed showing that the Bush administration had paid a man named Armstrong Williams $240,000. Williams had a syndicated newspaper column, and in exchange for the money, he was supposed to write positive articles about Bush's "No Child Left Behind" program—and to try to convince *other* African American journalists to do the same.

*

The Bush administration's attempt at media manipulation—including literally *buying* good coverage—was amateurish compared with what we can expect from Trump and his White House chief strategist, former campaign boss and head of the Breitbart Propaganda site, Steve Bannon.

Why was it that the Gannon and Williams scams didn't work?

They didn't work because they were too easy to spot in a crowd.

Solution: make the crowd bigger.

Move the White House press briefings next door and, as Reince Priebus says, you can quadruple "the amount of reporters that can cover the White House."

So what if you don't know if they're being paid to ask softball questions or to cheer, or just to serve as more useful idiots at a Trump rally? It's only the end of the First Amendment.

*

Oh, and by the way, the guy the Bushies paid for positive newspaper columns, Armstrong Williams? He's still around. He works with a Dr. Ben Carson, and when that nominee for secretary of housing endorsed Trump in March 2016, the endorsement was confirmed by . . . Armstrong Williams.

BOYCOTT THE INAUGURATION

Post date • **THURSDAY, JANUARY 19**

Boycott the inauguration.

It's very simple.

Don't go, don't watch, don't tweet, don't respond, don't spend money on it, don't spend one brain cell on it.

Depend upon this: if the Bible leaps from his touch or the authorities arrest him for violating the Logan Act, you'll hear about it. I'm headed for Los Angeles to be on Bill Maher's show inauguration night—we'll give you the info.

And if you're an elected Democratic official, under no circumstances attend—I don't want to hear about you working with him, unless you're working with him to move to the Caymans. I want to hear about your plans to impeach him or force him to resign.

An exception is offered to President Obama, though later, sir, you will regret having had anything to do with this man.

"I believe in forgiveness," Congressman John Lewis said. "I believe in trying to work with people. It's going to be hard. It's going to be very difficult: I don't see this president-elect as a legitimate president.

"I think the Russians participated in helping this man get elected and they helped destroy the candidacy of Hillary Clinton. I don't plan to attend the inauguration. It will be the first one that I'll miss since I've been in Congress.

"You cannot be at home with something that you feel is wrong.

"I think there was a conspiracy on the part of the Russians and others to help him get elected. That's not right, that's not fair. That's not the open democratic process."

Correct.

"To John Lewis, one of my heroes," wrote Nebraska senator Ben Sasse. "Please come to the Inauguration. It isn't about a man. It is a celebration of peaceful transfer of power."

Bullshit.

If you think, Senator, that handing over this country to the puppet of Vladimir Putin should be celebrated *and* should be a peaceful transfer of power, not only are you not loyal to this country, but you know nothing . . . about John Lewis.

If you *think*, Senator, that we will let you or anybody else *normalize* the transfer of power to a racist, psychotic Russian plant, perhaps you should look again at how heroes like John Lewis responded the last time the white supremacists of this country insisted that this was about power and that we must all accept its use—and its misuse—"peacefully."

"John Lewis once did very noble things," tweeted the editor of *The Wall Street Journal*'s Weekend Review, "but that shouldn't give him a pass for poor judgment now."

Irony. Poor judgment. A *Wall Street Journal* idiot invokes the language of apartheid. John Lewis—"we shouldn't give him a *pass*."

And of course:

"Congressman John Lewis should spend more time on fixing and helping his district, which is in horrible shape and falling apart (not to mention crime infested) rather than falsely complaining about the election results. All talk, talk, talk—no action or results. Sad!"

That's right: a hero who in the sixties literally put his skull where his mouth was, attacked by a clown who on a daily basis puts his *foot* where his mouth is.

If you ever needed evidence that Trump—not just some of his followers, not just some of his nominees—evidence that Trump was himself personally, always, and unchangeably racist and in tune with true white supremacy—he just confessed to it.

To racist scum like Trump, because Lewis is African American, his district *must* be in horrible shape and falling apart. In fact, his district contains Georgia Tech, Emory University, the busiest airport in the world, the Centers for Disease Control, and parts of the wealthy, 80-percent-white suburb of Buckhead, which likes to style itself as Beverly Hills East.

What a stupid, weak man Trump really is.

Bluntly, these tweets were written by a pig.

Boycott this pig's inauguration.

*

Actually . . . that's not fair.

Pigs are supposedly as intelligent as three-year-olds.

*

Lost in all this is that the true operative part of John Lewis's remarks is *not* his words about the Russian Conspiracy.

The Russian Conspiracy is obvious to everybody from this nation's true patriotic conservatives and Republicans to this nation's intelligence infrastructure to everybody but this crazy man Trump and his gullible supporters, even the smarter ones who are coming out of their trance and, according to the polls, beginning to understand that he has already fleeced them.

But that's not the key right this minute.

Nor is the key what Congressman Lewis said about Trump's illegitimacy. He is an illegitimate president; his name will someday appear with an asterisk, or it will be wiped from our history altogether.

No. *This* sentence is *the key.*

"You cannot be at home with something that you feel is wrong."

There's your rule.

Thank you again, John Lewis.

You do not open your door to the man, the thought, the act . . . that you know is *wrong*.

And you don't go to his home, to his speech, to his parade.

Happily, this message is getting across.

See this?

This is the Gallup poll on how Americans of all shapes, sizes, and parties are reacting to how Trump is handling the transition. And congratulations, Russia, he's now officially in the red . . . *51* percent disapproval, up from 48 percent disapproval the month before.

At this time in 2009, Obama—some of whose opponents believed he was the Antichrist—was at a disapproval of . . . *12* percent.

And Trump *got* to majority disapproval because of . . . the so-called independents who put us into this nightmare in the first place.

In December, *46 percent* of independents approved his handling of the transition.

Now? *33 percent.*

A quarter of his support among independents, gone in a month.

They have been seeing something with new eyes that the rest of us either concluded months or years ago or were standing too close to see.

They looked at the snot-nosed punk at the news conference, with the props, and the terrified woman from the winner of the Russian Law Firm of the Year award . . .

And they looked at those gratuitous, stupid, raving tweets about John Lewis on the weekend before Martin Luther King Day.

And maybe they saw a full-fledged racist, and maybe they didn't . . .

And maybe they saw a psychopath, and maybe they didn't.

And maybe they saw a Russian mole, and maybe they didn't.

But you know what they *didn't* see?

They didn't see . . . a president.

*

Boycott the inauguration.

KEYNOTE SPEECH TO MEETING OF DEMOCRACY MATTERS

Fort Lauderdale, FLORIDA

Post date • THURSDAY, JANUARY 19

Thank you.

Incidentally, when you come up here, you actually hear crickets. I just wanted to mention that before we start.

It is an honor to be here, it is an honor to see many old friends and to meet many new ones.

And now that my *affable* remarks are over, let me get down to the raw meat.

Let me begin with the worst-case scenario—or one of them, in any event. Imagine it is not January 19, 2017, but instead January 19, 2018. You and I are here, in these same circumstances, right here, and I repeat to you *then* what I am going to say to you *now*.

And as I finish, or earlier, or even as I begin, I am arrested. Or I am detained. Or I am put on a watch list. Or I am audited. Or I am denounced somewhere. Or I am who knows what happens to me. One year—and that is just an estimate; your punishment may vary. It could be two years from now, it could be two months from now, it could be tomorrow afternoon after the inauguration. And of course—if and when it happens—it will not be me alone. For the act of listening to me, you could be arrested. Or detained. Or who knows what.

I see some concern on some faces. "Political science fiction." "Hyperbole." "A paranoid dystopian view of January 19, 2018?" "A work of fiction." If, one year ago tonight, we had been here on January 19, 2016, and I had told you that in one year's time, a deranged, infantile, imbecilic, paranoid, sexist, racist, militaristic, fascist, perverted, vulgar, stupid, paper-thin-skinned man-baby would not merely be nominated for president by a major political party, in this country, but would swamp all of his rivals, including the brother and son of one former president, and if I then told you that, after unleashing all that is worst in America, he would be able to conjure the perfect electoral storm in the Electoral College to defeat, in the election, the wife of another president, who won 2,900,000 more popular votes than he did. And if I told you, further, that in one year's time, all we would be left asking here was not whether or not the Russians had tampered with our sacred election, but how *much* they had tampered with it—would you have called that political science fiction? Because I would have. And I like to think I'm smarter than I have turned out to have been on this.

So it's important—it's not happy, but it's important—to remember that we need to not assume that the nightmare ends in some way when Donald John Trump puts his hand on the Bible tomorrow and John Roberts says, "Do you solemnly swear that you will preserve, protect and defend the Constitution of the United States," and—presuming the Bible does not leap from his hand or spontaneously combust—Trump replies to this call of our history and our democracy by answering, "Whatevah." This is *not* the last scene of *The Manchurian Candidate*, nor *Seven Days in May*, nor *It Can't Happen Here*. There are countless possible nightmare scenarios ahead of all of us. We have seen some of them before, the last time we let the antiquated math of the Founders elect a Republican president in defiance of the will of the people.

We have seen a terrorist act and flames and collapses and ashes and pyres, and the immediate exploitation of that act by Republicans who demanded that we should do what they called "patriotic bipartisanship," which was in fact mono-partisanship, in which they were to make all the decisions and our role was to acquiesce to them or be branded disloyal. We know what they will do if the opportunity presents itself again. And we know, from a year of his lies and calumnies and gaslighting, and Orwell-grade perversions of light into dark and fiction into fact, that they are all now practiced and prepared and ready to create an opportunity if none presents itself—a phony threat that requires a curtailment of liberties. Some plot "he and he alone" could stop. And we must be prepared to call such a stunt exactly what it is, and to be patriots, and to wrap ourselves in the flag that we love, and shout from the hills why what has happened to this country—two months from now, six months from now, two years from now—why that has happened because there *is* a Donald John Trump.

And we know that this time they have tilted the playing field against us in advance in these areas: they have spent eight years delegitimizing a president, so that we might look foolish delegitimizing an actual illegitimate president. They have spent the length of a campaign refusing to promise to recognize a defeat, on the premise that it could have been obtained only by chicanery and dishonesty, so that we might look foolish refusing to honor a defeat that was actually obtained by actual chicanery and dishonesty. They have spent month after month insisting that the election, the media, the opinion polls, and now the polls about the transition are rigged and fixed, so that we might look foolish insisting that an election, the media, and the opinion polls are actually rigged and fixed. And we know that now we will and must play by rules that sicken us, against which our souls cry out. But we must. Our moral force, our moral high ground, our patriotic self-defense is simple. We did not seek any of these rules. We did not seek this battle. We did not seek this treachery. The rules, the battle, the treachery—are Trump's. We will fight him on his terms. And we will defeat him. And we will restore democracy.

And we will defeat Trump's Russian masters. Some of us have been warning since the beginning of the presidential campaign that Trump's connection and the connection of those around him to a dictator who has had the foresight to replace expensive, very complicated human war with the far more efficient cyberwar—invasion by remote control—we have noted that Trump's connection was not mere admiration, nor the perverted envy of a sick American monster gazing at a sick Russian monster. And we were right. The Russians did this. All we need to learn, and we will learn it, is how *much* they did. How many acts of war they directed against this country. How much they had on Trump. How much they expect him to deliver. How many of the mainstream Republicans will remain loyal not to the Constitution of the United States but to Vladimir Goddamned Putin!

*

I wish to quote three men and only three men tonight: Sidney A. Chayefsky, John Lewis, and, first, Winston Churchill. Churchill, speaking after what was, in his time, in his country, in his context, his Trump election. We know it in history as Munich. And from the wilderness of his Parliament, with a coalition government cheering itself deafeningly for having averted war, with the formal leadership of his nation shunning him and marginalizing him and giggling at him, when everybody roared how well they had done, Churchill began, in almost a whisper.

"Our loyal, brave people," Churchill said, "should know that we have sustained a defeat, without a war, the consequences of which will travel far with us along our road. . . . They should know that we have passed an awful milestone in our history"—and here I will briefly update Churchill's words, if I may make that offense—"when the whole equilibrium of the free world has been deranged, and that the terrible words have for the time being been pronounced against the American democracy: Thou art weighed in the balance and found wanting.

"And don't suppose," Churchill said, "that this is the end. This is only the beginning of the reckoning. This is only the first sip, the first foretaste of a bitter cup which will be proffered to us, year by year, unless, by a supreme recovery of moral health and martial vigor, we arise again and take our stand for freedom as in the olden time."

Churchill.

*

Tonight, in our country, which we all love in words and in ways that we cannot express—tonight is the end of the "olden time," in comparison to what Churchill said in 1938. Tonight is the night before the disaster. Tonight is the night that we will look back at, with some longing and some nostalgia. Tonight is the night to which the whole of our beings, and all of our priorities, and all of our efforts must now be focused, on getting our country back. Democracy, as we have known it, with the rules by which we have played, ends at noon. The fight—our fight—begins one second later.

*

And it begins—as you will hear this weekend—on a series of fronts.

The fight can begin in the media. You, everybody here, can confront anybody—reporter, anchor, spokesman, shill—who tries to publicly characterize all this as just some sort of political swing, as if it was not the seizure of power by the worst possible person to be found to serve as president, as if that person had not appointed the worst possible candidate to run each agency, as if Betsy DeVos was just some sort of an alternative to traditional education, when she is really an alternative to traditional education in the same way that stupidity is an alternative to traditional education. This weekend will show you ways to make this clear to the media, and it will introduce you to people whose job it will be to shine a constant, daily light on every broken promise, every shady nominee, every awful policy—and everything you can do to help directly.

The fight can also begin in the courts. Trump will come as close to privatizing the presidency as anybody in history, before sunset tomorrow, and whether he believes it or not, much of what he will try to do is actually illegal, and there are still laws, and this weekend will show you ways to pursue him and to have at the head of this fight—a cliché—Justice with her Shining Sword.

Or you can look at it more practically. Trump is coming for your money. You might as well spend some of it to prevent him taking *all* of your money.

And the fight certainly begins with a state of mind.

More than nine years ago, I ran into John Kerry in line to pick up World Series tickets at Fenway Park, in Boston. And as we came past each other, he congratulated me and he said thanks to me, and I said, "You're welcome—for what, by the way?" He said, "It was you who decided to run headfirst into the brick wall of the Bush administration. You said the terror color-code system was uncomfortably in sync with Bush's political needs. And then you said, 'I think they may be doing this,' just enough of that wall fell down, and the rest of us could storm through and start talking about it, and that's what turned around the 2006 midterms." And I said, "I doubt it, but I will defer to you, Senator." So never think, no matter what has happened in the last few months, that you individually don't matter. Or that an opportunity for you to prevail will not arise. Or that your state of mind does not matter. Or that even an act of symbolism by you doesn't matter.

To that point: John Lewis. I will contend that something he did on January 13, 2017, was just as important, or nearly so, and certainly just as dangerous, and will in the end prove just as saving and redemptive as was his agony on the Edmund Pettus Bridge. As you know, Congressman Lewis was asked if he planned to try to forge a relationship with Trump. And he said: "I believe in forgiveness. I believe in trying to work with people. It's going to be hard. It's going to be very difficult: I don't see the president-elect as a legitimate president. I think the Russians participated in helping this man get elected, and they helped destroy the candidacy of Hillary Clinton. I don't plan to attend the inauguration. You cannot be at home with something that you feel is wrong."

The questioner was stunned. "That's going to send a big message," my friend Chuck Todd said, "to a lot of people in this country that you don't believe he's a legitimate president."

And John Lewis—as always—would not back down, would not equivocate, would not protect himself. "I think it was a conspiracy on the part of the

Russians and others to help him get elected. That's not right, that's not fair. That's not the open democratic process." And John Lewis, in thirty seconds, moved "legitimacy" center stage. In the week since he said that, more than sixty elected Democrats have followed him. It should have been all of them. John Lewis leads us yet again—and there is the organizing principle of resistance.

It is simple: As hard as it may be to believe and to put into proper historical context, and just because none of us have seen it before, does not mean it cannot be true. It is simple: this is not a legitimate president. This *was* a conspiracy involving, to a great or small degree, another country! This is not the open democratic process. And you, as John Lewis said perfectly, cannot be at home with something that you feel is wrong.

Every day, we bring up Russia.

Every day, we shout Russia!

Every day, we SCREAM Russia!

Never do we speak this man's name without invoking what Churchill called the defeat without a war. Never do we criticize or discuss or analyze his actions—or those of his White House, filled with the crew of a pirate ship—without reminding everyone that the Russians put him there and that the Republicans who enable him to stay there are passively collaborating with a foreign enemy of the United States of America. At the other end of the extreme in terms of simplicity versus complexity: Never, ever do we refer to Donald Trump as "President." He is "Trump." Certainly that is sufficient, and accurate. And it is also easier for when it is time for us to *erase his name from history*. For now—we will erase what's left of his legitimacy. "I don't see the president-elect as a legitimate president," John Lewis said. "You cannot be at home with something that you feel is wrong," John Lewis said. Wise words stand the test of time, and the test of struggle, and these words from John Lewis are wise.

This weekend will be devoted to many means, practical and philosophical, with which we can fight this nightmare, on the terms the Republicans and their coalition partners the American fascists and the neo-Nazis have chosen. And to consider the first of the Republican hammers, which we can grab from their hands and which we can then use to chase them to hell, this weekend will be devoted to many means, practical and philosophical, with which we can resist Trump, reproach Trump, and ultimately "repeal and replace" Trump. Already we see the outlines of this: the boycott against the Breitbart advertisers was a spectacular success. It can easily be repeated, and it's fun for the entire family.

There are other media inroads to make: my *GQ* series just crossed 100 million views. A network—I don't know if this is a pipe dream of mine—that is largely liberal in its orientation, that I could speak to you from every night, would be a nice thing to have, but I don't know if we could ever see that. Why does it sound so vaguely familiar? But practically, again, with or without networks, we now know we are under no obligation to be nice, or cooperative, or Vichy, or bipartisan—that we can fight just as dirty and just as viciously, and we will beat them at their own game, because, as I have observed many times in my commentaries, democracy has survived not so much through the efforts of those who would protect it, as because of the stupidity of those who would destroy it—and this time the side that would destroy it includes Rudy Giuliani. We know the 2018 midterms must be fought on a wedge issue: "You, Congressman Rohrabacher; you, Congressman Chaffetz; you, Congressman Ryan—do you believe in democracy, or do you support Russia and Generalissimo Francisco Trump?" (You can tone it down as the circumstances warrant, district by district.)

We also know those midterms are of an importance that cannot be overstated, because while the Republicans may realize, sooner or later, maybe by this time tomorrow night, that they themselves may have to impeach Trump, or more likely use the Twenty-fifth Amendment on him because he's crazy, we must take no chances—we must have a Democratic Congress to impeach him two years from tonight. And we know that in the interim we must adopt the fighting style of Muhammad Ali. Yes, they will hit us. Yes, it will hurt. It has already begun to hurt. But each time they come in to land a blow—hit them back. As Richard Pryor phrased it, voicing Ali's inner dialogue during a fight, "Boom—and there you go, you take that with you." And we know that, yes, that means that Trump, the man-baby, the Stay Puft Marshmallow Man whose psychosis can be inflamed by trolling him on Twitter, must hear the words and phrases *weak, soft, lost the popular vote, no mandate, Russia, Putin, Assange, disloyal, treachery, videotape* every time he turns around. And we know that, yes, that means we shall actually have to learn from what we watched them do to Barack Obama.

So never again should Trump, or this Russian operative guy of his, Michael Flynn, or the native of the country of Exxon, Mr. Tillerson, or Kellyanne Con

Job, or any of them—never again will they get to speak in public without some-body rising and yelling, not necessarily rudely, to interrupt them, although you can do that if you want, but somebody rising somewhere when they say these things and respond with every fiber in their being—before, during, or after they speak—"You lie!" And yes, we know that nothing has ever changed for the good in the history of man without men and women rising up and saying—whether they whisper or yell—but starting by saying "This is *wrong!*"

However: behind all of this, behind every strategy, behind every plan made this weekend, behind everything we can do and everything we must do—to re-store our bloodied democracy, there must be one emotion with which our side of the political pendulum is seldom associated. This emotion must now in some ways become our animating principle. And about that animating princi-ple (and penultimately in my remarks), having already quoted Churchill and Lewis, I want to now quote—again with revisions, permissible I hope—Sidney Chayefsky. You may know him by his nickname, "Paddy," or you may know the name of the character he wrote for the movie *Network*, a Mr. Beale:

I don't have to tell you things are bad. Everybody knows things are bad. It's a coup d'etat. Everybody's out of hope or scared of losing their freedom.

Foreign governments buy influence at the White House, businesses are terrified of a Twitter account, shopkeepers keep a Klan hood under the counter, white supremacists are running wild in the street, and there's nobody anywhere who seems to know what to do—and there's no end to it! We know Trump is unfit to pass a sanity test and his enablers are unfit to lead. And we sit watching our TVs while some local news-caster tells us that today we had fifteen attacks on Obamacare and sixty-three racist bills, as if that's the way it's supposed to be.

We all know things are bad—worse than bad. They're crazy. It's like everything everywhere has gone crazy, so we don't go out anymore. We sit in the house, and slowly the world we're living in is getting smaller, and all we say is "Please, at least leave us alone in our living rooms. Let me have my steady income and my sanctuary cities and my warm Obama memories and I won't say anything. Just leave us alone." Well, I'm not go-ing to leave you alone. I want you to get mad. I want you to protest. I want you to write. I want you to call a Republican congressman, because we all know exactly what you should say to him. I know what to do about the depression and the inflation and the Russians and the corporate graft in the street. And I know that first you've got to get mad. You've got to say: "I'm an American citizen, goddammit! My! Democracy! Has! Value!"

So...

The rest of it—about going to the window, opening it, and sticking your head out and yelling—the rest of it you know. But to keep you motivated, and to keep you mad, and to keep you unwilling to take it anymore, as Howard Beale said, let me close by noting one overarching fact that has occasionally gotten lost since November 8, and that is the essence of everything, to my mind. Even with this nightmare that comes at sunrise. And even with the temporary end of much of our democratic experience in this country. Even with a gold dollar sign spray-painted on every American flag and spit on the grave of every patriot. Even with the confluence of Comey and the Russians and the lies and the greatest grifter in the history of this country. Even with the worst possible outcome that all that could produce. Even with the greatest possible grief. No matter what we have to face. No matter what we have to do. No matter how long the trip back is from tomorrow. Remember—and take strength from—and remind all those who forget—and remind all those who *deny*—and remind all those who lie—remember one thing.

We are the majority!

ANOTHER MESSAGE TO HIS SUPPORTERS— IT'S TIME FOR TRUMP TO RESIGN

Post date • MONDAY, JANUARY 23

It's time for Donald Trump to resign as president.

Admittedly, it's been an interesting couple of days.

But for any patriotic American capable of adding two and two and not getting one and a half million, this is enough.

If you voted for Trump or you support him now or are saying, "Give him a chance"—again, I'm not going to yell at you or call you names. I'm not going to try to argue policies. I'm not going to debate the size of his crowds, nor your conclusions about Saturday's marches. In fact, I'm going to compliment you on your generosity toward him, and the sincerity of your belief in his promises, and your natural and commendable desire to see him—and thus our country—succeed.

But this man is not of sound mind.

In office, faster and more frighteningly than at any point in the campaign—over the span of just a long weekend, really—Trump has proved that not only will he lie to America about anything big or small, but that, just as important, he will lie to *himself* about anything big or small. And more troubling yet, he will compel men weaker even than himself to lie on his behalf about anything big or small.

And worst of all, the lies *will* convince some people, and they will convince one especially dangerous person in particular: himself.

Because what Trump does not believe cannot be true.

And this way lies madness, and every evil imaginable, including the end of this country, in a literal sense—and perhaps the end of civilization, because, like somebody strung out on drugs or somebody living in a complete dreamlike state caused by profound, pulsating narcissism, he will *not* believe that the outcome of any of his actions could be failure or disaster or even something that could be harmful to *himself.*

A man who could accuse the Central Intelligence Agency of trying to undermine him and ask rhetorically of the conduct of that agency, "Are we living in Nazi Germany?" . . . a man who could do that and then, ten days later, go and stand in front of the shrine of its fallen agents and insist, with a straight face, with every word he said and motion he made suggesting he really believes this: "They sort of made it sound like I had a feud with the intelligence community. And I just want to let you know, the reason you're the number-one stop is exactly the opposite—exactly."

A man who could insist—to those same men and women at the CIA—that it got sunny the moment he started to give his inaugural address, when *you saw* the rain falling on him . . .

That is the kind of man who could convince himself that it would be fine to start a nuclear war, because *of course* he would survive the retaliatory attack, and so would his family, and so would whatever people he thinks are his friends—or, to use his word, his "fans"—*of course* they would all survive the retaliatory attack . . . because *he's* Donald Trump, and bad things cannot happen to Donald Trump.

*

At the CIA, Trump told the agents there that he has "a running war with the media."

He does *not* have a running war with the media.

He has a running war with *reality*.

His reality is what he says it is.

He has an adviser who came out and said Sunday that the opposites of factual truths aren't lies or deceptions but, quoting her, "alternative facts."

You try "alternative facts" in your life, for one hour.

Drive on whichever side of the road you want to. Stop wearing the safety glasses. Let the kids use the stove and the power tools. Write checks against money you don't have. Because ignoring the warnings and instructions isn't courting disaster—it's just a set of "alternative facts."

This is . . . crazy.

And even if—God willing—it never gets to the point where this kind of delusional thinking is employed during an international crisis, or here at home during some kind of threat or disaster—even if Trump's ability to turn off reality like a light switch never actually threatens us and our children and all we know . . .

What does it mean about the key promise that he made to you?

To unrig the system?

To level the playing field?

To defeat the candidate from Goldman Sachs?

Like he promised.

Like he *seemed* to promise.

Before he hired three people *from* Goldman Sachs and one from Wells Fargo and one from Rothschild Investments.

*

You *knew* this before that speech at the CIA or this crazy argument about how big the crowds at his inauguration were, or whether it was sunny and only *he* could *see* that it was sunny.

You may have *even* known this before you voted for him, and just hoped it was going to go away when he took over.

But it isn't going away.

It's getting worse.

He's. Crazy!

We will all be lucky to survive having had him in charge.

Even if we *do* survive, it will still be the greatest crisis of our lives. *All* our lives.

*

Look—I don't want a President Pence.

But I'll take him. And his policies. And I'll fight the policies. But the man? We can debate that in 2020. In the election. This isn't about policies or conservative or liberal or rigged systems or marches or making America great again.

This is about a man not in his right mind . . . who has nuclear weapons.

It *is* the greatest crisis of our lives, right now.

But together we can fix it, peacefully.

He just has to resign, or, if he won't, there are provisions for the Republicans to remove him because he is so sick.

We can fix it.

And then we can sleep at night again.

And you and I can go back to yelling at each other and enjoying ourselves again.

Thank you for listening.

THE MEDIA IS GOING TO HAVE TO RETHINK ITS RELATIONSHIP WITH TRUMP HERE

Post date • WEDNESDAY, JANUARY 25

Kellyanne Con Job says if the media continues to call the press secretary's lies "lies"—and, by extension, if it continues to call the *president's* lies "lies"— "we're going to have to rethink our relationship here."

Fine.

Do not *interview* Kellyanne Con Job.

*

Press Secretary Spicer comes out for what is allegedly a White House press briefing and shouts a bitter, angry statement at the media, then refuses to take questions?

Stop carrying his press briefings live on *television*.

*

Trump says the media "are among the most dishonest human beings on earth, right?"

Stop covering his speeches live.

Use a delay, employ a team of fact-checkers, play his rants, and each time he lies, stop the tape and state the facts. Resume the tape, wait for the next lie, stop the tape again, state the facts again.

*

Do not participate in Trump's propaganda game.

And do not reply that you are obligated to, because otherwise you could be accused of delegitimizing the presidency.

It is impossible to "delegitimize" something that was never legitimate in the first place.

And do not reply that you must cover these liars because of the marketplace of ideas, or because of commercial competition. In short order, nobody who *believes* Trump or Conway or Spicer or any of the other gangsters will be watching ABC, CBS, NBC, CNN, BBC, MSNBC, C-SPAN, or anything similar anyway.

*

In a time when democracy is being rapidly sabotaged by a lunatic president and his amoral flying monkeys, like Conway and Spicer, your market—and, incidentally, your *obligation* as citizens *in* that bleeding democracy—your market *and* your obligation are identical: to identify the lies and refute them, twice as often as they are told.

The hard-core Trump crowd—the fascists, corporatists, racists, and authoritarians—they are going to watch Fox News and read Breitbart and watch and read the new ones, Worse-Than-Fox and Worse-Than-Breitbart, that are going to pop up in the weeks to come, and there isn't eff-all you can do about it.

This was the exact scenario in the bygone days when George W. Bush was still widely believed about Iraq and *every* television news operation decided it was going to wave the flag just like Fox News—or try to outdo Fox; one of them put Michael Savage on TV!—and every one of them got smoked in the ratings, and then some guy at MSNBC said, "The emperor is not *wearing* any clothes," and all of a sudden the truth started pouring out and the hundreds of millions of dollars of profit started pouring *in*.

The danger to the society of for-profit journalism, especially in television, has been evident ever since the FCC equal-time rule—and, more important, the community-service provision—were repealed. *That* was when you could begin to say as much as you wanted on TV or radio, about any controversial topic, without ever being obligated to offer Floyd R. Turbo two minutes of airtime to give an editorial reply.

But the *blessing* to the society of for-profit journalism, especially in television, has been evident ever since the backlash against Bush a decade ago. Being state-run television is profitable. Being *anti*-state-run television is *nearly* as profitable.

To paraphrase the immortal Bill Hicks: The Gaslight Channel? Oh, they're going for that Gaslight marketing dollar. That's a good market. They're very smart . . . Wait . . . the *Anti*-Gaslight Channel? "Ooh, you know what Keith's doing now? He's going for the righteous-indignation dollar. That's a big dollar. A lot of people are feeling that indignation. We've done research—huge market. He's doing a good thing."

*

It would take a conscious—and conscientious—decision to leave those news consumers who believe an administration elected on, built on, and trading on nothing but lies.

But it is also *practice* for a worse time.

The previous Republican administration exploited a terrorist attack. It took the natural tendency of liberals at times of crisis to put aside party divisions and the natural tendency of conservatives at times of crisis to exacerbate them, and then multiplied it by their Fox-led Republican media echo chamber, and they insisted on something they branded "patriotic bipartisanship" but which was in fact *mono*-partisanship in which *they* were to make all the decisions and the role of Democrats was to acquiesce to them or be branded disloyal—and if they are given or they fabricate another such crisis, they will play the same card. You know, something, to quote Trump, that "I alone can fix."

Thus, now and especially later, there must be channels and sites and newspapers that devote huge swaths of their resources to blasting back the truth, toward the Trump Lies Factory. It must report the lies about health care, the release of tax returns, the inevitable attempts to use the mighty mechanisms of government against Trump's critics. It must report the *truths* about broken promises to release tax returns, and falsified government statistics, and passive-aggressive influence peddling.

It must learn, and it *will* learn, how *much* the Russians swung the election, even if it takes four years to learn it. And: how *many* acts of war the Russians directed against us and how *much* they had on Trump and how *much* they expect him to deliver and how *many* of the mainstream Republicans will remain loyal not to the Constitution of the United States but to Vladimir Goddamned Putin!

And until all that is found out, it can simply report all day—every day—that the investigation is still ongoing. Exactly the way Fox News spent nearly three years—all day, every day—insisting that Obama's birth certificate was an open question.

*

Those who own the news media—especially in television—are timid types and by nature conservative . . . *until* being either threatens their investments. Well, fellas, Trump has decided to *destroy* your investments. If you tell the absolute truth, he will try to bury you. If you tell his version and give airtime to his supporters but you also have others there to fact-check him . . . he will *still* try to bury you.

Appeasement will produce what appeasement always produces: the victims' wasting the resources and time that they *should* have used defending themselves.

The good news for the news media is, in fact, this little garage-band kinda series right here.

As of this one, we will have done sixty-five commentaries under the banner of either *The Closer* or *The Resistance*, and as of number sixty-three, last week, we had crossed the threshold of a hundred million views. That's a minimum of around 1.6 million views per commentary. And 1.6 million views of anything suggests there is a ready audience for the product in question, whether it's anti-Trump politics or learning how to tie your shoes; an average audience of 1.6 million is larger than the average audience at CNN or MSNBC.

So remember that thing before the election? "Trump TV"?

Well, it is now time for Anti-Trump TV.

It'll make somebody at least half a billion dollars in profits in the next four years—if he lasts four years.

And, yeah, oh, by the way, it also might be one of the few chances we have to stop the United States of America from descending fully into fascism.

*

You know. In case that still *matters* to anybody.

THE APOLOGY

Post date • MONDAY, JANUARY 30

To the people of Syria and Iraq...

And France and Germany...

And Mexico and Canada and...the world...

Permit me to apologize, on behalf of the citizens of the United States of America, for the unforgivable actions of the man who has assumed power here.

I speak for those of us who—unlike Trump, unlike the sycophants who surround him, unlike the hate-filled souls and conscience-optional bigots who applaud him, unlike the Russian puppeteers who manipulate him—I speak for those of us who have not forgotten and will not forget that *we* are the descendants of the immigrants—often the refugees. *We* are the modern equivalents of those whom this pig Trump has just banished and degraded and, in many cases, likely literally sentenced to death.

Our greatness and, more important, our goodness have, since the cliché of the arrival at Plymouth Rock, stemmed entirely from people who came here from elsewhere. The only true "natives" of this continent have been the victims of persecution and marginalization and genocide. If this gargoyle Trump really believed in "America First," he would lead the deportation of those who brutally stole these lands from their rightful inhabitants.

Indeed, if there is anything this country can offer as mitigating evidence against our original sin, it is that the land our forefathers invaded became a place of freedom, a destination for those who literally had no other place to turn. We became great and greater and greatest because to these shores came a world of brave men and women who could not be *certain* it would be better here but who knew it could not be worse than where they were.

They gained a sanctuary, and *we* gained their courage and their dedication and their hard work, and their belief that if life would not be better for them, it *would* be better for their children. In us, in this place, they saw the light of the world. And because of *them* . . . we *became* that light.

And now Trump . . . has extinguished it.

He has extinguished the light of the world not because it was necessary, not because it was protective—because it will indeed prove the opposite—but because many of those who support him cried out for scapegoats, and for people to hate because they believe a different religion, and for people to blame because they look different. And he, without conscience, soul, morality . . . he saw in their hate—his power.

He has extinguished the light of the world not because he wanted to prevent terrorism, nor reduce the flow of would-be terrorists, but because the political currency of twenty-first-century America is making the gullible afraid. Of convincing them that a foreigner lurks around every corner, when the risk of death to Americans is other Americans who have guns. Period.

The seven countries to whose residents visas will not be issued are Iraq, Iran, Libya, Somalia, Sudan, Syria, and Yemen. From data researched by the libertarian think tank the Cato Institute: the number of Americans killed in terrorism on American soil by people from those countries from 1975 through 2016 was . . . none.

The countries of the Middle East against which Trump did *not* act include the home nations of all the 9/11 hijackers, and those of the San Bernardino attackers—Pakistan and the United States—and, most cynically of all, those countries in which Trump has business dealings.

*

None of Donald Trump's grandparents were born in this country. Virtually none of his supporters who style themselves as "real Americans" are *not* the descendants of immigrants or refugees. The nation they know, the things here that have given them life—all of this has been built, entirely, by the children and grandchildren of exactly the kind of people whose banishment and punishment they now cheer.

My great-great-grandfather was a blacksmith, and he came here from Hamburg, Germany, and became a naturalized American citizen in 1854.

Donald Trump's grandfather was a scared teenager, and he came here from Bremen, Germany—sixty miles from Hamburg—in 1885.

Trump's grandfather was born with the name Friedrich and, once here, changed it to Frederick.

My great-great-grandfather was born with the name . . . Friedrich, and, once here, he changed it to Frederick.

A hundred twenty-five years after Frederick Olbermann got here, I became the first of his direct descendants to be able to afford to go to and graduate from college, and this is with me daily, and *I* consider myself the *child* of immigrants, and my eyes well with prideful tears that transcend time when I think of his sacrifices and efforts and the abuse he *bore* and the fact that *I* got to enjoy the fruits of his struggle.

A hundred thirty-two years after Frederick *Trump* got here, his grandson betrayed him. Friday, he changed the law in such a way that today, his own grandfather would not have been certain to get a visa waiver to get into this country.

And even *if* Frederick Trump had gotten here, and gotten a green card, he might not have been safe. For his own grandson—and his chief of staff, the *son* of a woman from Sudan—went after the green-card holders, *locked out* legal residents of this country, in what may very well be interpreted as the early, passive-aggressive stage of ethnic cleansing.

And *this* Trump also betrayed every other immigrant, and every other refugee, and every other man or woman the world over who looked to us then—or who looks to us now—and believed we *were* who we said we were.

I'm sorry.

Not like the brazen giant of Greek fame,
With conquering limbs astride from land to land;
Here at our sea-washed, sunset gates shall stand
A mighty woman with a torch, whose flame
Is the imprisoned lightning, and her name:
Mother of Exiles.
From her beacon-hand
Glows world-wide welcome; her mild eyes command
The air-bridged harbor that twin cities frame.
"Keep, ancient lands, your storied pomp!" cries she
With silent lips.
"Give me your tired, your poor,
Your huddled masses yearning to breathe free,
The wretched refuse of your teeming shore.
Send these, the homeless, tempest-tost to me,
I lift my lamp beside the golden door!"

*

Donald Trump has branded himself a traitor to everything this country has ever stood for.

We have already acted against him in the streets, and in the courts.

We will remove him.

We will welcome you again.

We will even again let you think that *you* are getting more from us, even though history proves, in generation after generation, with nationality after nationality, that it is *us* who are getting everything *from you.*

And until that day . . .

We, the citizens of the United States, beg your forgiveness.

Chapter 7

FEBRUARY 2017

TRUMP HAS NOW AIDED ISIS

Post date • WEDNESDAY, FEBRUARY 1

The first—perhaps the only—international organization of any kind to congratulate Trump on his Muslim-ban-in-sheep's-clothing was . . . the so-called Islamic State. ISIS. The terrorists.

It sent him no bouquets. It issued no press releases.

It didn't have to.

It has been celebrating him—and this plan, which will almost certainly instigate the deaths of American citizens—since the night of the election.

It—unlike so many of us—believed he would do what he said he would do.

And they could not be happier.

From BuzzFeed News:

"ISIS also sees Trump as an ideal enemy for propaganda purposes, the former and current members of the group said, believing that his campaign's heated rhetoric about Muslims will help the extremist group with recruitment by reinforcing its central narrative that America and the West are at war with Islam."

Of course.

Trump has just done the Islamic State's work *for* it.

What better recruitment tool could there be?

What better instigation to homegrown terrorists throughout the world to rise could there be?

What better confirmation of all the terrorists' insane immoral rationalizations for their blood lust could there be?

The United States of America, invoking exactly the kind of action that the Islamic State always said it would. Banning refugees because they are Muslim. Banning immigrants because they are Muslim. Banning those who live here with green cards—traveling outside the country—from returning because they are Muslim. Banning some British citizens because they are Muslim. And some French. And some German. And some Canadian.

An intelligent ten-year-old could tell you, could tell Trump, that what he enacted last Friday—criticized by John McCain and Lindsey Graham as a recruitment tool for terrorists; criticized by the organization of the infamous Koch Brothers as "the wrong approach"—*an intelligent ten-year-old could tell you* that the *last* thing the new Banana Republican government of the United States would want to do if it *wanted* to prevent radical Islamic terrorism would be to ban Muslims simply because they *are* Muslims.

*

Since it was, in fact, the *first* thing the new Banana Republican government of the United States *did* do . . . logic and simple common sense offer only two possible explanations.

Since it is the greatest possible gift to ISIS for recruitment, for confirmation, for rationalization, for instigating terrorist acts, here in America, it must either be that Trump does not understand what will almost inevitably follow . . . or that he *does* understand what will almost inevitably follow.

Let us put aside Trump's lunacy and stupidity for a moment and address the idea that the most obvious thing in the world is obvious *even* to Trump: that a Muslim ban will result in ISIS-inspired terrorism in the West. In—perhaps—this country.

Why would an American want that?

Not an American *president*—why would *any* American deliberately do anything to give terrorists a rationalization to commit terrorism *in* America?

*

We need only look to what happened the last time a Republican presidential administration and the Republican Party were confronted by large-scale terrorism here, in 2001.

For a time, that administration grieved, and that party was solemn. And that administration was somber, and that party promised unity. And both called for bipartisanship.

And within a year, the Republicans were using 9/11 as a phony pretext for war in Iraq. And for bullying dissenters. And for creating an extra level of bureaucracy with the Germanic-sounding invocation of the "Homeland."

And running political television advertisements against an incumbent Democratic senator—a triple-amputee Vietnam War vet named Max Cleland—that used images of Saddam Hussein and Osama bin Laden.

And outing a CIA operative because her ambassador husband wouldn't back up their lies at the United Nations. And manipulating the terror alert color-code warnings—and even the first Homeland Security secretary, Tom Ridge, later admitted this is how he read it—when political fortunes turned against them and toward the Democrats.

What was all that *for*?

Was it to make this country safer?

Or was it simply to make Republican possession of the *White House*...safer?

Is there anybody left who really thinks it was the former and not the latter?

*

It is instructive that one of the most chilling figures from the Bush administration, the vice president, Dick Cheney, condemned a Muslim ban within hours of Trump's first proposing it, in December 2015. It goes, Cheney said, "against everything we stand for and believe in."

Even Cheney understood it. *While* arguing for stronger vetting of refugees and immigrants. Still: Even. Cheney. Understood. It.

*

Trump and the anti-American louts around him, like Propaganda Barbie Conway and the Holocaust deniers and diminishers Bannon and Priebus, and the spineless, silent, power-mad Republicans enabling him, like Paul Ryan, either do *not* understand the implications, the *instigations*, of what they've now done—either do *not* see how ISIS can exploit this—or *do* understand the implications and instigations and the ISIS exploitation.

It must be the one thing or the other!

If it is the former—if none of them understands that Trump has made this country seem as evil as ISIS tells its cult members we are—then none of them has the minimum intelligence required to vote, let alone to lead a great nation.

But if it is the latter, and they *do* see the instigation for what it is, then they are *prepared* for that outcome. Terrorism, somewhere, blamed upon . . . Trump.

Now, why would they choose *that*?

Why would you take an action that itself forces you to take a second action of preparing for a terrorist attack?

*

When large-scale terrorism last presented itself, the last Republican administration exploited the horror, began to play with the fear of 285 million Americans, to try to consolidate its power here permanently.

What would *Trump* be willing to do—Trump, with less of a guiding moral force or understanding of the value of each human life than even Dick Cheney has—how far would Donald Trump be willing to go to get the opportunity to exploit the kind of immediate, genuine, heartrending, tangible fear and sorrow that smothered this nation in 2001?

How far would he be willing to go, to be able to go to war somewhere?

How far would he be willing to go, to be able to blame Democrats for lack of preparedness?

How far would he be willing to go, to be able to say, "I alone was right about terror and Muslims and banning them"?

How far would he be willing to go, to blame the judges who opposed his illegal order?

How far would he be willing to go, to begin pushing back against freedom of the press?

How far would he be willing to go, to begin denouncing critics as terrorist sympathizers?

How far would he be willing to go, to begin to make dissent and protest illegal or impossible?

How far would he be willing to go, to begin to make his reelection in 2020 seemingly guaranteed?

*

And as you ask yourself those questions, ask yourself one more.
How many of those things . . . has he *already* . . . started to do?

THE TOP FIFTY CRAZY AND/OR IMPEACHABLE THINGS DONE BY TRUMP SINCE THE INAUGURATION

Post date • MONDAY, FEBRUARY 6

There have been countless crazy and/or impeachable things done by Donald Trump—or in his name—since the inauguration.

These are *just* the top fifty.

Here they are, as fast as I can blow through them:

*

January 20:

Bounds into the White House, leaving the First Lady standing alone by the car.

Lies at an inaugural ball that the crowd extended to the Washington Monument.

*

January 21:

Goes to speak at the CIA Memorial Wall, bringing his own staff with him to applaud him.

Claims he holds the record for most *Time* magazine covers. He actually has eleven. Richard Nixon: fifty-five.

Claims that at the inauguration it stopped raining as he started to speak, when in fact it *started* raining as he started to speak.

Has his press secretary—a Melissa McCarthy character—shout a lie to reporters: "This was the largest audience to ever witness an inauguration—*period.*"

*

January 22:

Implies that none of the Women's March participants had voted.

After repeatedly promising that he would release his tax returns after an audit was complete, Kellyanne Conway—Propaganda Barbie—says, "He's not going to release his tax returns."

*

January 23:

Tells congressional leaders he would've won the popular vote if it hadn't been for three to five million illegal votes.

Places on the national security staff the man who added the infamous "sixteen words" to George W. Bush's 2003 State of the Union address.

*

January 24:

Tweets a panoramic photo of the inauguration as evidence of his crowd-size claims. Doesn't notice photo is dated January *21*—the day *after* the inauguration.

Claims "carnage" in Chicago, threatens to send in "the Feds" without saying if he means the military or Eliot Ness and the Untouchables.

*

January 25:

Makes up story about two people being murdered during Obama's Chicago farewell speech.

Threatens to cut off federal funds to sanctuary cities.

Demands investigation into nonexistent voter fraud—specifically, voters registered in more than one state.

Doesn't seem to realize that *among* voters registered in more than one state are: Steve Bannon, Sean Spicer, Steve Mnuchin, son-in-law Jared Kushner, and his own daughter Tiffany.

Cites Pew Research data to support his voter fraud claims . . . that actually *refutes* his voter fraud claims . . . then claims Pew researcher is "groveling" and suppressing the truth.

Tells interviewer about imaginary five million fraudulent votes, "If you look at it, they all voted for Hillary. They all voted for Hillary. They didn't vote for me. I don't believe I got one. Okay, these are people that voted for Hillary Clinton."

Ignores logic that his conspiracy theory requires that Democrats planted five million illegal voters around the country but forgot to put any of them in the states where just seventy-seven thousand votes cost Clinton the election.

*

January 26:

Reported to have personally pressured National Park Service to support his inauguration crowd exaggeration.

After campaigning against Clinton for slovenly handling of classified data and private email, is revealed to have tied the POTUS Twitter account to private email, to be using only one-step security, and to be tweeting from a five-year-old, non-secure phone.

*

January 27:

Cites voting fraud "expert" who claims three million illegal votes, but has never produced any of the evidence he has repeatedly promised.

Issues statement commemorating International Holocaust Remembrance Day that does not include the words "Jew," "Jewish," or "Judaism."

Institutes a Muslim and refugee ban—on a day that recalls how America turned its back on refugees from Nazi Germany.

*

January 28:

Muslim ban is so hastily introduced, no one knows about exceptions intended for those with green cards, and border and customs agents are left guessing what to do next.

In phone call with prime minister of Australia, becomes angered about agreed-upon refugee resettlement deal, reportedly *hangs up* on prime minister.

*

January 29:

Falsely claims Muslim ban is just an offshoot of a temporary immigration suspension once ordered by Obama.

Dismisses anti-ban statement by Senators Graham and McCain by calling them "former presidential candidates."

Is tweeting while authorizing raid on Al Qaeda camp in Yemen.

Says nothing when self-professed white supremacist Trump "fan" opens fire at a Quebec City mosque, killing six, injuring five.

*

January 30:

Claims weekend airport chaos owes not to his Muslim and refugee ban, but to Delta Airlines computer problems and the "fake tears" of Senator Chuck Schumer—ignoring that Schumer's great-grandmother and seven of her nine siblings were murdered by the Nazis after they were unable to *become* refugees.

*

January 31:

Among those confirming they were detained at a U.S. airport during Muslim ban crisis—because he once visited Iran—is the former prime minister of *Norway*.

*

February 1:

Commemorates start of Black History Month by implying he doesn't realize Frederick Douglass has been dead since 1895. Then complains about CNN.

Vice President *Pence* commemorates start of Black History Month by tweeting tribute to . . . Abraham Lincoln.

White House does not issue readout of weekend phone call between Trump and Vladimir Putin, reportedly because White House switched off the recorder.

Attacks Australian refugee deal, calling the 1,250 refugees "thousands of illegal immigrants."

Revealed by personal physician to be taking doses of the drug Propecia to promote hair growth. Possible side effects include "dizziness, weakness, feeling like you might pass out," and "abnormal ejaculation."

*

February 2:

At National Prayer Breakfast, asks for prayers . . . for Arnold Schwarzenegger's TV ratings.

Also at Prayer Breakfast, in front of seventy worldwide religious leaders, says, "What the hell."

Rescinds sanctions against sales of cybersecurity materials to the Russian FSB, the same spy agency accused of blackmailing him.

Administration claims Yemen raid was authorized by Obama; two Obama national security advisers publicly state that is not true.

Adviser Propaganda Barbie (Kellyanne Conway) complains that media has ignored one of the justifications for the Muslim ban, namely the "Bowling Green Massacre." There *was* no "Bowling Green Massacre."

Tweets that Iran has been "formally PUT ON NOTICE," even though the phrase means nothing diplomatically.

*

February 3:

Also tweets about a "new radical Islamic terrorist" with a knife at the "Louvre Museum in Paris." The attack was at the Carrousel du Louvre *mall*; there was one minor injury; the perpetrator is Egyptian and would not have been prevented from entering the United States by the Trump ban; Trump still hasn't mentioned the Quebec mosque attack.

Administration posts terrorist video supposedly obtained during Yemen raid, to prove raid was worth it. Administration *pulls down* terrorist video when it turns out video has been on the internet since 2007.

*

February 4:

In clip revealed in advance of Super Bowl interview, says he respects Vladimir Putin. Interviewer says, "But he's a killer, though. Putin's a killer." Trump replies, "There are a lot of killers. *We've* got a lot of killers. What, do you think our country's so innocent?" Pressed, he explains that among the killers were those "in the war in Iraq." Deputy editor of *Wall Street Journal* editorial page tweets, "Never in history has a President slandered his country like this"—and he's goddamned right.

*

February 5:

Finishes two-day-long siege of Twitter attacks against Washington State judge who ruled against the Muslim ban, writing of possible terrorism, "If something happens blame him and court system."

Is reported to have signed the executive order placing Steve Bannon on the National Security Council ... without fully reading it.

Super Bowl interviewer presses him for data to support illegal voting claims, and he replies, "Forget all that" and implies that *registration* rolls prove him right—suggesting he doesn't realize that not everybody who is registered votes.

*

February 6:

After one poll showing his first approval rating at a record-low 44 percent and a CBS poll showing his Muslim ban opposed by 51 to 45 percent and a CNN poll showing it rejected 53–47, tweets, right out of George Orwell: "Any negative polls are fake news."

*

In any other context, business, or country, Trump's *supporters* would now be organizing his removal from authority, even if it were only for *his* own good.

Get. Him. Out. Of. Here.

FOR TRUMP SUPPORTERS: MEET FATEMAH

Post date • WEDNESDAY, FEBRUARY 8

If you support Donald Trump, or his ban on travel from seven countries, let me ask you a few questions.

I'm not going to yell, not going to attack the policy.

Just ... a couple of questions.

*

Where is this beautiful little one from?

What is her nationality?

Where does her extended family live?

What kind of threat could she be to you?

And ... what would *you* do to save her life?

What does your religion tell you to *do* about her? What do your instincts tell you? What do your experiences with children of your own tell you? Your experiences of loss?

Look at her again.

If, when you die, no matter your religion, your idea of an afterlife is even remotely accurate, what happens if you are judged by what you did, or what you *would* have done, about *her*?

Because *she*, of course, is ...

All the children in the world.

She, of course, is ...

All the innocence in the world.

She *has* a name, obviously.

She is Fatemah, and she's four months old, and all three of her grandparents live ... in Portland, Oregon.

And all three of them are citizens of the United States of America.

And she has a heart condition—her heart is twisted; there are two holes in it—and she needs at least one operation.

And she and her parents live ... in Iran.

But they were on their way to Portland because open-heart surgery on an infant is always a mortal risk, and, frankly, her mother and father—and her grandparents, the American citizens, the proud American grandparents—they all agreed: *our* country is simply better at open-heart surgery for kids than is Iran.

They had filled out every document. They are not indigent; they asked no financial help. The family here—the three American-citizen grandparents and her American-citizen uncle, who is actually named Uncle Sam—*they* are paying. It's not a transplant; helping Fatemah does *not* mean . . . *not* helping an American-born child.

*

The family was leaving Iran to go to the Oregon Health and Science University Hospital, in Portland—just as the Trump ban was being announced.

That was when the U.S. embassy in Dubai canceled their visa appointment.

Because the president doesn't want to let anybody in from Iran.

Not even if their grandparents are citizens.

Not even if they need surgery to live.

Not even if they're four months old.

*

Her uncle says they told him to apply again in ninety days.

Her uncle says he's not sure Fatemah has that long.

*

The 9/11 hijackers were from Saudi Arabia, the United Arab Emirates, Lebanon, and Egypt—not on Trump's list of countries from which travel was banned.

The Boston Marathon bombers were from Kyrgyzstan—not on the list.

The man with the knife at the Carrousel du Louvre mall in Paris last week was from Egypt—not on the list.

The San Bernardino shooters were from Pakistan and Chicago. The Fort Hood shooter was from Virginia. The Orlando nightclub shooter was from New Hyde Park, New York.

Not on the list.

Fatemah Reshad—*she* was on the list.

*

Is this who you want us to be?

This decision was made in *your* name.

This. Decision.

To hell with you, Fatemah, you're from Iran. Try again in three months. If you're still alive.

Do we have to be cruel?

Is that what you want?

Whatever your fears or your concerns, whatever you think of this man Trump—Fatemah was banned . . . in *your* name.

And mine.

Luckily for you and me, a week into this nightmare, politicians swarmed this case and Fatemah and her family now reportedly have a waiver to come here to save her life.

But how many other Fatemahs are there, among the sixty thousand or more who had their visas revoked?

*

When you meet your maker and you say how pro-life you were, and how patriotic, and a faithful member of your church . . .

What are you going to say when he asks, "Great—but what did you do about Fatemah? And all the other Fatemahs?"

THE ARREST OF MICHAEL THOMAS FLYNN

Post date • MONDAY, FEBRUARY 13

I call for the immediate indictment of Michael Thomas Flynn on charges of—and his immediate arrest on *suspicion* of—violations of the Logan Act.

I call for his immediate suspension, resignation, or dismissal as the national security adviser to the president of the United States of America.

I call for the immediate investigation of whether his relationship with the Russian government is limited to activities covered *by* the Logan Act, or if he is acting as an agent of the Russian government or—as in the past—acting as a paid employee of companies affiliated *with* the Russian government.

I call for Senators Graham and McCain—and any remaining patriotic Americans on the Republican senatorial roster (if any there yet be)—to fulfill their promise of weeks ago to immediately conduct a full, open, and limitless investigation into:

- Russian hacking during the election
- Russian coordination with the Republican presidential campaign during the election
- the contact between the Russians and the transition team between the time of the election and the inauguration

And, last, I not only call for the grand jury to indict Flynn for his alleged violations of the Logan Act, but also for that grand jury to name at least one unindicted co-conspirator who may have been aware of—and may have colluded with—Flynn's improper conduct involving the Russian government.

I identify that potential unindicted co-conspirator as Donald John Trump.

The specific crimes included in the Russian hacking of and meddling in our presidential campaign of 2015–16, and in the Russian interference in our presidential *election* of 2016, are as yet unclear.

But in a series of events last week that seemed like mere individual explosions during a blitzkrieg of Trumpian evil . . . the outline of what has been done by Michael Flynn—who at this moment is still the man officially charged with advising a reckless and mentally unstable president on all national security issues—that outline became substantially more clear.

Flynn, lieutenant general, United States Army, retired.

On Thursday, December 10, 2015, in Moscow, he was photographed next to the Russian dictator, Putin, at a dinner for the Russian RT television network, by whom Flynn was paid.

Later he was seen leading a standing ovation for Putin at the same event.

On Wednesday, February 8, Mr. Flynn again denied that he had privately discussed U.S. sanctions against Russia with Russian ambassador Sergey Kislyak on December 28 and/or December 29, while Barack Obama was still president.

If proven, such discussions by Flynn would be illegal interference in stated American foreign policy under federal statutes referred to as the Logan Act.

If proven, such discussions would also indicate that Flynn misled—or *lied to*—Press Secretary Spicer and Vice President Pence, both of whom issued repeated public denials on Flynn's behalf.

On Thursday, February 9, Flynn's spokesman changed the general's story. Flynn now "indicated that while he had no recollection of discussing sanctions, he couldn't be certain that the topic never came up."

On the same day, *The Washington Post* quoted nine current and former holders of senior positions in U.S. agencies with access to U.S. intelligence about the Flynn-Kislyak conversations, including transcripts of their phone calls.

According to the paper, all nine insisted, "Flynn's references to the election-related sanctions were explicit." Two sources say, further, that the intelligence indicates Flynn urged Russia to *delay* any response to the sanctions until Trump was sworn in and could change them.

On Friday, December 30, 2016—after the Flynn-Kislyak conversations— the Russian dictator, Putin, said he would delay any response to the Obama sanctions.

Also on Friday, December 30, 2016, the then president-elect tweeted, "Great move on delay (by V. Putin)—I always knew he was very smart!"

*

The likelihood that Trump's message to Putin, Trump's close relationship with Flynn, and Flynn's conversations with Kislyak are all coincidental— reportedly after *and before* the election—is so small as to be almost laughable.

And if they are *not* coincidental, Trump had guilty knowledge of Flynn's conversations with Kislyak, and if Flynn can be indicted for violations of the Logan Act, Trump's awareness of this crime—and his cover-up of it—elevates him to the status of possible unindicted co-conspirator, with other implications relative to presidential impeachment.

On April 27, 2016, then candidate Trump gave his first major foreign policy speech. Seated in the front row of the audience at the Mayflower Hotel, in Washington, D.C. . . . Russian ambassador Sergey Kislyak.

As of 5:30 p.m. on Friday, February 10, a White House official quoted by the Associated Press says Trump has "full confidence" in Michael Thomas Flynn.

The interference by a foreign power in our government, in our country, is intolerable.

Collusion between a foreign power and representatives of our government— or representatives of a government yet to be—risks our independent existence as a nation, and renders those who commit such collusion—if not necessarily by legal definition, then in their hearts—*traitors.*

They will be exposed, rooted out of any position of responsibility in this country, and punished to the fullest extent of the law.

And that *begins* with the immediate indictment and arrest of Michael Thomas Flynn and the identification as unindicted co-conspirator of Donald John Trump.

GUADALUPE GARCÍA DE RAYOS

Post date • WEDNESDAY, FEBRUARY 15

First they came for the undocumented Americans . . . and I did not speak out because I was not . . .

You knew that original speech, from Pastor Martin Niemöller in 1946 . . .

And you knew you heard the first few letters of the first word of the confession of eternal guilt and regret as they began to echo over the last long weekend: In Southern California. In Atlanta. In Austin.

And you knew that ICE—Immigrations and Customs Enforcement—may have *said* there was nothing unusual about the round-ups.

And yet you knew that the barbarian in chief couldn't resist boasting about the truth—and making liars out of his gangs of deportation storm troopers.

And you knew that he would say something like:

"The crackdown on illegal criminals is merely the keeping of my campaign promise. Gang members, drug dealers & others are being removed!"

Others.

Like the mother of two Americans teenagers who has been living here since she was sixteen and who checked in annually for nine years with her immigration officer—just as they told her to—each time receiving work authorization. Until last week, when she checked in and they seized her and drove her to Mexico.

Gang member?

Drug dealer?

No. She was part of the cleaning crew at an Arizona water park.

Her name is Guadalupe García de Rayos.

And Donald Trump is proud of having removed the danger she represented to this country.

Because Donald Trump is a cowardly, hate-filled bully, who was elected on a promise to scapegoat people with dark skin.

Because whether from disease or abuse or—as Clarence Darrow said of the murderers Leopold and Loeb—because somewhere in the infinite processes that go to the making up of the boy or the man, something slipped . . .

For whatever reason . . .

Donald Trump thinks expelling people who will uncomplainingly do the jobs that people who were born here will *not* do is somehow to his credit, and is somehow to this nation's benefit—when in fact the whole history of this country is predicated on people who came here, like Friedrich Trump and Friedrich Olbermann, and uncomplainingly did the jobs that people who were born here would not do, in the hopes that their children or grandchildren or great-great-grandchildren might flourish in this nation of bounty and goodness.

Instead, we have this Trump adviser Stephen Miller, the one with the dead eyes, shifting side to side as if the eyes *themselves* were revolting against his racism and deception, insisting on television that "before a job is given to a foreign national, that job is offered first to an American worker."

Because they're going to be overwhelmed at that Arizona water park with American workers who want the job—for minimum wage, or less—of cleaning the shit from the toilet bowls.

And again, on behalf of Friedrich Trump and Friedrich Olbermann, I apologize.

To Guadalupe García de Rayos.

And her family.

And the world.

*

And I also have to apologize to Trump's supporters, so filled with misdirected rage about the failures in their own lives that they have never considered what happens to *them* if all the people who do all *those* jobs suddenly disappear.

Step back from Niemöller's lament for a moment and table the hatred and the racism and the scapegoating and the terror by night and remember, Trump supporters, who is now expected to *do* Guadalupe García de Rayos's job at the water park, or somebody else's job . . . in the kitchen, or yet another's job . . . in the crop fields on the farms.

You are.

Or your son.

Or the ex–factory worker who isn't getting his factory job back no matter what Trump promised him, because there's nobody, anywhere, who will *buy* the product the factory produces—not at those prices.

Take the emotion out of it—take the rightness and the wrongness out of this un-American spectacle, this Salem witch trial of 2017—and ask yourself what happens to the food on your table when the people who harvest it . . . aren't here anymore, because *you* decided they didn't *belong* here anymore.

That food rots in the field.

See, the thing is, this "throw out the illegals" purge has been done here before. In America. Recently. And the results were disastrous.

In 2011, the state of Georgia passed a bill called HB 87. The proud state representative from Peachtree City, Matt Ramsey, a coauthor, said at the time that the bill would give the police the right to demand immigration documents from anybody detained for any reason. It would also punish those who hired or harbored undocumented Americans. "Our goal," said Representative Ramsey, "is to eliminate incentives for illegal aliens to cross into our state."

And how well it all worked.

An estimated 425,000 undocumented Americans were employed in Georgia in 2010, but by the harvest of 2011 at least 40 percent of them . . . were gone.

The Georgia-born unemployed whose jobs those "illegals" had taken?

They not only wanted no part of the backbreaking labor, but those few who tried it were also no good at it.

Forty percent of the men and women who actually knew *how* to work the farms of Georgia and survive on minimal incomes suddenly vanished. And as Representative Matt Ramsey and the other racists cheered, an estimated $140 million worth of Georgia produce . . . rotted . . . in . . . the . . . fields.

By 2012, as farmers planted less due to the sudden labor scarcity, the state was forced to find new farmworkers.

Prisoners.

They bused in prisoners.

Georgia's agricultural economy still hasn't fully recovered.

Oh, and he's now *former* Representative Matt Ramsey.

*

So if you are so lacking in human soul that what this madman bigot Trump has just begun to roll out *doesn't* sear your flesh when you embrace it—forget the ethics for a while and think, instead, of what it will do to your wallet when the ticket to the water park doubles because Guadalupe isn't there to clean it for you, and the price of the meal at the fancy restaurant or the fast-food shack *triples* because her cousin isn't there to cook it for you, and the price of the food you buy at the supermarket quadruples because *none of them* are there to pick it for you.

You don't have to have the heart of Pastor Niemöller to have the *regret* of Pastor Niemöller.

In fact, you don't have to have a heart at *all*.

Just a wallet.

First they came for the undocumented Americans . . . and I did not speak out because I wasn't undocumented. And I didn't realize that without them . . . it would cost too much for me to feed my own family.

ARE THESE PEOPLE HIGH OR WHAT?

Post date • THURSDAY, FEBRUARY 16

Are these people high or what?

The Department of Education—whose new secretary, Betsy DeVos, begins her term acting like she's never *had* any education—tweets out a salute to the author and activist W. E. B. Du Bois . . .

By misspelling his name.

Department of Education.

Then, hours later, issues its apologies . . .

And misspells *apologies* . . .

Are these people *high*—or what?

On Instagram, Trump commemorates Abraham Lincoln's birthday—and the GOP does the same on Twitter—by posting his photo and attributing to him the quotation "And in the end, it's not the years in your life that count. It's the life in your years."

The quote is *actually* from an advertisement for a book about aging published in 1947—eighty-two years after Lincoln *died*.

Are these people high—or *what?*

Trump, in a private meeting with senators of both parties to talk about his Supreme Court nominee, wanders into his mental woods again, calls Elizabeth Warren "Pocahontas," and tells ex-senator Kelly Ayotte that she would've kept her seat in New Hampshire but for thousands of illegal votes cast there by people bused in from Massachusetts . . .

Are these *people* high—or what?

New Hampshire's former Republican chairman offers a thousand dollars for any proof of just *one* such illegal vote.

A federal elections commissioner appointed by President George W. Bush demands that Trump share whatever proof he has "with the appropriate law-enforcement authorities so that his allegations may be investigated promptly and thoroughly."

Whereupon Trump's Propagandist Flavor of the Month, Stephen Miller, goes on television and offers *as* proof . . . no proof!

"I've actually, having worked before on a campaign in New Hampshire, I can tell you that this issue of busing voters in to New Hampshire is widely known by anyone who's worked in New Hampshire politics. It's very real, it's very serious. This morning on this show is not the venue for me to lay out all the evidence."

Translation: You want proof?

I offer as proof—my opinion.

Because there *is* no proof.

*

Are *these* people high—or what?

Public Policy Polling asks 712 voters, "Do you agree or disagree with the following statement: 'The Bowling Green massacre shows why we need Donald Trump's executive order on immigration?'"

Roughly 51 percent of Trump voters answer yes . . . the Muslim ban is justified by the Bowling Green Massacre.

There *is* no Bowling Green Massacre—this is the nonsense that Kellyanne Conway made up.

*

Are these people high—or what?

Last August, the same pollster asked, "Would you support or oppose building a wall along the Atlantic Ocean to keep Muslims from entering the country from the Middle East?"

Thirty-one percent of those identifying themselves as Trump supporters said *yes*—to walling off the entire Eastern Seaboard . . .

To keep out . . . Muslims . . . coming in by . . . surfboard . . . or submarine . . . or swimming here from Baghdad.

*

Are these people *high*—or what?

Again, same pollster, asking, "Do you think Donald Trump should be able to overturn decisions by judges that he disagrees with, or not?"

Again, 51 percent said yes . . .

Another 16 percent aren't sure . . .

Only a third said no!

A democracy in which the president can overturn the rulings of judges is *not* a democracy. It is a dictatorship.

A majority of Trump voters are okay with replacing key parts of the United States of America with one-man rule.

*

Are these people *high*—or what?

And when all of these threads of madness join up, and the immigration history of this country is betrayed by a would-be tyrant looking for scapegoats . . . the picture changes.

From Americans acting as if intoxicated . . .

It becomes Americans acting . . . just like ordinary Germans did under the Nazis, or just as ordinary Russians did under the Communists . . .

JFK Airport. An Iraqi woman detained. Thirty-three hours. Handcuffed. Denied a wheelchair. She had come here to see her son. A sergeant in the U.S. Army 82nd Airborne Division at Fort Bragg.

Philadelphia International. A woman flies in from Iran to see her daughters—both American doctoral students. Her passport is seized. Somehow she doesn't have her cell phone anymore. Customs puts her on another flight to Iran, can't tell her daughters which flight.

Frankfurt, Germany. American customs there keeps Dr. Samira Asgari from flying to Boston, where the next day she is supposed to start her fellowship at Harvard Medical School.

Dulles Airport. Woman traveling with two citizen children. Reportedly detained for twenty hours without food, told the kids can stay but she will be deported to Africa. Handcuffed. Even when going to the bathroom.

Bush Intercontinental, Houston. Man coming in from Chile, forced to give his phone to customs. To give them the PIN number. To authorize them to copy its contents. He is a scientist at the Jet Propulsion Laboratory. The phone belongs to his employer, NASA. He works for an arm of the U.S. government. He was born in Los Angeles.

And back at Dulles. Five-year-old boy. U.S. citizen. Kept from his mother. Detained for four hours. Reportedly handcuffed by customs officials.

Sean Spicer's reaction? "To assume that just because of someone's age and gender that they don't pose a threat would be misguided and wrong."

Are.

These.

People.

High—or what?

*

Last month, as I sat next to him on his set, my friend Bill Maher managed to do something he hadn't done since 1978: he shocked me. He cited statistics that the fourteen states in this country with the highest number of painkiller prescriptions per person all voted last November for Trump.

Where Trump did the *best*? West Virginia. An average of 433 pain pills per person over the past six years.

Eighty percent of the states with the greatest heroin use—went for Trump.

Six of the nine Ohio counties that Trump flipped from Obama have opioid overdose rates high above the national average. *All* of the ones he flipped in Pennsylvania have *nearly double* the national overdose rate.

*

Madness surrounds us.

In the government...

In the behavior of its spokespeople...

In the amorality and brutality of those who enforce its decrees...

And in the rising disinterest in democracy of those who support it.

So, once more—much more solemnly.

Are these people high—or what?

THE SUICIDE OF A PRESIDENCY

Post date • **TUESDAY, FEBRUARY 21**

The suicide of a presidency occurred on Friday, February 17, 2017, at 4:32 p.m. Eastern Time.

"The FAKE NEWS media (failing @nytimes, @CNN, @NBCNews and many more) is not my enemy, it is the enemy of the American people. SICK!"

Donald Trump struck a fatal blow against his own presidency at that moment, with the use of those terms never heard before from an American president, not even from Richard Nixon, not ever.

The presidency, of course, did not end *with* those words.

But the inevitability that it will end, later or sooner—the truth that his position as president is no longer tenable—became fixed the moment he pressed "send" and promulgated those evil words.

And then he deleted them.

But he deleted them not because they were the spasmodic outburst of a man with no self-control suddenly understanding that he had just finally thrown everything he had achieved out the window and he was seeking to destroy the record, as Nixon destroyed the tapes.

No, he deleted them because he had *left out* some of the specific targets he wanted to smear with words that even the evil founder of the Soviet Union, Vladimir Lenin, waited until he was a month in power before using.

Sixteen minutes later.

"The FAKE NEWS media (failing @nytimes, @NBCNews, @ABC, @CBS, @CNN) is not my enemy, it is the enemy of the American People!"

There is no walking those words back.

A man holding the office of the president of the United States using the language of the totalitarian states of Russia, the language used to mark groups of people for removal and death.

A man holding the office of the president of the United States specifically attacking a group, specifically protected by the Bill of Rights, the first amendments ever passed to the Constitution to which he swore allegiance—apparently *falsely* swore allegiance—but a month earlier.

"Congress shall make no law respecting an establishment of religion, or prohibiting the free exercise thereof; or abridging the freedom of speech, or of the press; or the right of the people peaceably to assemble, and to petition the Government for a redress of grievances."

Freedom of the press—sandwiched in among the freedom from a state religion, and against government abridgment of free speech, and of the right of assembly, and of petition against grievances.

An attack on freedom of the press is an attack on all those other freedoms and all those Americans who *exercise* all those other freedoms.

It is an attack on the Constitution itself.

And that may not mean much to Trump or his wilder supporters, nor even to some of the men and women on the fringes of Congress to whom democracy has always been nothing more than a brand name.

But the most tepid of Democrats must realize—or be made to realize—that everybody else in the president's party now has to decide how to answer . . . *new* questions.

"Speaker Ryan—do you agree? Are *The New York Times*, NBC News, ABC, CBS, CNN, and many more the enemy of the American people?"

"Vice President Pence—a decade ago, you cosponsored a bill to let reporters protect confidential sources. Do you agree with the president—or do you believe in freedom of the press?"

"Majority Leader McConnell—can you defend the president of the United States' calling Americans, holding American jobs in American-owned businesses, 'the enemies of the American people'?"

"Senator McCain—do you believe the president should be calling *any* American citizens a phrase coined by the Communist Lenin?"

"Secretary of Defense Mattis—when people say that freedom of speech and freedom of the press exist because of the United States military, and that the military fights *for* free speech and freedom of the press, what, exactly, does that *mean*?"

"Judge Neil Gorsuch—do you believe in the First Amendment to the Constitution of the United States?"

"Republican candidate for the Senate, for the House, for the state legislature, for village mayor, for the school board—not condemning Donald Trump means not condemning his belief that the news media is the enemy of the American people. Do you support Donald Trump, or do you think the news media is the enemy of the people?"

These questions.

And similarly blunt follow-ups.

Again and again and again.

*

This is a door that Trump has closed behind himself—forever.

He cannot reopen it and go back through—even if he were smart enough to try to do so.

It is the suicide of a presidency.

Because whether all of those Republicans answer those questions now, or *next fall*, they *will* answer them, and they will not be able to nuance their answers, and if the country still believes in democracy and not fascism, it will punish any politician who does not repudiate Trump's authoritarian madness.

It does not mean his presidency ends today or tomorrow.

Richard Nixon committed the suicide of a presidency in the late morning of Friday, June 23, 1972, when he ordered the FBI to discontinue its investigation of the Watergate break-in of just six days earlier. The tape recording of his order did not become public, however, until August 5, 1974.

Nixon's presidency died of its two-year-old self-inflicted wounds at noon on August 9, 1974—just as Trump's presidency will die of the wound *he* inflicted on *it*, and for exactly the same reason.

Not because it was a crime against the United States of America and the Constitution.

But because . . . Republicans were going to have to answer questions about it in the midterm elections.

As the Republicans of 1974 would have had no choice but to run *against* Richard Nixon . . .

The Republicans of *our* day will have no choice but to run *against* Donald Trump.

*

We have always been very celestial about our motives in this country. The Constitution, the flag, American exceptionalism.

But ultimately, most of our internal decisions have come down to far less lofty issues—often they've come right down into the gutters and the sewers . . . of who is going to be reelected, and who is not.

And on Twitter, on February 17, Donald Trump guaranteed that Republicans would have to try to get themselves reelected *as* Republicans while a Republican president insisted that the free press was an enemy of the American people.

Those Republicans *can't* do that.

So they will not try.

So Trump will have to go.

And so, his presidency is, right now, dying—by his own hand.

The only question is: How *fast* will it die?

INTEL

Post date • WEDNESDAY, FEBRUARY 22

Do you think Donald Trump realizes that the American intelligence community has already started to kill and eat his presidency?

The leaks.

The drip, drip, drip.

The tiny revelation that cost Michael Flynn the national security adviser's job.

The slightly larger revelation that was the play-by-play of how and why his first three choices to succeed Flynn ... didn't.

The larger revelations that put the backbone in *New York Times* and CNN stories about the Trump campaign talking with Russia while still hiding the potentially disastrous details of what they said.

The far more meaningful—but far more *subtle*—revelation that the so-called British Dossier is gaining credibility within the intelligence agencies because they have been able to confirm so many little details, like how the claims of meetings and phone calls on specific dates are turning out to be exactly right.

Do you think Trump understands what all these things *are*?

*

They are ... *warnings.*

They are ... the cop letting the belligerent drunk see just the tip of the gun.

They are ... the poker player putting down the twenty-dollar chips, then smiling at the mark, then pulling *back* the twenty-dollar chips and replacing them with *hundred*-dollar chips.

They. Are. Warnings.

*

Stories based on sources usually bear no resemblance to what you see in the movies or on television dramas. It's not *All the President's Men* with indefatigable and annoying pests overwhelming reluctant individuals until the latter do the right thing.

You *might* have enough sources who are *around* the center, but not *at* the center, of a given story, and with all the circumstantial evidence they have provided you, you *might* be able to persuade the key source to confirm what you have already proved to them that you *know*.

But this is almost always true:

A source doesn't give you a story because *you* want *them* to give it to you.

A source gives you a story because *they* want to give it to you.

And there are sources—a lot of sources, very well placed, very well informed sources—who *want* to tell the world about Donald Trump.

The details they are doling out have a dual purpose. They get these stories out that confirm the correct perception that this administration is like a giant fire hose that the firefighters have lost control of.

But, more important, they are there to get the message to Trump and those around him that there is an iceberg, and it will be revealed one square foot at a time, so stop screwing around.

*

Maybe he's not smart enough to get it.

Maybe he's not *sane* enough to get it.

Maybe he's not experienced enough to *get* it—that individuals sitting on details potent enough to pick off his national security adviser, hours after Kellyanne Con Job said he had Trump's full confidence, are also clearly sitting on a hoard of far more embarrassing, far more destructive, far more lurid details.

*

So why aren't those lurid details known?

Well, this is entirely speculative, of course, but the way leaking in the intelligence community—or, as they sometimes phrase it, "story placement"—was explained to me, it's supposed to be done with the minimum expenditure of assets.

In other words, to go back to that analogy of the poker player pulling back the twenty-dollar chips and replacing them with hundred-dollar chips, you want to use as little of your stash as possible.

Each chip—each story you confirm or promulgate—involves something you then can no longer use for its original purpose. The essence of intelligence is secrecy: reveal a secret to a reporter and you may reveal within the worldwide intelligence community a thousand details of how you *learned* that secret.

Why spend the hundred-dollar chips when you might get the job done with the twenties?

*

And it is clear that the Oliver Stone version of the intelligence community is, at best, an exaggeration. Trump derided the IC, as it calls itself, during the campaign, insulted it after the election, impugned it during the transition—and yet, for the most part, the spies kept quiet.

Whatever they thought of Trump, with their great restraint, and to their great credit, they clearly wanted to grin and bear a Trump administration.

And then it became clear he wasn't going to stop.

What pushed them over the edge?

Again, just a guess, but I suspect that speech at CIA headquarters with Trump's disingenuous shallow fawning over them, while he brought his own employees to applaud, was certainly the end of the beginning as far as the intelligence community's forbearance was concerned.

And then came his disinterest in their product.

And finally came the night he took in the details of the North Korean missile test while the gawking patrons of NightMar-a-Lago—the Judge Smails and the Dr. Beeper and the Havercamps of Trump's real-life enactment of the movie *Caddyshack*—all took cell phone pictures.

And the next thing you knew, *The Wall Street Journal* had a story about how U.S. intelligence agencies are not telling Trump everything, for fear it "could be leaked or compromised" ...

And then CBS News had a story *about* Trump yelling *about* that story, at his CIA director ...

And *The Huffington Post* had a story about how the president wants only bullet points in his intel briefings and how he really likes maps ...

And *Newsweek* had a story about "one Western European ally" intercepting the Flynn phone calls with the Russian ambassador ...

And *Politico* had a story about a senior National Security Council aide criticizing Trump and his team and getting fired for it ...

And *The New York Times* just happened to be at a military conference when the general in charge of the United States Special Operations Command suddenly blurted out, "Our government continues to be in unbelievable turmoil," and, "as a commander, I'm concerned our government be as stable as possible"—remarks about as subtle as saying, "Golly, as service members who love and honor the Constitution, we'd *hate* to have to do a military takeover of the government, but Bullshit McGee over here is a wack job."

*

And none of it registers with Trump.

On he goes.

Threatening the leakers.

The leakers he compared to Nazi Germany.

The leakers who have all the chips.

The twenties. The hundreds. For all we know, the millions.

*

On he goes.

Tweets this a week ago: "Information is being illegally given to the failing @nytimes & @washingtonpost by the intelligence community (NSA and FBI?). Just like Russia."

"The real scandal here is that classified information is illegally given out by 'intelligence' like candy. Very un-American!"

"Un-American."

"Just like Russia."

"Nazi Germany."

*

Whereupon somebody asks John Schindler, a former NSA guy who left under embarrassing circumstances but whose tweets about Trump and the intelligence community have been consistently prescient, "What do you think is going on inside NatSec right now after Trump's 'intelligence' tweet this morning?"

And Schindler tweets:

"Now we go nuclear. IC war going to new levels. Just got an EM fm senior IC friend, it began: 'He will die in jail.'"

Do you think Donald Trump realizes that the American intelligence community has already started to kill and eat his presidency?

HE MUST GO

Post date • THURSDAY, FEBRUARY 23

He must go.

He must go because he does not believe in democracy or the supremacy of the judiciary.

He must go because his spokesman asserted that his powers "will not be questioned."

He must go because he believes that Republican congressmen are obligated to represent only . . . Republican constituents.

He must go because he is here only after the interference of an enemy nation in our election.

He must go because he believes in conspiracy theories, and in his own intuition instead of facts and reality.

He must go because he publicly spews those conspiracy theories, which would get anyone else marginalized in society, yet television covers him live and without fact correction, and when asked why, a CNN reporter answers blankly, "He is the president of the United States."

He must go because not only do his actions simplify the task of known terrorist organizations, but in many cases his actions also qualify as the emotional definition *of* terrorism.

He must go because he burns with hatred toward people of color and, as shown in several statements by his administration, toward those of the Jewish faith.

He must go because the crudeness of his words about women have been exceeded by the coldness of his actions in office *against* women.

He must go because he has found an environmental secretary who wants to pillage the environment, a health secretary who wants to gut the ACA and

Medicare and Medicaid, and an education secretary who seems dedicated to making sure most children are stupid.

He must go because he has chosen to make his job not about serving the people of this nation, but about hearing applause and being reelected.

He must go because he can, in one breath, promise not to use Air Force One as a political prop, and in the next give a campaign speech while standing in front of Air Force One.

He must go because from the first minute of his presidency, it has been about leveraging this sacred democracy for his own personal financial profit.

He must go because he has summoned from ordinary Americans, as certainly as if he were invoking devils, the worst of what is inside them.

He must go because his ill-informed and provocative "last night in Sweden" comment showed he can't—or won't—tell the difference between terrorism and ordinary crimes committed by legal immigrants.

He must go because he has caused alarm and dismay among our allies abroad and given considerable comfort to our enemies.

He must go because, whether insane or diseased or drugged or syphilitic or intellectually challenged or simply evil, he is not in control of his own mind.

He must go because he called the media "the enemy of the American People"—like Stalin or Hitler would have.

And he must go because his next "enemy of the people" . . . could be you.

He. Must. Go.

TELL IT TO THE GRAND JURY

Post date • MONDAY, FEBRUARY 27

I call for a federal grand jury to be empaneled to determine whether crimes have been committed by the Trump presidential campaign, the Trump presidential transition, and now the Trump presidential administration, involving Russian attempts to influence American democracy—specifically, the presidential election of 2016.

I call on that grand jury to look specifically at the actions of Trump attorney

Michael Cohen, Trump business associate Felix Sater, Trump's former campaign manager Paul Manafort, and former national security adviser Michael Flynn—specifically in regard to contacts with agents of the Russian government in 2016 and 2017.

I call on that grand jury to hear evidence as to whether or not indictments should be returned against White House officials—Chief of Staff Reince Priebus, Press Secretary Sean Spicer, or others.

I call on that grand jury to ascertain specifically whether Priebus, Spicer, or others violating the 2009 Department of Justice regulation requiring that White House contact with the FBI about investigations be made only by the president, the vice president, the White House counsel, or the primary deputy White House counsel is evidence of prohibited criminal behavior, such as aiding and abetting, conspiracy, or misprision of a felony.

I call on that grand jury to determine whether indictments should be returned against House Intelligence Committee Chairman Devin Nunes, Senate Intelligence Committee Chairman Richard Burr, or officials at the FBI and the CIA.

I call on that grand jury to ascertain specifically whether Nunes and Burr and the others mishandled classified information about investigations of the Trump-Russian connection by the intelligence services when Nunes and Burr made anonymous-source phone conversations to reporters on behalf of the White House.

I urge that grand jury to carefully review the actions already publicly acknowledged or reported—

Such as the contact between General Flynn and Russian ambassador Sergey Kislyak...

Such as the meeting between Ambassador Kislyak and the president's son-in-law...

Such as the involvement of Trump attorney Cohen, and the five different stories Mr. Cohen has told about that involvement, in delivering a plan to General Flynn to destabilize the government of Ukraine...

Such as the efforts by Mr. Priebus to influence FBI Deputy Director Andrew McCabe and FBI Director James Comey to "knock down" the Trump-Russia story through leaks or announcements to the media.

I urge that grand jury to ascertain whether these confessed actions already constitute evidence of illegal contact among the Trump campaign, Trump transition, and Trump administration and representatives of the Russian government—possibly rising to the level of misprision, conspiracy, or espionage—and additionally to ascertain whether they already constitute an overarching attempt to cover up these involvements and to obstruct justice.

*

Trump's involvement with Russia obscures—perhaps dictates—every other aspect of this existentially dangerous presidency.

We have to have answers.

The answer we should have gotten from Trump and his gang was simple— it should have been "We have done nothing wrong. We will give the FBI full license to interview anybody and read anything we have."

The answer we have gotten from them was instead Trump telling us he "hasn't called Russia in ten years," and to get on with our lives, and branding as "sore losers" those who believe that he either is a Russian operative or has been compromised by Russian intelligence, and declaring war on the FBI and on news organizations that publish stories about this topic using leaks from anonymous sources—while we now have Mr. Priebus trying to get the FBI and other intelligence community figures and elected officials, like Congressman Nunes and Senator Burr, to act as off-the-record leakers to news organizations to get them to publish positive spin about this topic.

The answer we should have gotten from Nunes, in his role as chairman of the House Intelligence Committee, with access to classified intelligence, and Burr, in his role as chairman of the Senate Intelligence Committee, with access to classified intelligence, was simple: "We will immediately begin open and full investigations—preferably a select joint committee—to determine to what degree Donald Trump knew of, or colluded with, the Russian government to decide the last presidential election."

The answer that we instead have gotten from Mr. Nunes was that there is no evidence of Russian contacts, but "major crimes" were committed by those who leaked about Russian contacts—which is impossible if there were no contacts.

The answer that we have instead gotten from Mr. Nunes and Mr. Burr constitutes their violating their oaths of office, and compromising their personal ethics and the codes of honor required of every public servant in this nation, and completely compromising any congressional investigation. They began actively serving as press agents to try to influence media coverage in order to suppress investigation, and to suppress truth, and to suppress our ability to know whether our foreign policy, our domestic policy, our school policy, our self-defense policy—whether our *government* is being run by Americans or being run by Russians.

*

We. Have. To. Have. *Answers.*

*

In short, Senator Burr...
    Representative Nunes...
    Mr. Priebus...
    Mr. Spicer...
    Mr. Manafort...
    Director Pompeo...
    Director Comey...
    Deputy Director McCabe...
    Mr. Cohen...
    Mr. Sater...
    General Flynn...
    Mr. Kushner...
    Mr. Trump...
    We need to know from you... if we are still Americans... or if we are now merely living in a colony of Russia.
    Tell it to the grand jury!

CALL THEM WHAT THEY ARE: A MUSLIM BAN AND A PURGE OF HISPANICS

Post date • TUESDAY, FEBRUARY 28

Trump's travel ban is a Muslim ban.

And his immigration enforcement order is a purge of Hispanics.

And I'm tired of hearing the radical-right bullshit that they are anything else.

And I don't believe a word about them coming out of this racist's mouth, whether at CPAC or this insane address to Congress . . .

And, most important, they are useless, they add nothing to the safety of this country, they are sadistic, they are turning ordinary, unthinking Americans into a mindless gestapo—Donald Trump's gestapo.

*

When you detain an American born in Philadelphia and ask him over and over again, "Where did you get your name from?" and "Are you Muslim?" and the man's name is Muhammad Ali Jr.—it's a Muslim ban!

When ICE agents wait across the street from a Virginia church refuge designed to save the homeless from freezing to death on the streets, and they grab six men as they leave the place—it's a purge of Hispanics!

When a white supremacist reportedly asks two engineers from India in a bar in Kansas City about their visas, then allegedly shoots them while shouting, "Get out of my country"—and Sean Spicer says that the thought it had anything to do with Trump is "absurd"—it's a Muslim ban!

When you end a program designed to prevent the deportation of spouses and parents and children of active U.S. military personnel—it's a purge of Hispanics!

When you tell the Oregon family of a four-month-old girl that, no, no matter who approved what, she can't come to Portland for lifesaving surgery because she's from Iran—it's a Muslim ban!

When you go into a Texas courtroom and nab an undocumented woman, a victim of domestic abuse who was there getting a restraining order, and her lawyer speculated that the tip for the arrest may have come from the domestic abuser—it's a purge of Hispanics!

When you detain a seventy-year-old woman and interrogate her at LAX for two hours because somebody somewhere thinks there's something wrong with her American-issued visa when there isn't, and she turns out to be the author of children's books with titles like *Possum Magic* and *With Love, at Christmas*, and this is her 117th trip to this country, and her name is Merrion "Mem" Fox . . . it's a Muslim ban!

When you detain a Mexican man at the border and, even though he's in apparent emotional distress, you deport him anyway, and he goes to a bridge a few hundred feet into Mexico and throws himself to his death—it's a purge of Hispanics!

When you ignore the report from the Department of Homeland Security that the ban on travel from the seven countries will do nothing to enhance American security—it's a Muslim ban!

When you seize a man being released on bail and detain him for three days and you tell him he's an illegal immigrant and you're going to deport him and you don't care that his birth certificate and state ID say he's from Puerto Rico—which is part of the goddamned United States—it's a purge of Hispanics!

When you detain a historian, a visiting scholar at Texas A&M and formerly at Harvard and Dartmouth, for ten hours, because he was born in Cairo sixty-three years ago, and he was coming here to speak about the French Vichy government that collaborated with the Germans in World War II and how all those lessons have been forgotten—it's a Muslim ban that now tracks directly back to the Nazis.

And when you propose loosening employment requirements for hiring new border agents—congressionally mandated requirements—loosening background checks; loosening the use of polygraph tests; loosening entrance examinations . . .

And when you tell passengers on board a domestic flight from San Francisco to New York that they need to produce "their papers" or they won't be allowed to get off the plane, because you're looking for somebody who has a deportation order against them, it's no longer just a Muslim ban.

It is a series of acts intended to terrify Americans into submission. It is a series of acts intended to silence those who would object, and turn them into human sheep. It is a series of acts intended to turn respect for authority into fear of authority. It is a series of acts intended to give the rank-and-file customs and ICE employees both the false sense that they are doing something moral and the appetite for sadism and brutality on which authoritarianism feeds. It is—in fact—a series of acts of terrorism against the people of the United States of America. And Donald Trump, it is your doing—and in due time, you will atone.

Donald J. Trump ✔
@realDonaldTrump

 Follow

How low has President Obama gone to tapp my phones during the very sacred election process. This is Nixon/Watergate. Bad (or sick) guy!

4:02 AM - 4 Mar 2017

↩   ⇄ 25,050   ♥ 68,593

Chapter 8

MARCH 2017

THE COCOON AND ANOSOGNOSIA

Post date • FRIDAY, MARCH 3

It is, in retrospect, amazing that Trump spoke to the two houses of Congress at all.

Because the address did not take place inside his cocoon.

Six weeks into his presidency and he has already silenced virtually all stimuli coming from outside that cocoon . . . the evidence that could tell him the truth—that he is already hated more, by more people, than any other incoming executive in our history; that efforts to remove him from office are already coalescing and sharpening; and, especially, that much of his own administration has turned on him and is dividing quickly into two camps: those trying to clean up his messes by routing around him and those who are actively undermining him through leaks and even with on-the-record contradictions.

Trump, of course, cannot—literally cannot—hear any of this.

He must be loved, worshiped, obeyed. That's why there is a cocoon.

That's why there is a cocoon where there were lines "six blocks long" to get into his speech at CPAC, when the public wasn't even admitted to CPAC, so there couldn't have been any lines. That's why he had to cancel on the White House Correspondents' Dinner before the correspondents could refuse to invite him, or he'd be faced with venturing outside the cocoon and getting mauled by a comic. That's why his staff reportedly feeds him only stories he'll like from propagandist sites like Fox and Breitbart.

That's why the Baltimore Orioles denied us a test of the density of the co-coon when the team president said he wouldn't invite Trump to throw out the ceremonial first pitch on baseball's Opening Day. What a choice! Forty-six thousand screaming fans who could cheer him: To be cheered—perchance to be booed; ay, there's the rub!

And then there are the leaks.

Trump is insane enough that he could repeatedly scream about "the illegal leaks" when he spent the campaign—literally every one of the last thirty days (164 times in one month)—quoting the "illegal leaks" provided by Russia and Julian Assange and WikiLeaks.

He loves WikiLeaks.

He could rail about catching the leakers and investigating them and pun-ishing them—while Reince Priebus was begging the FBI to leak about Trump and Russia, and while the White House got Congressman Nunes and Senator Burr to leak about Trump and Russia.

He could attack the FBI and the CIA—self-destructively and specifically—about leakers inside their organizations, while his own house is such a sieve that his faithful toady Sean Spicer collects all his staffers' phones to check whether they've been leaking. And not only does that story itself leak out within days, but when it does, it contradicts Trump's mindless assertion that the news media just makes up stories about him—if they're making them up, why are you checking who's leaking them? And when Trump wants specific outlets banned from news briefings, Spicer does it, even though just two months ago Spicer said they only do that in dictatorships.

This makes no sense—not even for a crazy man in a cocoon. Confirming what you ardently deny; retroactively declaring your presidency a "dictator-ship"—it makes no sense unless we postulate that what Trump calls leaks and what the rest of the world calls leaks are different things.

He's not obsessed with leaks from inside the cocoon . . . getting out . . .

He's obsessed with leaks . . . from outside the cocoon . . . getting in.

The Russian scandal is not a problem because it could send him to an im-peachment trial or the penitentiary or both. It's a problem because stories about it leak into the cocoon and damage his perfect world, in which he was elected because everybody loves him.

The same with the loss of the popular vote. To him, that's not about presidential legitimacy or a mandate. He cannot permit it to be true because it means he finished second in something.

What he calls leaks—are in fact reality permeating the wall of the cocoon.

As historians and medical researchers gain new information and new insight, the evidence mounts that the primary intellectual damage done to President Woodrow Wilson during his stroke in October 1919 was that it short-circuited the part of the brain that would normally have allowed Wilson to understand the reality and gravity of the damage to his brain. It's called anosognosia, and it is, in essence, a physical form of denial.

As the psychologist David Dunning once told *The New York Times*: "An anosognosic patient who is paralyzed simply does not know that he is paralyzed. If you put a pencil in front of them and ask them to pick up the pencil in front of their left hand they won't do it. And you ask them why, and they'll say, 'Well, I'm tired,' or 'I don't need a pencil.'"

Maybe Trump has that.

If not, he has manufactured a cocoon for himself—in which he might as well have it.

It can be tragic for the nation—many historians believe that Wilson's anosognosia made it impossible for him to compromise about the League of Nations. His stroke may have in part led ... to the Second World War.

Our tragedy with a president who will not—or cannot—allow reality to leak into his cocoon?

Who knows which nightmare we will get.

But it is axiomatic that authoritarians in power—even the ones who don't have anosognosia or regular old denial—begin by shutting out dissenting voices, and invariably end up ... by shutting down dissenting voices.

RUSSIA, CONTINUED

Post date • MONDAY, MARCH 6

Not only is the putative president of the United States being investigated for illicit contact directly or through intermediaries with representatives of an enemy nation, but the head of the Federal Bureau of Investigation reportedly asked the Department of Justice to essentially let him call the president a lying gossipmonger.

Trump's madness and his weekend of channeling his persecution complex and disseminating it as a deflection from his own perfidy is the obvious headline.

However—the true story is the moving parts of his regime's treachery with Russia—especially those moving parts that have become the wheels now flying off the vehicle!

*

To dodge those wheels and review the headlines as they land—

Foremost: Trump's White House counsel, Don McGahn, reportedly spent the weekend combing the U.S. intelligence services trying to gain access to any FISA Court–ordered surveillance related to Trump or his associates.

That would be twice in a little over a week that the White House directly tried to interfere with the investigation of the Trump Gang and Russia. The first was when Chief of Staff Priebus got the chairmen of the House and Senate intel committees to spin the media on Trump's behalf, and tried to get intelligence officials to do the same.

Stuff like this is what Nixon's White House tried to do with the FBI and the CIA throughout Watergate.

*

Second headline: Longtime Trump confidant Roger Stone confessed—indeed, publicly boasted—over the weekend of knowing in advance about the coming WikiLeaks attacks on Hillary Clinton last October. "Have never denied that Assange and I had a mutual friend who told me WikiLeaks had the goods on HRC and would begin disclosures in Oct. . . . Assange does NOT work for Russians and no one has proved otherwise. Although I never had direct contact with him, such contact would be neither illegal or improper."

Even if Stone is correct about that—this is damning circumstantial evidence. The most generous interpretation is that a key Trump adviser looked the other way before the dissemination of emails stolen in what the American intelligence community asserts to this day was a Russian cyberattack against this nation!

Third headline: Yes, attorney general and former Trump campaign flunky Sessions did the right thing and recused himself from any investigations of Trump and Russia. But he also gave a series of nonsensical interview answers. Asked if anybody in the Trump campaign thought the Russian government favored Trump over Clinton, Sessions answered, "I have never been told that."

The follow-up question: "Do you think they did?"

The Sessions answer: "I don't have any idea . . . You'd have to ask them."

At his confirmation hearing—the one at which he forgot to mention his meetings with the Russian ambassador—the subject of Russia being guilty of interfering with the election came up twice, and Sessions first said, "At least that's what's been reported," and then, "I have no reason to doubt that and have no evidence that would indicate otherwise."

Sessions is coming off as either a bad liar paralyzed with guilt, or a moron.

Fourth headline: Carter Page—the second man Trump ever mentioned as one of his foreign policy advisers—keeps changing his story.

Said on February 15, "I had no meetings, no meetings" with Russian officials in 2016. Said on March 2, about meeting Russian ambassador Sergey Kislyak at the Republican Convention in Cleveland, "I'm not going to deny that I talked to him."

Fifth headline: Campaign national security lackey J. D. Gordon changed his story about how the Republican platform at the convention was 180'd from defending Ukrainian rebels to kissing them off.

Sixth headline: Michael Cohen, Trump's personal lawyer, who has already changed his Russian story at least four times, did not change it a fifth.

However, the businessman Alex Oronov, who organized the controversial "Ukrainian peace plan" that Cohen reportedly hand-carried to General Flynn—he suddenly turned up all dead.

Seventh headline: Whatever it is, it's catching: When the popular ambassador to the UN Vitaly Churkin keeled over at his desk last month, he became the sixth Russian diplomat to die since the day Trump was elected.

Eighth headline: Trump himself was reportedly so outraged by the recusal of the attorney general from the Russian investigation that he went into a three-day spasm of Whataboutism. He began with a demand for an investigation of a 2003 photo of Senator Chuck Schumer with Vladimir Putin, which turned out to be them literally at the ceremony christening a Russian-owned Lukoil service station in New York City.

Schumer and Putin were at a gas station opening—as if they were the cohosts of some radio station morning-zoo program.

The ninth Trump-Russia headline: Trump then tweeted, "The first meeting Jeff Sessions had with the Russian Amb was set up by the Obama Administration," adding—without realizing he was making his own argument look ridiculous—"under education program for 100 Ambs." When that didn't work, Trump moved on to repeating the right-wing radio nutjob patter that Obama had tapped Trump's phone.

When that blew up in Trump's face, there came a tenth headline: The reaction to the conflation of Russia, Obama, and imaginary wiretaps so screwed up the White House that at 8:51 Eastern Time Sunday morning, Press Secretary Spicer declared that, until there was a congressional investigation of Trump's crazy talk, "Neither the White House nor the President will comment further."

Eighteen minutes later, Deputy Press Secretary Sarah Huckabee Sanders went on ABC's *This Week* to comment further.

And twenty-five minutes after that, Spicer commented further on Twitter.

And by late Sunday afternoon, Trump was, according to Maggie Haberman of *The New York Times*, "frustrated by the Sunday shows today/felt people didn't defend him strongly enough on his Obama claim, per ppl close to him."

And at 7:06 Eastern Time Monday morning, the White House—still not commenting further—commented on ABC again, via the deputy press secretary.

Last, the eleventh headline: A question posed in many different quarters. At least seven Trump campaign figures had contact with Russia. Even if every last second of all the interaction was benign, did any of them, at any time, ask their Russian pals if they could lay off the international cybercrime? All of this one-to-one conversation, and did anybody in the Trump Gang say, "You know, you should probably stop hacking our computers and screwing with our election"?

The wheels haven't just come off the bus—the tires have now formed a pile and started a fire!

And of course, Trump, who blamed "the generals" for the loss of the Navy SEAL in Yemen and suggested that threats on Jewish centers had been made by Jewish people . . . None of this panorama of disloyal, amoral interaction with an enemy nation during a presidential election—none of this is his fault.

And you know what, Republicans—he's right!

This is no longer his fault.

This is your fault!

Look to our history. Look to the Civil War, when the entirety of one political party, the Democrats, opposed intervention against slavery, and for personal politics and the evils of omission.

Look to the years before World War II, when the entirety of another political party, the Republicans, opposed intervention against Hitler, and for personal politics and those evils of omission.

What happened to all those men?

They took the fall.

Not one prominent figure in either party in either century . . . survived the political apocalypse that followed their amorality!

They took the fall—as all you gutless Republicans of today will take the fall for enabling this treason involving Russia to remain unrevealed, and this lunatic Trump to remain unimpeached.

THE CONSPIRACY PEDDLER IN CHIEF

Post date • TUESDAY, MARCH 7

We no longer have a president of the United States.

We have an executive for dismissing the facts he doesn't like and believing the lies he does.

We have a head of state-of-paranoia.

We have a conspiracy peddler in chief.

There are positives underlying this insanity: few, but potent.

Such a damaged personality cannot discern that while every new falsehood may bind to him more tightly those who already trust him, they inevitably drive more people away.

Such a narcissist cannot realize that every time he invokes Russia and close ties and wiretaps and the intelligence services and investigations, he does not decrease—he only increases—the chances that the investigations by the intelligence services of the close ties to Russia will be not about others, but about him.

Such a messianic individual cannot fathom that his rumormongering is so dangerous—merely to himself—that even the director of the FBI feels compelled to publicly get out his conclusion that Trump is lying.

But these positives still sit under a pile of excrement, of radioactive waste, of what even a Republican senator correctly describes as a "civilization-warping crisis of public trust."

The immediacy of such a danger—the active crisis of fantasy-based reality in a president—is obvious:

Any man—no matter how immorally or illegally he attained the Oval Office—is still, as Lincoln said, "president of the United States, clothed with immense power."

For the unthinking, the uneducated, the unbalanced who sincerely believe him—or who have chosen to, as if they have a menu of realities from which to select—a lie, a calumny, a slander, a preposterous fiction is automatically less a lie, less a calumny, less a slander, less a preposterous fiction just because he said it.

Thus the flunkies, like House Intelligence Chairman Nunes, and the bottom-feeders of filth, like Fox News and Breitbart and Alex Jones and Mark Levin, line up to endorse and reinforce the lies.

And thus the mighty engines of investigation with which Congress is clothed, and the free press is clothed, are not turned on the obvious, gigantic, irrefutable, horizon-blocking truth that Trump and Manafort and Stone and Cohen and Kushner and Flynn and Sessions and Gordon and Page and Trump Jr. all interacted with the Russians in some nefarious way, great or small, during the campaign and after it.

No. Those investigative engines are turned instead on a previous president and something there is no evidence he did, something there was never even a rumor that he did, something that has been propagated nationally—by the paranoiac in chief, without any substance, governmentally or journalistically—a desperate and manufactured slander designed as part of a cover-up of true and traitorous crimes, containing exactly the same probability of truth as something that would have come to Donald Trump in a dream.

That they will investigate.

And now not even logic and motive are still necessary. Even on the one-in-a-billion chance that none of it is criminal, Trump's connection to Russia is plausible if only because the Russians wanted a president who would give them a free hand in Ukraine and elsewhere, and Trump's desperate ego would let him pay any price—even the freedom of this country he falsely purports to love—to gain ultimate power.

But Trump's Obama claim? What is the theory here? What is the motive? What is the purpose? As Obama's former speechwriter Jon Favreau tweeted: "Barack Obama's master plan: 1) Wiretap the opposition 2) Gather damaging info 3) Say nothing 4) Let him win 5) Ride off into the sunset."

It is as nonsensical as Trump's claim of the Democrats enabling three million illegal votes—all for Hillary Clinton—and none of them in the counties where seventy-seven thousand votes would have swung the election to her.

There are paranoid, insane, unsupported conspiracy theories, but even they divide into the good ones and the bad ones—and the man holding the executive power of the nation can't even tell the difference between them.

He who has already sold birtherism conspiracies, and vaccination conspiracies, and inauguration crowd-size conspiracies, and illegal-vote conspiracies, and a carnage of immigrant-violence conspiracies, and 40-percent-unemployment conspiracies . . . has now sold the-last-president-tapping-his-phone-and-stealing-his-secrets-and-doing-nothing-with-them-before-the-election conspiracies.

This is the immediate danger—the active crisis of fantasy-based reality—into which Donald Trump has pushed this nation with his peddling of the ludicrous.

But the true danger is—which insane conspiracy and which resultant crisis is next.

Trump has already sold to the gullible the snake oil that ISIS is pouring across the nation's borders.

Trump has already sold the stupid on the falsehood that immigrants commit virtually all violent crime and push virtually all drugs—when an immigrant is *less* likely to break the law.

Trump has already sold the racist and the hateful on the idea that a then sitting president of the United States is behind the leaks from his administration, and now that he tapped his phone, apparently just for the hell of it.

What will Trump try to sell next?

What would stop him from announcing that there is a terrorist plot, and behind it is a judge he doesn't like, or a newspaper he doesn't like, or a senator he doesn't like, or a religion or race he doesn't like, or a member of your family he doesn't like?

What would stop him from using that immense power to declare an imminent threat against an institution, a city, a state, the nation as a whole, and this time not merely tweet but act—and close borders, or detain critics, or arrest protesters, or suspend laws and liberties?

What would stop him?!

Who would stop him?!

His enablers?

His cabinet?

His supporters?

His political party?

His FBI director?

His conscience?

His news sources?

Nothing... would stop him.

Except—removal from office.

THAT SPEECH AGED WELL

Post date • THURSDAY, MARCH 9

I am old enough to remember the high-water mark of the Trump presidency.

Can you cast your memory back that far?

The speech?

The one to the joint session of Congress?

The one so measured, so majestic, so devoid of pants-pooping that it prompted a conservative television pundit to say, "I feel like tonight [he] became the president of the United States" ... and it prompted a liberal television pundit to say, "He became president of the United States in that moment, period"?

Remember *all the way back to that?*

That was a week ago.

That was *last* Tuesday.

That speech has not aged well!

Tuesday: forty-eight words in:

"Recent threats targeting Jewish community centers and vandalism of Jewish cemeteries . . . remind us that . . . we are a country that stands united in condemning hate and evil in all its forms."

Tuesday, same day:

Trump implied to a meeting of state attorneys general—according to the one from Pennsylvania—that such anti-Semitic attacks were false flags. Josh Shapiro quoted Trump as saying, "'Sometimes it's the reverse, to make people—or to make others—look bad,' and he used the word 'reverse' I would say two to three times in his comments."

The next Monday? Another anti-Muslim travel ban.

Tuesday? "Dying industries will come roaring back to life. Heroic veterans will get the care they so desperately need."

Tuesday.

Friday?

The Trump regime deported Clarissa Arredondo back to Mexico, more than two weeks after unmarked SUVs showed up at her home near San Diego on Valentine's Day and captured her.

Ms. Arredondo is the mother-in-law of a heroic Navy veteran now working as a contractor in Afghanistan. And the other grandmother of that heroic veteran's two toddlers is on active service with the Army, and she will now have to retire and become a veteran to take over the deported grandmother's role helping raise the kids.

What made Ms. Arredondo so dangerous, so needing to be urgently thrown out of here? She may have once falsified paperwork to get her family a welfare check.

Tuesday: "We have cleared the way for the construction of the Keystone and Dakota Access pipelines—thereby creating tens of thousands of jobs—and I've issued a new directive that new American pipelines be made with American steel."

Tuesday.

Thursday? Fox News: "The Keystone XL oil pipeline won't use American steel in its construction . . ." Turns out Trump wanted you to think he meant the Keystone would use American steel when the truth was, his executive order is only for the *next* "new American pipelines," because Republicans in the Senate voted down an amendment requiring American steel in the Keystone— an amendment proposed by Democrat Al Franken.

Tuesday: "We will soon begin the construction of a great wall along our southern border. It will be started ahead of schedule . . ."

Tuesday.

Thursday?

Reuters discovers that Trump's promise to use existing funds to "begin the construction" has a problem. The only existing funds the Trump regime has been able to find is $20 million.

Twenty million dollars will build you a Mexican wall that is . . . four miles long.

Tuesday: Trump says his government "will be guided by two core principles: Buy American, and hire American."

Tuesday.

Also Tuesday?

Ivanka Trump tweets a photo of herself in the dress she wore to the speech. It is identified by experts as having been designed by a Frenchman, and having been manufactured in the United Kingdom.

Buy American, hire American.

Tuesday: "I have ordered the Department of Homeland Security to create an office to serve American victims. The office is called VOICE—Victims of Immigration Crime Engagement. We are providing a voice to those who have been ignored by our media and silenced by special interests."

Tuesday.

Wednesday? Countless writers and commentators note that before taking power in Germany, the Nazis published a feature called "Letter Box" in their official newspaper, which provided a voice to those who had been ignored by the media and silenced by special interests and had been the victims of crimes by Jews. Once in office, the Nazi government began publicly disseminating the details of crimes by Jews.

Tuesday: "We are blessed to be joined tonight by Carryn Owens, the widow of U.S. Navy Special Operator Senior Chief William 'Ryan' Owens. . . . Ryan is looking down right now, and he's very happy because I think he just broke a record [for the length of an ovation]."

Even though it had been Trump who gave the order that sent Chief Owens to his death, in a raid the previous president would not approve, in a plan so controversial that Owens's father has demanded a formal investigation, pundits—particularly on television—fell all over each other to praise Trump.

"I feel like tonight," said Chris Wallace on Fox, "he became the president of the United States, and everyone is going to have to accept that fact."

"That was one of the most extraordinary moments you have ever seen in American politics, period," said Van Jones—until that moment a liberal—on CNN.

"For people who have been hoping that maybe he would remain a divisive cartoon, which he often finds a way to do, they should begin to become a little bit worried tonight . . .

"He did something tonight that you cannot take away from. He became president of the United States in that moment, period."

Tuesday.

Insight that would last a lunchtime.

Not a divisive cartoon. Became president. Have to accept that fact.

Saturday?

"Terrible! Just found out that Obama had my 'wires tapped' in Trump Tower just before the victory. Nothing found. This is McCarthyism!"

"How low has President Obama gone to tapp my phones during the very sacred election process. This is Nixon/Watergate. Bad (or sick) guy!"

No. Not a divisive cartoon!

As I said: this speech hasn't aged well.

Tuesday: "My job is not to represent the world. My job is to represent the United States of America."

Tuesday.

Thursday?

Trump's attorney general is forced to recuse himself from any investigations of the Trump presidential campaign's interactions with Russia, because—at best—he personally failed to reveal his interactions with Russia while part of the campaign, at a meeting he got to by spending campaign money.

Tuesday: "We can only get there together. We are one people, with one destiny. We all bleed the same blood. We all salute the same flag. And we are all made by the same God."

Tuesday.

Thursday?

A Facebook and Twitter storm about Jeff Sessions—and about the nearly 66 million people who voted for the Democratic candidate: "This whole narrative is a way of saving face for Democrats losing an election that everyone thought they were supposed to win. The Democrats are overplaying their hand. They lost the election, and now they have lost their grip on reality."

"We can only get there together.... We all salute the same flag... we are all made by the same God"—except you 66 million people who voted for Hillary.

Tuesday: "The time for small thinking is over. The time for trivial fights is behind us."

Tuesday.

Saturday?

"Arnold Schwarzenegger isn't voluntarily leaving the Apprentice, he was fired by his bad (pathetic) ratings, not by me. Sad end to great show."

The time for small thinking is over.

The man is not going to change.

The man is not going to improve.

The man is not going to be cured.

The man is not going to become presidential.

The man is not going to devote himself to anything except his own extraordinary, irrational, unquenchable, insatiable, unslakable, immeasurable, bottomless, endless, eternal need...to...

Keep Trump First!...and...

Make His Ego Great Again.

SEVEN YEARS

Post date • MONDAY, MARCH 13

To Donald Trump:

My father died seven years ago.

March 13, 2010.

He died after seven months in hospitals and six months in the surgical intensive care unit, and after a fight against death so extraordinary that it caused the chief of that unit to mistake him for a professional trained athlete, when in fact he hadn't exercised since 1951, and when I told him about it, my dad laughed, even though there was a breathing tube down his throat.

He died with my sister and me having to make the decision to let him go, and he died with her holding his hand and me reading him his favorite James Thurber story and him—I swear—waiting until this very long story was over, and only then profoundly sighing and leaving us.

He died leaving me a hospital bill—for six months of twenty-four-hour-a-day surgical intensive care, another month in standard care, one four-hour operation, and thousands of procedures and scans and drugs and consultations—a bill, if I remember correctly, of approximately one thousand dollars. Most of that was for a television he had rented for a few days, early on. My father had a little private policy. And something he got for being in the Army. And government-issued insurance, Trump—a thing called Medicare. Our out-of-pocket costs: about five dollars a day.

He died after seven months in which we talked every day—as the debate raged around us, and as we could hear the practical impact on the lives and finances of the other patients and families in that hospital of what was then called health care reform or insurance reform, and which shortly after my dad's death became known as the Affordable Care Act and, less officially, Obamacare.

*

Obamacare, which, Trump, you idiot—and that idiot Ryan, and this liar Price, and that liar Chaffetz—now want to undo.

Because, confronted with an independent calculation that repeal by your

Republicans will end insurance for at least fifteen million Americans, and asked how many will lose their coverage under his plan, this sniveling little man Ryan who sucks up to you says, "I can't answer that question. It's up to people . . . People are going to do what they want to do with their lives, because we believe in individual freedom in this country."

Individual freedom—like the freedom to die because you don't have health insurance. The way 122 Americans died every day because they didn't have health insurance before the ACA was passed as my father was dying.

Individual freedom, Trump.

Go to hell, Paul Ryan.

*

Individual freedom, Trump.

Like freedom from taxes for the rich.

The Joint Committee on Taxation, a nonpartisan arm that crunches numbers for Congress, calculated that the Republican gutting of health care that you are leading, Trump, will in the next decade reduce the taxes of those making a million or more a year . . . by $157 billion.

Individual freedom, Trump, or, as this condescending jackass Chaffetz put it, "Americans have choices, and they've got to make a choice. So rather than getting that new iPhone that they just love and want to go spend hundreds of dollars on that, maybe they should invest in their own health care."

The price of an iPhone would not cover those few days my father rented a hospital television, never mind something like cancer drugs or surgery, or the price you are billed to have your father officially declared dead.

Go to hell, Jason Chaffetz.

*

Individual freedom, Trump.

Like the freedom to end the insurance of the 700,000 new Medicaid recipients added just since the reform of 2010, just in Ohio, per the Republican governor there, John Kasich. Kick them off and instead throw them an insurance tax credit of $3,000, and Kasich asks rhetorically, "What kind of insurance are you going to buy for three thousand dollars?"

That's individual freedom, or, as this liar and con man your health and human services secretary, Tom Price, put it, "I firmly believe that nobody will be worse off financially." And of course he's right—if by "nobody" he means insurance companies and Republican donors and the wealthy.

Go to hell, Tom Price.

Individual freedom, Trump, like your budget director insisting that you are focused on health care, not insurance coverage, as if, when they hand you your bill at your hospital or your doctor's office, you could hand it back and say, "I'm focused on care, not on paying you."

Trump—you said, on September 27, 2015: "Everybody's got to be covered... I am going to take care of everybody."

Trump—you said, on February 19, 2016: "You're going to end up with great health care for a fraction of the price. And that's going to take place immediately."

Trump—you said, on January 15 of this year: "We're going to have insurance for everybody."

Only now your budget director says—because you don't have the courage to say it yourself—that "insurance for everybody" means health care, not insurance, which means—nothing. Which means you're on your own.

Go to hell, Trump.

*

Months before my dad died seven years ago, the likelihood that he would became tangible to me. And in that hospital, every day, twice a day, as we talked about that and we talked about health care reform, it began to dawn on me what we were all really debating.

I wrote much of what follows in October 2009.

It's true again, Trump.

Since you evidently think you're immortal, have a sane grown-up explain to you what this next part means.

*

This, ultimately, is about... death.

About preventing it, about fighting it, about resisting it, about grabbing hold of everything and anything to forestall it and postpone it even though we know that the force will overcome us all—always will, always has.

Health care is at its core about improving the odds of life in its struggle against death, of extending that game which we will all lose, each and every one of us, onto eternity, extending it another year or month or second. This is the primary directive of life, the essence of our will as human beings . . .

And when we go to a doctor's office or a hospital or storefront clinic in a ghetto, we are expressing this fundamental cry of humanity: I want to live. I want my child to live. I want my wife to live. I want my father to live. I want my neighbor to live. I want that stranger I do not know and never will know to live . . .

And there is the essence of what this is. What on the eternal list of priorities precedes health? What more obvious role could government have than the defense of the life of each citizen?

We cannot stop every germ that seeks to harm us any more than we can stop every person who seeks to harm us, but we can try, damn it. And government's essential role in that effort—facilitate it, reduce its costs, broaden its availability, improve my health and yours—seems ultimately self-explanatory.

We want to live.

What is government for if not to help us do so?

*

I issue this warning to you, Trump.

Take these steps and you will inherit the wind.

Gut health care in this country so millionaires can save sixteen billion a year in taxes, and you will be killing American citizens.

And before we let you do this, Trump, we will defend ourselves.

Protests? Nonviolent resistance? Good.

A mass refusal to pay insurance premiums? Perhaps—risky.

A general strike? Yes.

Shut the country down, rather than let you kill people.

Health care, Trump, is about life and death.

And right now, you are on the side of death.

And we will not permit this.

RUSSIA, RUSSIA, RUSSIA

Post date • TUESDAY, MARCH 14

"There's a lot more shoes to drop from this centipede," said John McCain about Trump and Russia, shortly after Trump got rid of the United States attorney in New York, as part of what might have been a political purge that Trump saw Sean Hannity suggest on cable, only this U.S. attorney wouldn't resign, so Trump fired him in a Saturday massacre—you know, like Watergate—and then we were reminded that the guy he fired had prosecuted and put into prison a Russian spy who was based in New York, posing as a banker, and another Russian mobster who ran New York's highest-stakes illegal poker game, usually in an apartment at Trump Tower, and then the guy he fired was banned from Russia by Vladimir Putin.

It's not just that McCain's analogy is apt. It's as if there are no shoes on the Trump Human Centipede that aren't about Russia.

*

Russia, Russia, Russia.

Trump claims his phones were tapped.

Then Kellyanne Conway emerges from wherever she was hiding to suggest that—never mind Trump's crazy claim—there may have been wholesale surveillance of the Trump campaign, possibly including "microwaves that turn into cameras. We know that that is just a fact of modern life." Microwaves, you say. Obama was spying on Trump, using microwave ovens, to find out about Russia, Russia, Russia.

*

Meanwhile, Trump's boy, Russia expert and frequent-flier-to-Russia Carter Page, the second name Trump ever dropped as a foreign policy adviser, writes a letter to two senators claiming that his phones were also tapped. Doesn't that mean that Trump is part of the investigation of his gang's connections to Russia? *No reason to believe there's any investigation by the Justice Department!* says Trump's press secretary. *He didn't get that from us!* says the Department of Justice—off the record. *I didn't say no,* says Trump's press secretary. *I said we weren't aware.* Russia, Russia, Russia.

*

Trump Gang members Flynn, Sessions, and J. D. Gordon deny meeting with Russian ambassador Kislyak.

Turns out they all met with him.

Then they all fudged the truth about meeting with him. Then CNN turns up a video of Kislyak last October—and he's fudging the truth about meeting with them. Russia, Russia, Russia.

*

Trump henchman Roger Stone boasts about trading admiring messages with the hacker Guccifer 2.0. Not only does the American intelligence community believe Guccifer is the front for the Russian spies who hacked the Democratic National Committee, but Stone himself believes Guccifer is the front for the Russian spies who hacked the Democratic National Committee. In fact, he wrote a piece stating this for Breitbart on August 5, nine days after the news conference in which Trump said, "Russia, if you're listening, I hope you're able to find the thirty thousand emails that are missing."

Russia, Russia, Russia.

*

Of course, days before he boasted about contact with Guccifer, Stone had already boasted about having a back channel to Julian Assange, who posted the hacked DNC files at WikiLeaks.

And last August, Stone boasted that he knew the DNC materials were about John Podesta. The presumption is that there's a middleman between the Russian spy hackers and Assange, and just about the only thing Roger Stone has yet to boast about would be if he were that middleman.

Russia, Russia, Russia.

*

Then there's Trump's pet Englishman, the Brexit conspirator Nigel Farage.

March 7, WikiLeaks releases documents purporting to reveal CIA hacking tools. March 9, Farage is photographed coming out of the London embassy of the nation of Ecuador—where, for the past five years, has lived Julian Assange! Asked if he had met with Assange presumably moments earlier, Farage says he can't remember why he was in the building. Later, a source in Farage's right-wing extremist political party confirms that Farage met with Assange. March 10, Assange holds a news conference pimping his supposed CIA documents and promising new revelations.

The same day, a British newspaper prints non-WikiLeaks correspondence showing five years of support for Assange by Farage's political party. By the way, as late as October 10, Donald Trump gave a speech in which he bellowed, "I love WikiLeaks." And Trump did not say a thing about the presumed purloined CIA docs as WikiLeaks released them. And as recently as February 28, Nigel Farage had dinner with . . . Trump.

Russia, Russia, Russia.

*

And there's Trump and the Russian fertilizer billionaire. A Florida newspaper wondering why, nine years ago, Dmitry Rybolovlev bought a Palm Beach mansion from Trump, reportedly for about $50 million more than it was worth. And why, twice during the campaign and again as recently as last month, Rybolovlev's private plane landed at a U.S. airport just before, or just after, Trump's private plane landed at the same airport.

Russia, Russia, Russia.

*

And last of all, there was the former director of national intelligence James Clapper . . .

Who was so pissed off that Trump claimed he had been phone-tapped that Clapper went public with the news that in January, days after he briefed Trump about the existence of the Russian showers dossier compiled by the former British spy Christopher Steele, Trump called him and asked him to publicly say the dossier wasn't true.

He wouldn't.

Russia, Russia, Russia.

*

Everything Trump touches turns into a story about Trump and Russia.

*

Oops! I take that back. General Michael Flynn! The very briefly tenured national security adviser who was paid to appear on a Kremlin-controlled television propaganda outlet. The very briefly tenured national security adviser who was paid to go to Moscow to be part of a standing ovation for Putin. The very briefly tenured national security adviser who told the Russians not to worry about sanctions for allegedly meddling in our election. The very briefly tenured national security adviser who either lied to the vice president about Russia or got the vice president to lie for him about Russia.

While he was sitting in on the classified U.S. intelligence briefings Trump was getting as the Republican presidential candidate, Flynn was a paid lobbyist for the nation of *Turkey*.

Turkey, Turkey, Turkey.

*

Only partially obscuring the fact that Flynn, like Trump's call to Clapper, like the sale of the Palm Beach mansion, like Farage's visit to Assange, like Stone's contact with Guccifer, like Kislyak's denial, and Gordon's denial, and Sessions's denial, and Trump firing the United States attorney personally banned by Vladimir Putin . . .

All mainline back to Russia, Russia, Russia.

RUSSIA/WIRETAP/COMEY TESTIMONY

Post date • MONDAY, MARCH 20

We may have just heard the most carefully crafted sentence structure in American political history—and that sentence structure has condemned Donald John Trump.

According to its director, the FBI is "investigating the nature of any links between individuals associated with the Trump campaign and the Russian government . . ." Not "possible links." Not "if there were links." Links. *Any* links. Period.

The FBI's investigation is about the *nature* of the links.

Director Comey used a caveat a minute at that hearing. He made no such disclaimers about links between individuals associated with the Trump campaign and the Russian government.

To him—under oath, before Congress—they exist.

*

Thus, the intelligence community is investigating links between the victorious presidential campaign and the Russians. Thus, the intelligence community has been investigating links between the victorious presidential campaign and the Russians since last July. Thus, the intelligence community will be investigating links between the victorious presidential campaign and the Russians—indefinitely. No time frame. No end date. What's the normal length of such an investigation? "There is no normal," says Comey.

I firmly believe that almost any other American politician hearing these words from the director of the FBI to the House Permanent Select Committee on Intelligence would have resigned the presidency before noon: "I have been authorized by the Department of Justice to confirm that the FBI, as part of our counterintelligence mission, is investigating the Russian government's efforts to interfere in the 2016 presidential election." I also firmly believe that almost any other American politician hearing Comey's next words would have not just resigned the presidency before noon—but fled the country before nightfall:

"And that includes investigating the nature of any links between individuals associated with the Trump campaign and the Russian government, and whether there was any coordination between the campaign and Russia's efforts."

Again, note carefully the grammar.

To paraphrase the old insult: the links—we know what they are, now we're just arguing about the price.

When Representative Jim Himes of Connecticut came back to the point of coordination and collusion and asked whether we should or shouldn't dismiss it, Comey confirmed that this sentence structure—"any links"—was no accident.

Comey answered, "All I can tell you is what we're investigating. Which includes whether there was any coordination between people associated with
the Trump campaign and the Russians." For Comey—keeping his cards not
just close to his vest but sealed inside the deck—these comments were extraordinary.

And that was just the start of Donald Trump's first day of reckoning. Comey
dismissed Trump's wiretap hoax. "I have no information that supports those
tweets." Comey said his bosses dismissed Trump's wiretap hoax. "The Department of Justice has no information that supports those tweets." Admiral Mike
Rogers, the head of the NSA, dismissed the news gossip, cited by Press Secretary
Spicer, that the British had surveilled Trump. Pressed by Congressman Pete
King of New York to agree with former director of national intelligence Clapper
that he had not seen proof of any collusion between the Trump campaign and
Russia, King got nothing more from Rogers and Comey than "No comment."

And Director Comey and Admiral Rogers repeatedly swatted away attempts by majority members like Chairman Nunes and Representative Trey
Gowdy to elevate any procedural leaks, or their publication, to the level of an
investigation of a foreign government's efforts to alter the outcome of our elections, and the information they are investigating that a foreign government
may have coordinated those efforts with the winning presidential campaign!

And in terms of the optics, all this took place the same morning as a series
of panicked, hysterical tweets by Trump insisting, "The Democrats made up
and pushed the Russian story as an excuse for running a terrible campaign."

"This story is FAKE NEWS and everyone knows it!"

*

"The FBI, as part of our counterintelligence mission, is investigating the Russian government's efforts to interfere in the 2016 presidential election, and
that includes investigating the nature of any links between individuals associated with the Trump campaign and the Russian government, and whether
there was any coordination between the campaign and Russia's efforts."

The story is not fake news. The story was not made up by the Democrats. It
is not a "story." It is an investigation by the FBI—and its targets are Donald
Trump's men.

In short, Trump got nothing from Comey or Rogers or even any of the

Republican congressmen backfilling on his behalf who went so far as to imply that the Russians have always supported Republican presidential candidates. Sure—like Ronald Reagan.

Nothing. There was nothing to keep Trump from sinking. The best news he got was that there is an investigation—but that it hasn't reached its conclusions yet. The best news is that the drip-drip-drip of Trump and Russia, and Russia and Trump, and what did Trump know and when did he know it—will continue indefinitely. That was the *best* news. The only way that hearing could have gone worse for Trump was if Vladimir Putin, Michael Flynn, Roger Stone, and Vladimir Ilyich Lenin had been sworn in and confessed.

*

In the past, Trump has claimed that his favorite motion picture of all time is the Orson Welles classic *Citizen Kane*. Might be true, might not; for all we know, he might never have seen it. But one piece of dialogue from that film kept playing in my head as I watched this hearing.

The corrupt politician whom Kane has promised to lock up has discovered Kane's own corruption that will cost him the election. He offers Kane a way out—"you're so sick that you've got to go away for a year or two"—but Kane can't see the reality in front of his face, doesn't know it's over, doesn't save himself and his supporters from humiliation and disaster. And the corrupt politician says to Kane: "If it was anybody else, I'd say what's going to happen to you would be a lesson to you. Only you're going to need more than one lesson. And you're going to get more than one lesson."

Were Trump smart, he would flee the country.

Now.

DONALD TRUMP, LOSER

Post date • TUESDAY, MARCH 21

Sixty days into his presidency and there is only one conclusion: Donald Trump is a loser.

Amid the kaleidoscope of the past two months of prejudice, hatred, revenge, gluttony, dishonesty, corruption, protofascism, and corporate statism this is, perhaps, the only unexpected development—the only true surprise: these people are idiots.

What have they thus far accomplished?

They have left such a bad taste in the mouths of their own supporters that the Gallup tracking poll—showing as late as the 25th of January that Trump approval was at 46 percent and disapproval at 45—has now collapsed to approval at 39, with disapproval at 55 percent.

With control of the White House and the Senate and the House, they got an intelligence hearing Monday that confirmed that the FBI "is investigating the nature of any links between individuals associated with the Trump campaign and the Russian government." They have a Republican member of that committee and the Republican deputy majority whip both insisting that Trump owes Barack Obama an apology for Trump's wiretapping hoax story. They have Trump still propagating this hoax, even as it roots back through an uninformed Fox talking head to an anti–Michelle Obama conspiracy theorist and back further to the Russian propaganda network RT, and they not only still can't get him to let it die, but he tried to draw the German chancellor into supporting his paranoid delusion at a news conference and she looked at him like he was a dick.

They have let Trump attack the free press, the intelligence community, the judiciary, the right to protest, the opposition party, and the vote totals in an election in which he prevailed. They have let Trump go out in public day after day, in setting after setting, acting as if he is not a governmental executive working for this nation, but the owner of a company, and we are all his employees, and if he doesn't like what we do, he will fire us.

They have produced a budget that is cruel, draconian, stupid—and yet have somehow managed to lose the narrative on it so badly that it is actually perceived as worse than it is. They have sent out a profoundly and exhaustingly stupid man named Mick Mulvaney, the budget director, to publicly explain cuts by saying, "Can we really continue to ask a coal miner in West Virginia or a single mom in Detroit to pay for these programs?" without ever thinking that people would respond by wondering why it's okay to ask the coal miner and the single mom to pay the half a million dollars a day it costs to keep Melania Trump living in New York, or to pay the three million a trip it costs to let her husband go play golf. Every weekend. Every goddamned weekend. They have so little idea even how to manipulate public opinion that they have let stand the conclusion that this budget eliminates Meals on Wheels for the elderly and veterans, when it does not—but the damage has left Trump looking like Scrooge in *A Christmas Carol*, asking "Are there no prisons? Are there no workhouses?"

They have tied themselves to gutting health care, changing their own promises about insurance for everybody, then *access* to insurance for everybody, then, finally, no—nothing for anybody.

They have sent an amateur dressed up as a secretary of state into the middle of a hornet's nest in North Korea and China, and when the story gets out that he canceled a dinner because he was fatigued, they can't refute that story, because they themselves banned the press from accompanying him on the trip.

They have had a national security adviser resign, and prove to have been a paid representative of the governments of Russia and Turkey while receiving classified American intelligence. They have had an attorney general misrepresent the truth at his confirmation hearing and thus be forced to recuse himself from key investigations. They have had a senior adviser come under investigation for allegedly wearing a pro-Nazi, anti-Semitic Hungarian medal and tunic to an inaugural ball.

They have tried and failed twice to impose a Muslim ban, with Trump's own words and the words of his minions being quoted back to him by the courts that stopped him. They have insisted that the ban could not wait a day, let alone a week, for implementation—and then they waited weeks to introduce a revised version.

They have been so amateurish using those entry laws that already do exist that their operatives have twice detained the son of the legendary boxer Muhammad Ali, and have kept for questioning the former police chief of Greenville, North Carolina, whose first name is Hassan. They have been so ham-handed at the border that they publicly advertised that they would separate toddlers from their parents at detention centers. They have threatened to deport a man with a Hispanic name who was born in Puerto Rico. They have staggered from insisting that the border wall would be paid for by Mexico to insisting that it would be paid for by us, with reimbursements from Mexico, to explaining that it would be paid for with available funds to having to acknowledge that they only have enough money to build a wall four miles long.

Under their inspiration, the Secret Service has become so dispirited or incompetent that it had a laptop full of Trump Tower floor plans stolen, was found to have had agents who took selfies with Trump's sleeping grandson, and needed seventeen minutes to find a fence jumper at the White House.

They have been so slovenly about security that passersby at Trump's Mar-a-Lago resort were able to photograph him studying data about North Korea, and last weekend one gawker boasted of eluding the Secret Service there in order to take a selfie with one of Trump's endless portraits of himself.

They have done all this . . . in just sixty days.

These people are idiots.

*

This is no longer merely about Trump's substandard and dysfunctional mental, psychiatric, or intellectual status. This is now—most urgently—about his unadulterated and unceasing incompetence, and the unadulterated and unceasing incompetence of those he has brought with him into government. This is about the realization by his opponents and supporters—a realization seemingly growing geometrically every single day—that the worst-case Trump scenario is going to be the standard operating procedure—until we remove this incompetent and unstable individual from office and rush to save this nation while there is still a chance to do so.

I ALONE CAN BREAK IT

Post date • WEDNESDAY, MARCH 22

"I alone can fix it."

July 21, 2016, at the Republican convention in Cleveland, the five Trump words that officially proclaimed his bid to overthrow the traditional government of the United States of America and replace it with him. As I have argued here this week, you can look at the first sixty-plus days of his presidency as a succession of losses and incompetence and humiliations that would have sent almost any other human being who found himself in Trump's shoes fleeing for the Cayman Islands.

But one comment by one woman with the improbable name of Charla Mc-Comic has me wondering if this—this chaos-monger, this embarrassment, this petulant little boy refusing to shake Angela Merkel's hand, this doer of this latest stuff he did today, this imbecile in imbecile's clothing—has me wondering if all this is actually the plan.

"I alone can fix it."

Charla McComic is the woman from Lexington, Tennessee, whom Jenna Johnson of *The Washington Post* found. Ms. McComic is fifty-two years old, her son lost his job and the health insurance that came with it, and yet his health insurance premium dropped from $567 a month to $88 a month. "A blessing from God," said Ms. McComic—a blessing from God via Donald Trump. Quoting her again: "I think it was just because of the tax credit."

That's the Trump-Ryan-Republican plan to in part replace the Affordable Care Act with a series of tax credits.

She thinks her son's insurance premium plummeted because of the Trump plan that hasn't even been passed by the House and Senate, let alone become law.

She thinks Trump did this for her.

In fact—Obama did this for her. Her son's insurance premium dropped $479 a month due to Obamacare.

But not in her mind. Nope. Trump brought her God's blessing.

"I alone can fix it."

Do you remember that a majority of Iraqis—this is in the twenty-first century, mind you—believed that Saddam Hussein wore a magical stone around his neck, or had one implanted in his arm, that made him invulnerable to attack? And that if somehow he was killed, chaos would consume Iraq?

"I alone can fix it."

Have you watched Turkey in the past year? A country riven with terrorism and sectarianism, coming apart at the seams. And then this lunatic bully Erdoğan either fomented a coup against his own government, which included insurgents who just happened to not shoot down the plane he was in while they were next to it—or, if it wasn't a false flag, he just happened to be in position to almost immediately exploit it, to detain, arrest, or dismiss as many as 150,000 of his own citizens and blame everything on a dissident living in Pennsylvania, and put to a national vote his bid to eliminate the remnants of democracy and place all power in his own hands.

"I alone can fix it."

"I'm a Leninist," Steve Bannon told a reporter from *The Daily Beast* in a 2013 conversation he now claims he does not remember. "Lenin wanted to destroy the state, and that's my goal, too. I want to bring everything crashing down and destroy all of today's establishment."

Thus "I alone can fix it" would actually just be shorthand for a longer quote: "I alone can fix it . . . after so many of you never notice that I alone broke it."

Mind you, I'm not *convinced* of this.

Most of the fascists who have popped up to seize power in this country's history have been pretty easy to analyze. The question "Why in the hell are they doing this this way?" does not usually come with a series of multiple-choice answers. I'm still not convinced that Trump and his cronies are not just morons who have tried to apply the simple rules that always worked for them in corporate ownership to the mega-complexity of geopolitics. I'm still not convinced they're not all crazy. I'm still not convinced they're not all stoned.

They sure *act* stoned.

But what if this is the plan?

Claim the British tapped his phones, threaten North Korea and China, insult the German chancellor, try to drag her into his paranoid wiretapping hoax, quote a bozo from Fox for it, turn around and throw the bozo from Fox under the bus, blame the rest of the news media for painting the Merkel meeting as bad, and himself paint Merkel as some kind of deadbeat—all in a span of twenty-four hours. What would all that mean to Ms. Charla "God's Blessing" McComic in Lexington, Tennessee?

Why—it would mean her president is under attack.

By the British. By the Germans. By the North Koreans. By the Chinese. By Obama. By fake news. By Fox News. By the judges. By the Democrats. By the paid protesters. By the Muslims. By the Hispanics. By the non-Christians.

"I alone can fix it."

And when it's broken? Will it matter who is really at fault to Charla McComic? When some atrocity from this medieval budget gets through? When, say, the Delta Regional Authority and two similar agencies that Trump wants to cut *get* cut—the agencies that fix the roads and the sewers and fund the health clinics and support the local small businesses in 698 rural counties, including in Charla McComic's Tennessee, 698 rural counties that Trump won by 16 percent—what happens when the Delta Regional Authority goes away?

Trump blames somebody else.

And Charla McComic blames somebody else. The Democrats did it. The Republicans did it. The career politicians did it when they altered his budget.

That'd never *work*, though. Of course not. He could never get away with being "President I Didn't Do It." And he could never pitch—for nearly three weeks—a hoax that Obama tapped his phones. Or insist it was reported in *The New York Times*. Or that he used quote marks on his tweets about it when half his tweets had no quote marks. Or claim that he disproved birtherism. Or insist that the generals lost the Navy SEAL in Yemen. Or contend that the judiciary had no right to interfere with his idea of legal and illegal travel bans, or what is safe and what is terroristic. And he could never get people thinking the way they thought in Iraq, or the way they think in Turkey. He could never get Charla McComic to convince herself, by herself, that her son's insurance dropped $479 a month due not to Obamacare but to Trump tax credits that don't exist yet. And even if she did start thinking that way, so what? She's obviously on the fringes of society, not very bright, not very . . .

She's a retired schoolteacher.

*

Charla McComic and her friends, by the way, campaigned for him, started a motorcade, shouting his name at passersby. "We said: 'Who else would we do this for, besides Trump?' We agreed on the Lord. We would stand here for the Lord, but that's about it." So what happens if McComic's son now actually loses his insurance because of Trump? Presumably all Trump would have to do is . . . blame somebody. Anybody. She believes him. He could probably convince her he has a magic stone under his skin.

But—if this is the plan—maybe the stone is for later.

Maybe that's for when there is a real crisis that Trump fostered, and he ignores the courts and the Congress and the Constitution and blames somebody else for it.

Right now, the only thing he has to do is just say it again to her:

I alone can fix it . . .

After so many of you never notice that I alone . . . broke it.

FIRST TO FLIP GETS LESS JAIL TIME

Post date • MONDAY, MARCH 27

Trump couldn't make a deal on health care, but Michael Flynn might have made a deal with the FBI?

The Russia story continues to grow grimmer and bigger and deadlier, like a funnel cloud, moving like a living thing out at the horizon.

- The word "treason" has been invoked by the unlikeliest of sources;
- By process of elimination, it seems as if Flynn—or somebody from the Trump Gang—may be ready to testify against the rest of them;
- The White House seems to be setting up Flynn and maybe a second guy as its scapegoats;
- And . . . the Chairman of the House Intelligence Committee has been engulfed in a full, weeklong spasm of panic.

Part by part.

I. "FBI UNCOVERING EVIDENCE OF TREASON. THERE IS NO OTHER WORD FOR IT"

That's a helluva statement.

I couldn't just make that statement, even just as commentary.

But that was one man's comment when he retweeted the McClatchy news report that FBI investigators probing Russian sabotage of the presidential election were now looking to see whether Breitbart, Infowars, and maybe other American right-wing sites were knowingly involved in Russian cyber operations. "FBI uncovering evidence of treason. There is no other word for it."

Who wrote that? Professor Richard W. Painter, of the University of Minnesota Law School, who from February 2005 to July 2007 was President George W. Bush's chief ethics lawyer. He uses the word "treason." *Seven* times. Like after the CNN report that the FBI is culling through evidence that Trump associates communicated with suspected Russian operatives to possibly coordinate the leaks damaging to the Clinton campaign. Painter, Friday: "Despite mounting evidence of collusion and treason, President Trump is still spouting the Kremlin line."

So, to cite the full quote from sixteenth-century British courtier and author John Harington:

Treason doth never prosper: what's the reason?
Why, if it prosper, none dare call it treason.

None dare call it treason.
Except the ethics lawyer for President George W. Bush.
So you are probably okay using the term.

2. LET'S MAKE A DEAL

So, there's a good chance you may have committed some light treason. What should you do now?

To again paraphrase the former NSA and Naval War College figure John Schindler: First ones to make a deal usually get the lightest prison sentences.

Friday: security expert, Harvard lecturer, and somebody I was proud to help bring to MSNBC, Juliette Kayyem, put together three mildly interesting facts and realized that one other name was missing, and that name and why it was missing was way more interesting.

Former Trump campaign manager Paul Manafort volunteered for a limited interview with the House Intelligence Committee.

Longtime Trump henchman Roger Stone demanded to make an appearance before the House Intelligence Committee.

The second man ever named by Trump as a foreign policy adviser, Carter Page, also said he would talk to the House Intelligence Committee.

Monday morning, *The New York Times* revealed that Jared Kushner—whose only known skill is that he has survived being Trump's son-in-law—has been asked to testify to the Senate Intelligence Committee.

But, as Juliette Kayyem realized, the other key actor in whatever the Trump-Russia Dance of Deceit really is—*he* hasn't said boo about testifying anywhere.

General Michael Flynn.

Thus, says Juliette, the question in the intelligence and security circles in which she travels is: Could Flynn be cutting a deal with the FBI?

Flynn, of course, was briefly national security adviser until it turned out not only that every wild report about him and Russia was true, but that some of them were sanitized versions of true . . .

Then it turned out that he was also on the Trump campaign team and the Turkish payroll simultaneously . . .

Now, former CIA director James Woolsey says he was at a meeting last summer at which Flynn, on the Trump campaign team, talked to Turkish officials about "removing" the Muslim cleric on whom Turkish dictator Erdoğan has blamed all of his country's problems.

You can translate "removing" as "kidnap a legal resident of the United States from his home in Pennsylvania and take him to imprisonment and/or death in Turkey."

Making a deal to flip and tell all he knows about Trump or whomever is Flynn's only way out, since he could be charged with some traitorous offenses involving two different foreign countries.

His reaction? His spokesman told a reporter that, to this story, Flynn is not "responding."

3. SCAPEGOAT TIME

As Humphrey Bogart cooed to Mary Astor in *The Maltese Falcon,* "Don't be silly—you're taking the fall." Funny that Juliette Kayyem thinks that Mike Flynn may have made a deal with the FBI. Seen the blood-curdling cover of the Trump-friendly tabloid the *National Enquirer*?

"Trump Catches Russia's White House Spy!"

"How He Tricked the Bungling FBI."

"'23 agents have infiltrated Congress, federal bureaus & the military!'"

Spoiler alert: They mean General Mike Flynn.

But there are plenty of buses, under which plenty of the Trump-Putinistas can be successfully thrown. The Associated Press story that Paul Manafort signed a $10 million contract with a Russian oligarch in 2006? The deal Manafort said would "greatly benefit the Putin Government"? The Trump government responded by dismissing Manafort's role with the campaign as a "volunteer"—as somebody "who played a very limited role for a very limited amount of time," as somebody there only to "count delegates."

Paul Manafort was Donald Trump's second campaign manager.

All that's missing for Manafort is the bus. And remember what Mom always said: Never run for the bus—there will always be another one.

4. WALKING IN THE NUNES OF LIFE

And finally: in American politics, we've seen guilty suspects panic and innocent suspects panic and vindicated suspects panic, but not since Ken Starr have we seen somebody who is, in effect, the prosecutor panic.

Devin Nunes, chairman of the House Intelligence Committee, is acting as if he is about to flee the country. He told the media he had some kind of intelligence information that somehow backstopped Trump's wiretapping hoax—possibly violating the law just by saying that. He then took that information to Trump—like a prosecutor handing over evidence to a defendant, or at least the associate of a defendant—possibly violating the law again. He explained that he did this amazingly stupid thing because Trump had been "taking a lot of heat in the news media."

He did this before sharing any of whatever the intel was with the rest of his own committee. He had to apologize to his own committee. He then was unable or unwilling to deny that this information that supposedly supported Trump had originated with Trump.

Then *The Daily Beast* quoted three unnamed committee officials and a former national security official who said that the night before all of this started, Nunes was in an Uber with a staffer, got a call or a text or an email, and immediately bolted out of the car, and for hours nobody knew where he was.

Then, Monday morning it was reported that Nunes had been at the White House that day to meet his intel source—but his spokesman said that while, yes, he was on the White House grounds, he didn't go to the White House itself.

Because this is what happens when you elect Inspector Clouseau to Congress. This is the guy nominally leading the congressional investigation! Who, of course, was also a member of Trump's presidential transition team and just happened to be at one of General Flynn's meetings with the Turkish foreign minister. And all of this while my friend Andrea Mitchell reported that there were "a lot of former transition team members in and outside of the White House now purging their private phones." And all of this while the Russian propaganda website Sputnik may get credentials as part of the foreign press, covering the White House.

*

This is not blowing over.

This has not stopped expanding.

This is not something for which we can't use the big words.

This is about whether the man elected president is loyal to the United States of America, or whether he is loyal to the Russian Federation.

This is about—to quote George W. Bush's White House ethics lawyer—each of the seven times he has used the word:

Treason, treason, treason, treason, treason, treason—and Treason.

COULD TRUMP PASS A SANITY TEST?

Post date • WEDNESDAY, MARCH 29

His daily behavior getting weirder and weirder and weirder—like today, after his candidacy was nearly ended by the pussy-grabber tape, he has now been reported to have become, as president, verbally and grossly fixated on the breasts of the Japanese prime minister's translator.

His grasp of history doubted during the campaign when he repeated the tabloid gossip that Senator Cruz's father was involved in a presidential assassination, he has now given a speech suggesting he believes that nobody knows which political party the first Republican president belonged to.

His intellectual capacity questioned during the transition, when he reportedly revealed that he thought NATO members paid dues to the United States, he—as president—reportedly directly demanded to the chancellor of Germany that her country pony up $375 billion.

His campaign manager convinced that microwave ovens—not microwaves, but microwave ovens—can turn into cameras, and his transition team on the record asking about using tanks during the inaugural parade, as if this was May Day 1962 at the Kremlin, and a guy on Fox News who used to be Glenn Beck's vacation relief insisting that Trump told him he was on the short list for the Supreme Court.

With all that, I want to ask a question I first asked a year ago:

Could Donald Trump pass a sanity test?

*

With the help of a couple of professionals in the field and using only Trump's own words and actions, I scored him on an actual twenty-question screening test for psychopaths. The most you could get was 40 points. The threshold for probably being a psychopath was 30 points. Trump's words and actions got him 32 points. He could still finish life as high as 36, since two of the questions pertain to criminal record and violation of parole, and there's plenty of time for him on both.

Short answer: he couldn't pass a sanity test, then or now. Open book.

This little problem is, of course, disastrous in a presidential candidate, though the minority of 63 million who voted for him either didn't notice he was the craziest nominee of all time or chose to ignore it. But in a president, the problem escalates to, you know, the possible end of the world. First, the thing with the purported invoice he handed, literally or figuratively, to Angela Merkel—the thing that happened just before this happened, according to *The Times* of London, which has kept its credibility more or less intact since 1785, or which didn't happen according to a White House that has already spent all of its credibility as of day 68.

This isn't hard to grasp, and anybody sane whose parents were alive during World War II grasped it as kids, because they saw the Germans as Nazis and even they understood why suddenly we had to accept the Germans as friends. Geographically, Germany is essential to American security—it is our symbolic front line against Russia, and Russia's primary geopolitical goal since 1945 has been to break up the German-American alliance. Politically, Germany is essential to American security because the last time we pushed it away, after World War I, when it rose again it was powerful enough by itself to start World War II. If we help it with its self-defense—even if we pay a little more of the freight than Germany does—we are in fact paying for our self-defense. Instead—and, by the way, the source for the London *Times* story is a minister of the German government—Trump handed Merkel a bill for a supposed short-fall since 2002—with compound interest.

This is nuts—done by a guy who's nuts.

*

Then there's the translator story.

Graydon Carter, the publisher of *Vanity Fair*: "Vintage Trump is not going anywhere anytime soon. A couple of weeks earlier, during a visit by the Japanese prime minister, Shinzō Abe, the president told an acquaintance that he was obsessed with the translator's breasts—although he expressed this in his own, fragrant fashion." You can decide which of several vulgar terms Trump used about the woman—which bit of "locker room talk," the euphemism by which Trump so cynically and successfully made his boasts about sexual assault vanish during the campaign. The point is—nobody at the White House even bothered to deny this. Why would they?

Trump is already disconnected enough from reality to presume that he has the right to talk that way—and disconnected enough from reality that not only did he get the prime minister's name wrong, but the tweet in which he got it wrong and called him "Prime Minister Shinzo"—as if he wanted you to call him "President Donald"—is still in his timeline, uncorrected.

As is every other crazy thing he's done just since becoming president— uncorrected: the Obama-wiretapped-me hoax; blaming the Muslim-ban air-port chaos on Delta computer problems; bringing his own fanboys with him to applaud during his speech at the CIA; the whole inauguration-crowd-size delusion; the three-million-illegal-votes delusion; the five-million-illegal-votes delusion; praying at the National Prayer Breakfast for Arnold Schwarzenegger's ratings; not knowing Frederick Douglass is dead, when he's been dead since 1895.

And what is, to me, the surest sign of reality disconnect—the craziest thing so far, possibly worse than all the other ones combined. If you haven't heard about this yet, please sit down, surrender a few seconds of your life that you'll never get back, and pray there is a God to help us, and let Trump fill you in on one of the great secrets of American history, about arguably our greatest president, Abraham Lincoln. "Great president. Most people don't even know he was a Republican, right? Does anybody know? Lot of people don't know that."

No.

Hadn't heard.

Who knew?

Let. That. Sink. In.

Huge if true.

Game-changer.

I'll just leave that here.

Life comes at you fast.

Mic drop.

*

Are you effing kidding me?

Lincoln, the first Republican president, on Mount Rushmore, face on the five and on the penny, only president on the front page of the GOP website besides Trump, and Trump thinks that "most people don't even know he was a Republican"?

And in context it's even worse. He made this claim to the *National Republican Congressional Committee fund-raising luncheon.*

"Hey . . . did you guys ever hear about this fella Reagan?"

That was the moment I thought back on that sanity test and wondered if maybe he could score not 32 out of 40, but 42 out of 40.

Chapter 9

APRIL 2017

TRUMP IS PANICKING OVER RUSSIA

Post date • MONDAY, APRIL 3

Trump is panicking.

About Russia.

It is often hard to be sure what you are actually seeing when you look at him. There is so much going on. So little of it makes sense to ordinary, sane eyes. But this? This is obviously panic. And the reasons he is panicking may include a man named Mikhail Kalugin, also a growing understanding that the key to Trump's fatal Russian scandal is less about fake news and more about hacking the voter registration rolls in about twenty different states before the election.

First, the panic. Twitter, bright and early in the morning. Turning to his private intelligence service, *Fox & Friends*. Can't stop bringing up spying. Can't stop bringing up Russia. But now unable to find anything else to deflect whatever his people did by invoking Hillary Clinton's campaign chairman's brother's company's legal lobbying. For a bank, for $28,000 a month. And then: panicking, defined:

"Did Hillary Clinton ever apologize for receiving the answers to the debate? Just asking!"

You wouldn't get the answers to a debate.

You'd get the questions.

*

There are times when Donald Trump must make no sense *even to Donald Trump*. And in two other tweets, less than twenty-one hours apart over the weekend, he contradicted himself, first applauding news reporting based on government leaks to anonymous sources, then condemning news reporting based on government leaks to anonymous sources.

But the panic wasn't limited to Twitter. Common sense would dictate that Trump should never mention any of the following things again: surveillance, wiretapping, intel, leaking, Russia, or, say, "outside things changing the course of a presidential race."

Trump, Sunday, talking to the *Financial Times* about the French presidential race:

Question: "In France, Marine Le Pen has a very similar message to you, not identical. Do you think a victory for her would validate what you have done here?"

Don't answer it / don't answer it / don't answer it / don't hint about Russian interference / don't hint about Russian interference / don't hint about Russian interference.

"I don't know what is going to happen. I know that some outside distractions have taken place which have changed that race. . . . You know, some outside things have happened that maybe will change the course of that race."

What's the French word for "panic"?

*

Trump is not panicking solo.

The Devin Nunes story—a Profile in Panic if ever there was one—is now well documented: that the supposedly exculpatory surveillance intel Nunes rushed to the White House to loudly share with Trump was reportedly shared with him the night before at the White House by two or three White House lawyers.

And you may have seen a couple of Sean Spicer's Baghdad Bob news conferences last week, in which he twisted himself into such knots that—as the former Justice Department spokesman Matthew Miller put it—"according to Spicer, Hillary Clinton has such close connections to Russia that they intervened in the election to elect her opponent."

That's panic. From Trump. From his White House. From his pet congressman. Because of somebody named Mikhail Kalugin? Head of the economics section at the Russian embassy in Washington, Kalugin went home to Russia last August after a six-year stint in this country. Last week, the impeccable BBC reporter Paul Wood reported that U.S. officials have confirmed that Kalugin was, in fact, "a member of one of Russia's spying organizations, the SVR or GRU." And so what? There are a lot of spies here under diplomatic cover from a lot of countries—except Mikhail Kalugin may have been the only one who was first identified as a spy in a little thing called the Christopher Steele dossier, the one with Trump and the Moscow prostitutes and the bathroom stuff and all that. "A leading Russian diplomat, Mikhail Kulagin," Steele wrote in the dossier, getting the man's name wrong, "had been withdrawn from Washington at short notice because Moscow feared his heavy involvement in the U.S. presidential election operation . . . would be exposed in the media there." In other words, it appears that the investigation James Comey of the FBI confirmed at the House hearing two weeks ago has not only nailed Kalugin as Russia's key man in Washington working on the American election, but in so doing confirmed yet another critical detail in the Steele dossier.

And if that story by itself didn't cause Trump or somebody close to him to fly into full-scale existential panic, something else Wood of the BBC reported must have: "The U.S. government identified Kalugin as a spy while he was still at the embassy. . . . A retired member of a U.S. intelligence agency told me that Kalugin was being kept under surveillance before he left the U.S."

Surveillance?

Of the Russian operative in Washington trying to help Trump win the election? Dates of meetings, transcripts of conversations, maybe recordings? Last August and earlier? Oops. Who else would be on those transcripts or recordings?

*

And then there's what Wood of the BBC—and several other, less mainstream news sites—report that American intelligence has finally figured out about what the Russians were actually trying to do to help Trump win. Remember the mysterious news last August that hackers had accessed the computers containing voter registration records in Arizona and Illinois? And then the

ABC report that this was tried in at least twenty different states? And then the director of national intelligence said there had been probing and scanning of registration rolls, "in most cases originated from servers operated by a Russian company," and we were all left wondering: why just scan the voter polls? Just to prove you could hack the computers? A test run for something?

No.

The voter rolls were the goal.

Copying them.

The Russians probing and scanning and copying the names of American voters. The names, the email addresses, the party affiliations of voters. Each could then be sent—by email, on Facebook, in a tweet—only the stories most likely to keep them from voting for Hillary Clinton. Stories based on materials the Russians had already hacked from the Democratic National Committee. Stories based on materials hacked from the emails of John Podesta. Stories not based on anything.

Microtargeting, it's called. But this would be microtargeting with the best, most specific list of registered voters that a political campaign could ever get: the actual official government list of registered voters. The kind of stuff that would be gold to a political data-mining company like, say, Cambridge Analytica, whose vice president and board member is, or was, Steve Bannon. Cambridge Analytica—up to $5 million of the equity of which is or was owned by Steve Bannon. Cambridge Analytica—which has its headquarters in New York, eight blocks down from Trump Tower.

Moscow's man in Washington in charge of trying to help Trump win. Wiretapped, to borrow somebody's favorite phrase. Along with whoever he talked to. Evidence that Russians hacked the names and online identities of voters in twenty key states. And did so to steal the data that companies like the one Steve Bannon was vice president of would kill for.

Ohhhhhh, Donald . . .

This is bad.

I'd panic, too.

FLYNN AND THE DOG THAT DID NOTHING IN THE NIGHTTIME

Post date • TUESDAY, APRIL 4

Perhaps the most crucial break in Trump's Russia scandals comes to us fresh from the pages of *The Strand Magazine* and its new issue for December 1892.

Inspector Gregory of Scotland Yard asks Sherlock Holmes, "Is there any other point to which you would wish to draw my attention?"

Holmes replies: "To the curious incident of the dog in the nighttime."

Gregory states: "The dog did nothing in the nighttime."

Holmes concludes: "That was the curious incident."

*

Publicly, the attorney for General Michael Flynn—agent of the Turkish government, Russian television contributor, and not-briefly-enough national security adviser in this shambles of a presidency—*publicly*, Flynn's attorney volunteered Flynn to testify to the intelligence committee of the Senate or the House or both and confirmed discussions about testifying and even revealed that he might not be asking for full immunity for his client . . .

And by the following morning he and Flynn had been turned down.

First, a "senior congressional official" said off the record that the Senate committee viewed Flynn's bid as "wildly preliminary," and that immunity was "not on the table," and a second source added, "at this time." By the next morning, the ranking Democrat on the House Intelligence Committee, Adam Schiff, in essence said, "too soon," and after Trump's crazy tweet suggesting Flynn should seek immunity from what Trump wants us to believe is a fake-news witch hunt, Schiff added, everybody should meet Flynn's offer with skepticism. The headline here is not so much Flynn's offer—but the reaction to it from both intelligence committees.

In short: The dog did nothing in the nighttime.

That was the curious incident.

Because other, similar dogs, in other, similar nighttimes, have barked the house down. In 1973, as the unraveling of the Watergate cover-up began to accelerate, White House counsel John Dean realized he was being set up as the scapegoat. President Nixon asked Dean to write a report summarizing everything he knew about the scandal. Dean—then, as now, no dummy—quickly figured out that Nixon could use the document as a shield and say the report was the first time he had heard these details, and also as a spear against Dean by noting that it was odd that Dean knew all this stuff, when he, Nixon, didn't. Dean knew he needed to make a deal—with somebody. His lawyer initially approached federal prosecutors with Dean's offer to testify—in exchange for immunity—testify not against the president but against his immediate supervisors. As Dean's attorney Charles Shaffer colorfully quoted Dean: "We can't talk about 'The P!'" The feds thought about it, and turned him down.

Then Nixon fired Dean.

Dean's lawyer then went to the new committee that the Senate had formed to investigate Watergate, which also had the right to request immunity for its witnesses. When Dean told them he was now ready to "talk about 'The P,'" Dean got his immunity.

He got it immediately.

He also got something else immediately—he went right into the Federal Witness Protection Program. They moved him out of his home. They moved him to another state. The day two months later when the Senate committee found a witness willing to confirm Dean's suspicion that Nixon had secretly taped all the conversations in the Oval Office? Committee counsel Sam Dash had to get Dean to come back from a secure, undisclosed location in Florida just to tell him and get his reaction. Starting in the spring of 1973, John Dean spent a total of 540 days as a protected witness.

Those dogs didn't just bark the house down.

They barked the White House down.

*

But Flynn's offer didn't get so much as a tail wag.

I had breakfast with John Dean last Saturday morning. I've known him for nearly twenty years and consider him both a friend and a true American hero. Happily, we had so much to talk about that Michael Flynn barely took up five minutes—but as usual, John made the most of them. Yes, the obvious reaction to Flynn's offer to make a deal is the suspicion voiced by Adam Schiff and reinforced by this child Trump's tweet. His lawyer may have offered nothing and demanded everything. Less obviously, these unusually public comments—by the attorney and by Congressman Schiff—could be opening gambits, each man staking his ground for the battle to come over what Flynn testifies to, and what he gets for it.

Except that Flynn's lawyer is named Robert Kelner, and his bachelor's degree was in politics and Russian studies, and he wrote his thesis on the black sheep of the Russian Revolution, Trotsky, and he was a Never-Trumper, and in June he tweeted, "Spy novel script: Russia hacks #DNC for @realDonaldTrump oppo. Trump says nice things about #Putin. Hmmm." And three weeks before the election, Kelner blasted Trump for claiming the voting was rigged, saying, "The only real threat to this election is the reported effort by Russian intelligence services to hack election systems, which is something that Trump himself has failed to condemn."

Not only does that *not* sound like a lawyer offering nothing and demanding everything, but Kelner's letter sounds like he's not *asking* for everything. It ends: "No reasonable person, who has the benefit of advice from counsel, would submit to questioning in such a highly politicized, witch hunt environment without assurances against unfair prosecution."

"Unfair."

Not "assurances against prosecution." Assurances against *unfair* prosecution.

John Dean reminded me that even he didn't get blanket immunity and didn't ask for it. He got "use" immunity—they can't use what you say while testifying against you, but everything else you've done is still fair game.

So Flynn's offer to testify is made by an anti-Trump, Russian-conspiracy-believing student of Russian history, whose law firm biography identifies his areas of expertise as including: "Federal and state campaign finance, lobbying disclosure, pay to play, and government ethics law . . . the Federal Election Campaign Act, Lobbying Disclosure Act, Ethics in Government Act, Foreign Agents Registration Act, and Foreign Corrupt Practices Act." In short, it sounds as though Mr. Kelner was born specifically to represent Michael Flynn. And the Senate and House intelligence committees aren't climbing over each other to make a deal with Flynn and his anti-Trump lawyer?

*

John Dean smiled.

It may be very simple, he said. You immunize somebody to get him to testify against somebody bigger. Flynn would not be given any kind of immunity to testify against Paul Manafort or Carter Page, probably not even against Jared Kushner. The only person bigger than Flynn in this scandal is Donald Trump. Why wouldn't they jump at a chance to get a witness to testify against Trump, even if they had to let Flynn get away with whatever he did?

The likeliest reason?

They don't need him to make the case against Trump.

They don't need anybody to make the case against Trump.

They may have made the case against Trump *already*.

Turns out the dog may not be doing nothing in the nighttime.

He may be reading through all the transcripts and listening to all the recordings of the Russian embassy economist whom American intelligence has reportedly identified as the spy Putin put in Washington to supervise Russian efforts to get Trump elected.

And it may also turn out that the witness vital to convicting Donald Trump is actually Donald Trump.

SO—NEW ELECTION?

Post date • WEDNESDAY, APRIL 5

So.

New election?

Our last one was influenced by a foreign power, coordinated with the victorious presidential campaign—influenced and coordinated, that is, barring the most extraordinary and unexpected vindication, one so sweeping that not even Trump's most ardent supporters have successfully hinted at it, let alone articulated it.

So—new election?

Obviously, it will be impossible ever to prove that Russian cyberwarfare, an internationally managed disinformation campaign, targeted marketing tied to hacked and stolen voter registration records, and maybe even laundered money caused the seventy-seven thousand Americans who decided the Electoral College count to actually vote the way they did, and that they otherwise would not have voted. We cannot examine the brains of every voter in the country, and Lord knows that with the ones who voted for Trump we wouldn't have much to examine anyway.

But the mechanics of the interference—and let's call it what it was: a Russian act of war, a virtual invasion of the United States, with the collaboration and support of Americans who would be, by legal definition, traitors to this country—the mechanics of how that war was successfully waged against our election and our freedoms and our way of life: that can be proved.

So . . . new election?

Not only are those who oppose Donald Trump getting closer to connecting every link in that chain, but each time he opens his mouth about how he was "wiretapped" and how his campaign was spied upon, he is also connecting every link in that chain. Humpty Dumpty over there is simply so focused on his unquenchable, existential need to make himself the victim that he has begun to resemble the proverbial defendant charged with killing his parents who complains he is being persecuted even though he's an orphan.

So: new election?

There is no philosophical construct in which, were the Russian conspiracy proved and Trump impeached and removed from office, the Republican Party should be rewarded with continued control of the White House. The Republicans not only had ample opportunity to derail Trump's nomination, and even his victory in the Electoral College, but he gave them a dozen reasons and opportunities to do the right thing. They did not. To hell with them.

*

So—new election?

Well, we don't do it that way. We have had a presidential vote of some kind every fourth year since 1788. We have held a presidential election when nobody knew what the rules were and only six states had popular voting. We have held a presidential election while the British were forming a blockade of our ports. We have held a presidential election in the middle of the Civil War.

Every. Four. Years.

You want a new election? You'll get it. In 2020.

*

And none of that is in the Constitution.

Article 2, section 1, clause 6. It is amazingly vague. It was later clarified by the Twenty-fifth Amendment—but the pertinent part is as vague today as when the Framers wrote it: "In Case of the Removal of the President from Office, or of his Death, Resignation, or Inability to discharge the Powers and Duties of the said Office, the Same shall devolve on the Vice President, and the Congress may by Law provide for the Case of Removal, Death, Resignation or Inability, both of the President and Vice President, declaring what Officer shall then act as President, and such Officer shall act accordingly, until the Disability be removed, or a President shall be elected."

"Until the Disability be removed, or a President shall be elected"? Not *"until the term of the elected president shall expire."* The Constitution specifies that an elected president serves four years. In the scenario in which the elected president is out . . . it specifies . . . nothing. No "every four years." No serving out the term. That's just the custom. And in fact, the first time a president did not make it to the end of his term—when William Henry Harrison died after just thirty-one days in office in 1841—there were those who argued that the vice president, John Tyler, should act as caretaker in chief until another election could be held. While this was being debated, Tyler simply had himself sworn in as president and basically told his opponents to try to do something about it.

That—"the Tyler Precedent," as they call it—is the entirety of the reason that President Mike Pence would presumably finish Trump's term. Or that President Paul Ryan would presumably finish Trump's term if Trump and Pence were both swallowed up by the Russian scandal. Or President Orrin Hatch, who's third in line. Or President Rex Tillerson, who's fourth. Or President Betsy DeVos, who's fifteenth.

President Betsy DeVos!

So—new election?

A new presidential election before 2020 is entirely constitutional, though presumably politically impossible, because some legislation would have to be passed by the Senate or the House and presumably affirmed by the Supreme

Court, and all three bodies would have to be hit by lightning simultaneously to knock enough patriotism and morality into the Republicans who control them to get them to actually hold a 2017 or 2018 presidential election.

However.

This could be opening Pandora's box, like turning off all the gravity. If we somehow were able to break the tradition—the Tyler Precedent—the industry into which we have made politics and government could conceivably generate a new presidential election every six months. Elect a president, swear him in, impeach him and his successors, pass legislation for another new election, lather, rinse, repeat. I mean, imagine what the Republicans would do with this.

Well, of course, we kind of already know. If a Democratic president had been elected as part of a secret Russian war against this country—the Republicans would impeach that president and the vice president and everybody on the Democratic chain of succession and embrace the cry of "New Elections Now" rising from the streets—Wall Street and K Street, specifically. Hell, in 1998, Newt Gingrich reportedly had dreams that he would impeach and remove Bill Clinton, then President Al Gore would pardon Clinton, and Gingrich could then impeach Gore for pardoning Clinton. That would have made the Speaker of the House—Newt Gingrich!—president. Instead of what he is now: a guy whose last presidential campaign defaulted on debts of $4.6 million.

You missed the sunrise today because somebody put something in your drink last night? You can't go back in time to see it, and you can't declare a second sunrise at four p.m. You have to wait. But you don't have to wait three and a half years.

So—new election??

It would be unprecedented and dangerous. And unprecedented and dangerous is where we are *now*, with this disloyal punk in the White House. Thus, to me, we should keep a new election on the table. Despite the risk, and, more obviously, despite the near impossibility that it would be, politically.

However, if you want a guaranteed new election to take the government out of the hands of these thugs; if you want, after Trump's removal, to keep our freedoms safe from the fourteenth in line to succeed him—that'd be President Rick Perry, who would serve just before President Betsy DeVos; if you want a new election—you've got a bunch of them this November. I don't care if it's the two state governorships up for grabs or the mayoralties in twenty-one major cities, or balloting for the head of whoever in your city government supervises the Visiting Nurse Association. Throw the Republicans who profited from this—and they have all profited from this, and they all knew who they signed on with—throw them out and put their party out of business this fall, and next year in the midterms.

Concentrate on voting out every single Republican from the House and Senate in 2018.

Run them into the ground.

So—new election?

That's your new election.

Matter of fact—that's your new sunrise.

THE SYRIA STUNT

Post date • MONDAY, APRIL 10

Trump's bombing raid in Syria was a stunt.

The heartfelt policy change? The secrecy? The element of surprise? The retaliation? The neutralization? The mission itself? . . . A stunt. And much of the news media and who knows how much of the public believed every stupid word! Swallowed it like mother's milk. Object: distraction. And they fell for it.

The Trump Gang publicly confirmed that the Russians were warned in advance, per the terms of a deconfliction agreement. ABC News reports that the Syrians guessed, or knew far enough in advance to move personnel and equipment out of the targeted air force base. How in the hell could that have happened? Maybe the Russians told them? And while the Russians knew, and the Syrians knew, did Congress know? Did the American people know? They didn't even tell the State Department.

It. Was. A. Stunt.

And what do you call a stunt in which the Americans make sure the principal ally of the targeted nation knows in advance that it's coming, but our own Congress and State Department don't? It's called Collusion with the Enemy. It was a stunt—a glorified fireworks show—which did nothing to impede the

Assad regime from again using chemical weapons against its own people. It was a stunt that did nothing to impede the Trump regime from using propaganda weapons against its people.

Four years ago, Trump sent out a fistful of tweets about Syria, condemning exactly the stunt he just pulled in Syria. Two months before Trump's stunt, he banned refugees from Syria from coming here—so the kids and the adults who died such horrible deaths had one fewer place to run to, because of Donald Trump. And four days before Trump's stunt, his government said removing Assad wasn't the plan anymore. And three days before Trump's stunt, as the children still lay there choking to death, he blamed Barack Obama for it.

And two days before Trump's stunt, he cut the U.S. contribution to the United Nations Population Fund by nearly half and threatened to cut it completely, and last year 48,000 pregnant women in Syria were able to deliver their babies in safety because of that funding Trump just cut, so don't tell me he had some kind of change of heart because of the video of those dying kids, because by the end of the year, more children may have died in Syria because of Donald Trump than because of Bashar al-Assad!

And less than twenty-four hours after the last of the bombs hit the ground, the Syrians were running more missions out of the same base. Bombing more civilians. We dropped a reported $94 million worth of bombs, and we didn't even put a hole in the runways, and nobody noticed, because seventy-eight senators publicly said that this stunt—this meaningless, dangerous, cynical, exploitative, bullshit stunt that didn't even slow Assad's bombers down—was a good thing.

And then Trump also claimed it was the plan. "The reason you don't generally hit runways is that they are easy and inexpensive to quickly fix (fill in and top!)" Right. When you bomb air bases, you *never* try to destroy the runways to keep the planes from taking off. And the media bought all of this. A TV anchor giddily quotes Leonard Cohen lyrics about the beauty of the video of the missiles. A TV analyst says, "I think Donald Trump became president of the United States last night," which is exactly what another analyst on the same network said a month earlier, after Trump's speech to the House and Senate, because every time this idiot Trump doesn't crap his pants or pay one of his companies another million dollars of taxpayer money, apparently that makes him Abraham Goddamned Lincoln. The retired anchormen who won't go away and the ex-generals making TV per diem and the war correspondents who have nothing to do if there's no war congratulated Trump on getting "away with this one without having an escalation of the conflict," and *USA Today* wrote about Trump's "successful week" and asked if he would continue his "winning ways."

Just like in the three years after 9/11, the news media in this country is right now suffering from a kind of journalistic post-traumatic stress disorder. Everything around them is so outside their own experience, so different and alarming and real, so existentially threatening, that none of their clichés fit anymore and none of their default story lines work anymore, and by God, when something vaguely familiar happens—like American missiles taking off and blowing stuff up in the Middle East without congressional authorization—they feel like the tiny little world inside the Beltway, the only thing simple enough for them to digest and regurgitate and pretend they know what the hell they're talking about, they feel like that's back—that the unique nightmare of a president who has something wrong with his brain and tells you he's been in office thirteen weeks when it's only been eleven is finally pivoting—just like they predicted!—into an ordinary president who just blows stuff up, and they can revert to rewriting what they wrote in 2010 or 1996 or 19-*goddamned*-12!

It was a stunt!

And the media believed every stupid word! Object: distraction! And they fell for it!

Let me fully explain the media in two rules.

Rule one is: "Bombs = Easy to Understand." *Swoosh, kaboom,* "boots on the ground," Greatest Generation? Easy to understand.

Rule two is: "Russian Cyberwar ≠ Easy to Understand."

Disinformation, collusion, hacking, voter registration rolls, microtargeting? Not easy to understand.

And what did those corners of the political media miss while they fell for it? They missed nearly four dozen tweets from Trump in 2013 and 2014—virtual messages in a bottle from the Trump of Christmas Past to the Trump of Christmas Present, like this one:

"Again, to our very foolish leader, do not attack Syria—if you do many very bad things will happen and from that fight the U.S. gets nothing!"

And they also missed all of Trump's 2017 cheerleaders, in the Senate, in the House, in the media, praising him for this stunt when they condemned Obama for even proposing action four years ago. Sean Hannity, September 2013: "Glad our arrogant Pres. is enjoying his taxpayer funded golf outing after announc-ing the US should take military action against Syria."

And in falling for it—again—much of the media missed the real lessons of Trump's Syria stunt. Less than twenty-four hours later, what was the pro-Trump super-PAC Great America—the one run by the eternal Republican Ed Rollins, a man who told me to my face that I was right, that Trump is crazy—what was that PAC doing? Fund-raising off the children dead in Syria from sarin gas, and off Trump's stunt!

Fund-raising off a stunt that accomplished nothing except make the stupid people of this country fall for it just like they fell for it in Iraq in 2003 and just like they'll fall for it next time, because the actual outcome of the Syrian stunt was that Trump learned that whenever he can convert true international out-rage and heartbreak into a publicity photo-op stunt, he will get applause and support and prestige—and people from all around the nation willing to pretend he's a president and not an unstable egomaniac; people willing to pretend he's a leader and not a charlatan who, while in the middle of being investigated for electoral collusion with Russia, decides it's the perfect time for military collu-sion with Russia by staging a phony bombing run that saved no children, deliv-ered no message, drew no line, showed no leadership, provided no hope, resolved no crisis, and did not even produce potholes in the runways!

*

Author's note: Just after this piece was recorded and posted, Eric Trump told Britain's The Telegraph, *"If there was anything that Syria did, it was to validate the fact that there is no Russia tie."*

A MESSAGE TO PRESIDENT JACKASS

Post date • WEDNESDAY, APRIL 12

(Voiceover announcer: "And now a message to the President of the United States.")
You are a jackass.

There have been many words used to describe you during these first two and a half months of this human waste treatment plant of an administration of yours, and I've used most of them: demagogue, liar, idiot, despot, simpleton, traitor, schmuck, asshole, buckpasser, puppet, lunatic, toddler, fascist, jerk, schmo, schnook, dope, dipstick, lamebrain.

But after prolonged consideration . . .

You are a jackass.

You are President Jackass.

Who else but a jackass would look at the dying children of Syria and, as your first reaction, blame your predecessor when your predecessor did exactly what you urged him to do at least forty-seven different times just on Twitter?

Who else but a jackass would, as your second reaction, do nothing—just stick to the policy that most benefits Russia?

Who else but a jackass would, as your third reaction, put the international balance of power at risk in case our troops happened to kill a Russian in Syria because your daughter—the schlockmeister one who tries to turn everything she can touch into a marketing opportunity—she ran to Daddy and said she was heartbroken and you should go kill some people?

Who else but a jackass would, as your fourth reaction, warn Russia that our planes were coming, knowing that Russia would warn Syria, and then put the lives of American service personnel at risk so they could run a farcical stunt attack on an air base, with instructions that they should not try to destroy the runways from which the Syrian jets carrying the sarin gas that killed those kids took off?

Who else but a jackass would, as your fifth reaction, when America finally woke up to the nauseating reality that you put our people's lives at risk to run a phony photo-op bombing raid that didn't bomb anything, tweet that everybody knows when you bomb an air base you never bomb the runways because they're so easy to fix.

You are a jackass! You are President Jackass!

Who else but a jackass would rely on his nitwit son-in-law to do anything on behalf of the American government, when he just happened to fill out the forms for the top-secret security clearance he doesn't deserve in a million years and he came to question 20B.6, which asks about substantial meetings with foreign governments, and he forgot to mention his meetings with the Russian ambassador to the United States?

Who else but a jackass would trot out this Kushner, this triumph of double nepotism, after this? To borrow names from Louise Mensch's Twitter feed: Oliver Northface somehow acting in the name of our democracy, wearing Flaks Fifth Avenue and a pair of Jamokely Sunglasses?

Who else but a jackass would say how many weeks he'd been in office—and get it wrong by a margin of 15 percent?

Who else but a jackass would accuse Susan Rice and Barack Obama and the intelligence community of crimes, without one shred of evidence among them, but continually defend Vladimir Goddamned Putin?

Who else but a jackass would claim that an eleven-term Democratic congressman from Baltimore had told you, "You will go down as one of the great presidents in the history of our country," and leave off the part where he said that to perhaps become great, first you'd have to stop dividing and harming the country and start truly representing everybody?

You are a jackass!

Who else but a jackass would demote a man like Steve Bannon not because he has no business being involved in running anything more important than a popsicle stand, but because you reportedly were embarrassed that *Saturday Night Live* made him look like your boss, and you weren't—quoting, of all places, Fox News—"happy with the way Bannon had been grabbing the limelight"?

Who else but a jackass would let Homeland Security try to trample the First Amendment to unmask one of his critics on Twitter?

Who else but a jackass would have escaped disaster during the campaign after the *Access Hollywood* sexual assault tape, yet still publicly defend a serial sexual harasser like your pal Bill O'Reilly and claim he had done nothing wrong?

Who else but a jackass could accuse a *New York Times* reporter of being the PR person for Hillary Clinton, and when she replies, "Mostly by you, though," you say, "No, no, no, mostly by a lot of people," like you're twelve freaking years old?

Who else but a jackass could have a collection of pet television hosts, propagandists so stupid that they would try to delete four-year-old tweets that prophesied your nitwitted policy? "Glad our arrogant Pres. is enjoying his taxpayer funded golf outing after announcing the US should take military action against Syria."

You are a jackass!

President Jackass!

And worst of all, worst of all, maybe worse than everything else combined: who but a jackass would approve his first military mission, and see a Navy SEAL named Ryan Owens lose his life while fulfilling that mission, and exploit his widow during a speech to both houses of Congress, and then say, "This was a mission that was started before I got here. This was something that was, you know, just, they wanted to do. . . . My generals are the most respected that we've had in many decades, I believe. And they lost Ryan."

Jackass.

You worthless jackass.

You President Jackass.

THE TALE OF THE TAPE

Post date • MONDAY, APRIL 17

The British may have already nailed Trump on Russia.

On tape.

No—not that tape.

It was the thirty-fourth and final paragraph in a long and pretty staid review of the role British spies have played in connecting the dots between the Trump presidential campaign and the Russians. And then, as if it were merely the best available way for Britain's newspaper *The Guardian* to end its useful but modest story, came paragraph thirty-four: "One source suggested the official investigation was making progress. 'They now have specific concrete and corroborative evidence of collusion,' the source said. 'This is between people in the Trump campaign and agents of [Russian] influence relating to the use of hacked material.'"

Oh.

Shouldn't that have been presented, I don't know, a little more *prominently*? "Specific and corroborative evidence of collusion . . . between people in the Trump campaign and agents of Russian influence . . . relating to the use of hacked material."

Not only did the Republic not grind to a halt, but nobody, not even *The*

Guardian itself, followed up with the appropriate screaming headlines. No screaming headlines, even in light of what Eric Trump told another British newspaper, *The Telegraph*, in the wake of his father's impotent missile attack against that Syrian air base. "If there was anything that Syria did," the Trump spawn protested, too much, "it was to validate the fact that there is no Russia tie."

No screaming headlines as a British magazine—*Prospect*—quoted that nation's former chief spy Richard Dearlove as speculating, "What lingers for Trump may be what deals—on what terms—he did after the financial crisis of 2008 to borrow Russian money when others in the west apparently would not lend to him."

No screaming headlines, even as *The Washington Post* reported that the FBI did indeed get a judge to issue a FISA warrant (permission under the Foreign Intelligence Surveillance Act) to track the actions of and communications with Russians by Carter Page, who was the second name Donald Trump ever gave when asked who his foreign policy advisers were.

No screaming headlines, even though the story that the FBI had sought, and gotten—a FISA warrant of some kind against somebody directly linked to Trump and/or his campaign—had been widely reported in nontraditional media ever since the former British member of Parliament Louise Mensch published a sourced story before the election.

No screaming headlines, even though the essence of Mensch's November 7 story was that, while looking at suspicious Russian banking activity, foreign intelligence services had tripped over contacts between the Russians and the Trump team, and the FBI needed that FISA warrant because without it they couldn't even read what, say, the British had come up with. "It is thought in the intelligence community," Mensch wrote in November, "that the warrant covers any 'US person' connected to this investigation, and thus covers Donald Trump and at least three further men who have either formed part of his campaign or acted as his media surrogates."

Mensch's report was not so much dismissed as ignored.

Now Ms. Mensch is back. On her own blog, Sunday night: "Sources with links to the intelligence community say it is believed that Carter Page went to Moscow in early July carrying with him a prerecorded tape of Donald Trump offering to change American policy if he were to be elected, to make it more favorable to Putin. In exchange, Page was authorized directly by Trump to request the help of the Russian government in hacking the election."

Well, you have to admit, a tape of Donald Trump personally saying he would trade American policy decisions in exchange for nefarious Russian intervention in the election would probably fit *The Guardian*'s thirty-fourth paragraph about "specific and corroborative evidence of collusion . . . between people in the Trump campaign and agents of Russian influence . . . relating to the use of hacked material."

Mensch also identifies three Trump associates named in the FBI FISA warrant application—Russian-born reportedly ex–Trump TV spokesman Boris Epshteyn, former Trump campaign manager Paul Manafort, and Carter Page. "A recording exists of all three men discussing the possibility of Page taking the tape of Trump to Moscow as an earnest of good faith. There is a minor dispute over whether Trump himself is also on that tape . . ."

So, if Mensch is correct, there may be two tapes of Trump personally making a promise to a foreign government, to help it out if that foreign government broke American laws in order to get him elected.

In the abstract—in the theoretical—that would be treason.

On tape.

Where Ms. Mensch has been again dismissed, three criticisms have been raised. First, that she was not exactly right when she was the first to report that the FBI had gone to the extreme lengths of seeking FISA warrants against the Trump team, before the entirety of the world's mainstream media was even close to the story *The Washington Post* just got last week.

Second, there is the disbelief that anybody would be stupid enough to not just leave "specific and corroborative evidence of collusion," of Trump saying, "Let's make a deal," but to actually, deliberately create that evidence.

If you have seen Carter Page interviewed, you should have no doubt that he is stupid enough to have done something exactly like this. In one interview on the question of whether or not he had ever met the infamous Russian ambassador Kislyak, he managed to contradict himself about five times in about five minutes before confessing with the immortal words "I may have met him—possibly. It might have been in Cleveland."

And of course, if you have ever heard Donald Trump talk, and forget which country he attacked the day before but remember what kind of cake he was eating while he was telling the premier of China about the attack, you should have no doubt that he, too, is stupid enough—and, more relevant, so convinced of his own invulnerability—to have done something exactly like this. And indeed this underscores my repeated contention here that democracy has survived less because of the hard work and dedication of people like you and me who are committed to its preservation, and more because of the unfailing and eternal stupidity of those who would destroy it.

But last, and most important, Louise Mensch's story has been criticized because no matter how unfailing and how eternal that stupidity may be, who could ever rise to the position of president of the United States, no matter how insane, or paranoid, or certain that the ordinary odds that they might get caught did not apply to them?

No president would be stupid enough to *put it on tape*.

Richard Nixon?

THE PRESIDENT IS GETTING CRAZIER

Post date • TUESDAY, APRIL 18

Lost in the cacophony of launched missiles in Syria and dropped bombs in Afghanistan and rattled sabers in Korea; drowned out by the clamoring dissonance of conflicting policies about China and Assad and NATO; shouted over by the crises of Sean Spicer and Paul Manafort and Eric Trump; and always—forever—distracted from by the little whir and click sounds of a recorder switching on and off, supported by the remorseless background drumbeat of the Russian election scandal, there is a terrifying new fact: The president is getting crazier.

This statement is somewhat akin to rhetorically asking if today here in hell it is hotter than it was yesterday. But in the last week—just in the last week—the featherlight grip on reality of Trump's tiny hands has seemingly gotten much looser—and much looser, much faster.

The most obvious, though hardly the most disturbing, evidence of some kind of deepening illness or damage or madness or what-does-the-cause-matter-any-longer was the latest barrage of tweets, like the "Fake Media (not

Real Media)" tweet Monday morning, but especially the string of them on Easter.

In eighty-three short minutes, Trump started with a simpleton's rationalization of his complete 180 on Chinese currency manipulation to boasting about his election as if it were the answer to everything, to using that election as an excuse for reneging on one of his campaign promises, to paranoid fantasies about paid protesters, to then insisting that his election should *not* be the answer to everything, to a random boast about American military strength, which, if it were connected to the previous tweet, could easily and terrifyingly be read as a tacit threat to suppress American protesters with American military force.

The president is getting crazier.

It is possible that this string of five "word explosions" could be only that. Merely a sign of a lazy, damaged, unfocused mind wandering off on its own—again. Attention deficit hyperactivity disorder, or adult attention disorder, or not-really-an-adult sanity disorder, taking a stroll on a lazy holiday weekend. But this wasn't a lazy holiday weekend. Literally twenty-four hours earlier, there was urgent reason to think we might be bombing North Korea. There had been no accord. There had been no stand-down. And had there been no Korean missile self-destructing and dropping impotently into the sea, there would have been no relief from the crisis.

And the next morning, the quote-president-unquote was obsessed about how many votes he got in the Electoral College five months ago, as if anyone, anywhere, at any time—besides him—thinks that his weak victory there is by itself an explanation for his broken promises about releasing his taxes.

And North Korea? North Korea went from inspiring a joke on *Saturday Night Live*—with Melissa McCarthy as Sean Spicer suggesting we should eat all the chocolate eggs we want, because it was to be our last Easter on earth—to being relegated to almost an afterthought to the real Trump's rationalizations about his other broken promises about designating China as a currency manipulator. In the disordered mind of the commander in chief, North Korea had been figuratively, if not literally, the end of the world. Overnight, it was reduced to being not nearly as much of a threat as the Trump tax return protesters.

The president is getting *crazier.*

And it's not as if he had spent the preceding week—or even the preceding seventy-two hours—focused just on North Korea. In our collective national trip inside the kaleidoscopic, roller-coaster mind of this unstable man, does anybody even remember the MOAB? The 21,000-pound Mother of All Bombs dropped in Afghanistan? Or the stunt attack on the Syrian missile base that didn't even disable the Syrian missile base? That was one week before Syria. The MOAB was Thursday. Thursday has apparently become Blow-Stuff-Up Day.

And of course, Trump had already forgotten into which country he had those missiles fired. "So what happens is, I said 'We've just launched fifty-nine missiles heading to Iraq, and I wanted you to know this.' And he was eating his cake. And he was silent." And Maria Bartiromo, who used to be a journalist, interrupts and says, "To . . . *Syria*—"

"Yes. Heading toward Syria. In other words, 'We've just launched fifty-nine missiles heading toward Syria.'"

No.

Those aren't "other words." Those things—"We've just launched fifty-nine missiles heading to Iraq" and "We've just launched fifty-nine missiles heading toward Syria"—are not two different descriptions of the same thing. They are two different things with two utterly different, world-changing sets of consequences. And they are two things that a president says in an interview in which he also expresses his amazement about the unmanned missiles, as if there were manned missiles, and the only thing he says with clear conviction or un-muddied memory is "We had the most beautiful piece of chocolate cake that you've ever seen."

They are two things a president says when he is getting crazier.

Only a president who is getting crazier would admit going into a meeting with the premier of China with a long-standing assumption that the Chinese could just wave a magic wand and stop North Korea, but figuring out this was not true after only ten minutes of conversation, while not realizing that there are ten-year-old children in this country with a better grasp on North Korea than he has.

Only a president who is getting crazier would flip-flop on the Export-Import Bank. And flip-flop on NATO. And flip-flop on his own promise on

Chinese currency manipulation. And flip-flop on his own promise on his tax returns. And flip-flop on his Syria policy. And flip-flop on his top adviser. And all of that in just barely over a week, while bombing two countries and threatening a third, and correctly remembering only two of their three names!

*

We don't like to admit this, but it has often served our purposes, just as certainly as it has served Kim Jong-un's, to have leaders, or indeed even commanders in chief, who verged on seeming madness. Kissinger used to tell the Russians that Richard Nixon was a madman. Ronald Reagan let the same country believe he viewed it as the "evil empire" from *Star Wars.* Barry Goldwater wouldn't rule out nuking North Vietnam, and George Wallace's vice presidential candidate was an ex-general who wanted to nuke Vietnam, Russia, and China, and the Russian records from the Cuban Missile Crisis suggest that Khrushchev thought John F. Kennedy might have been literally insane.

It can be a tactic. But it can work only if there remains the likelihood that the president really is not crazy. And with every passing week and every passing day and every passing hour, there is less and less evidence that this president really is not crazy.

What is rapidly becoming the paramount fact of the twenty-first century, the event overshadowing everything else from 9/11 to climate change, continues to be largely ignored—ignored even though it is an existential threat to the future of mankind. There are millions of Americans, millions of others around the world—even millions who despise these policies and hate that man—who are standing so close to the bark, they can't see the trees, let alone the forest.

President Let-Me-Eat-Cake over here is crazy, and getting crazier, and he will descend quickly into full-on hallucinatory, meet-my-invisible-friend, why-do-we-have-nukes-if-we-don't-use-them crazy, while our only hope to remove him, our political system—destroyed by twenty-five years of utter partisanship and complete denial and the placement of a price tag on virtually everything and everybody in our country—is no longer capable of even pulling off a successful White House Easter egg hunt.

He is getting *crazier.*

A GILDED COACH, YOU SAY?

Post date • THURSDAY, APRIL 20

The president of the United States insists on being brought to Buckingham Palace alongside the queen of England, in a golden coach drawn by six royal white horses.

Like goddamned Cinderella.

Like a man unaware of the security nightmare he will create. Like a man unaware of the massive public protest that all the king's—or, in this case, queen's—men and all the queen's horses might be able to keep nonviolent, might be able to contain, but cannot keep from happening.

When *The Times* of London reported this latest evidence of the nexus of narcissism and madness meeting inside the addled brain of the demented man a minority of voters have cursed us with, it caused barely a ripple here, because it was only the fifteenth- or sixteenth-craziest thing Trump has done this week. Reminder: the newspaper reporting this, quoting security sources and making references to London's Metropolitan Police and the U.S. Secret Service, is owned by Trump's latest hanger-on, Rupert Murdoch. This is not a story designed to harsh Trump's buzz. This is reality so real that even Murdoch gets it. *The Times* reported that "the White House has made clear it regards the carriage procession down the Mall as an essential element of the itinerary for the visit currently planned for the second week of October."

The story, by its crime-and-security editor, dripped with warnings. As recently as 2003, Vladimir Putin's state visit saw the foreign leader and the queen ride the seven-tenths of a mile with the carriage top down. Six years ago, President Obama had the presence of mind to thank the British for the option of the ceremony but ride in his own armored limousine.

Even when the president of Mexico and the Chinese premier visited—separately—in 2015, each had the common sense to ride in a closed carriage. It is not clear that Trump has even agreed to that. "If he is in a golden coach being dragged up the Mall by a couple of horses, the risk factor is dramatically increased," *The Times* quoted its primary security source. "There may well be protections in that coach such as bulletproof glass, but they are limited.

In particular it is very flimsy. It would not be able to put up much resistance in the face of a rocket propelled grenade or high-powered ammunition. Armor-piercing rounds would make a very bad show of things."

But we're not even talking about those scenarios. This is a president who would not throw out the ceremonial first pitch at the Washington Nationals' Opening Day baseball game, obviously out of fear that he would be booed. This is a president who has yet to appear anywhere in public in which he might *not* be loudly cheered. This is a president who collapses into paranoid accusations of paid agitators when protesters, demanding he release his tax returns, force him to alter his motorcade route, from his fantasyland of a golf course he owns but can charge the taxpayers each time he uses it, to his other fantasyland of a country club he owns but can charge the taxpayers each time he uses it.

This is the world's ultimate snowflake living inside the world's ultimate snow globe of his own creation to prevent the slightest chance that his delusion that he is universally beloved will come into violent contact with the reality that he is hated—insisting that he ride to the palace in a golden coach moving so slowly that he would have to hear and see at least some of those who despise him, for as long as ten minutes.

Twenty years ago, I had a stalker, and while I worked, ironically, for Rupert Murdoch, the woman appeared to be getting crazier and crazier. For everything else they do wrong, Fox does protect its employees from stuff like this. Murdoch gets a serious death threat a day, his head of security—a former Scotland Yard chief—told me when he flew from London to Los Angeles to coordinate a game plan to keep me safe. He had assessed my case on the plane, and he said that while he did not suspect the woman was going to turn to violence, he wanted to enact several protective measures, because her behavior reminded him of the story of a prominent actor being stalked by a woman fan.

This woman's delusion about the actor was different from most. She didn't need to actually inject herself into his life. She was content to simply mirror his life. If he spent the weekend in, say, Miami, she would weasel the information about where he was staying and what he was doing—something at which stalkers are adept—and she would go to Miami herself. She'd stay at a hotel near his, follow him at a discreet distance, and never once interact with him, but on Monday morning she could go home and go to work and say, "Mike"—we'll call him that—"Mike and I were in Miami. We went to South Beach. We even saw that funny game you bet on, jai alai."

When it was all over, her coworkers were absolutely astonished. Everything she had told them was factually correct and rich in detail. They never realized it was only literally correct. "Mike" had indeed gone to Miami and South Beach and jai alai, and this woman, his stalker, had gone to Miami and South Beach and jai alai, and the parts she left out were that she had stayed a hundred yards away from him at all times, and he never knew she existed. The stalking ended, Murdoch's head of security told me, in Minneapolis or somewhere, when Mike left his hotel on foot and his stalker followed at a safe distance—and then suddenly Mike realized he'd left something at his hotel and turned around to go get it.

And the stalker was faced with disaster. Mike was now approaching her. She couldn't run away—that would be admitting to herself that Mike wasn't actually her boyfriend. She couldn't cross to the other side of the street. She couldn't stop him and introduce herself. She certainly couldn't let him walk past her without so much as looking at her. The entire elaborate, self-delusional fantasy was about to crash down upon her.

Unless...

Murdoch's man said that as soon as Mike got to within a few feet of her, this woman, whom he had never met and who had never contacted him, but who had built a complete and intricate and expensive relationship with him, saved herself from the confrontation with reality—the end of her world—in the only way left to her. She reared back and punched him in the face. She could now smile and explain—to the police, to her coworkers, to herself—that she and Mike *had had a fight, and they had broken up.*

*

In our little nightmare, of course, Donald Trump is Mike's stalker. And Mike is the reality in which Trump the Stalker is failing and old and paunchy and fooling a thousand fewer people right now than he fooled an hour ago, a reality in which the world mocks him and the politicians use him, and his judgments are entirely wrong, and those closest to him try to calculate the exact date it becomes to their advantage to sell him out over Russia and impeach and jail him.

And mostly, Mike is the public that *hates* Trump the Stalker.

The public that Trump the Stalker has decided to expose himself to, from a slow-moving golden carriage on the way to Buckingham Palace in October. What happens when reality approaches Trump and he cannot avert that confrontation?

What kind of punch to the face does a thwarted stalker throw when he has nuclear weapons?

THE WHITE HOUSE RUSSIA COVER-UP

Post date • TUESDAY, APRIL 25

It went by so quickly and in such a cacophony of five interviewees all on at the same time, that its importance seemed to go right past everybody, maybe even the man who was saying it. "There is serious belief, in the FBI, in the congressional committees in the House and the Senate, that there is an active cover-up going on, involving trying to keep investigators from finding out what happened in terms of the Trump campaign—Trump associates near the top of the campaign—and what happened in their associations with Russians, and that there is an active cover-up going on . . . One of the things that the congressional committees are very concerned about, as is the FBI, is that they don't have the resources to conduct a proper investigation, and the White House is taking advantage of it."

An active White House cover-up to keep the FBI and Congress from finding out what the connections between All the Trump's Men and Russia really mean. It is a startling conclusion, it was attributed by the CNN guest to FBI and Capitol Hill sources, and it was said by who?

Carl Bernstein.

*

Being dead right about Watergate forty-three, forty-four, and forty-five years ago doesn't mean he's automatically right about Trump and Russia. But it does mean Bernstein's reporting gets a faster and more durable benefit of the doubt than anybody else's. And while Bernstein underscored that there yet may prove to be nothing to the Trump-Russia links, the unalterable fact of history is that Richard Nixon was forced from office not by the Watergate break-in but by the cover-up.

People went to jail during the infamous Teapot Dome scandal not because of the oil or the money, but because of the cover-up! They got Big Tobacco because of the cover-up. Iran-Contra. The Dreyfus Affair! And even Bill Clinton was impeached not based on what he said or did or didn't say or didn't do, but because of the cover-up. And Bernstein says FBI and Capitol Hill sources believe there is an active cover-up being undertaken right now by the Trump administration. If that's true, the cover-up by itself might be impeachable—even if there is no Russian smoking gun, or it is never produced.

What would it look like? What would the signs of a cover-up *be*? I mean, apart from the nuclear-detonation-size obvious ones like the Jeff Sessions recusal, or the self-defenestration of Congressman Devin "You Haven't Heard from Me Lately, Have You" Nunes.

Well, how about the principals all backing away from one another? Like, oh, the new head of the CIA branding WikiLeaks a "non-state hostile intelligence service often abetted by state actors like Russia." Or like WikiLeaks tweeting, "Trump's breach of promise over the release of his tax returns is even more gratuitous than Clinton concealing her Goldman Sachs transcripts." Or the Justice Department reportedly seeking to charge Julian Assange and even perhaps trying to pry him from his hidey-hole at the Ecuadorian embassy in London, where he's visited by Nigel Farage and Pamela Anderson. Separately—please, God. Or maybe Vladimir Putin's primary TV mouthpiece, Dmitry Kiselyov, telling his Russian viewing audience, "Trump is more impulsive and unpredictable than Kim Jong-un," and "more dangerous." Or the younger of the moron twins, Eric, telling a British newspaper, of the missile strike in Syria, "If there was anything that Syria did, it was to validate the fact that there is no Russia tie." Or, most recently, Trump telling the Associated Press that in 2016 "WikiLeaks came out . . . never heard of WikiLeaks, never heard of it." Except that on December 2, 2010, asked by this Fox clown, "You had nothing to do with WikiLeaks?" Trump said, "No, but I think it's disgraceful. I think there should be like death penalty or something."

So Trump denounces WikiLeaks and WikiLeaks denounces Trump and

Trump threatens to arrest Assange and the Russians denounce Trump as more dangerous than Kim Jong-un and Eric Trump makes it look like Daddy fired fifty-nine missiles just to show he's not a Russian marionette and then Trump never heard of WikiLeaks until last year, except he did in 2010.

Boys, don't everybody run out of the room at the same moment—you'll all get crushed trying to get through the exit.

Cover-up!

There are other, slightly more subtle signs. Notice that odd story that turned up on CNN? "The FBI gathered intelligence last summer that suggests Russian operatives tried to use Trump advisers, including Carter Page, to infiltrate the Trump campaign, according to US officials.

"The new information adds to the emerging picture of how the Russians tried to influence the 2016 election, not only through email hacks and propaganda but also by trying to infiltrate the Trump orbit."

See what they're doing there? Carter Page is no longer a Trump foreign policy adviser—the second one he ever mentioned. Page, who has denied all wrongdoing, is also no longer an alleged courier carrying a reported audiotape of Trump to Vladimir Putin in an offer to swap Russian-friendly policy changes for election-roll hacking by the Russians so Steve Bannon could microtarget American voters. He's no longer a possible traitor. Now he's the *victim*.

"U.S. officials." That'd presumably be current U.S. officials, you know, like Trump, or somebody appointed by Trump—suggesting the Russians tried to infiltrate the Trump campaign by using people too dumb to realize it, like Carter Page. And thus Page becomes not a conspirator but the injured party—the way, if Trump or his buddies are indeed on tape because they happened to be talking to Russians that foreign intelligence services were spying on, Trump and the Trumpettes are not disloyal monsters willing to sell out this nation; they were the victims of wiretaps and Barack Obama and Susan Rice and maybe the Devil himself.

Carl Bernstein's comments last Friday about serious belief at the FBI and the House and Senate intel committees that Trump is, at this moment, perpetrating an active cover-up of his people's ties to Russia underscore the necessity of an independent prosecutor—a necessity so important that Democratic candidates for the House next year ought to run on it and pin down their Republican opponents on it by waving the flag and asking: Who is running this country—us or the goddamned Russians?

And another thing about Bernstein and Watergate and trying to make Page and Trump—and whoever is next—into the victim rather than the perpetrator. Early in the Watergate cover-up, Richard Nixon tried to make it look like the whole thing was John Dean's idea, that Nixon was the victim, that there was a witch hunt. McCarthyism. Communists. We ran out of gas! We got a flat tire! We didn't have change for cab fare! We lost our tuxes at the cleaners! We locked our keys in the car! An old friend came in from out of town! There was an earthquake! A terrible flood! Locusts! It wasn't our fault, we swear to God!

It's a cover-up.

WHAT ARE WE DOING?

Post date • THURSDAY, APRIL 27

The Trump Gang, already shaming us for all of history by rounding up good, honest, law-abiding Americans without criminal records and with families who they have started and raised here, and forcibly sending them back to countries they barely know or do not know at all, may shortly begin rounding up judges and forcibly sending them to the immigration detention camps at which our neighbors are being scapegoated and uprooted from our country so Trump can fulfill his credo of hate, sadism, and barbarism.

Literally forcing judges out of their homes so they can throw Americans out of *their* homes—for the sake of Trump's pointless, racist brutality. This is being done in our name. Shame on us!

The day this was reported by the Reuters News Agency, it largely slipped under the radar: a letter, from the Department of Justice, asking for fifty immigration judges to volunteer to go—the word used is "deploy"—to New York, L.A., Miami, New Orleans, San Francisco, Baltimore, the Twin Cities of Minnesota, El Paso and Harlingen, Texas, Omaha, Phoenix, and Imperial, California, and perhaps elsewhere, so as to dispense with due process as quickly as possible. Start deporting scapegoats at six a.m., continue deporting scape-goats until ten p.m., on split shifts. For a month or two at a time.

Not enough volunteer judges? Quoting Reuters: "If the department can-not find enough volunteers, the department would assign judges to detention centers, the sources said." *What* are we doing? What are we *doing*?

You've heard the horror stories already: Mothers. Mothers-in-law of mili-tary veterans. Grandmothers. Parents. Natives of Puerto Rico—and their captors are too stupid to realize Puerto Rico is a territory of the United States. Crime victims. People outside homeless shelters. Roberto Beristain, described by its mayor as one of the model citizens of South Bend, Indiana; a restaurant owner there; a criminal because at Niagara Falls one time, he accidentally crossed into Canadian territory. And the husband of a Trump voter. Trump fooled her. "He did say the good people would not be deported, the good people would be checked." Madam, he lied to you. Your husband was deported because he was easy to find.

What are we doing?

What are we doing to Catalino Guerrero, who got a sixty-day extension be-fore what is still a scheduled deportation next month? He's been here more than twenty-five years, has two jobs, owns his own home in New Jersey, pays taxes, has four children, four grandchildren, has type 2 diabetes, recently had a stroke, has heart problems, uses a cane, and has no criminal record. In fact, he has been the victim of a crime in our country—a home invasion.

Why is Trump's ICE trying to deport him? Guerrero claims he got bad legal advice and filed for asylum. And if you file for asylum and don't get it, you have to leave. He filed for asylum in 1992, and the ruling against him came seven-teen years later. On May 22, we may throw him out because he's replicating what my great-great-grandfather did. Making his way here—because in 1992, as in 1854, we were the light of the world. Because both Catalino Guerrero and Friedrich Olbermann wanted freedom and better lives, maybe not in time for themselves, but for their children. Catalino Guerrero and Friedrich Olber-mann and how many of your ancestors? And how many of the ancestors of the unthinking humanoids who are cheering the Trump raids? And how many an-cestors of Trump?

And we are now relocating judges to the concentration camps, with in-structions to speed it up. What are we doing? What are *we* doing?

Exactly what we are doing has been expressed poignantly a thousand times through history, but never more so than by a thirty-six-year-old man who faced expulsion from the country he had called home for half his life but whose government now insisted he was illegal. He was not a professional writer, and the plea he made to the prince of his home region was not written in English. A historian found it last autumn, 111 years after it was written. The translation is by Austen Hinkley of *Harper's Magazine*, and I have made minor edits to the text for simplicity and clarity and to remove the fluffy flattery toward that royal prince.

It is painful. But in its own way, it is also beautiful. And it should be heard by everyone in this country—as long as this purge goes on in our name.

My parents were honest, plain, pious vineyard workers. They strictly held me to everything good—to diligence and piety, to regular attendance in school and church, to absolute obedience toward the high authority.

After my confirmation, in 1882, I apprenticed to become a barber. I emigrated in 1885, in my sixteenth year. In America I carried on my business with diligence, discretion, and prudence. God's blessing was with me, and I became rich. I obtained American citizenship in 1892. In 1902 I met my current wife. Sadly, she could not tolerate the climate in New York, and I went with my dear family back [home].

The town was glad to have received a capable and productive citizen. My old mother was happy to see her son, her dear daughter-in-law, and her granddaughter around her; she knows now that I will take care of her in her old age.

But we were confronted all at once, as if by a lightning strike from fair skies, with the news that the . . . Ministry had decided that we must leave our residence . . . We were paralyzed with fright; our happy family life was tarnished. My wife has been overcome by anxiety, and my lovely child has become sick.

Why should we be deported? This is very, very hard for a family. What will our fellow citizens think if honest subjects are faced with such a decree—not to mention the great material losses it would incur. I would like to become a . . . citizen again.

> *In this urgent situation I have no other recourse than . . . the most humble request that the highest of all will himself in mercy deign to allow the applicant to stay.*

It is signed: "Your most humble and obedient, Friedrich Trump." Trump's grandfather. He was, in his native Bavaria, deemed "illegal"—and rounded up, and deported, and sent back to New York with his pregnant wife, Elizabeth, where, literally within months, she gave birth to Donald Trump's father, Fred.

From the grave, Friedrich, Elizabeth, and Fred Trump, and Friedrich Olbermann and millions of deportees and exiles and refugees and millions more who had nowhere to turn but here, are asking us: What are we doing? And they are asking Donald Trump: What are *you* doing?

THE ONE HUNDRED DAYS ARE REALLY JUST SIXTY

Post date • FRIDAY, APRIL 28

As we hit the hundred-day benchmark of the Trump "presidency," let's review his accomplishments. Not by our standards—not by human standards—just by the stuff he promised to do for those greedy, hateful, and/or naive people who voted for him. Let's list all he's done—for them.

(Author's note: Forty seconds of silence follow.)

Yep.

In "the first hundred days"—he's gotten nothing done for them. With a Republican House and a Republican Senate and a Russian election in "the first hundred days"—he's gotten nothing done. With the great nationwide—*world*wide—liberating effects of the populist wave to throw the baby out with the bathwater . . . in "the first hundred days"—he's gotten nothing done. With one television network dedicated to lying on his behalf, to deliberately falsifying reality to make it fit his addled mind as he sits in a bathrobe watching it, with other networks wasting live coverage on his public speeches—his garbled, nonsensical stream of semi-consciousness—as if they were actually news in "the first hundred days," he's gotten nothing done.

This truth—utter impotence—is, of course, his greatest fear.

He confessed it, on Twitter, last Friday: "No matter how much I accomplish during the ridiculous standard of the first 100 days, & it has been a lot (including S.C.), media will kill!" You don't need to be a psychoanalyst to decode the sense of failure in that, though it helps to remember the context of that phrase "the ridiculous standard of the first 100 days."

Who set the ridiculous standard of the first hundred days?

He did.

Here is candidate Trump's Contract with the American Voter, his "100-day action plan to Make America Great Again." Contract—his word. Just sign here, like you were enrolling in Trump University. There's lots of LOL-worthy failure on the first page. Column one ends with "THIRD, I will direct the Secretary of the Treasury to label China a currency manipulator."

"Why would I call China a currency manipulator," he asked on Twitter, "when they are working with us on the North Korean problem?" Well, because you put it in the contract that you would—in the first hundred days. *Tick, tick, tick, tick, tick.* (By the way, for the uninformed, you've just gotten a taste of doing business with Trump: "But it's in the contract!" "So? Sue me.")

The second column ends with "suspend immigration from terror-prone regions where vetting cannot safely occur. . . ." Yeah—how's that going for you, Sparky?

What's funny is, the thing he boasted about in that desperate tweet? "It has been a lot (including S.C.)." The "S.C." part, of course, is the confirmation of Gorsuch to the Supreme Court. Wow. A Republican president got a Republican Senate to approve a Republican nominee because the Republican majority leader is such a craven turtle that he destroyed two pillars of the democracy. Getting that new nominee confirmed? That isn't even in the Trump contract! Only: "begin the process of selecting a replacement for Justice Scalia . . ."

As I said, there are some good laughs on this front page of yet another worthless Trump contract, about all the things he guaranteed he would do during his "ridiculous standard of the first 100 days"—that he's just outright failed at.

But it's the back page where the fun really begins. Here's all the legislation he was going to, at minimum, get introduced into Congress: A bill to create 25 million new jobs. Nope. A bill to punish sending jobs out of the country. Nope. A bill to spend a trillion dollars on infrastructure. Nope. A bill to give parents total choice on schooling, even religious schooling, presumably at government expense. Nope. A bill to repeal Obamacare. And how's that going for you, Sparky?

Why, when I think of him threatening to defund Obamacare unless Democrats support the border wall—why do I get an image of Cleavon Little in *Blazing Saddles* holding a gun to his own head and saying, "Hold it! The next man that makes a move, the . . ."

Moving on. A childcare and eldercare act that hasn't been written. A bill to fund that wall that not one congressman or senator from the states where the wall would be has said he'll support. An anti-gang bill. A bill preventing international cyberattack. (Yeah, kinda "swing and a miss" right there.) And finally, the "Clean Up Corruption in Washington Act. Enacts new ethics reforms to Drain the Swamp and reduce the corrupting influence of special interests on our politics." Presumably, that was to be commemorated by a series of "Ivanka Trump Signature Brand Drain the Swamp Formal Wear and Accessories," manufactured in China and available exclusively at the "Spa by Ivanka Trump," at Trump Old Post Office Hotel for Wayward Diplomats, Washington, D.C., 20004.

He's. Gotten. Nothing. Done.

And remember—nobody, nobody said to him, "You have to do this in the first hundred days or you'll be a failure." *He* said that! So what do you do when the homework has to be handed in, in the morning, and you haven't even found your textbooks yet?

You claim there *was* no such homework: "I think the hundred days is, you know, it's an artificial barrier. It's not very meaningful. . . . Somebody, yeah, somebody put out the concept of a hundred-day plan."

You put it out!

The somebody with the concept of a hundred-day plan was you!

That's *your* name, moron—moron! T-R-U-M-P, moron!

So what do you do when your denial that there was homework fails utterly?

You claim the teacher got the due date wrong! "The hundred days is just an artificial barrier. The press keeps talking about the hundred days..."

"I've only been working on the health care, you know, I had to get like a little bit of grounding, right? Health care started after day thirty, so I've been working on health care for sixty days... we're very close."

See, this isn't really one hundred days.

This is only *sixty* days.

Who you gonna believe?

Me? Or your lying calendar?

*

If ever you needed additional confirmation that this man's brain does not work, there it is.

At the hundred-day mark that was so important to him that he wrote up a phony contract predicated on it, he is such a failure that he is blaming the hundred days on the media, and actually claiming that it isn't really a hundred days anyway. "No matter how much I accomplish during the ridiculous standard of the first 100 days, & it has been a lot (including S.C.), media will kill!"

His greatest fear. So let's help him celebrate the hundred-day mark. He doesn't desperately search Twitter for compliments as much as he used to—but it's clear he still does it once in a while. Let's flood it with tweets congratulating him on having completely failed at everything in the first hundred days—including counting to a hundred days. Let's have him, figuratively, wading knee-deep in tweets at the White House. And don't forget! Since he claims this isn't really a hundred days, but only sixty—we get to flood Twitter again and congratulate him on even more failure on the "Hundred-Day Mark in Alternative-Facts Land," which I calculate to be Thursday, June 8.

Mark your calendars.

Unless by then he's ordered that we change all the calendars. Which would make that date Trumpday, the third of Trumpvember.

Chapter 10

MAY 2017

TRUMP'S PLAN: SUE DISSENTERS

Post date • MONDAY, MAY 1

In the span of one weekend, a man who usurped the office of the president of the United States with the assistance of this nation's most powerful and venomous enemy . . . has himself attacked the structure of our Senate and our House of Representatives because their rules are archaic and they inconvenience him; has himself dismissed the two-party system because he believes it is "obstructionist"; has himself attacked the constitutionally protected freedom of the press because the media has repeatedly caught him lying; has himself let his chief of staff confirm that he may try to eradicate those freedoms of speech and yours.

In sum, this man has himself so endangered the freedoms and the liberties of this country that if anyone does not understand that they and you and I and every individual in this country, and everything we love, and everything for which every American soldier has ever fought, *all of it*, is under attack, *right now*, by this crypto-fascist Trump—if they do not see that their freedoms hang by a thread, they are sheep headed to the slaughter—or collaborators leading the rest of us there—

For the sake of Trump.

"'The failing *New York Times* has disgraced the media world,'" Jon Karl of ABC said, reading Trump's tweet from March 30. "'Gotten me wrong for two solid years. Change libel laws?'" To Trump's chief of staff, Reince Priebus, Mr. Karl continued, "That would require, as I understand it, a constitutional amendment. Is he really going to pursue that? Is that something he wants to pursue?"

And Priebus answered, "I think it's something that we've looked at. And how that gets executed or whether that goes anywhere is a different story. But when you have articles out there that have no basis or fact and we're sitting here on 24/7 cable companies writing stories about constant contacts with Russia and all these other matters that have no basis at all . . ."

Here Mr. Karl interrupted, to refocus Priebus on whether or not Trump should be able to sue *The New York Times*. Priebus replied: "And I already answered the question. I said this is something that is being looked at."

Wrong goddamned answer. The correct answer is that freedom of speech is the purpose of the United States of America. And every time this country's government has tried to alter that fact, or has ignored it in the slightest, it has met with disaster. The correct answer is that constitutional change to limit free speech would not just be a step on a slippery slope, but would be putting the entire nation in an eighteen-wheeler and driving it full-speed down that slippery slope. The correct answer is never. Never!

Do not be sidetracked by Priebus's milquetoast disclaimer about "whether that goes anywhere." Do not be reassured that, at its worst, this so-called government would only attack the news media. Do not "settle down" because a constitutional amendment is the longest of long shots; this is about the threat, the chilling effect, as much as the execution. Priebus started by saying, "It's something that we've looked at," and then upgraded the threat to the present tense by saying, "This is something that is being looked at."

For the sake of Trump.

If—as Trump first suggested more than fourteen months ago—"We're going to open up those libel laws"—it would not be *The New York Times* or ABC News that would be the victims; it would be you. *The New York Times* and ABC News and the like could, even in those nightmare scenarios, be able to defend themselves legally—at least for a time.

Would you?

If the libel laws were "opened up"—if writing or publishing a story the government found was merely inaccurate now subjected the writer or publisher to a libel lawsuit, with financial damages—or worse—exactly who would be a writer or a publisher? Would writing a blog post be writing or publishing? Would sending a tweet be writing or publishing? Would speaking at a protest be writing or publishing? Armed with changed libel laws, Trump's target would be you. What he would stop would not be a newspaper article or a cable news story that his supporters would never read, nor see, nor believe even if they were forced to do so. What he would stop would be dissent. What he would create—what his attacks on the media on Twitter, and at that white nationalist circle jerk in Pennsylvania Saturday night; what that little rat Priebus was getting at—was invoking fear inside you, a hesitation before you protested or spoke out or wrote or tweeted or posted a comment. That moment in which you ask yourself, "Is this going to get me sued?"

It has worked for Trump all his life. Family members, ex-wives, business contacts, customers, the suckers of Trump University. Lawsuit after lawsuit. The blight of financial ruin if you violated the nondisclosure clause. That is how Trump has gotten away with nearly every crooked deal and every broken contract and every threat to the middle wife that nobody talks about anymore, because if she says anything, she and her Trump child get cut off or sued. That's what Trump and his minions like Priebus want for America.

Before you criticize—even if every fact is on your side—they want an America in which a voice inside your head screams: Remember that the government could sue you for libel, and keep you in court, with lawyers, for years, indefinitely—and even if you prevailed, the government could ruin your life, erase your savings, destroy your family, and that's *if you win.*

And as you envision that nightmare, something else not to be missed in the snarling little throwaway comment by Trump's toady Mr. Priebus: what was the first example he gave, of what kind of free speech needs to be erased? You know, for the sake of Trump?

Which topic just happened to come up when phrases like "change libel laws" and "constitutional amendment" were invoked? The first story to which the Trump brand of fascism turns, the first story about which they want to criminalize dissent, is the Trump connection to the Russians. And that just happens to come up as Trump invites the murderous strongman of the Philippines, this pig Duterte, to the White House. Duterte, who said last year, "Just because you're a journalist, you are not exempted from assassination, if you're a son of a bitch."

Coincidences, no doubt.

"You look at the rules of the Senate, even the rules of the House," Trump said on Fox on Saturday. "It's really a bad thing for the country, in my opinion. They're archaic rules. And maybe at some point we're going to have to take those rules on, because, for the good of the nation, things are going to have to be different. You can't go through a process like this. It's not fair. It forces you to make bad decisions."

And now we change the rules of the House and the Senate. Because they don't move fast enough for the sake of Trump. Because the bureaucratic delay—built into our system by the Founding Fathers to prevent despots or foreigners from changing our way of life overnight—is keeping Trump from changing our way of life overnight.

Oh, and that two-party system, the right of the opposition to exist? That has to be changed, too, for the sake of Trump. "I also learned, and this is very sad, because we have a country that we have to take care of," he said on CBS. "The Democrats have been totally obstructionist. Chuck Schumer has turned out to be a bad leader. He's a bad leader for the country. And the Democrats are extremely obstructionist. All they do is obstruct . . . and you know what that's hurting? It's hurting the country."

Change the House and Senate rules for the sake of Trump.

Get rid of the rights of the Senate minority—even if they represent the rights of the majority of voters in the last election—for the sake of Trump.

Instill the fear that to speak or write or tweet or ask, "What is this with Russia?" will get you sued for libel—for the sake of Trump.

This man, already, as of 102 days in office, the worst president in the history of the United States, already the symbol of betrayal and treachery and the willingness to whore himself out to whichever foreign nation will give him a "win"—in the media or at the ballot box—this pitiful excuse for a man is a thug bent on destroying the freedoms of this country as we know them, and, God damn it, we are not going to let him do it.

TRUMP IS PANICKING AGAIN ABOUT RUSSIA

Post date • TUESDAY, MAY 2

On Russia, Trump appears to be running out of excuses. He may also be running out of time. He is not, however, running out of panic.

Two developments this week underscore that. The first involves one of those excuses, and...you guys are kidding, right? General Michael Flynn, who campaigned for Trump, who spoke at Trump's convention, who guided the formation of Trump's policy on Russia, who was briefing the Russian ambassador while on Trump's transition team, who Kellyanne Conway said still had Trump's full confidence as of four p.m. on February 13, who resigned as Trump's national security adviser at ten p.m. on February 13, who is—in the best-case scenario—guilty only of lying to Trump's vice president, who has offered to testify, somewhere, presumably against Trump, in exchange for immunity...He's Obama's fault.

Uh-huh.

"I just heard where General Flynn got his clearance from the Obama administration," Trump told CBS. "When he went to Russia, it was 2015 and he was on the Obama clearance. When General Flynn came to us, as you now know, he already had the highest clearance you can have."

Go *on.*

"They're so devastated because this only came up two days ago...I watched one of your other competitors and they were devastated by this news, because you know what? That kills them. That's the end of that subject."

And then there was a ruling. And the ruling said Flynn wasn't my fault. And the ruling also said he was Obama's fault. And so you can't ever talk about Russia again. Because the ruling is final. It's a ruling. And China ate my homework.

What are you, six?

Trump—Mr. Business, Mr. Extreme Vetting, Mr. Full Confidence in Flynn—has just admitted that when he brought Flynn on, he and his entire team, his government-in-waiting, had no idea whether or not Flynn had the necessary national security clearance to become national security adviser.

Although he knows Flynn traveled to Russia in 2015, on the payroll of Kremlin propagandists, to sit alongside Vladimir Putin, at the same table with Jill Stein, and he knows that Flynn was director of national intelligence until Obama fired him, he seems to think the idea that Flynn had gotten security clearance while Obama was president means that anything Flynn did after Obama fired him is somehow Obama's fault.

Trump also believes—literally believes—that the fact that Flynn worked for the government while Obama was president somehow ends the story of the growing evidence of his campaign's connections to the Russian interference with the 2016 election. "That ... kills ... them," he said. "That's the end of that subject."

And this remarkable overconfidence dovetails with the sudden return to Trump's early campaign pledge to change the Constitution so he can sue anybody who writes a news story he doesn't like. When his henchman Reince Priebus went on ABC's *This Week*, the first story Priebus used as an example of media irresponsibility—the only story Priebus used as an example of media irresponsibility—was that same saga of the Trump campaign and Russia.

I would leave it to John Dean or a historian to analyze the twelve stages of a massive political cover-up. But somewhere in them there has to be this succession of emotions: first comes utter panic at some development that might not be publicly visible, followed by a complete rationalization that you had managed to blame an outside party for it and were now and forever free, followed, in turn, by a public declaration that the subject was now closed.

We saw this with Watergate. "I believe the time has come to bring that investigation and the other investigations of this matter to an end," said Richard Nixon in his 1974 State of the Union address. "One year of Watergate is enough!" The Republicans applauded, and Nixon almost smiled, and—a note to Trump—less than two weeks later, the House voted 410–4 to authorize the Judiciary Committee to investigate impeachment charges against Nixon.

If we are in the "utter panic at some development that might not be publicly visible" stage—what has caused it? Shoes continue to drop at a steady pace. Two of the shoes belong to Sebastian Gorka—reported to be leaving the White House. He was the guy who came up through the Fox News/Breitbart pipeline who showed up at the inaugural ball as an incoming Trump national security aide, wearing what might—or what might not—have been the ceremonial medal of a Hungarian group that was pro-Nazi during World War II. More pertinently, he was one of Trump's loudest defenders about Russia.

Meanwhile, there is also a Russian shoe. A Russian national named Peter Yuryevich Levashov has been indicted on eight counts in Connecticut for, according to the Justice Department, "alleged operation of the Kelihos botnet—a global network of tens of thousands of infected computers, which he allegedly used to facilitate malicious activities . . ." The former member of the British Parliament Louise Mensch—who beat all of American media by five months to the story that the Justice Department had gotten a FISA Court order relating to Trump's associates—has now posted, "Sources linked to the intelligence community say it is believed that a Russian hacker of the election, Pyotr Levashov, was paid directly by Boris Epshteyn on behalf of both Trump and the FSB."

Pyotr Levashov! Why, *that's Peter Levashov's name!*

The FSB is one of the many Russian spy agencies. Epshteyn, who has denied both the allegations and the assertions that he is an FSB agent, is the Russian-born former Trump communications team member who just left the White House.

Mensch also quotes sources who say that the botnet that Levashov operated had a "command and control center" in Trump Tower.

And yes, with Mensch, and the British agent Christopher Steele, of the Steele dossier, and the British newspaper *The Guardian* leading world coverage of this story—and the BBC reporter Paul Wood, who isn't far behind—yes, the British just may be your cousin who is just far enough away to see clearly that your girlfriend or boyfriend is no good and you need to get them out of your life immediately.

And then there is a shoe I wouldn't ordinarily mention.

It is a story from a man named Claude Taylor, who identifies himself on Twitter as a "Veteran of three presidential campaigns, served on White House staff (Clinton)." He tweeted on Friday, "This just in from a source with knowledge of Comey's investigation. 'two grand juries have convened and I know that one is almost complete.'" Thin gruel under ordinary circumstances . . .

But Taylor's seeming bombshell was then retweeted by a man named Rick Wilson, with just one word added: "Same." Wilson is not just *not* a Democrat, as

Taylor is, he is a former Rudy Giuliani adman and adviser, he dreamed up the awful ad linking Georgia senator Max Cleland to Osama bin Laden in 2002, and he tied then Senator Barack Obama to Reverend Jeremiah Wright in 2007.

Take Wilson and Taylor for whatever you think they are worth, but I am not ready to dismiss them, especially not after Taylor came back on Sunday to describe one of the alleged grand juries as having supposedly focused on violations of the Foreign Agents Registration Act, RICO racketeering, and the Russians and Trump Tower.

Are there grand juries ready to hand up, hand down, or hand out indictments?

I would not dare claim to know. But I do know what I see: Trump—at escalated levels of panic. Trump—floating a constitutional amendment that would keep us from talking about his Russia problem! Trump at the point of pretending that a not very interesting fact about General Michael Flynn and his security clearance, which Trump should've known and anybody who had ever thought about it could probably have guessed, is somehow the final judgment on his Russia problem, that it "kills" those covering his Russia problem, and concludes for all time any discussion of his Russia problem—quoting him again about his Russia problem: "That's the end of that subject."

I do not dare to claim to know the whole story of Trump and Russia. But I willingly dare to claim that this is *not* the end of that subject.

A PLEA TO THE FREE WORLD: FOR GOD'S SAKE, ASK TRUMP!

Post date • WEDNESDAY, MAY 3

This is a plea from what's left of the United States to the rest of the free world, specifically to the news media of the rest of the free world. Please—what happened in Berlin to Ivanka Trump has to happen everywhere any of the Trumps or the secretary of state or the vice president or anybody else connected to this misbegotten, evil man stops long enough to take questions.

Our media has been all but frozen out, replaced by propaganda outlets where nothing, no matter how outlandish or un-American—not even attacks on the very freedom of speech under which they operate—gets a follow-up question. On those few occasions when there is an opportunity to state that Donald Trump is an existential threat to the United States and the free world, our media has largely choked. It asks him questions not designed to be challenging to his fact-free worldview, but designed to be played on television. Or it self-censors, overcome at the crucial moment by desperate, stupid, and ultimately pointless attempts to, as a source at one cable outfit reportedly put it, "focus on Trump voters."

Last Saturday, Trump compared immigrants to "snakes." He called the rules of the Senate and the House "archaic." His chief of staff would, the next morning, propose a constitutional attack on the First Amendment. He invited the murderous strongman of the Philippines to the White House. He held a rally apparently openly attended by white nationalists.

And after all that, this was the headline in the Sunday *Philadelphia Inquirer* (right under "Winner of 20 Pulitzer Prizes"): "Touting Progress." Touting *progress*? Touting *fascism*!

We here, the liberal media, Trump's "Fake News"—we pretend this is just another presidency and just another difference of opinion. Even *The New York Times*. As Robert Duvall called it in the movie *Network*, "The holy goddamn *New York Times*." The same morning: "Remaking the Presidency, Trump Has Changed, Too. Expanding Power and Shunning Norms, Yet Adapting to Realities, After 100 Days."

The hell he has! Adapting to *what* realities? As that newspaper hit the streets, his spokesman was talking about a constitutional libel amendment so that—as Trump put it eleven months before his inauguration—"we can sue them and win lots of money."

In interviews preceding his hundredth day in office, Trump showed a succession of reporters the county-by-county map of his election—five months after that election—and at least half-seriously suggested to a reporter from *The Washington Post* that the paper print the map, now, on its front page. Instead of an article asking how crazy anybody who would do such a thing would have to be, this became an anecdote for the *Washington Post* reporter to joke about much later, on television.

Trump told a *Washington Examiner* reporter about his admiration for Andrew Jackson and how Jackson "was really angry that he saw what was happening with regard to the Civil War. He said, 'There's no reason for this.'" Jackson left the presidency twenty-eight years before the Civil War started, and in fact had nearly precipitated a civil war thirty-two years before it started. Trump couldn't have been more wrong about him if he had claimed Jackson rode to his inauguration in an automobile. And yet the American news media continues to treat Donald Trump as just another story, as the wacky neighbor who just happens to have nukes, and it continues to treat the Trump Presidential Crime Family as just another collection of White House relatives.

So again, my plea to the journalists of the world: Do what Miriam Meckel, the editor in-chief of a German business magazine, did. "You're the first daughter of the United States," began Ms. Meckel as she moderated a business panel featuring Ivanka Trump, "The German audience is not that familiar with the concept of a First Daughter. I'd like to ask you, what is your role, and who are you representing? Your father as president of the United States? The American people? Or your business?"

Ms. Trump, whose confused-beauty-pageant-contestant-grade stupidity has largely been hidden from the American audience, stumbled through her answer. Incredibly, she then began to laud her father's treatment of *women*. "I'm very proud of my father's advocacy... He's been a tremendous champion of supporting families, and enabling them to thrive..."

The crowd began to hiss, boo, and make other verbal equivalents of eye-rolling.

"You hear the reaction from the audience," moderator Meckel observed. "I need to address one more point. Some attitudes toward women your father has displayed in former times might leave one questioning whether he's such an empowerer for women..." Since Trump's election, no one in this country has asked a question that pointed or that realistic or that challenging of him or his spawn or his key appointees, and Miriam Meckel asked two of them.

"I've certainly heard the criticism from the media," Ivanka Trump replied, again startled by reality and sounding surprisingly like her father, "that's been perpetuated." Miriam Meckel deserves all the Pulitzer Prizes, the Murrow Awards, the Cronkite Awards, the Emmys, the Peabodys, and any other trophy we can hand her. And she and other reporters and editors and just other citizens in Germany or England or France, or those foreign correspondents who are reporting from the United States for the BBC or Agence France-Presse or the *Aardvark Daily* of Wellington, New Zealand—or anyone who is anywhere that members of this family or this government might not be able to elude the media—you need to keep asking pointed, doubtful, skeptical questions that our reporters are too afraid to ask.

Ask Trump if he's ever had a CAT scan. Ask Trump if he's experiencing headaches or blurred vision or hallucinations. Ask Rex Tillerson if he's worried that evidence continues to mount connecting his boss's campaign to Russian electoral hacking while his boss has resumed blaming China. Ask UN Ambassador Nikki Haley if it's a problem that Trump invited Duterte to the White House and congratulated Erdoğan on destroying democracy in Turkey. Ask any of the Trump children why their father has simultaneously enraged North Korea and South Korea and China. Ask them about the *Carl Vinson* Armada Bluff, and ask them about the conflation of Kim Jong-un with Kim Jong-il, and ask them about the White House education story on Snapchat that misspelled the word "Education," and ask them about how the First Lady seemingly had to physically nudge Trump to put his hand over his heart during the national anthem. Or take anything from that crazy Associated Press interview where he said off the record that he watched CNN and then said on the record, two minutes later, that he never watched CNN—and ask him! Or that crazy Reuters interview where he admitted that he thought life as president would be easier than being a seventy-year-old con man who inherited his money from his daddy!—and ask him! Or take that crazy rally in Pennsylvania where he called immigrants "snakes," when his own grandparents were immigrants and his mother was an immigrant and two of his three wives have been immigrants and four of his five kids are the children of an immigrant—and ask him!

Ask him! For God's sake, *ask him.* Because the media of this country is too terrified of being accused of not being balanced to come out and state the obvious: that emotionally, the president is not at all balanced! And that while all of our lives depend on whether he gets less crazy or more crazy, apparently it is no longer worth the risk to American reporters to ask just how crazy he is at this moment!

THE HEALTH CARE REPEAL

Post date • THURSDAY, MAY 4

The well-dressed man in the neatly trimmed beard was one of the last of the 558 people to testify to the commission. He had been chosen by his colleagues to represent them all, and none of them disavowed what he said—nor ever would. His colleagues had been willing to paralyze the nation, to not just affect at least 10 percent of the economy but to, at best, inconvenience and, at worst, literally threaten the lives of virtually all of its citizens. No matter what entreaties had been made to them—no matter what evidence of inhumanity had been presented, no matter the pleas and protestations, no matter the "moving spectacle of horrors," as one of their opponents termed it—they would not listen. They had a mandate to protect what their side believed.

And their side had the money. And then the well-dressed man in the neatly trimmed beard said something that you can still find in the history books today. Of the victims of the inhumanity he and his moneyed colleagues were inflicting, he testified, "These men don't suffer! Why, hell, half of them don't even speak English."

The man was named George F. Baer, and he was the president of the Philadelphia and Reading Railroad. His testimony was to the first real public hearing about the hellish, murderous virtual slavery facing the coal miners of this nation, called the Anthracite Coal Strike Commission.

This was in the year 1903. In Pennsylvania. The miners worked ten hours a day, six days a week, for which they would be paid $2.75 an hour. The boys who worked in the mines made thirteen cents per hour. And George F. Baer was—as were all the moneyed men of the coal and railroad industries—defending this. Baer had become their spokesman because a letter he had written had leaked and been published. "The rights and interests of the laboring man will be protected and cared for—not by the labor agitators, but by the Christian men of property to whom God has given control of the property rights of the country . . ."

This made him a hero.

He would defend the millionaires who sent boys of twelve and eleven and ten and nine and eight years old to straddle a conveyor on which traveled the shale their fathers were sending up from the pits half a mile below the surface. They literally broke up the oversize pieces. Or, if they did it wrong, the oversize pieces would break *them* up and, as the commission heard, could easily take off a boy's hand or arm or leg. For thirteen cents an hour.

"These men don't suffer! Why, hell, half of them don't even speak English."

I have been thinking a lot lately of George F. Baer and the other demons of the 1902 coal strike. I hope there is a hell solely for people like them. They exist in all generations, their view of man's duty to other men twisted and perverted and unimaginable to nearly all of us—and roundly cheered by the sadistic and the money-obsessed and the comfortable. They exist today. They are the people like Donald Trump. And Paul Ryan. And the others involved in the repeal of the often ineffective, far-from-finished first step toward establishing the absolute and inalienable right of every man woman and child in this country to have their health minimally protected through the intervention of the government, that first step they have derisively called Obamacare.

Trump and his ilk look at the transplant recipients who gained new life under it, and will now have no means of paying for the drugs to keep themselves alive, and they shrug and congratulate themselves on tax cuts for themselves. Trump and his ilk look at the special-needs kids who will have no insurance and see only "liberal tears." Trump and his ilk will look at the as-yet-uncountable number of poor people who will die because of the greed of the rich, and they will celebrate what they actually believe is a victory. These men don't suffer! Why, hell, half of them don't even *vote Republican.*

George F. Baer died 103 years and one month ago, and I hope he's still suffering somewhere. All that he knew—the railroad industry and the coal industry that used to dominate this nation—it's all gone. Without the government, there would be no train service in this country. And coal mining is an afterthought, no matter Trump's false promises. And child labor is, in retrospect, impossible to believe. But man's inhumanity to man lives on, in Donald Trump. And Paul Ryan. And in every other so-called human being who voted to repeal the Affordable Care Act.

Be heartbroken. Be terrified. Be angry. But mostly, be vengeful—quietly, persistently, permanently vengeful. To Trump and Ryan and every man and woman who voted for this medieval act, this barbarism: we know your names, we will destroy your careers, we will make you suffer, and—like George F. Baer and the mine owners—if any of the religions are correct, future generations will comfort themselves and move forward driven in part by the comfort of knowing that you, Paul Ryan, and you, Donald Trump, will burn in hell.

YATES PROVES TRUMP'S TREASON

Post date • MONDAY, MAY 8

Sally Yates, American hero.

A little oversimplistic. And in some respects, damning the American government with faint praise. Because all she has testified to the Senate that she did, that she said, that happened to her, used to be the minimum standard for public servants in this country, but now, in the era of Trump, she stands out like a champion. You are the goddamned president of the goddamned United States and your acting attorney general tells your White House counsel that your national security adviser "essentially could be blackmailed by the Russians" and "you don't want [him] to be in a position where the Russians have leverage over him"—and you . . . *fire* the acting attorney general? Not the national security adviser. You fire the acting attorney general? The person warning you that a man charged with giving you arguably the most important advice in the world—what to do to keep this nation secure from international threat—is ripe for blackmailing by this country's primary national enemy. A person of extreme importance in our White House, who can influence you, who *could* influence you on behalf of the Russians—*and you fire her and keep him*?

Which are you? An idiot? Or a traitor?

What Sally Yates testified to; what Jim Clapper testified to; the pathetic redirections and sad obfuscations of Chuck Grassley and John Cornyn and Ted Cruz and the other Republican Trumpian lapdogs desperate to change the subject, desperate to talk about "unmasking"—the Trump-Russia equivalent of saying that the true victim of Watergate was Richard Nixon, because those audiotapes of him betraying democracy made him sound bad, because people got to hear him swearing all those *expletives deleted*—all that was important.

But the meat of that Senate committee hearing was the timeline . . . the cynical, disloyal, amoral timeline. November 10: President Obama warns Trump not to make Flynn his national security adviser. NBC reports Trump explains that he thinks Obama is kidding. January 26: Acting Attorney General Yates warns the White House that National Security Adviser Flynn has been compromised by the Russians, does so in order that the White House can take action. January 27: Yates goes back and repeats to White House Counsel McGahn that Flynn's been compromised, could be blackmailed by the Russians, has lied to other White House officials; that the Russians know about the conversations with Flynn. January 30: Trump fires Yates, claiming he is doing so because she would not defend his Muslim ban in court. January 31: Trump does not fire Flynn. February 1: Trump still does not fire Flynn. February 2: same. February 3: same. The fourth. The fifth. The sixth. Seventh, eighth, ninth, tenth, eleventh, twelfth: the same. February 13: *The Washington Post* breaks the story of the Yates warning that Flynn has been compromised by the Russians and the Russians could be blackmailing the man who tells the president how to preserve our country from destruction by a foreign power, and only then is Flynn forced out.

If the *Post* had not broken the story, how long would Flynn have remained in this White House? Iago, pouring whatever lies the Russians might be blackmailing him into telling into the ears of Trump. Even if Trump is somehow innocent of everything implied and inferred about collusion with Russia, he is not innocent of choosing a Russian stooge, a Russian vessel like Flynn, and defending him to the last, even to the point of veiled threats. Like the one just hours before that hearing began: Trump tweeted, "Ask Sally Yates, under oath, if she knows how classified information got into the newspapers soon after she explained it to W.H. Counsel."

As Congressman Ted Lieu of California noted, there is a law—18 U.S. Code 1512—which defines "intimidation" of a witness to "influence" testimony in an "official proceeding" as a federal crime, the perpetrator of which "shall be fined under this title or imprisoned not more than 20 years, or both." Trump chose Michael Flynn, a blackmailing victim waiting to happen, over Sally Yates, an honest American public servant, on January 26, and he has chosen Flynn and smeared Yates every day since. And today he adds intimidation—possibly criminal intimidation—to the list.

Once again: if *The Washington Post* had not broken the story, how long would Flynn have remained on the job? He'd still be there now, wouldn't he?

Potentially being blackmailed by the Russians. To influence the president.

It is treachery of the highest order, and no matter who is the puppet and who is the puppeteer, our country is *not* safe in the hands of these idiots, and Trump and all of them must go, and must go *now*.

FOLLOW THE MONEY

Post date • TUESDAY, MAY 9

Follow the money.

Follow, say, a hundred million dollars as it reportedly went from Russia to Trump in 2014.

"Follow the money" is the most famous line in political history, said by Deep Throat to Bob Woodward in *All the President's Men*. And of course, Deep Throat never said it. Doesn't mean it wasn't true, then or now. Then it was true—as we investigated a corrupt president's attempt to subvert the two-party system, but he was dumb enough to leave a paper trail of endorsed checks. Now it is true—as we investigate precisely how much Russia and Donald Trump may have subverted our 2016 election exactly six months ago, and he and his son were perhaps dumb enough to leave a verbal record of how Russians allegedly gave them a hundred million dollars.

Follow. The. Money.

James Dodson is a golf writer. An expert. The coauthor of Arnold Palmer's autobiography. And over the weekend he was featured on the regular sports segment on the Boston Public Radio station WBUR, where he recounted being invited to play golf with Trump at Trump's new club in Charlotte, North Carolina, three years ago, in 2014, to play with Trump and Eric Trump, and to immediately not just wonder how Trump was financing all his golf courses, when the world of golf never really recovered from the 2008 recession, but to *ask* him how: "When I first met him I asked him how he was—you know, this is the journalist in me—I said, 'What are you using to pay for these courses?' And he just sort of tossed off that he had access to a hundred million dollars."

Donald Trump had "access to" a hundred million dollars, for what James

Dodson knew was one of the diciest investments in the world? Luxury golf courses? Three years ago? That wasn't all of it. Dodson says he was paired with Eric Trump for the first nine holes. "So when I got in the cart with Eric, as we were setting off, I said, 'Eric, who's funding? I know no banks—because of the recession, the Great Recession—have touched a golf course. You know, no one's funding any kind of golf construction. It's dead in the water the last four or five years.'"

You still have time to make your guess—and grab your popcorn.

"And this is what he said. He said, 'Well, we don't rely on American banks. We have all the funding we need out of Russia.' I said, 'Really?' And he said, 'Oh, yeah. We've got some guys that really, really love golf, and they're really invested in our programs. We just go there all the time.'" Donald Trump boasting to a golf writer that he alone had "access" to $100 million to invest in golf courses, and Eric Trump explaining that "we have all the funding we need out of Russia" and "we just go there all the time."

And you and I are listening to the ground and sniffing the wind for evidence that the reported possible Trump-Russia grand jury met in the Eastern District of Virginia today. And we are parsing the new testimony of the former acting attorney general, who tried to warn Trump about the treachery of General Michael Flynn. And we are sifting through the claim that there are anywhere from twenty-eight to forty-two names on the FBI Trump-Russia target list. And while we're expending all that energy, between them, Donald and his son Moron Twin Number 2 may have told a golf writer at a Trump golf course (my God, it's always him and some goddamned *golf course*) that as of three years ago, the Russians gave them a hundred million dollars.

Follow the money. I mean, at minimum, if this is true, Eric Trump makes his father out to be a liar. February 7, Trump tweets, "I don't know Putin, have no deals in Russia . . ." Is this the part where we take him seriously but not literally?

That he thinks of a Russian-funded golf course in Charlotte not as a "deal in Russia" but as a "deal in North Carolina"?

In addition to all the non-mainstream-media coverage of what Comey is doing behind the scenes, and how many FISA warrants were granted last year, and what's up with the Russian company Alfa-Bank and its disputed links to computers inside Trump Tower . . . there is just as much media coverage of this labyrinth of financial connections between Trump and Russia. Like the old (but true) cliché goes, they didn't send Al Capone to jail for killing people—they sent him to jail for cheating on his tax returns. And oh, by the way, a respected golf writer says Donald Trump and Eric Trump told him three years ago that the Russians gave them a hundred million dollars. Which might have inspired this in a Sunday-morning tweet: "When will the Fake Media ask about the Dems dealings with Russia & why the DNC wouldn't allow the FBI to check their server or investigate?"

On January 9, I noted that Trump could not leave the subject of Russia alone, and I predicted that it would—sooner or later—destroy him. A week ago, he said that the so-what news about Michael Flynn getting security clearance while Obama was president had "devastated" everybody questioning Trump's ties to the Russians, "because you know what? That kills them. That's the end of that subject." Less than three days later, while attacking FBI Director Comey on Twitter, he added, "The phony Trump/Russia story was an excuse used by the Democrats..."

He cannot leave Russia alone. It will destroy him. It *is* destroying him.

And it will be especially delightful if it destroys him on, or because of, one of his goddamned golf courses.

Follow the money.

"Deep Throat," by the way, never said that to Bob Woodward.

Bill Goldman said it. Wrote it, actually. Bill Goldman wrote the film adaptation of *All the President's Men*, and everything else from *Butch Cassidy and the Sundance Kid* to *The Stepford Wives* to *The Princess Bride*. And I know him—he lives about ten blocks from me, and he's got one twelve-foot-high apartment wall full of political books, and the most famous line in political history isn't in any of them, because the guy who wrote it is sitting there! And it's still true. Follow the hundred million dollars in Russian golf money!

And you know what would really help Trump now? If he had some way of proving the James Dodson story wasn't true, or was misinterpreted, or if a hundred million was a drop in his golf ball bucket, or if it really was just golf money and the guys who gave it to him weren't Putin spies and if he didn't agree to sell out our country for a hundred million. You know—if only there was some *tax record* or *tax data* or, I don't know, *tax return* he could release to clear his good name and stop people from connecting a hundred million in Russian golf money to, you know, treason. But alas, I guess his tax returns from 2014 are still under audit, so we have no way of seeing them, so he can't clear himself, so we'll just have to assume the worst and that the hundred million is the tip of the iceberg and if Trump doesn't do what Putin wants, Putin will take a lot more than a hundred million dollars from him.

Follow the money.

Oh, and one last word: *Fore!*

YOU CANNOT FIRE THE MAN WHO IS INVESTIGATING YOU

Post date • WEDNESDAY, MAY 10

Donald Trump has declared war on the legal system, moved to overrule the spirit of the Constitution, and enacted a coup against the ideals of the United States of America. And at this hour, one of two things is, already and irretrievably, under way: either the end of Trump or the end of American democracy—because both cannot continue—because, simply: You cannot fire the man who is investigating you. It is axiomatic, it is simple, it is eternal, it is proven: You cannot fire the man who is investigating you.

Even the dumb people will understand what you are trying to get away with. No matter what excuse you provide. No matter who you get to agree with you. No matter what you think it will accomplish for you. No matter what you think it will protect you from. No matter if you are the president of the United States and the man you have fired may be guilty of something: You cannot fire the man who is investigating you.

To do so is to inherit the wind. To do so is to immediately, and irreversibly, take whatever problems you face, whatever investigations you have to suffer, whatever crimes you may or may not have already committed, and to magnify them by a number so large it almost cannot be counted: You cannot fire the man who is investigating you.

It is, by itself, a cover-up. Not just part of an already extant cover-up. Not another drop in a bucket of corruption and dishonesty. It's an entirely new bucket. Donald Trump fired the man who was investigating him. That, by it-self, without further explanation, without further evidence—that alone imme-diately is a cover-up. Donald Trump should be impeached, today, for this one act. No Russian collusion needs to be proved. No financial records need to be assayed. No Michael Flynn, no Carter Page, no Paul Manafort, no Ambassador Kislyak, no Steele dossier, no Trump tapes, no Eric Trump tapes, no Pence tapes, no hacking, no sanity hearing, no hundred million golf course dollars from Russia, no last-minute Comey requests for a larger Russian investigation budget.

You cannot fire the man who is investigating you.

Trump is effectively guilty today of an impeachable offense, and if enough of the Republican members of the House and the Senate are anything other than political whores and the fully owned lickspittles of corporations and other special interests, Trump will be impeached. Within two hours of Trump's strategically inexplicable blunder, Republican congressman Justin Amash of Michigan tweeted: "My staff and I are reviewing legislation to es-tablish an independent commission on Russia. The second paragraph of this letter is bizarre."

Amash was referring to this, in Trump's dismissal notice to James Comey: "While I greatly appreciate you informing me, on three separate occasions, that I am not under investigation, I nevertheless concur . . ." "Bizarre" is an un-derstatement; it is suicidal. Trump simply says, "I am not under investigation." He never mentions under investigation for what. And there is no evidence that Comey ever told him anything of the sort—or that Comey made a distinction to him between an investigation of his campaign and him personally.

James Comey testified last week that the FBI is coordinating with two prosecutors, one at the Department of Justice and one who is the U.S. attorney for the Eastern District of Virginia, in their investigations of possible collu-sion between Trump's campaign team and the Russian government. The non-mainstream observer Claude Taylor had claimed that there was already a Trump-Russia grand jury sitting near Washington, and CNN reported last night that indeed there was a grand jury in Alexandria, Virginia, and it had is-sued subpoenas to associates of Michael Flynn "in recent weeks."

It is fair to assume that some part of this news was what got Comey fired. And whether or not, in his hazy grasp of reality, Trump really thought he could somehow put the Russian toothpaste back in the FBI tube, he clearly thought—CNN reported this Tuesday night—that there would be no political blowback. Trump's ham-handed, falsely lighthearted tweets Wednesday morning about "when things calm down" and how "Republican and Democrat alike" will be thanking him confirm this. His next round of tweets—criticizing the Vietnam service controversy of a senator, without remembering that this would also invoke his own five deferments from Vietnam—confirmed the mixture of rage and panic that had been reported earlier, that he had raged over how much television coverage Comey was getting, and he had been screaming at television coverage of his Russian scandal and Comey's refusal to make it all disappear. At minimum, somebody told this unstable president—or he told himself—that any fallout would be less damaging to him than letting Comey proceed. This is not true, because of the simplicity of the only takeaway from this naked power grab:

You cannot fire the man who is investigating you.

So we have a Tuesday Night Massacre for our time. And for those of you who always wondered what it felt like to live through Watergate, welcome. That catch in the throat, that intake of breath that doesn't go all the way through, that repeated sensation that the future of democracy in this country rests on the events not of an administration, nor a year, nor a month, but on those of the next few weeks—that's what October 20, 1973, felt like. Richard Nixon had been able to get a new attorney general approved by the Democratic Senate only when that attorney general, Elliot Richardson, swore to name a special Watergate prosecutor. On Saturday, October 20, 1973, Nixon decided that prosecutor, Archibald Cox, had to be fired. The attorney general wouldn't do it, and resigned. The deputy attorney general wouldn't do it; Nixon fired him. The third man at the Justice Department, the solicitor general—he fired Cox.

When the sun rose that beautiful Saturday morning, Nixon may have had enough political capital, enough House and Senate support, enough public approval, to survive. When the sun rose the next morning, most of that was gone. Politically, he was a dead man walking. Because you cannot fire the man who is investigating you.

Republican Representatives Amash, Comstock of Virginia, Curbelo of Florida, and Senators Burr, Corker, Flake, and McCain had, by breakfast, made correct and patriotic responses to the crisis. Nevertheless, it may require still more evil from Trump to shake the remaining disloyal or disbelieving

Republican political whores loose from the tree. But if the Comey firing doesn't do it, Trump will provide that evil, and even the Republicans will abandon him. But will they abandon him in time? You cannot fire the man who is investigating you, because the next man will now also have to investigate you for *that*.

"Whether ours shall continue to be a government of laws and not of men," read the entirety of Archie Cox's statement after Nixon fired him in 1973, "is now for Congress, and ultimately the American people."

AN APPEAL TO THE WORLD'S INTELLIGENCE SERVICES

Post date • THURSDAY, MAY 11

I appeal to the intelligence agencies and the governments of what is left of the free world—to them as entities, entireties, as bureaucracies making official decisions, and to the individuals who make decisions of conscience, to GCHQ and MI6 in the UK, to the BND in Germany, the DGSE in France, the ASIS in Australia, and even to the GRU in Russia, where they must already be profoundly aware that they have not merely helped put an amoral cynic in power here, but an uncontrollable one, whose madness is genuine and whose usefulness even to them is over.

To all of them, and to the world's journalists, I make this plea: We, the citizens of the United States of America, are the victims of a coup. We need your leaks, your information, your intelligence, your recordings, your videos, your conscience. The civilian government and the military of the United States of America are no longer in the hands of the people, nor in the control of any responsible individuals on whom you can rely. The first step toward compromising our FBI occurred Tuesday with the unilateral firing of its director by the president, prompted by the attorney general, both of whom are—or were, at least in theory, possibly to be—under investigation by the FBI as led by that director.

Our CIA is run by one of that president's political appointees. The first national security adviser was fired and may have been a Russian stooge. The second national security adviser has reportedly been yelled at by the president because he had the temerity to disagree with him. Our State Department is in the hands of useless amateurs. Our United Nations mission is bereft of power and uninformed. And the White House is run by a cabal of an amoral family syndicate that has spent its first three months slapping a dollar sign on anything that stood still long enough. A cabal with, at its head, a man with seemingly no interest in our laws, in our rights, in our Constitution, and with a brain that appears to not work properly.

Through our own negligence, the resentments and stupidities of millions of us, and the boundless greed of our elite class, our democracy has all but slipped away from us. It hangs today by a thread, and those who could protect it and restore it and fight for it, even at this late date—the Republican politicians whose voices today could force Trump out of office tomorrow—they are all but silent. Owned by special interests and silenced by a power that exceeds even whatever dedication to freedom they once had, all but a few of them fall back into platitudes about the leader of the country firing the head of the FBI and precipitating a constitutional crisis in order to shut down the investigation of his possible high crimes and misdemeanors. Our majority party impotently wrings its hands about "timing" and how "troubled" they are, and then they go back to calculating how they will most easily get reelected—with whose money; by whose instructions.

We, the citizens of the United States of America, are the victims of a coup. For months we have heard that your organizations have damning evidence against Donald John Trump. Whatever evidence you may have, you cannot conceal it any longer. Whatever we in this country are to you now, wherever you are now, you know that this nation has been a savior to you at some point in the past, and that our stability and our freedom and a government controlling this country that is at least sane are your surest guarantees of a prosperous future—indeed, perhaps your surest guarantees of any future at all. Now: We. Need. Your. Help.

Whatever there is, on Trump: reveal it. Issue it officially if you can; leak it if you cannot. If your directors and your governments want you to wait, look to the last days here and ask yourselves—plumb your consciences—if there is any time left to wait. Give it to a reporter, give it to an American friend, put it on the internet, leave it outside somebody's back door. There is no time left for proto-cols and estimations of long-term impacts and tradecraft.

A dictator-in-training has betrayed our Constitution, and nevertheless survived two nights in office. The dictatorship he may want—the dictatorship he may feel is the natural extension of his past life, the dictatorship he may believe he has earned—has gone, in this week, from crawling to taking its first few tentative steps. What you have, we need, and we need it *now*.

And to the intelligence community of this country: your patriotic duty is clear. In many respects, in the months since the election, you have provided your greatest service in our history. A democracy that has lost its political way staggers down the street like a drunk and lurches toward the gutter, yet you have walked a virtually bipartisan straight line, and have followed your rules, and the rules of the civilians—and yet the evildoers still exist, regardless.

The greatest threat to the freedoms of this nation that this nation has ever faced—the Trump administration—the Trump *junta*—is playing by no rules. They just offed the FBI director and let him find out about it by reading a TV news crawl in the back of the room in which he was addressing his Los Angeles office.

They have no rules. For now, the rest of us, who only want our democracy back, we can have no rules, either. We will take the risk of reestablishing the rules later. What you in the FBI, in the CIA, in the Justice Department have on Trump, we need now. Because by tomorrow it may disappear, and your ability to do anything with it may disappear as well. Some of us on the outside have tried the best we could to prevent this day, others less so—now it doesn't matter who did how much, when. You, in the FBI, the CIA, the other intelligence agen-cies, the Justice Department—you must be the patriots now. You, in the "Five Eyes," in the PSIA in Japan, in the outfits too secret to have their names known to us, you must become, for the moment, Americans. We need what you have, and we need it now, and we need it made public.

It is more than just the fate of this sloppy country that is at risk. For all our faults, for good or bad, we cannot be left as a fascist, rogue state and an enemy of freedom and international comity. The fate of all freedoms may rest in your hands and your willingness to not merely hint, but show what you know.

If we go under, you are next.

The freedom you save *will be* your own.

THE TRUMP-RUSSIA COVER-UP CASE

Post date • MONDAY, MAY 15

And so we conclude a week that began with the Trump-Russia scandal as a complicated, labyrinthine, bizarre international tangle of questions about computer hacking and money laundering and collusion, but ended with the Trump-Russia scandal as a simple, straightforward, traditional American, easy-to-digest set of questions about obstruction of justice and witness intimidation and presidential cover-ups. "Trump and Russia" is no longer about Trump and Russia. He could be as pure as the driven snow about Russia. He and he alone has made the Trump-and-Russia story about covering up the Trump-and-Russia story.

In articles of impeachment—and, if he leaves or is removed from office, perhaps in criminal prosecution afterwards—Trump could theoretically wind up being accused of eighteen separate counts of six separate crimes in just the past week.

Working backwards: Friday's tweet—"James Comey better hope that there are no 'tapes' of our conversations before he starts leaking to the press!" That could be prosecuted as a blackmail threat to a private citizen. That tweet could be interpreted as intimidation of a possible witness in an official proceeding—18 U.S. Code 1512—which carries a sentence of up to twenty years. That's two possible crimes in the Trump-Russia Cover-up.

Plus—the reference to "tapes"? In the District of Columbia, there's nothing illegal about taping your own conversation. But as Richard Nixon learned, to his chagrin, a president doesn't own the recording. If Trump destroys the recording—or can't prove he was just lying in the tweet and it never existed—that could be a charge of destruction of government property. And the third of the three articles of impeachment against Nixon in 1974 was entirely about the president's refusal to turn over secret White House tapes that Congress had subpoenaed. His handling of evidence—the tapes—was believed to fit the Constitution's definition of "high crimes and misdemeanors."

So—one tweet—four possible charges.

The day before, Thursday the eleventh, came the *New York Times* report that Trump had brought Comey to the White House for dinner on January 27.

That was when Trump reportedly asked if he was being investigated, and asked Comey for his loyalty. That loyalty pledge, Trump has only partly denied, and his adviser Kellyanne Conway has endorsed. As the Harvard professor and scholar of constitutional law Laurence Tribe noted, "That is clearly, on its face, obstruction of justice. What it really means is 'Can I count on you not to make me a target of this investigation?' That's clearly an impermissible question." So there's a fifth potential charge: obstruction of justice in the possible investigation of Donald J. Trump.

But here's a sixth. That dinner was the day after the acting attorney general, Sally Yates, first warned the White House that Michael Flynn had been compromised by Russia. So was Trump also trying to get Comey to obstruct justice for the sake of Flynn?

It's more of a stretch, but here's a seventh. Could Trump be charged with trying to get a threat or warning to Yates to lay off Flynn, via Comey? And a can of worms Trump opened that might be bigger even than whether or not he has recorded White House conversations. When the report came that he had reportedly asked Comey to, in essence, swear loyalty, another question bubbled up: Did Trump ask anybody *else* to do that? Each time he asked someone who may have been involved in the investigation, it could be another count of obstruction of justice. And, just as important—did anybody say yes? Because once somebody else says yes, you could then have a *conspiracy* to obstruct justice. Just one of each here charge, and there are already nine counts in the Trump-Russia Cover-up—just against Trump.

And we're still not done with Thursday the eleventh.

Trump's interview with NBC that evening, in which it almost seemed as if he had deliberately unraveled the stonewall defense his staff had used for forty-eight hours—insisting Comey's firing had nothing to do with Russia, and happened only because the attorney general and the deputy attorney general recommended it: "Regardless of recommendation, I was going to fire Comey . . . and in fact, when I decided to just do it, I said to myself, 'You know, this Russia thing with Trump and Russia is a made-up story.'" Not only could this be yet another obstruction-of-justice charge, our tenth charge of the Trump-Russia Cover-up, but you could go out on a limb and accuse anybody in Trump's administration—Trump included—who advanced the claims that it was about Comey's competence, or the Hillary Clinton emails, or the recommendations of others, of obstructing justice again if they knowingly lied about why Comey was fired, essentially obstructing justice about obstructing justice! So that's an eleventh charge. And a conspiracy to do that—with Sean Spicer, Sarah Huckabee Sanders, Vice President Pence, and Trump all involved in that original story—conspiracy makes twelve.

Moving back to Wednesday, May 10, there's a thirteenth possible charge. McClatchy news quoted White House sources who say that when Attorney General Sessions and his deputy, Rod Rosenstein, went to see Trump two days earlier to complain about Comey, Trump had asked them to write the letter that he had originally cited as the cause for firing Comey. That's now another possible tentacle of conspiracy in the Trump-Russia Cover-up Case: Trump asking the Department of Justice to give him a weapon with which to fire the head of the FBI.

The day before, Tuesday the ninth, had the most obvious of the possible charges, number fourteen: Comey's firing itself. You can't fire the criminal investigator investigating you for possible criminality, in the middle of his criminal investigation. It's obstruction of justice, and, as a reminder, the first article of impeachment against Richard Nixon was a string of obstructions of justice. As Obama's presidential ethics czar, Norm Eisen, tweeted, "Newly revealed demand for loyalty was the obstruction—firing was consummation of the threat." Legally, the loyalty demand and the firing could be viewed as separate events.

But there's still one more. On Monday the eighth, before her dramatic testimony to the Senate Judiciary Committee, Trump tweeted about the once acting attorney general. "Ask Sally Yates, under oath, if she knows how classified information got into the newspapers soon after she explained it to W.H. Counsel." Well, we are back where we started: just like Friday with Comey, Monday with Yates, Trump may have violated Section 18 U.S. Code 1512—intimidating a witness in an official proceeding, and maybe intimidating a whistle-blower and a private citizen.

Seventeen possible charges, for Trump, in the theoretical articles of impeachment pertaining to the Trump-Russia Cover-up Case. There's one each for possible destruction of government property and in the hypothetical, possible refusal to turn over subpoenaed evidence. Two for intimidating witnesses, two for threatening private citizens, two for threatening whistle-blowers, one for threatening the acting attorney general. Maybe two more for separate conspiracies to commit obstruction of justice. And perhaps seven for obstruction of justice.

It's staggering, but it may still be burying the lede: As he started to compose his tweet about Sally Yates on the eighth, Trump faced terrifying and solemn accusations about Russia. But they were also complicated, confusing ones. Frankly, how many Americans know what Alfa-Bank is? How many might not be certain if Carter Page is a guy or a document? What can cause even well-informed citizens to check out faster than a bunch of Russians all named Sergey? Donald Trump has eliminated his own benefit of the confusion. The Trump-Russia Cover-up Case is now about threatening people and firing people and pressuring people to keep them from investigating you and your colleagues. The most immediate threat to his presidency is no longer about Russian smoke that not everybody can see and even fewer can trace. It is now about "When I decided to just do it, I said to myself, 'You know, this Russia thing…'" It is now about "Ask Sally Yates." It is now about "James Comey better hope that there are no 'tapes' of our conversations." The smoke doesn't matter anymore.

Who needs Russian smoke, when the White House is on fire?

"SOME KIND OF PARANOID DELUSION"

Post date • TUESDAY, MAY 16

"Across Washington," wrote Philip Rucker of *The Washington Post*, "Trump's allies have been buzzing about the staff's competence as well as the president's state of mind. One GOP figure close to the White House mused privately about whether Trump was 'in the grip of some kind of paranoid delusion.'"

Ya think?

What you and I have been not debating but quantifying—me for eighteen months—seems finally to have gotten through, even to the occasional Republican: Donald Trump is not well. "Some kind of paranoid delusion" is as good a placeholder as anything else. Trump could have a psychiatric condition. It could be physical. It could be an illness. It could be substance-related. It could be the long-term effects of concussions. This is apart from questions of good and evil. This is about whether the equipment works. "After President Trump accused his predecessor in March of wiretapping him," wrote *The New York Times*, "James B. Comey, the F.B.I. director, was flabbergasted. The president, Mr. Comey told associates, was 'outside the realm of normal,' even 'crazy.'"

Crazy—another good placeholder.

The point is that only in the past couple of weeks has much of the media-political complex in this country been willing to even hint at what has been perfectly obvious to many of the rest of us: Donald Trump is not well. "Trump has two complaints about Cabinet members," wrote Mike Allen of *Axios*. "Either they're tooting their own horns too much, or they're insufficiently effusive in praising him as a brilliant diplomat, etc. . . ." "White House and former campaign aides," reported *Politico*, "have tried to make sure Trump's media diet includes regular doses of praise and positive stories to keep his mood up— a tactic honed by staff during the campaign to keep him from tweeting angrily." So occasionally his staff prints fake *Time* magazine covers off the internet, or articles torpedoing each other, to give to Trump. This crazy stuff originates from *inside* Trump's White House.

Donald Trump is not well.

As a whole, the country has appeared to be unwilling to address this, even as a possibility. It's understandable. We have gradually grown as a society to understand the nature of mental illness—physically based or otherwise. Even in my childhood, this was a subject of fear and confusion and blame, and now, finally, we are sympathetic. But for fifty years, we have asked our mental health professionals not to diagnose our presidential candidates from afar. Unfortunately, this is like saying that you can't call it a forest fire unless you work for the National Park Service, at the specific forest, and you've been personally singed by the fire.

Our refusal, out of sympathy and fairness, to call "some kind of paranoid delusion" "some kind of paranoid delusion" could destroy this country. The last Quinnipiac poll asked recipients to give a description of Trump, using the first word that came into their heads. Not multiple choice, just "give me the word that best describes him."

Forty-six different words were given five times or more. The leaders were *idiot, incompetent, liar, leader, unqualified, president, strong, business-man, ignorant,* and *egotistical. Asshole* just missed the top ten, tied with *stupid. Arrogant, trying* (excellent, thoughtful word there, "trying"), *bully, business, narcissist, successful, disgusting, great, clown, dishonest, racist, American, bigot, good, money, smart, buffoon, con-man, crazy, different, disaster, rich, despicable, dictator, aggressive, blowhard, decisive, embarrassment, evil, greedy, inexperienced, mental, negotiator, patriotism.* Only three words that even hint at psychiatric issues: *crazy, mental,* and *narcissist.* Used just a combined 23 times from a total of 527 people.

Trump's aides spend forty-eight hours violently insisting that Comey's firing had nothing to do with Russia; he gives an interview and says of course he was thinking about Russia, destroying the argument, and the aides. He hints at a secret taping system in the White House—something even Richard Nixon hid for more than four years. He uses the phrase "priming the pump" about the economy and claims he just made it up, and he asks the interviewer "Do you like it?" even though there's documentary evidence that "prime the pump" has been used to describe government action to energize an economy since at least 1933, and he thinks he just coined it last week!

But nobody will call him crazy.

That one little quote from *The Washington Post* might be a harbinger of increased belief among his supporters that Trump is dangerously unstable. "One GOP figure close to the White House mused privately about whether Trump was 'in the grip of some kind of paranoid delusion.'" But they can't admit that. If *you* supported a candidate, and he was elected president, and it turned out you were wrong and all your opponents were right and he *was* crazy—would you admit it?

Nevertheless, it might be leaking out over the sides. In the Quinnipiac poll on February 7, 88 percent of Republicans said they approved Trump, and 75 percent said they strongly approved Trump. In the Quinnipiac poll on May 10, 82 percent of Republicans said they approved Trump, but only 63 percent still said they strongly approved Trump. Same thing in an NBC poll: 90 percent

Republican approval on February 5, 67 percent strong approval; 88 percent Republican approval on May 11—virtually no change—but just 54 percent strong approval. Two polls in which, in three months, about 20 percent of Trump's Republican support has sunk from *strong* approval to just approval.

Maybe the Trump "thing"—his mental health, the chaos of his administration, Russia, whatever—is slowly creeping into the awareness even of the Republicans. They had better figure it out fast, because there is also something new—and I don't think this has been reported anywhere else—that suggests what happens when you don't act quickly to check the Trump effect. Until I sold last year, I lived in Trump Palace. Well, "fled" is a better word than "sold." I took a 10 percent loss to get out, and weeks after I sold last July, the buyer put it back on the market, and he's finally been able to find a buyer, and he has lost 5 percent.

And this is nothing less than a letter from the owner of the Grand Penthouse, the one at the top, who has been trying to sell for two years. According to the real estate listing, Laurence Weiss has cut his price at Trump Palace by 35 percent, and he has written to his fellow condo owners in the building: "Several realtors say that part of the problem is the Trump name on the building. Just this week a potential buyer dropped out when their teenage daughter refused to live in a Trump building . . . This problem is real and will not go away any time soon. We, the owners, can change the name if 2/3 of us agree . . . Our homes are worth more without the Trump name . . ."

The Grand Penthouse owner is putting his money where Trump's mouth is. "Since I perceive a direct financial benefit from a name change I am prepared to underwrite the costs of a name change disproportionately. Specifically, I am prepared to spend 10% of the cost of signage changes . . ." He is willing to pay his neighbors to help him take Trump's name off the building. If there isn't a metaphor in that for this country, I don't know my metaphors:

A 10 percent Trump loss, then a 5 percent Trump loss, then a 35 percent Trump loss, then *I'll pay you to get rid of his name.*

Or, to go back to *The Washington Post*: "One GOP figure close to the White House mused privately about whether Trump was 'in the grip of some kind of paranoid delusion.'"

THE TAPE

Post date • TUESDAY, MAY 23

Barring the unforeseen, Donald Trump is finished.

The unforeseen? Like: some imaginary or inflated threat. National calamity. Terrorism. War. Or another impossible long shot—Trump telling the truth. Otherwise: Something has happened, the finality of which few have noted, that will end—sooner or later—the Trump presidency. It happened in two stages, and when the second stage hit, the smarter Republicans began to at least look to see where the exits were, and some, like Jason Chaffetz and Paul Ryan and Ben Sasse and Mike Pence, edged imperceptibly toward them.

It's the threat he made against James Comey. About a tape.

Combined with the revelation from one of Comey's associates. About a memo.

There are only so many ways out for Trump, and only one of them is good, and the others are all proof of lies and impeachable offenses, and the chances that the good one is real are about one in a billion. This registered with Brian Beutler of *The New Republic*, and I'm indebted to what he wrote on this, because he saw it and I did not. And amid the tsunami of Trump stories in the past week, it was easy to miss. Remember the tweet: "James Comey better hope that there are no 'tapes' of our conversations before he starts leaking to the press!"

So Comey reportedly has a series of memos of the conversations, which would document his version of his conversations with Trump. Presumably noting, in real time, Trump asking Comey to discontinue the Michael Flynn investigation (a potential violation of the so-called "Take Care" provision of the Constitution, article 2 section 3), asking Comey to be loyal to him first and, by extension, to the Constitution second (violation of the presidential oath of office), asking Comey when the FBI was going to announce it wasn't investigating him about Russia (potential obstruction of justice, violations of the White House/Justice Department contacts policy), and Lord knows what else.

It is a one-witness impeachment trial waiting to happen. Either Comey is lying and lying and lying, or Trump's presidency is already over and we just don't know whether the Republicans will bury it soon, in hopes of recovering by the midterms, or they will wait for the possibility Democrats will get to do it early in 2019. Comey has that and all that *that* implies.

And Trump has a tape—maybe.

Option one: Trump's only hope is that his schoolyard-bully tweet means there is a tape. And it had better be a tape on which every reference to Michael Flynn and Russia and loyalty and the FBI and Comey and his claim that Comey exonerated him—it had better be a tape on which every reference to every single thing is as Trump has publicly claimed it is, and not as Comey has reportedly written it is. Trump can't be wrong once.

If he's wrong once and Comey is right once, that brings us option two: one article of impeachment. All you need is one. Ultimately, all that those thousands of hours of Watergate tapes needed to show was Nixon, on June 23, 1972, plotting to stop the FBI investigation of the break-in. Just as all this scandal would need would be, say, Trump talking to Comey about the Flynn case and asking him to "let this go." That's if there *are* tapes and if they produce only one pro-Comey fact. And if it's more than one? All of them?

That's option three: Given not just Trump's hundreds of lies just since assuming office, but his seeming complete disinterest in and unawareness of the difference between lying and telling the truth, the safe guess is that Trump has no idea what would be on the tapes, if they exist, and they are likely to prove him repeatedly violating the law and vindicating Comey, in which case it's not just impeachment, as in option two, but it would then suggest other impeachable acts and several articles.

Of course, it can still get worse—in option four: There are tapes, but Trump refuses to let anybody listen to them, claiming executive privilege or personal property or whatever he comes up with. At which point he would presumably be in violation of subpoenas from the Justice Department and maybe both houses of Congress, and a very public legal case goes up to the Supreme Court, which heard this exact story forty-odd years ago and voted unanimously against the president.

So he's humiliated and he still has to go back to face option two or option three.

And still it can get worse, as in option five: Trump claims there were tapes, but he has destroyed them to protect executive privilege and national security.

Don't laugh—several advisers told Nixon to destroy his tapes. His former treasury secretary, John Connally, said he should do it in the Rose Garden with the press looking on. Apart from the fury from Capitol Hill, destroying the tapes might deplete much of his political support. If Comey's memos accuse Trump of impeachable offenses, and Trump has tapes that he claims clear him, and he destroys those vindicating tapes—how many of even Trump's voters and, more important, his supporters in Congress, would see the ultimate stupidity of that? You threatened him with the tapes; he's lying about you; so you destroyed the tapes?

And still it can get worse. Option six: For whatever reason—desperate, last-chance self-protection, or finally listening to better advice, or thinking he can win the world back to his side—Trump announces that there are no tapes and there were no tapes. He now might be guilty of fabricating evidence to aid obstruction of justice. Worse yet, he would have to admit that something he implied . . . was not true. So far Trump has been asked only once about the purported Comey tape, in a Fox interview, and he adamantly refused to comment: "That I can't talk about," he said. "I won't talk about that." But to *have* to talk about it? To have to concede that what he has said previously was not entirely correct? Never mind not true—not correct? He's Trump—when was the last time he admitted that he was *not correct*? The admission alone might destroy him from within.

And still, there is one last outcome that is worse than all the others. Option seven: Trump for once does the smart thing and comes down from his self-decorated cross of being the most unfairly treated politician in the history of the galaxy and he backs down from his threat and puts his tail between his legs and reveals, quietly or loudly, that there are no tapes—and then somebody else in the administration, some operations guy at the White House who is under oath and who really doesn't want to go to jail for perjury to protect Trump, testifies somewhere that, no, there are tapes of Trump and Comey, and not just Trump and Comey, but Trump and everybody else from whom he asked loyalty, and everybody he asked to interfere with this investigation or to help him get dirt on this person he fired, and tapes of Trump and the Russians last week, and on and on and on. After all, we didn't find out about the Nixon tapes from Nixon. We found out about them because a Republican attorney asked a White

House operations guy named Alexander Butterfield. Nixon had never been asked if he was taping everybody who came through his office door. Come to think of it, Trump has yet to be asked if he is taping everybody who comes through his office door.

But that's because we don't have to ask—we have that stupid tweet he stupidly sent to stupidly threaten Comey to stupidly make himself feel better—and until and unless Trump can prove the tapes vindicate him, or until and unless Trump can prove the tapes don't exist and never have existed, the Republicans in Congress have to assume that there are tapes, and if tapes could destroy Nixon two years after he won forty-nine out of fifty states, they sure as hell can destroy Trump and take half of the Republicans seeking reelection next year with him!

It was hours after the *New York Times* story about the Comey memo that Jason Chaffetz tweeted that he was ready to subpoena it, and only hours more until the chair of the House Republican Conference endorsed that, and only hours until Speaker Ryan said he was fine with that, and only hours more until the appointment of Robert Mueller as the Justice Department's special counsel on Trump and Russia, and only hours after that that Fox couldn't find any Republican congressmen to come on and defend Trump, and only hours after that that Mike Pence filed the paperwork with the Federal Election Commission for his own PAC, because, sure, it doesn't look bad that, not four months into a new administration, with the president already running for reelection, the *vice* president is launching a separate PAC!

The Republicans are not fleeing, and the room is not yet on fire. But if you think all of what we have seen them do since Trump decided to threaten, with secret intelligence and hidden recording devices, a man who is in the secret-intelligence-and-hidden-recording-devices business . . . it all becomes clear.

At 8:26 a.m. on May 12, Trump hit "send." In terms of his presidency, he might as well have hit "delete." And, like us, the Republicans now know it is no longer a question of *if,* but of "Donald Trump better hope that there are no 'memos' of our conversations before he starts threatening." . . . Oh, right, there *are*!

WHEN WILL RUSSIA "BREAK"?

Post date • WEDNESDAY, MAY 24

So when will the Trump-Russia story break?

When will we know, when will we hear—when, already?! Indictments? Impeachments? Confessions? Trumps fleeing to Elba? I am actually asked these questions even more than I ask them myself. And it has recently occurred to me that, while the Trump-Russia story might indeed be the proverbial iceberg that is 90 percent underwater, what we now see is still immense. There are the gigantic headlines everybody knows: Trump boastfully giving the Russians Israel's classified intelligence about ISIS; Trump boasting to them that he had "relieved the pressure" by firing James Comey; the *Washington Post* report that the Trump-Russia investigation has now reached somebody actively serving in the White House; Michael Flynn's attorney saying his client would take the Fifth in front of the Senate.

But we also know so much more. We know that the fired head of the FBI testified to the House Intelligence Committee that it is investigating, and that it is not investigating *if* there are links between the Trump campaign and the Russians, but rather it is "investigating the nature of any links" and "whether there was any coordination." We know that James Comey testified to the Senate Judiciary Committee that the Bureau is coordinating with "two sets of prosecutors: Main Justice, the National Security Division, and the Eastern District of Virginia U.S. Attorney's Office," and that there's reason to believe that this coordination means a U.S. Attorney's Office might already have a grand jury sitting about the Trump campaign and Russia. According to CNN, we know that a grand jury sitting in that district issued subpoenas to associates of General Michael Flynn for business records. We know that two non-mainstream observers, first Claude Taylor and then the former intel officer John Schindler, said the number of FBI targets in its Trump-Russia probe ranges from about twenty-eight to about forty-two, when Watergate resulted in forty Nixon administration figures or associates jailed or indicted.

We know that Carl Bernstein reported on CNN that the FBI and the Senate and House investigators believe there is an "active cover-up" of Trump and

Russia being run by the White House, and that at least the FBI also believes its work is being "impeded" by All the Trump's Men.

We know that Acting Attorney General Sally Yates warned the White House about National Security Adviser Flynn's vulnerability to Russian blackmail, and the next day Trump reportedly asked James Comey whether or not he was under investigation about Russia, and he reportedly asked for Comey's loyalty. We know that Trump promptly fired Yates, and then tweeted about her in such a way that led some to think he may have broken a federal law against witness intimidation.

We know that Trump ultimately fired Comey, and then tweeted about him in such a way that led some to think he may have broken a federal law against witness intimidation.

We know that former director of national intelligence James Clapper said the Russians should consider the firing of Comey another triumph for them. We know that Trump claimed Clapper had cleared him of any collusion with Russia, while Clapper said he never said any such thing.

We know that the White House seems to be trying to throw General Flynn under the bus and portray him as the man who gave the appearance of Russian influence on Trump's administration even while Trump himself is somehow still claiming Flynn is the victim of Democratic McCarthyism. We know that not only has Flynn offered to testify, possibly against Trump, in exchange for immunity, but that he has hired a lawyer trained in Russian history, who is also an expert in the various laws for foreign agents and lobbyists, and who was one of the last Republican Never-Trumpers still standing. We know that to date, nobody has taken Flynn up on his offer, and in the view of the best analyst you could have on presidential scandals and cover-ups, John Dean, that could only mean prosecutors don't need Flynn's testimony, not even if it will nail Trump. We know from CNN and NBC reports that President Obama personally warned Trump not to make Flynn his national security adviser. We know from a *Daily Beast* report that even after Flynn's ouster, Trump repeatedly asked White House lawyers whether it was okay for him to again contact Flynn anyway.

We know that the Senate Intelligence Committee has asked for four Trump associates to turn over all of their emails and documents about Russia voluntarily or it will subpoena them, and that Carter Page and Roger Stone have confirmed they've been asked, and *The New York Times* has reported that so, too, have Flynn and Paul Manafort. We know that Manafort's bank records have reportedly been sought by the Justice Department and that, as reported by NBC, the "Senate Intelligence Committee has requested documents on Trump from Treasury's money laundering unit."

We know that Carter Page wrote a nine-page letter to the Senate committee, angrily denying any wrongdoing while noting that the guy U.S. officials believe is a Russian spy, Victor Podobnyy—Page admits to meeting with him in 2013.

We know that the chairman of the House Intelligence Committee had to recuse himself from the Trump-Russia investigation after putting on this bizarre Kabuki theater thing involving trying to ride to Trump's rescue with evidence it sure looks like the Trump administration provided to him, and then virtually disappearing from public view. We know that the attorney general had to recuse himself from the Trump-Russia investigation because he stepped in his own borscht by not telling the truth about meeting the Russian ambassador.

We know that the White House initially identified the opinion of the attorney general as one of its reasons for firing FBI Director Comey—and thus the attorney general may have violated his own recusal from all investigations of Trump and Russia. We know that the Trump campaign denied there had been any meetings between campaign officials and Russian ambassador Kislyak— which Kislyak denied, too. And then CNN turned up evidence of him meeting with the attorney general, and with General Flynn and Trump aide J. D. Gordon . . . at the Republican convention.

We know that Trump produced a "certified letter" from a lawyer claiming he'd had no business dealings with Russia in the past decade—oh, wait, that says, "with a few exceptions," meaning he's had some business dealings with Russia in the past decade, worth more than a hundred million dollars. We know that the lawyer was the same one from the January news conference with all the folders supposedly full of documents, and that last year her company's Moscow office actually won an award as Russia's top law firm.

We know that a prominent golf writer now says that in 2014, Trump boasted of having access to a hundred million dollars in funding for golf courses, and that his son Eric—though he now denies saying this—explained: "We don't rely on American banks. We have all the funding we need out of Russia . . . We just go there all the time."

We know . . . that one of the men reputed in the Steele dossier to be a key figure in Trump-Russia, an obscure Russian diplomat named Kalugin, was confirmed to be a key figure by U.S. intelligence, according to the BBC. We know that the preelection hacking attempts of voting registration rolls in Arizona, Florida, Illinois, and maybe other states was done allegedly by Russians, and was no dry run, but could have been efforts to procure the email addresses of voters so they could be microtargeted by specific campaign advertising—this also according to the BBC.

We know that last month, the British newspaper *The Guardian* concluded a forty-three-paragraph summary of the Trump-Russia saga with this stunner: "One source suggested the official investigation was making progress. 'They now have specific concrete and corroborative evidence of collusion,' the source said. 'This is between people in the Trump campaign and agents of [Russian] influence relating to the use of hacked material.'"

In short, we know a helluva lot about Trump and Russia. And no matter what they all say, the only person who could look at this 10 percent of the iceberg and say, "There's nothing there," and really believe it is Trump himself, and he's nuts. I don't know when there are indictments or somebody cracks or somebody cuts a deal, or all three. Could be six hours from now, could be six months; there could be sealed indictments now. But if the Trump-Russia scandal is an iceberg, and the ratio of 10 percent to 90 percent holds, Trump-Russia is an iceberg big enough to sink about two hundred *Titanics*—and nearly as many Trumps.

THE ARREST OF JARED KUSHNER

Post date • TUESDAY, MAY 30

I call for the immediate arrest of Jared Kushner.

If he should not be suspected of money laundering, racketeering, and influence peddling, then he should be suspected of obstruction of justice and espionage and possibly worse.

There is no other option that can be reasonably entertained.

18 U.S. Code 794. Gathering or delivering defense information to aid foreign government, section A: Whoever, with intent or reason to believe that it is to be used to the injury of the United States or to the advantage of a foreign nation, communicates, delivers, or transmits, or attempts to communicate, deliver, or transmit, to any foreign government, or to any faction or party or military or naval force within a foreign country . . . either directly or indirectly . . . information relating to the national defense, shall be punished by death or by imprisonment for any term of years or for life . . .

That is from the Espionage Act.

Arrest. Kushner. Now.

The rest of that statute limits use of the death penalty to the exposure of the identities of American agents or defense plans or communications intelligence.

The Russian ambassador to the United States reportedly told his superiors that on December 1 or 2 of last year, in the building on Fifth Avenue in New York City called Trump Tower, Jared Kushner proposed using Russian communications facilities in a Russian embassy or a Russian consulate to contact the Kremlin directly, to make certain the lawful government of the United States could not prevent, interfere with, or know of those communications.

Arrest. Kushner. Now.

The proposal was so startling, so unprecedented, that even the ambassador, Sergey Kislyak, "reportedly was taken aback," according to *The Washington Post. The New York Times* printed the Kushner side's cover story. This was a means by which Kushner could get information from the Russians about Syria. The cover story given to the Associated Press was that this was so that General Michael Flynn could talk directly to Russian military leaders about Syria. Having already twice chosen not to mention his meetings with Russians on the SF 86 forms he swore under oath in order to gain security clearance, Kushner was reportedly himself willing to enter, or willing to have other Trump transition officials enter, diplomatic facilities—which have privileged legal status within the United States—and talk directly to officials of the Russian government.

Even if this Syria Excuse is somehow true, Kushner was still intending to communicate with a foreign nation—a foreign *enemy* nation—about a second foreign nation: a second foreign enemy nation. And he would not have been asking about the Russians' assessment of the weather in Syria. This would have pertained to Russian military involvement there and could likely have delivered "either directly or indirectly . . . information relating to the national defense." The Syria Excuse could still be espionage.

Arrest. Kushner. Now.

If the Syria Excuse is not true, the banking story may be. The Reuters News Agency, quoting "seven current and former U.S. officials," reported that Kushner had a minimum of three previously undisclosed contacts with Ambassador Kislyak during and after the presidential campaign. It cited one current U.S. law enforcement official in reporting that "FBI investigators are examining whether Russians suggested to Kushner or other Trump aides that relaxing economic sanctions would allow Russian banks to offer financing to people with ties to Trump." NBC and *The New York Times* are reporting that Kushner met last December with a Russian banker named Sergey Gorkov, and Gorkov's bank is the Russian government's national development bank, and Gorkov graduated from the academy that trains Russian intelligence personnel, and that our intelligence personnel consider Gorkov a "Putin crony." CNN is reporting that Russian government officials even claimed to have "derogatory" financial information to use against Trump and his staff during the election campaign.

The Banking Story could be money laundering or racketeering and/or influence peddling. It ties together all too cynically with the renewal of EB-5 visas, a renewal stuffed into page 734 of House Resolution 244, signed by Trump on the fifth of May, offering permanent residence in this country to rich foreign investors who put money into things like American real estate projects. It ties together all too cynically with the impression Kushner's family company left with Chinese investors just two weeks later, that if they bought in to Kushner real estate deals in New Jersey, their immigration process could be expedited. And it further ties together all too cynically with the CBS report that when word spread that the FBI investigation of Trump had expanded from potential electoral collusion to finances and investments, Kushner became a "prominent voice advocating Comey's firing," and when it is all tied together, what that "prominent voice" was advocating might reasonably be considered obstruction of justice.

Arrest. Kushner. Now.

And if the Syria Excuse, which could still be espionage, is not true, and if the Banking Story, which could be money laundering or racketeering or influence peddling and obstruction of justice, is not true, what is left? For what other evil purpose did Jared Kushner want a covert, secure means of direct spy-tested communication to the Kremlin? After a presidential campaign in which his father-in-law encouraged Russians to hack into the computers of his electoral opponent, why would Jared Kushner want to go inside the Russian embassy or consulate—the centers of Russian espionage in this country? After an election about which the Russians would boast of their influence, why would Jared Kushner need means to avoid the detection of the government of the United States? After the direct evidence of contact between his father-in-law's campaign and Ambassador Kislyak throughout 2016, why would Jared Kushner want to keep his contact with the Kremlin secret from the intelligence services of the United States? After the mounting circumstantial evidence of collusion between his father-in-law's campaign and the government of Russia, what would make Jared Kushner willing to tempt prosecution under the Espionage Act to avoid his contact with Russia becoming known to the president of the United States?

Arrest. Kushner. Now.

Jared Kushner brings us not just into the White House; he brings us both figuratively and literally to the door of the Oval Office. Inside that door, there are people who appear not to understand why they are not permitted to break the law when they think it's a good idea. Inside that door, there are people for whom running this nation is not a solemn and nearly religious responsibility, but an opportunity for wins and power and financial corruption. Inside that door, there is a man in charge who has never been stopped by rules and never been held accountable when he breaks them.

These people do not believe in the law. These people do not believe in patriotism. These people do not believe in the United States of America. These people—Kushner, his wife, Trump, General Allen, General McMaster, General

Flynn, the others—are in their souls, if not under the law, traitors to this country, and no matter which excuse Jared Kushner has for proposing to talk to Russia using secret Russian communications surrounded by Russian spies inside Russian territory, there is but one answer:

Arrest. Kushner. Now.

Chapter 11

JUNE 2017

THERE ARE BUT TWO PARTIES NOW

Post date • THURSDAY, JUNE 1

Today—every day—the presidential administration of Donald John Trump looks, a little bit more than it did the day before, like a bomb disposal operation.

And the Republican Party owns the bomb.

Our alliances are in tatters, the president gives away intel to whomever he wants, his budget proposal has a $2 trillion math error, the Germans say Europe must go on without us, Trump wanders off a stage in Israel, shoves aside one European leader and all but arm-wrestles another, starts spontaneously boasting about the Montana congressional outcome in Sicily, offers to trade personal cell phone numbers with the new French president, is believed to be angry at the EU because it was so difficult to build golf courses there, the Russians reportedly boast of having had financial leverage against Trump during the campaign, words like "collusion" and "corruption" and "emoluments" and "espionage" and "treason" echo across the country, and Trump identifies the true enemy: the news media, and on and on and on.

And nearly all the Republicans say nothing, as if they cannot hear the ticking of the bomb. The few who speak nearly all buck-pass back, with a tepid "You'll have to ask the White House," or offer transparently asinine rationalizations for a growingly unfit president who threatens the freedom and the safety of every American, and indeed of every living thing on the planet. As if letting the bomb go off is just one of a series of political options.

I warn the leaders of the Republican Party: Donald Trump's candidacy was his fault. Donald Trump's election, no matter how much the Russians aided it, was this broken society's fault. Donald Trump's supporters are everybody's fault. But Republicans: Donald Trump's continued presidency is entirely your fault. And unless this man actually manages to literally destroy this country or this world, this simultaneous nightmare, shared by hundreds of millions here and abroad, will forever damn you in history—just as the Democrats who were willing to sell out our freedoms during the Civil War are damned in history, just as the southerners of all parties who sanctioned Jim Crow are damned in history, just as the traitors in law or in deed throughout our national life are damned in history.

Donald Trump might as well be a Russian spy, or clinically diagnosed with any of a thousand psychological illnesses, or diseased, or in an altered state of consciousness, or . . . the specifics almost no longer matter. In just over four months in power, he has virtually erased historical comparison. He's beyond Nixon, he's beyond Woodrow Wilson after his paralyzing stroke, he's beyond the afflicted King George—if there's anybody to whom he can now be compared, perhaps it is the disastrous first-century Roman emperor Nero.

An alt-right Trump supporter echoes the campaign and hurls abuse at two teenaged girls, one wearing a hijab, on a commuter train, and two American heroes—one from the political right and one from the political left—intervene to save them and are killed for doing so, and Trump ignores it for more than three days but finds time to tweet about the news media being the enemy. Paul Ryan—you don't hear the bomb ticking? To hell with you. Now you *own* the bomb, Ryan.

The Republican chair of Multnomah County, Oregon, says that to protect his Republican staffers in public, maybe he should hire right-wing militia like the Oath Keepers or the Three Percenters as "security." Orrin Hatch—you don't hear the bomb ticking? To hell with you. Now you *own* the bomb, Hatch.

Trump tells the butcher of the Philippines about our nuclear subs near North Korea, blows the cover of Israel's vital ISIS lead to the Russians, and somebody gives away the details of the Manchester terrorist attack to the newspapers. John McCain—you don't hear the bomb ticking? To hell with you. Now you *own* the bomb, McCain.

The Kushner family all but offers to sell green cards to rich Chinese who'll invest in their private real estate deals, the Russians reportedly say Kushner wanted to use their spy communications systems to talk directly to the Kremlin, and he reportedly meets with a banker who is tied to Russian espionage. George W. Bush—you don't hear the bomb ticking? To hell with you. Now you *own* the bomb, Bush.

Trump attacks a late-night television host. The windows of a newspaper office are shot out in Kentucky. A reporter is arrested after asking a question of the secretary of Health and Human Services. Another is body-slammed by a congressman-to-be the night before the election. The president meets with Russians in the Oval Office and no American media is admitted. A protester is convicted of laughing at the testimony of the attorney general. The president tweets about news: the enemy. Hugh Hewitt—you don't hear the bomb ticking? To hell with you. Now you *own* the bomb, Hewitt.

Long ago, Trump lost any hope of controlling himself. The Republicans, who could get him out of office with the Twenty-fifth Amendment before sunrise, do nothing. As Churchill once said: They "go on in strange paradox, decided only to be undecided, resolved to be irresolute, adamant for drift, solid for fluidity, all-powerful to be impotent." Republicans—you don't hear the bomb ticking? To hell with you. Now you *own* the bomb, Republicans.

On the twenty-first of April, 156 years ago, a failed soldier, farmer, bill collector, and firewood salesman wrote his father a letter: "Whatever may have been my political opinions before, I have but one sentiment now. That is, we have a Government, and laws, and a flag, and they must all be sustained. . . . There are but two parties now, traitors and patriots, and I want hereafter to be ranked with the latter, and I trust the stronger party." The writer was Ulysses S. Grant, and he was explaining to his father why, when he had just finally gotten up on his feet in civilian life, he had to go back to the Army. Because on that twenty-first of April 1861, there *were* but two parties: traitors and patriots.

And as this, our modern-day Nero, tweets while a nation burns, those who are not patriots salt away all the financial spoils they can grab, and roll back every statute of progress they can repeal, and exploit every fear they can locate, and put every dollar they can find into the pockets of the corporations that own them. And the bomb in the White House continues to tick, and the infamy continues to adhere more and more strongly to the party at which we will one day soon look back and say, "They could have stopped this." The reality is simple, and it requires that General Grant's letter to his father be altered only by the measure of one pair of words: "There are but two parties now: Republicans . . . and Americans."

ANYBODY ELSE WOULD'VE BEEN FIRED BY NOW

Post date • MONDAY, JUNE 5

Let me apologize again to the world, particularly the United Kingdom, on behalf of the United States of America. Donald Trump is not of sound mind; we are working to correct the problem as soon as possible.

Amid all that he creates—confusion, charges of corruption and collusion—there is a stark reality. In almost any other job in this country—assuredly in any other private sector job—no matter the financial cost, no matter the upheaval, no matter the blowback, Donald Trump, our national embarrassment, our international disgrace, would have been fired by now. His complete incompetence, his complete failure, and his complete inability to see his incompetence and his failure as anything except brilliance would get him fired everywhere from the board room at Microsoft to the deep fryer at McDonald's.

His tweet: "At least 7 dead and 48 wounded in terror attack and Mayor of London says there is 'no reason to be alarmed!'"

The mayor of London didn't say that.

"Londoners will see an increased police presence today and over the course of the next few days," said Mayor Sadiq Khan. "No reason to be alarmed—one of the things the police and all of us need to do is make sure we're as safe as we possibly can be." Mayor Khan was urging Londoners not to be alarmed at additional police presence. Trump proclaimed himself the law-and-order candidate. He is symbolized by additional police presence. He is in agreement with Mayor Khan.

But Donald Trump is not the kind of man who will take "yes" for an answer. He has now doubled down on his delusion. "Pathetic excuse by London Mayor

Sadiq Khan who had to think fast on his 'no reason to be alarmed' statement. MSM is working hard to sell it!"

Simply: this is a lie. Mayor Khan's statement was made, complete, before Trump's reaction. Trump took a part of it out of context, and is now lying to imply that the part about the police presence came separately. It did not. Trump is lying. It may be a lie that is explained by the liar's inability to admit he was wrong, or understand context, or process reality, as opposed to what he wants to have had happen—but it is still a lie.

Trump must confound, contradict, exploit, boast, and insult, and he has to do it so compulsively, he cannot even see when somebody from outside his tiny, self-obsessed world is agreeing with him. For that kind of knee-jerk thinking, the lunchroom manager of a middle school would be fired.

Another tweet about the London attack: "Do you notice we are not having a gun debate right now? That's because they used knives and a truck!" *What?* A London Bridge kind of attack here in America, where terrorists can easily buy American guns and rifles—and have bought American guns and rifles, and have killed Americans with American guns and rifles—that kind of attack would not see men jumping out of a van brandishing knives; they would be carrying automatic weapons and mowing down Americans with guns and rifles bought in America. For behavior that obstinate, that slow-witted, that overflowing with bad guesswork—an attorney at any law firm in this country would be fired.

"We need to be smart, vigilant and tough. We need the courts to give us back our rights. We need the Travel Ban as an extra level of safety!" Trump sent that tweet about forty-eight hours after Justice Department attorneys went to the Supreme Court and asked them to overrule lower courts and instate Trump's new regulations on foreigners entering this country, and the central premise of their argument is that it isn't a travel ban. And Trump not only publicly cuts their legs out from under them, but reminds the Supreme Court justices that one of the reasons the travel ban was stopped by the other judges was that, while the lawyers insisted it wasn't religion-based, or a travel ban, Trump and his associates made, and kept making, public comments about how it was religion-based, and a travel ban.

And then he doubled down on it: "People, the lawyers and the courts can call it whatever they want, but I am calling it what we need and what it is, a TRAVEL BAN!" Were he the head of a company that had decided upon a vital policy, and a strategy to defend that policy legally, and he acted so contradictorily and destructively to that policy—the CEO of any Fortune 500 corporation in this country would be fired.

"Despite the constant negative press covfefe." Those of us who are repelled by this man got a rare laugh at this absurdly meaningless, stupid tweeting mistake. Meanwhile, Trump and his littlest flying monkey, Sean Spicer, actually tried to seriously claim it was some kind of brilliant communication strategy, intended perhaps to distract and confound his critics.

Neither side fully understood the nightmare behind this. The man acting as president of the United States went to his favorite platform of public communication, at 12:06 a.m. prevailing local time, got to the thirty-seventh character and sixth word of a tweet, misspelled something—probably the word "coverage"—and somehow managed to hit "send." The meaninglessness, the lack of focus, the carelessness, the self-pity, the irresponsible redefinition of the language itself that has symbolized this fifth-rate administration from the moment of Trump's inaugural address was summarized in five words plus some kind of typographical error. And no great leap of imagination is required to presume that it was transmitted, because, just as he was misspelling "coverage," he suddenly—phone in hand—fell asleep or otherwise lost awareness, and pressed "send," or reached for "delete" and instead hit "send," and then fell asleep, or otherwise screwed up, and checked out. And Trump says nothing about this remarkable and sudden disconnection from reality—for six hours. And when something is finally said, it is a lie a kindergartner wouldn't believe.

And the context is lost as well. Just two nights earlier, he had tweeted: "The Fake News Media works hard at disparaging & demeaning my use of social media because they don't want America to hear the real story!"

Evidently the real story is "covfefe."

For behavior that irresponsible, that incoherent, that utterly self-unaware, any employee, in any company or in any branch of government service that wasn't the presidency, would either be fired or immediately tested for substance abuse or their psychological health or both.

For more than a year, I have anguished over what's wrong with Donald Trump: stupidity, madness, evil, disease, injury. I no longer care which. Attacking a mayor who agreed with him. Attacking him again and, in so doing, attacking a city still reeling from a terrorist attack. Insisting on a travel ban while his lawyers are trying to convince the Supreme Court it isn't a travel ban. Announcing he doesn't care what the lawyers call it, and threatening the courts. Tweeting gibberish while half-asleep or half-conscious or half-sane.

This is not about policy. It is not about conservatives versus liberals. It is not about Republicans or Democrats. It is not about Make America Great Again or Grab Them by the Pussy. It is not about Russia, and it is not about Pittsburgh or Paris or both. It is about absolute baseline incompetence. We all know that we have, occupying the office of president of the United States, a man doing the simple, easy, isolated, no-brainer parts of the job so badly, so strangely, so destructively even to his own perverse goals, that were he in any other job in this country, somebody would fall back on Trump's hackneyed television catchphrase.

They would invoke that nitwitted blurt that made him famous to many, infamous to others, and plausible to just enough of this country, and we would be freed from this self-perpetuating nightmare of a chief executive who cannot even handle Twitter, let alone reality.

WHEN DONNIE MET SERGEY

Post date • TUESDAY, JUNE 6

FBI and congressional investigators are reportedly scouring evidence that Donald Trump may have met privately thirteen months ago with the Russian ambassador who is at the nexus of all of the Trump-Russia scandals. This was reported last week by NBC News and CNN, but it fell between the cracks that were the covfefe tweet and the (abandonment of) the Paris Climate Accord, and it got no traction, and it is kind of important—it is weapons-grade important.

In short, it's: When Donnie Met Sergey.

The date was April 27, 2016, the locale the Mayflower Hotel, in Washington, the sponsor the Center for the National Interest, which is run by the Russian émigré Dimitri Simes, who has long maintained a connection to the Kremlin and Vladimir Putin, along with neocon Richard Burt, who, among other things, is an adviser to the controversial Russian outfit Alfa-Bank. This was not some casual event. The Mayflower speech was the first major foreign policy address of Trump's presidential campaign, and in the front row for it—you can see him in the pictures and the video—is Russian ambassador Sergey Kislyak. Also in attendance: Jared Kushner, and Jeff Sessions. It is also no secret that before the speech, there was a VIP reception at which, *The Wall Street Journal* reported, "Trump warmly greeted Mr. Kislyak and three other foreign ambassadors who came to the reception."

But just how warmly? "Five current and former U.S. officials said they are aware of classified intelligence suggesting there was some sort of private encounter between Trump and his aides and the Russian envoy," NBC reported, "despite a heated denial from Sessions." And we all know how much credibility a denial from Sessions about meetings with Russians should be given.

It is also unclear whether the VIP session and the so-called private encounter between Trump and Kislyak are the same thing or separate meetings. But if you read a little between the lines, you get a sense that there's some evidence somewhere—maybe from our intelligence people surveilling Kislyak, or another country's spies surveilling somebody else—that at some point on April 27, 2016, there were more words between Trump and his entourage and Kislyak than just the pleasantries of a receiving line, as described this past March by a spokesman for that pro-Kremlin group that hosted Trump's speech.

Moreover, those would seem to be words that are just now ringing bells. NBC quotes an official who says, "The FBI is interested in who was at the event and what was said, in the context of the counter-intelligence investigation into Russian election meddling." Timing is, as always, everything. April 27, 2016, is around the time that the Democratic National Committee would begin to realize that there was unusual activity on its computer network. This would soon be confirmed as the Russian hacking.

All the NBC sources emphasized that they only know there is classified intel about the Trump-Kislyak meeting or meetings; they don't know what it confirms or that it confirms anything. They—and everybody else—know that this week Trump is up to his neck in former FBI directors, what with James Comey scheduled to testify to the Senate Intelligence Committee Thursday and his predecessor—the new Justice Department special counsel, Robert

Mueller—reportedly taking over what had been a separate criminal investigation into Paul Manafort and Russia, and also reportedly considering expanding still further into investigating the roles of Attorney General Sessions and Deputy Attorney General Rod Rosenstein in Trump's firing of Comey, and the Associated Press's source on whether or not Mueller legally can investigate Sessions and Rosenstein is a pretty good one—Rosenstein himself.

As you will recall, Trump has reportedly at least mulled invoking executive privilege to keep Comey from testifying, but my friend John Dean and others have pointed out that Comey is now a private citizen, and anyway, the subject of what Trump and Comey talked about was discussed by Trump publicly—on Twitter, no less—so if there was any executive privilege, Trump piddled it away.

The Trump-Russia Octopus is so large that his apologists, like Fox News, have even gone so far as to offer a doomsday defense. "Collusion is not a crime, only an antitrust law," said Gregg Jarrett. "You can collude all you want with a foreign government in an election. There's no such statute." So Trump's not guilty of joining with an enemy foreign government to fix the presidential election—or, oh well, maybe he is, but so what, there ain't no law against it. In fact, if Trump colluded with the Russians, *PolitiFact* reported, he could be guilty of fraud, public corruption, conspiracy, and receiving illegal foreign campaign contributions. And if he traded something to the Russians for their help, like a vow to lift sanctions against Russia or destroy NATO, well, we move into the territory of espionage and treason charges.

The original point here: The reporting on FBI and congressional investigations of what happened when Donald Trump and Sergey Kislyak met in Washington on April 27, 2016, might be the most important break yet. Or it might mean nothing. Because not only does it get lost in the latest giant bag of manure generated just this past week by this man occupying the presidency—it also gets lost in the amazing number of individual Trump-Russia scandals. You may have seen this on the internet: As best I can find, it tracks back to early April and a repost on a political cartoon website by somebody calling himself Radish. Let me read you a part of this:

I don't know it's hard for me to see any U.S. ties to Russia . . . except for the Flynn thing and the Manafort thing

and the Tillerson thing
and the Sessions thing
and the Kushner thing
and the Carter Page thing
and the Roger Stone thing
and the Felix Sater thing
and the Boris Epshteyn thing
and the alleged Rosneft thing
and the supposed Gazprom thing
and the Sergey Gorkov banker thing
and the Donald Trump Jr. thing
and the Russian Affiliated Interests thing
and the Russian Business Interests thing
and the Alex Shnaider thing
and the hack of the DNC thing
and the Guccifer 2.0 thing
and the Mike Pence "I don't know anything" thing
and Trump's public request to Russia to hack Hillary's email thing
and the Trump house sale for $100 million at the bottom of the housing
    bust to the Russian fertilizer king thing
and the Russian fertilizer king's plane showing up in Concord, NC,
    during Trump rally campaign thing
and the Nunes sudden flight to the White House in the night thing
and the Cyprus bank thing
and Trump not releasing his tax returns thing
and the Republican Party's rejection of an amendment to require
    Trump to show his taxes thing
and the election hacking thing
and the GOP platform change to the Ukraine thing
and the Steele Dossier thing
and the Leninist Bannon thing
and the intelligence community's investigative reports thing
and Trump's reassurance that the Russian connection is all
    "fake news" thing

and Spicer's Russian Dressing "there's nothing there" thing so there's
probably nothing there since the swamp has been drained, these
people would never lie probably why Nunes cancels the investigation
meetings
all of this must be normal
just a bunch of separate dots with no connection.

And all that was before the Trump-Kislyak thing.

TRUMP IS NOW UNDER INVESTIGATION FOR COLLUSION AND OBSTRUCTION OF JUSTICE

Post date • THURSDAY, JUNE 8

We are at the darkest moment of the history of representative government in this country.

James Comey has now implied, under oath, that the president of the United States is being investigated by the Justice Department for possible collusion with the Russian government in tampering with the 2016 election, and that the president of the United States is also being investigated for possible obstruction of justice. Comey said none of these things so starkly nor directly in his testimony to the Senate Intelligence Committee. He might as well have.

The Republican senator Tom Cotton asked it bluntly: "Do you think Donald Trump colluded with Russia?" Comey's reply: "That's a question I don't think I should answer in an open setting... But that's a question that will be answered by the investigation, I think."

Logic exercise: *How* would Special Counsel Robert Mueller answer that question? By investigating. *Whom* would you investigate to see if Trump colluded with Russia? Trump. And all around him. Conclusion? Special Counsel Mueller *is* investigating Donald Trump, today, about collusion with Russia.

The Republican chairman, Mr. Burr, asked about Comey's conversation with Trump about General Flynn. Comey's reply: "I don't think it's for me to say whether the conversation I had with the president was an effort to obstruct. I

took it as a very disturbing thing, very concerning, but that's a conclusion I'm
sure the special counsel will work toward, to try and understand what the
intention was there and whether that's an offense."

Second logic exercise: *How* could Special Counsel Robert Mueller do that?
By investigating. *Whom* would he have to investigate to do that? Donald Trump.
Thus, *what* is he investigating? Whether or not Trump obstructed justice.

If it *is* obstruction of justice, it was directed at least in part at James
Comey, to get him to, at minimum, as Comey quotes Trump, "let Flynn go." The
Republican senator Jim Risch asked whether Trump directed Comey to do
that. Comey answered: "Not in his words, no." Risch followed up: "He did not
order you to let it go?" Comey answered, "Those *words* are not an order," and
later added, "I took it as a direction. This is a president of the United States,
with me alone, saying, 'I hope this.' I took it as: this is what he wants me to do. I
didn't obey that, but that's the way I took it." And Comey added that he was so
clear about what Trump was trying to do that he didn't want to tell his FBI
"troops" what Trump had said, for fear that his words would have a chilling
effect on their investigation.

And for the completion of the attempt to obstruct justice, its intended victim
had no doubt about the cause and effect. "I take the president at his word . . ."
Later, he said, "I was fired because of the Russia investigation. I was fired in
some way to change, or the endeavor was to change, the way the Russia investigation was being conducted." Fired, it seems, not just because he would not close
the Flynn investigation but also, perhaps, because he would not publicly pro-
claim that Trump was innocent of all suspicion, innocent of collusion with the
Russians, innocent of everything about the election, innocent about everything
in the Steele dossier, down to "hookers in Russia." Fired because he was ordered,
in words that, out of context, would not seem like an order, to close at least the
Flynn investigation in a manner that reminded him of the infamous phrase attributed to King Henry II of England about the Archbishop of Canterbury. Quoting Comey again, "It rings in my ear as kind of 'Will no one rid me of this
meddlesome priest?'" Fired, and left to the mercies of Republican senators who
somehow went into this hearing seemingly thinking that if they could get Comey
to say that Trump only tried to obstruct the Flynn investigation, Trump would
somehow be vindicated; who somehow went into this hearing thinking that if
Comey told Trump there was no investigation of him in January, then Trump

couldn't be guilty of trying to obstruct anything; who somehow, seemingly, at this hearing, managed to ask questions that permitted Comey to pronounce the most damning things ever spoken about any president in our history; who somehow, at this hearing, made it urgently necessary to know if Trump did indeed tape his conversations with Comey; tapes—the mere threat of which Comey said induced him to reveal that he had taken notes on some of his conversations in hopes that a special counsel would then be appointed; tapes about which he testified: "Lordy, I hope there are tapes." And then, later, "The president surely knows whether he taped me. If he did, my feelings aren't hurt. Release all the tapes, I'm good with it."

Trump's attorney, the one who misspelled "president," now says he believes Comey all but cleared Trump. Based on Comey's testimony, it looks all but certain that the actions of the president of the United States are under investigation; under investigation by the Justice Department's special counsel on Trump and Russia; under investigation as possible collusion with the Russians and possible attempts to obstruct justice; perhaps under investigation right now; and that a target of some of that attempt to obstruct justice completely believed—in the moment—that Donald Trump was trying to obstruct him from pursuing justice.

These are the only possible conclusions after the testimony to the Senate Intelligence Committee by former FBI director James Comey.

WHAT WAS THAT AGAIN ABOUT RUSSIAN HOOKERS?

Post date • MONDAY, JUNE 12

An afterthought on the testimony Thursday of former FBI director James Comey. Not what he said that appropriately grabbed all the headlines, but what he put only in his written testimony that never directly came up at the hearing.

What was that again about Russian hookers? "On the morning of March 30, the President called me at the FBI. He described the Russia investigation as 'a cloud' that was impairing his ability to act on behalf of the country. He said he had nothing to do with Russia, had not been involved with hookers in Russia, and had always assumed he was being recorded when in Russia."

Wait—what?

I know this was covered when Comey's opening statement was released in advance, and during and after his testimony, but isn't there something even more amiss here than has yet been publicly recognized? You call up a guy whom you're desperately trying to convince to publicly clear you, whom you will later fire, whom you will later threaten with a vague claim that you may have taped your conversations with him, and who will thus be required to talk about what you said to him, in public venues and probably under oath, and you say something like "I have not been involved with hookers in Russia and I always assumed I was being recorded when in Russia"?

Seriously?

Even in the cascading madness of the seven months since the election—is this not just the craziest thing ever attributed to any president of the United States, but the craziest choice of topics ever raised by any president of the United States? Is it not evidence that, within Trump's desperate obsession to get somebody to clear him personally about Russia—and, boy oh boy, do you and I understand Trump's desperate need to get somebody to clear him personally about Russia—inside that, doesn't it seem there is an obsession within an obsession? I mean: What? *The whole election thing isn't true, but Mr. FBI Director, make sure you clear me about the Russian hooker thing?*

And this wasn't even the first time that Trump brought this up to Comey. January 27: "During the dinner, the President returned to the salacious material I had briefed him about on January 6, and, as he had done previously, expressed his disgust for the allegations and strongly denied them. He said he was considering ordering me to investigate the alleged incident to prove it didn't happen. I replied that he should give that careful thought because it might create a narrative that we were investigating him personally, which we weren't, and because it was very difficult to prove a negative."

To be fair, as Comey said in his statement, it was he who brought this up first. He brought the Steele dossier—including the Russian hypothetical hookers, in all their glory—to Trump's attention when they first met in New York on January 6. But three weeks later, Trump was going to order Comey to disprove it somehow? To have the FBI conclude something didn't happen? And in Russia?

And that's still one of Trump's first concerns when he phones Comey eighty-three days later? "He said he had nothing to do with Russia, had not been involved with hookers in Russia, and had always assumed he was being recorded when in Russia."

And in a speech in Australia, overnight, between Comey's statement and Comey's testimony, the former director of national intelligence, James Clapper, said he had phoned Trump on January 11 to encourage him to stop comparing the American intelligence community to the Nazis, and, quoting Clapper, "ever transactional, he simply asked me to refute the infamous dossier, which I couldn't and wouldn't do."

I am not for a moment suggesting that this detail from this rancid presidency is as important as all the times Comey's words supported accusations of obstruction of justice against Trump, or Comey's joy at the prospect that there might be tapes of his meetings with Trump, or his implication that Trump is under investigation now by the special counsel, or certainly the weight that Comey's testimony added to the evidence necessitating Trump's impeachment, not even Trump's attorney misspelling "president" in his response to the hearing and thus calling him "Predisent Trump."

But it's not just that there's something wrong here. There's something *wronger* here! When Comey's opening statement was first released, Trump attorney Marc Kasowitz issued a forty-three-word victory lap that included the phrase "The President feels completely and totally vindicated." And before the paint was dry on that statement from that Trump attorney, another statement came from another Trump attorney: "Comey's statement released today needs to be carefully scrutinized," Michael Cohen asserted, "as his testimony claims the president was concerned about the dossier. It must be noted that the dossier has been debunked even by the author himself, Christopher Steele."

Well, except (a) Christopher Steele did *not* debunk his dossier; he wrote, as he submitted it, that a lot of it was unverified. That it was raw intelligence that needed further investigation. And (b) what the hell!? The dossier? That's what you want to underline after a statement from the fired FBI director about how he was to testify under oath to facts that could conceivably end a presidency? The dossier? You just put the dossier, and the Russian hypothetical hookers back under the public nose again? Why? Because Comey referenced them only twice and somehow that wasn't enough times?! Why? Because you wanted to make sure every news organization in the world has to bring up the Steele dossier and the hookers, even the ones who never mentioned them in the first place?

I mean, what's hidden within the Steele dossier that could conceivably be more damaging to Trump than, you know, impeachment or evidence of treason, or both? What could it contain, that on January 27 and March 30 and June 7, the president—and then one of his attorneys—seem more concerned with it than with anything else? What could possibly be in the Steele dossier?

Well . . . Russian hypothetical hookers.

Move over, Richard Nixon. Before all this ends, "I am not crook" may be replaced in presidential lore by "I am not a john."

SELF-DESTRUCTION

Post date • MONDAY, JUNE 19

The president of the United States is self-destructing.

We need to give him all the help we can in his task.

This is not said lightly. Even with this president, even in this atmosphere of daily if not hourly crisis—this is an issue of deep regret. Ordinarily, the last thing in the world any American would want is a leader bent on destroying himself and ending his presidency. But the threat to our freedoms, our heritage, our way of life—our lives themselves—is so overwhelming and unprecedented that, putting aside the almost immeasurable anger and resentment that this childish, petulant, selfish man engenders, it is still with genuine sadness that we must look at his self-destruction and say it simply and resolutely:

Better him than our country.

"Trump advisers and confidants describe the president as increasingly angry over the investigation, yelling at television sets in the White House carrying coverage," wrote Julie Pace and Jonathan Lemire of the Associated Press on June 16. "He has watched hours of TV coverage every day—sometimes even storing morning news shows on his TiVo to watch in the evening—and complained nonstop," wrote Josh Dawsey of *Politico* on June 15.

We will ignore for a moment the thought that somebody still has a TiVo.

The president *is yelling at television screens*, evoking the probably apocryphal story of Richard Nixon, in his last days, arguing with the White House paintings of Kennedy and Lincoln. Yelling at television screens. Let's just hope the sets are actually on.

"Trump, for months, has bristled almost daily about the ongoing probes," Dawsey continued. "He has sometimes, without prompting, injected 'I'm not under investigation' into conversations with associates and allies."

That was written Thursday, June 15. On Friday, June 16, Trump threw the ship fully into reverse in a tweet that seemed to confirm the opposite of that and included the direct quote "I am being investigated for firing the FBI Director by the man who told me to fire the FBI Director!" After ceaseless denials about this, Trump could now adjust his inaccurate worldview to accept what has been obvious to everybody else since at least the appointment of Robert Mueller as special counsel.

And then he couldn't.

By Sunday, June 18, Trump had to have one of his mouthpieces go on three network shows and tell one of them that Trump is being investigated and then, when pressed for detail, say that, no, Trump isn't being investigated. Same interview. Yes and no. Trump is so sick that he cannot continue to accept on Sunday what he had seemed to have begun to accept on Friday. Trump still had to preserve a corner of his fantasy world in which not only is he never at fault, but if indisputable reality disagrees with his delusions, indisputable reality must be wrong in some way. In the June 16 tweet, Trump blamed a "man who told me to fire the FBI Director!" On May 11, Trump had claimed, "Regardless of recommendation, I was going to fire" the FBI director. Now, in his mind, that first statement never happened.

You know, of course, about the subsequent terrifying cabinet meeting in which Trump claimed, "Never has there been a president, with few exceptions… who has passed more legislation, who has done more things," when in fact next to nothing has passed or been done. And you know about the twenty-three minutes of praise he asked for and got from such reeking toadies, such Self-Servatives, as Rick "My Hat Is Off to You" Perry and Reince "Blessing to Serve You" Priebus and Mike "The Greatest Privilege of My Life" Pence—although in Pence's case, that might be true.

It evoked the councils of North Korea, or perhaps the flattering of the Roman emperor Caligula to keep him from killing everybody in the room, or maybe images from the episode of *The Twilight Zone* where the six-year-old boy has the power to destroy everything on earth merely by wishing it, and the remaining adults vie to appease him. Or—less chillingly and perhaps more in accordance with the farce of this administration—the governor that Mel Brooks plays in *Blazing Saddles* who tells his cabinet they must protect their "phony-baloney jobs," and they all join him in saying, "Harrumph, harrumph." And then Brooks stops and points at one of them and says, "I didn't get a 'harrumph' out of that guy!" and the holdout finally says "Harrumph," and Brooks stares and points at him and says, "You watch your ass."

You know of his meeting this week with the president of Panama, in which he said, "The Panama Canal is doing quite well; I think we did a good job building it," as if it had just been finished. It opened on August 15, 1914.

And maybe most disturbing of all, there is this. Buried in a June 13 opus from Glenn Thrush, Maggie Haberman, and Julie Hirschfeld Davis of *The New York Times*, what would have been, in any other time, in any other presidency, a sign of desperate personal, emotional, psychological, or physical distress, but which in this one—this presidency of self-destruction—was almost an afterthought. About the conflicting stories wafting out of the White House that he might or might not fire the special counsel: "The president was pleased by the ambiguity of his position on Mr. Mueller and thinks the possibility of being fired will focus the veteran prosecutor on delivering what the president desires most: a blanket public exoneration."

This is where the sane, patriotic people of this country must see that we are dealing not with a president who occasionally strays into madness, but with a madman who occasionally successfully pretends to be sane. To look at a special counsel, a man with a long, respected, and lucrative career behind him and, if he wants it, more of the same ahead after this assignment, and to think for a moment that you could get him to clear you, even if you are guilty, by threatening to fire him from a job he did not want and does not need—to assume that your only motive, money, is also everybody else's only motive—is as rational as going to the roof of the White House and, to prove yourself invincible, jumping off—because you've always believed that when it was necessary, you could fly, because you have a lot of money.

And right now, in this atmosphere of daily if not hourly crisis, his critics, his sycophants, his Self-Servatives are not going to be able to convince Trump that he cannot fly.

So the country will have to hope for the best. And let him jump.

DOES TRUMP HAVE TAPES? DOES ANYBODY?

Post date • TUESDAY, JUNE 20

Are there tapes of Donald Trump's White House meetings and phone calls with James Comey and perhaps others, or not?

If there are, what do they say?

If there are *not*, did Trump destroy them?

It is now more than five weeks since this issue was first raised by, naturally, Trump tweeting his mouth off. May 12: "James Comey better hope that there are no 'tapes' of our conversations before he starts leaking to the press!" Since then, we have gotten from Trump and his sycophants misdirection, obfuscation, and cuteness, when it is for this man's presidential life or death to either produce tapes that validate his versions of conversations with Comey and others, or prove that tapes never existed in the first place, and thus he has not destroyed possible evidence in a criminal case.

There seemed to be new insight into this during the wall-to-wall coverage given last Sunday of a part-time radio host, part-time guitarist, and full-time Nathan Thurm look-alike named Jay Sekulow. Mr. Sekulow, one of Trump's attorneys, is the man who told Chris Wallace of Fox News that the president was indeed being investigated for firing Comey, and then, in literally the next breath, said no, he *wasn't* being investigated for firing Comey. Sekulow also appeared the same morning on CBS. John Dickerson asked, "The president said last week he would release the tapes of—if there were tapes—of his conversation this week. That hasn't happened. Where is that?" Sekulow replied, "I think the president is going to address that in the week ahead. There were a lot of issues this past week; this issue will be addressed in due course and, I suspect, next week."

"Next" week, as of June 18, being, obviously, *this* week.

Except—don't count on it. Exactly a week earlier, on June 11, Jay Sekulow was on ABC and said the *same thing.* "That's a decision that the president will make in consultation with his chief lawyer, Marc Kasowitz," said Sekulow, adding that Trump would "address it next week."

"Next" week, as of June 11, now being, obviously, last week.

Suggesting that next week, as of June 18, probably means "Next week I'll just say 'next week' again."

Thus is the Trump Gang continuing to kick the can down the road on the issue of just confirming or denying that there are tapes. As I have noted here previously, Trump has put himself in an impossible position. Sooner or later, at an impeachment or in a courtroom, Trump will need those tapes, will need them to validate his version and not Comey's. If he can't produce them, he will either be asking us to believe he would not release something that would exonerate him, or he will have to confess that his tweet of May 12 was an empty threat, or, worst of all, he will have to prove that there aren't tapes, never were tapes, and he didn't destroy them, and frankly, I don't know how you ever prove that vast a negative. To give you a time frame on this, the House Intelligence Committee had given Trump a deadline of Friday, June 23, to voluntarily produce any tapes.

*

There are two known potential outside sources for Trump tapes, or at least information about Trump tapes. The Secret Service says it does not have any—this was in reply to a Freedom of Information Act request by *The Wall Street Journal.* Then there is the long-standing assumption that for security reasons, all phone calls to the White House, no matter who the president is, are automatically recorded, in case somebody makes a threat. Is that true? Is it also done for outgoing calls? If there are recordings, are they kept? Is there a tape of the March 30 call in which Comey claims Trump talked about the "cloud" he was under and pushed him to publicly clear him about Russia? Is there a tape of the April 11 call in which Comey claims Trump wanted to know what Comey had done about publicly clearing him? Depending on the language used, tapes of either of those phone calls could be submitted as evidence of Trump trying to obstruct the FBI investigation and thus obstruct justice, or even of Trump threatening Comey, or of trying to induce him to lie.

We only know that the Secret Service says it doesn't have any recordings. We only know that two weeks ago, Trump said we'd soon find out and be disappointed by the answer. We only know that this goober Sekulow has now gone on talk shows on consecutive Sundays and predicted resolution next week, leading me to wonder if Sekulow is not, in fact, an actual person but is himself simply a recording.

There is another way to clear this up, at least in part, and I hardly think I'm the first person to realize this. The big issue of recordings and the little one of who does or doesn't have them—White House operations, Secret Service, Trump himself—can be ascertained, by the Justice Department's special counsel, using a little technical device known inside the world of audio—and inside other worlds—as a "subpoena."

Finally, there is one other possibility that, to my surprise, I haven't seen raised anywhere else. In the District of Columbia, it is legal to record conversations in person or on the phone so long as one of the people in the conversation knows it is being recorded. Down the block from Ford's Theatre, just before you get to that Chop't salad place, at its office, doesn't the FBI record all the phone calls that come into its headquarters?

I mean, never mind Trump-Comey tapes. Are there—could there be, legally *can* there be—FBI-Comey tapes?

FIRING THE SPECIAL COUNSEL

Post date • FRIDAY, JUNE 23

It ultimately does not matter whether the president does, doesn't, has, or hasn't fired the special counsel who is investigating him. Obviously this is a simplified overview. The grinding wheels of justice and truth would be better served with Robert Mueller on the job, rather than with his being just the latest body on the pile of men Trump has fired as they gathered the damning facts about him. But in a larger sense, firing Mueller might actually speed Trump's demise. Because, whatever breathing room Trump might gain from cashiering Mueller and declaring the investigation over and himself vindicated, it would be more than counterbalanced by the degree to which the headline "Trump Fires Another Investigator" will move the story of his alleged corruption, obstruction, and madness into the center of the American view.

It is hard for you and me to really grasp this. We have fought this man, and fought what he meant, and saw clearly what he would do for more than one year (some of us, exactly two years). But we are not average Americans, and I'm not talking about our political viewpoints. I'm talking about our political viewership. I have never seen a study of just how much time the average American spends thinking about politics each day, but I would suspect it's a lot shorter than it takes to read the shortest of these commentaries. For better or for worse, to the average American, even the average American voter, it just isn't necessarily a priority.

A president fires the U.S. attorney in New York investigating his associate's business dealings? How many million Americans *didn't* know this happened? A president then fires the FBI director investigating his campaign? How many million Americans don't know *that* happened? Far fewer. A president *then* tweets that he's being investigated for firing the FBI director, then fires the special counsel doing that investigating? How many million Americans won't know *this* has happened? Far fewer still.

There is a tipping point in everything in American culture, from reality-TV popularity to political scandal. It is almost always: a lot of people who didn't know about something suddenly finding out about that something.

You can't really establish a single tipping point in the Watergate scandal, but the "Saturday Night Massacre" is probably the closest thing. On a Friday, Richard Nixon said he would refuse a court order to surrender his White House tapes, and he ordered the special prosecutor to drop the Watergate case. On Saturday afternoon, in a news conference carried live on television, that prosecutor said he would continue the investigation anyway, and continue to challenge the president in court. Later that day, the president ordered the attorney general to fire the special prosecutor for defying him. The attorney general refused and resigned. The deputy attorney general refused and either resigned or was fired; it still isn't 100 percent clear. Saturday night, the third-ranking figure in the Justice Department, the solicitor general, finally fired the prosecutor.

And all hell then broke loose.

On the Friday before the Saturday Night Massacre, there had been ten different stories on the front page of *The New York Times*, from the Yom Kippur War to a shootout in midtown Manhattan to Game 5 of the 1973 World Series. Nothing about Watergate. By the Sunday after the Saturday Night Massacre, there was an eight-column, three-line headline about Watergate and four separate front-page stories, including one just about impeachment.

By the Monday after the Saturday Night Massacre, White House and congressional and senate offices were flooded with telegrams. The Watergate scandal—front of mind for millions of Americans but, in its sixteenth month, still an irrelevant shape on the horizon to most of us—suddenly became the only topic in politics, and just as quickly politics became the only topic in America.

Would "Trump Fires Mueller" unfold precisely that way? It's impossible to tell. The world of media is utterly changed. We have a thousand more distractions now than we did when Richard Nixon had Archibald Cox fired in 1973. We have another president who will lie about anything, but, unlike Nixon, the one we have now can do so instantaneously via social media, and his true believers will happily reject the insights of Rosenstein and Mueller to instead swear by those of Diamond and Silk.

But to fire Mueller is to tempt a repetition of the Saturday Night Massacre—and the spread of public awareness of the investigation—which might not destroy Trump but cannot possibly help him. And just as important is to risk a repetition of the aftermath of the massacre—the part very few people noticed or talked about, then or now.

Within twelve days after Nixon fired the special prosecutor, the pressure and the outcry had grown so loud that Nixon had to hire *another* special prosecutor—the one who would ultimately help force him from office.

THE APPEASEMENT OF TRUMP

Post date • TUESDAY, JUNE 27, 2017

The president of the United States has admitted that the Russians "meddled" in the election that put him in power, and he has blamed his predecessor in essence for not stopping him, and he has admitted to intimidating the FBI director who was investigating this treachery, and he has resumed his veiled threats of intimidation against the special counsel now investigating his treachery—and yet this "president" has not yet been removed and arrested.

We are appeasing Trump.

The mind reels, and our democracy if not dead is in suspended animation because the Republican Party is now actively shielding this traitorous megalomaniac because he will sign whatever they put in front of him, and their actions should be identified for what they are: being accessories after the fact to the worst set of crimes in American history.

We are appeasing Trump.

The nation, which should be in the streets, holding a general strike, fighting to restore the rule of law that is dissolving in front of its eyes, is instead utterly divided or distracted or both. Republican legislators wholly owned by corporations are dismantling the already porous health care net in order to fund tax breaks for the wealthiest and greediest bastards among us, even though every group from those legislators' own constituents to every hospital and insurance organization opposes the action. The president's sycophantic base is happy because though a few of them may have noticed that society is still hitting them in the head, they look with perverse joy at the reality that this society is hitting women and minorities harder.

We are appeasing Trump.

The elected Democrats, who should be the voice of resistance against every legislative rape by Trump and his gang as well as the base for all the defenses of the democracy, are instead jockeying for position and cynically calculating whether keeping Trump in office next year will give them a better chance of election—cynically calculating whether it's better to let the country burn until autumn 2018 rather than to put out the fire now. These Democrats are offset by others who argue one vote in one special election means they need to ease up on the "Russia thing" and must "stand for something," as if the "Russia thing" didn't threaten everything we hold dear and standing for a restoration of representative government weren't "something."

We are appeasing Trump.

And the media are obsessed not with the lies of a president who is gifted only at lying, and news conferences of his lying spokespeople that contain no news, no truth, no reality, and no morality, spun by cretinous deceivers who make the farcical propaganda of the infamous Iraqi Baghdad Bob look like the revealed word; the media are obsessed not with recognizing that war has been declared on them and that Trump's goons are playing them like the proverbial two-dollar banjo—the media are obsessed that the White House won't let them record the press briefings that are nothing but lies, and instead of getting up and walking out and no longer participating in this desecration of freedom of the press, they stay there and still report the lies and still put the White House liars on the Sunday shows and still pander to the Trump audiences that were not watching them, are not watching them, and will *not be* watching them, and calculate only how the lack of a live feed from the White House press room will impact their ratings instead of how the lack of truth from the White House press room will impact whether their children live in freedom or slavery.

We are appeasing Trump.

*

Resist—because these people are *not* going to do it for you.

Peace.

Epilogue

Well, thank goodness we all know how this whole thing turned out. To try to button this up in midsummer was to be forced to place a wager on the outcome even while the percentage of those firmly believing in this would-be Emperor and his New Clothes was still so high that the amount of time left in the Revenge Porn of Administrations could range from about four years to about four minutes.

But as I put down my abused and overworked laptop, it was beginning to seem clear that there were four inevitable outcomes for Trump. Each would be terminal to his presidency. It was plausible that he could elude the consequences of one, two, or maybe even three of them. Yet barring the most unforeseen and calamitous of national crises—like Trump stumbling into war with North Korea because he shot off his big bazoo and said something like "Fire and Fury," which his puppeteer Steve Bannon had remembered from his days monetizing the video game World of Warcraft—Trump was not going to escape. Nobody has that much dumb luck, and Trump clearly went way over his limit long before he took office.

The first inevitable and inescapable trap was his deteriorating control of his personality/mental health/impulsiveness/brain trauma/whatever. The domestic terrorism in Charlottesville not only revealed his decades-long leanings toward racism, anti-Semitism, and worse, but reflected his prioritizing of his own refusal to be "controlled" over everything else—to say nothing of his mindless rage. In mid-July, he had taken three mutually exclusive positions on the second failure of the health care Repeal and Replace legislation in just forty-eight hours. His hazy, dreamlike grip on reality was sliding from loose to intermittent to only periodic. And maybe worst of all: He was beginning to repeat himself. When he hopped into the cab of a big fire truck rolled out for Made in America Week and pretended to drive it, America remembered he had done exactly the same thing, in almost exactly the same suit, photographed at almost exactly the same angle, in another big rig, back in March. The unstated question was, did *he* remember?

Trump's second bottomless pit was Obstruction of Justice. Apart from the repeated pleas/requests/threats to have everybody in authority except Putin publicly clear him about Russia, and apart from the attempt to get Mike Flynn a legal pass, and apart from whatever he actually did to Jim Comey, and apart from whatever Bob Mueller was collating, there was the small matter of that little June 2016 meeting attended by Trump Junior, Jared Kushner, and Paul Manafort. The surface details were bad enough: their own emails said they believed they would be hosting middlemen delivering dirt on Clinton from the Russian government. Trump himself boasted about new "corrupt dealings" by Hillary three hours after Donnie Junior had confirmed the confab, and he adopted a new number for her total of emails in a tweet ten minutes after the meeting ended. Worse yet, the initial Trump Junior denial about how they only talked about adoption was reportedly composed by Trump himself *aboard Air Force One*. They unnecessarily dragged the cover-up of that meeting (and thus the entire Trump-Russia thing) from the comparably arm's-length distance of Trump Tower directly into the Oval Office.

The third patch of quicksand was, obviously enough, at the end of the route marked Russia. We might never know exactly how much Putin did to mess with the 2016 election, and we might never know exactly how much Trump and his gang knew in advance and conspired with the Russians. But that Trump Tower meeting with Natalia Veselnitskaya, Rinat Akhmetshin, Ike Kaveladze, and everybody but Boris and Natasha meant that the Trumps had *tried* to conspire with the Russians—and just because maybe you don't completely betray your country doesn't mean you don't get charged for trying to do that. The Trumps seemed to have forgotten that there is a crime known as *attempted* murder.

And the last and maybe the most perilous long walk off Trump's marina full of short piers was the indication of cracks in his political base. His approval numbers in the Rust Belt counties he had so unexpectedly flipped had dropped underwater. Nothing less than a *Fox* poll showed disapproval edging approval in his handling of the economy and even Iran and Syria, and getting blown out of the tub on immigration, health care, and Russia. The same mid-July numbers suggested that although 41 percent considered Junior's clambake with the Russkies was "no big deal," 55 percent found it "troubling." Part of the base was seemingly looking for a climb-down, an amazing development considering that it required them to acknowledge—if only to themselves—that they were wrong about him, that he was elected nefariously, that they couldn't continue to enjoy their revenge against liberals, and that there was no middle ground and if they left Trump's side they could never go back. Were they to become genuinely remorseful and make noises about punishing the Republicans in the midterms, their congresspeople wouldn't be doing any climbing down. They'd simply jump.

Oddly, the thing that seemed to be sustaining Trump was the media's continuing refusal to acknowledge that what the rest of us were all seeing—and what they were pretending wasn't happening—was something that was outside their collective experience. I spent twenty years in sports news and then twenty years mostly in political news, and it never ceased to amaze me that sports reporters were constantly expecting and even hoping to cover things that had never happened before, while their political counterparts seemed to have been constructed from the conviction that nothing that hadn't happened before in American history could possibly happen now. There *couldn't* be a candidate who sold his soul to another country to get elected, because they had never covered one before. There *couldn't* be a semi-functioning disturbed psyche occupying the White House, because they had never run into one in the Senate or House or whatever county board they broke in covering. And they certainly *couldn't* write any of these things. Bill Safire, Tom Wicker, Christopher Hitchens, and Merriman Smith never wrote these things. So onward they marched, surprised by every rake they stepped on, awaking each morn fully convinced things would get back to normal and they could simply rework something they had written in 1999, unwilling to invoke the words "treason" or "madness" because they weren't legal or psychological experts—as if you needed to be an electrical engineer to write about how the wiring had just caught fire.

Happily, you and I and the rest of us, *saw*. So, at the worst, from the ruins, at least we could say we told you so.

Photography credits